Lecture Notes in Computer Science   7127

Commenced Publication in 1973
Founding and Former Series Editors:
Gerhard Goos, Juris Hartmanis, and Jan van Leeuwen

Tuomas Aura   Kimmo Järvinen
Kaisa Nyberg (Eds.)

Information Security Technology for Applications

15th Nordic Conference on Secure IT Systems,
NordSec 2010
Espoo, Finland, October 27-29, 2010
Revised Selected Papers

 Springer

Volume Editors

Tuomas Aura
Kimmo Järvinen
Kaisa Nyberg
Aalto University
School of Science
Konemiehentie 2, 02150 Espoo, Finland
E-mail: {tuomas.aura, kimmo.jarvinen, kaisa.nyberg}@aalto.fi

ISSN 0302-9743   e-ISSN 1611-3349
ISBN 978-3-642-27936-2   ISBN 978-3-642-27937-9 (eBook)
DOI 10.1007/978-3-642-27937-9
Springer Heidelberg Dordrecht London New York

Library of Congress Control Number: 2011945062

CR Subject Classification (1998): D.4.6, K.6.5, D.2, H.2.7, K.4.2, K.4.4, E.3, C.2

LNCS Sublibrary: SL 4 – Security and Cryptology

Typesetting: Camera-ready by author, data conversion by Scientific Publishing Services, Chennai, India

Printed on acid-free paper

Springer is part of Springer Science+Business Media (www.springer.com)

Preface

The Nordsec workshops started in 1996 with the aim of bringing together computer security researchers and practitioners from the Nordic countries. The event focuses on applied IT security and, from the beginning, its goal has been to encourage interaction between academic and industrial research. Over the years, Nordsec has developed into an international conference that takes place in the Nordic countries on a round-robin basis. It has also become a key meeting venue for Nordic university teachers and students with an interest in security research.

The 15th Nordic Conference in Secure IT Systems took place at Aalto University in Finland during October 27–29, 2010. The program of this year's conference was a cross-section of the security research at Nordic universities and industrial research centers with some contributions from around Europe. The themes ranged from the enforcement of security policies to security monitoring and network security. There were also papers on privacy, cryptography, and security protocol implementation. The conference received 37 submissions, of which 13 were accepted for presentation as full papers and three as short papers. In the original workshop spirit, the authors were able to revise their papers based on discussions at the conference.

The keynote talk at Nordsec was given by Erka Koivunen from CERT-FI with the title "Why Wasn't I Notified?": Information Security Incident Handling Demystified. An invited paper based on the talk is included in the proceedings. Furthermore, a large number of students presented their work at a poster session and competition.

The proceedings also include three selected papers from the OWASP AppSec Research 2010 conference, which focuses on Web application security. These papers were originally presented in Stockholm during June 21–24, 2010. The authors of the selected papers were invited to submit revised papers for a joint conference publication and to give talks at Nordsec.

We would like to thank the authors, members of the Program Committee, reviewers, students presenting posters, the Organizing Committee, and all conference attendees for coming together and making Nordsec 2010 a successful scientific and social event for both security researchers and practitioners.

October 2011

Tuomas Aura
Kimmo Järvinen
Kaisa Nyberg

Organization

Nordsec 2010
October 27–29, 2010, Espoo, Finland

Program Chairs

Tuomas Aura   Aalto University, Finland
Kaisa Nyberg   Aalto University and Nokia Research Center,
         Finland

Local Organizing Committee

Tuomas Aura   Aalto University, Finland
Kimmo Järvinen   Aalto University, Finland

Program Committee

N. Asokan   Nokia Research Center, Finland
Tuomas Aura   Aalto University, Finland
Catharina Candolin   Finnish Defence Forces, Finland
Mads Dam   Royal Institute of Technology, Sweden
Simone Fischer-Hübner   Karlstad University, Sweden
Viiveke Fåk   Linköping University, Sweden
Dieter Gollmann   Hamburg University of Technology, Germany
Christian Damsgaard Jensen   Technical University of Denmark, Denmark
Erland Jonsson   Chalmers University of Technology, Sweden
Svein Johan Knapskog   Norwegian University of Science and
         Technology, Norway
Audun Jøsang   University of Oslo, Norway
Peeter Laud   Cybernetica AS and University of Tartu,
         Estonia
Helger Lipmaa   Tallinn University, Estonia
Vaclav Matyas   Masaryk University, Czech Republic
Chris Mitchell   Royal Holloway, University of London, UK
Kaisa Nyberg   Aalto University and Nokia Research Center,
         Finland
Christian W. Probst   Technical University of Denmark, Denmark
Hanne Riis Nielson   Technical University of Denmark, Denmark

Michael Roe   University of Hertfordshire, UK
Nahid Shahmehri   Linköping University, Sweden
Einar Snekkenes   Norwegian Information Security Lab, Norway
Alf Zugenmaier   Munich University of Applied Sciences,
                                    Germany

Reviewers

Naveed Ahmed   Hans Hedbom
Waleed Alrodhan   Aapo Kalliola
Musard Balliu   Atefeh Mashatan
Stefan Berthold   Davide Papini
Joo Yeon Cho   Emilia Käsper
Nicola Dragoni   Andrea Röck
Olof Hagsand   Ge Zhang

Table of Contents

Policy Enforcement

Selected OWASP AppSec Research 2010 Papers

Cryptography and Protocols

BloomCasting: Security
in Bloom Filter Based Multicast

Mikko Särelä, Christian Esteve Rothenberg,
András Zahemszky, Pekka Nikander, and Jörg Ott

{mikko.sarela,andras.zahemszky,pekka.nikander}@ericsson.com,
chesteve@dca.fee.unicamp.br, jo@netlab.tkk.fi

Abstract. Traditional multicasting techniques give senders and receivers little control for who can receive or send to the group and enable end hosts to attack the multicast infrastructure by creating large amounts of group specific state. Bloom filter based multicast has been proposed as a solution to scaling multicast to large number of groups.

In this paper, we study the security of multicast built on Bloom filter based forwarding and propose a technique called BloomCasting, which enables controlled multicast packet forwarding. Bloomcasting group management is handled at the source, which gives control over the receivers to the source. Cryptographically computed edge-pair labels give receivers control over from whom to receive. We evaluate a series of data plane attack vectors based on exploiting the false positives in Bloom filters and show that the security issues can be averted by (i) locally varying the Bloom filter parameters, (ii) the use of keyed hash functions, and (iii) per hop bit permutations on the Bloom filter carried in the packet header.

1 Introduction

Recently, a number of routing and forwarding proposals [25,16,32] are re-thinking one of the most studied problems in computer networking – scalable multicast [12,23]. The unifying theme of these proposals is to use Bloom filters in packet headers for compact multicast source routing. This makes it possible for the multicast architecture to scale to the billions, or even trillions, of groups required, should the system need to support all one-to-many and many-to-many communications, such as tele and video conferencing, chats, multiplayer online games, and content distribution, etc.

While the Bloom filter is a space efficient data structure and amenable to hardware implementations, it is also prone to false positives. With in-packet Bloom filter based packet forwarding, a false positive results in a packet being erroneously multicasted to neighbors not part of the original delivery tree. Consequently, false positives lead to reduced transport network efficiency due to unnecessary packet duplications – a fair tradeoff given the potential benefits. However, false positives have also security implications, especially for network availability.

T. Aura, K. Järvinen, and K. Nyberg (Eds.): NordSec 2010, LNCS 7127, pp. 1–16, 2012.

Earlier work [26] has identified three forwarding anomalies (packet storms, forwarding loops, and flow duplication) and two solutions that provide fault tolerance for such anomalies, namely, varying the Bloom filter parameters and performing hop-specific bit permutations. Our contribution is to analyze the anomaly related problems and solutions from security perspective. It has also been shown [13] that Bloom filters can act simultaneously as capabilities, if the hash values used for the Bloom filter matching are cryptographically secure and depend on the packet flow.

In this paper, we concentrate on the security issues of Bloom filter based multicast forwarding plane. We analyze service and network infrastructure availability. The contributions of this paper are a characterization and evaluation of the security problems and solutions related to Bloom filter based forwarding. Other security issues for multicast, such as key management, policy, long term secrecy, ephemeral secrecy, forward secrecy, and non-repudiation are out of scope for this paper.

Additionally, we propose BloomCasting, a source specific multicasting technique that integrates the provided security solutions together. In BloomCasting, group membership protocol is carried from the receiver to the source. This pushes both the costs and the control of the multicast group management to the source. The Bloom filter used to forward the traffic is gathered hop-by-hop along the unicast path to the group source.

The rest of the paper is organized as follows. In Section 2, we review the principal aspects of Bloom filter based forwarding and scope the problem of secure multicast for the purposes of this paper. We present BloomCasting, a secure source-specific multicasting technique in Section 3 and in Section 4, we describe the security solutions in more detail. We evaluate our approach In Section 5, review the related work in Section 6, and conclude the paper in Section 7.

2   Security Issues in Bloom Filter Based Multicast

As with unicast, securing multicast communications requires considerations in two orthogonal planes: the data plane (protecting multicast data forwarding) and the control plane (securing multicast routing protocol messages), although the problems are more difficult because of the large number of entities involved. While secure multicast data handling involves the security-related packet treatments (e.g., encryption, group/source authentication and data integrity) along the network paths between the sender and the receivers, control plane security aspects involve multicast security policies and group key management i.e., secure distribution and refreshment of keying material (see e.g. [22,11,23,18,24]). Ultimately, control plane security must be handled individually by each multicast routing protocol to provide authentication mechanisms that allow only trusted routers and users to join multicast trees (e.g., PIM-SM [3]).

Our focus in this paper, however, is elsewhere – on the *availability of the multicast infrastructure* in an open and general source specific multicast model [9]. A source specific multicast group is defined by the source and group address taken together. We assume that multicast groups can contain receivers anywhere in the network. This means that hierarchical addressing [19] cannot be used to scale up the system with sub-linear growth in routing table size in relation to the number of groups. The number of potential source specific groups grows exponentially with the number of nodes in the network – compared to quadratic growth in the number of potential unicast connections and logarithmic growth in the size of routing table based on hierarchical addressing. State requirements create a potential for denial-of-service (DoS) attacks as described in 'stateless connections' [4].

Bloom filter based source routing has been proposed as a solution to scaling multicast into large networks and number of groups [25,16,32,13]. Such an approach places the state requirement at the source, instead of the routers alleviating the potential for DoS attacks against the network infrastructure.

2.1 Forwarding with in-Packet Bloom Filters

The Bloom filter [10] is a hash-based probabilistic data structure capable of representing a set of elements S and answering set-membership questions of the type "is $x \in S$?". The insert operations consist of, given a bit array of size m, for each element x in a set S of size n, $k \ll m$ independent hash values are computed $H_1(x), ..., H_k(x)$, where $1 \leq H_i(x) \leq m, \forall x$ and the corresponding bit array locations are set to 1. Conversely, asking for the presence of an element y in the approximate set represented by the Bloom filter involves applying the same k hash functions and checking whether all bit positions are set to 1. In that case, the Bloom filter returns a 'true', claiming that y is an element of S. The Bloom filter always returns the right answer for each inserted elements, i.e., there are no false negatives. However, due to hash collisions, there is some probability $p(m, n, k)$ for the Bloom filter returning a false positive response, claiming an element being part of S even when it was not actually inserted.

In-packet Bloom filter based multicast [25,16,32,13] is based on the idea of turning the forwarding operations into a set-membership problem. The basic idea consists of encoding a multicast tree by inserting the appropriate link identifiers into a Bloom filter carried in the packet header. Forwarding nodes along the path process the packet and check whether neighboring link identifiers are present in the Bloom filter. Then, a copy of the packet is forwarded along the matching interface(s).

Inherited from Bloom filters, false positives cause packets to be unnecessarily duplicated over some extra links. When a router receives a falsely forwarded packet for which it does not find a matching forwarding directive, the packet is simply discarded. Hence, Bloom filter forwarding guarantees packet delivery to all intended destinations but introduces a degree of wasted resources due to unnecessary packet duplications – a tradeoff worth to consider given the benefits in terms of space efficiency (i.e., reduced state) and performance (i.e., fast forwarding decisions).

2.2   Threat Model and Existing Attacks

We restrict the scope of this paper to security issues of the Bloom filter based forwarding plane of one-to-many multicast, also referred to as source-specific multicast (SSM) architectures. We assume an attacker who may control large number of hosts (e.g. botnet) that wishes either to disrupt the network infrastructure, or deny service to target host or network links. We also evaluate available possibilities for *controlled multicast*, i.e. ensuring that only authorized senders and receivers are capable of sending to and receiving from a particular multicast group.

Our adversary model assumes malicious end hosts and benign routers. Consequently, *packet drop attack* or *blackhole attack* fall out of the scope. This assumption is coherent with the wired networking scenario under consideration where trust among routers and the management plane is provided by e.g. pair-wise shared secret techniques. Moreover, we assume an end-to-end security mechanism to provide payload confidentiality, authentication, and integrity (e.g., as discussed in [15]). Attacks related to these security mechanisms are not discussed further in this paper.

While false positives represent a well-known limitation of Bloom filters, the security implications of (random) false positives in packet forwarding are far reaching and less understood. Our main security goal is to guarantee *forwarding service availability* of Bloom filter based data planes under malicious attacks. Hence, we seek for data plane mechanisms that ensure that only packets from authorized users are forwarded, i.e., providing resistance to (potentially distributed) DoS attacks .

DoS can be divided into attacks on infrastructure availability and (end) service availability. These can be disrupted by bandwidth, state, or computation consumption attacks (cf.[7]). Any unauthorized sending of multicast data can be construed as a DoS attack. For instance, *flooding attacks* would cause an escalating of packets filling the network links to an extend that legitimate packets end up discarded due to massive link congestion. Such denial of service may affect a greater proportion of the network due to the "multiplier effect" of false-positive-prone multicast packet distribution.

Chain Reaction Attacks. False positives can cause forwarding anomalies that greatly increase the amount of network traffic. These include packet storms, forwarding loops, and flow duplication [26]. We review these anomalies that an attacker could do here. We highlight the fact that if Bloom filters are assigned per multicast tree or per flow, the anomalies will affect every packet in a given multicast tree or flow.

Packets storms are caused when, for sizable part of the network, the average number of false positives per router exceeds one. Should this be the case, then on average each false positive causes more than one additional false positive, creating an explosive chain reaction. The average number of false positives is $\rho^k \cdot (d - b - 1)$, where ρ is the fill factor of the Bloom filter, k is the number of hash functions used, d is the number of neighbors, and b is the number of actual

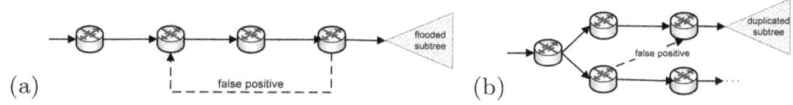

Fig. 1. (a) Forwarding loop and (b) flow duplication

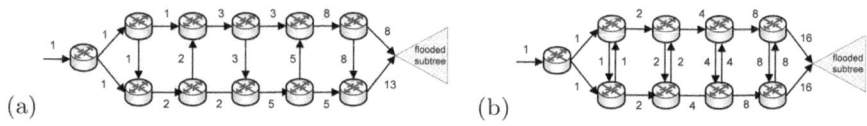

Fig. 2. (a) Flow duplication with Fibonacci number growth in the number of packet copies and (b) exponential growth in the number of packet copies

branches in the multicast tree at that node. After the first false positive $b = 0$. As an example, considering $k = 5$ and $\rho = 0.5$, a nodes with degree $d > 32$ would produce more than one false positive per node.

Forwarding loop happens, if a set of false positives cause the packet to return to a router it has already visited. The router will then forward the packet again to all the nodes downstream of it, including the false positive links that caused the packet to loop. As a result, not only will the packet loop, but every loop causes a copy of the packet to be sent to the full sub-tree below the router. A forwarding loop is shown in Figure 1.

Flow duplication is another possible anomaly as shown in Figure 2. Figures 2(b)-(c) show that even flow duplication can cause the number of packet to grow – according to Fibonacci sequence and as the powers of two.

The above attacks can also be combined. If link identifiers are common knowledge, the attacker can form a Bloom filter that corresponds to the Figure 2(c) which also includes one or more links back to the first router, causing the packet load to explode both in network and in all receiver hosts.

Target Path Attack. An attacker controlling a large number of hosts can try to coordinate as many packet flows as possible to a single link or a particular path. If link identifiers are common knowledge (1), then this is simple. Each host just computes a forwarding tree that goes through chosen link. If however, the link identifiers are secret and static (2), then the attacker has a few potential attacks available: *injection attack* – where she tries Bloom filters that get traffic forwarded along a certain delivery tree, *correlation attack* – where she attempts to infer workable link identifiers from a collection of legitimate Bloom filters, and *replay attack* – where a valid Bloom filter is misused to send unauthorized traffic (i.e., with different content or flow identifiers). [13]

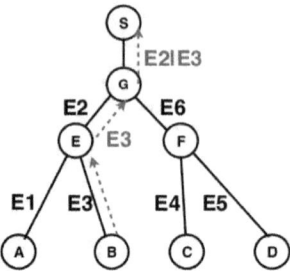

Receiver	BF
A	E1|E2
B	E2|E3
C	E4|E6
D	E5|E6
ABCD	E1|E2|E3| E4|E5|E6

Source S

Fig. 3. The left side shows multicast Join message using iBFs. The right side shows a simplified Membership Table MT(S) that contains the Bloom filters for A, B, C, and D. The separated bottom row shows how to combine the Bloom filters in to an iBF.

3   BloomCasting

BloomCasting is a secure source specific multicast technique, which transfers the membership control and per group forwarding state from the multicast routers to the source. Similar to [25,16,32], it uses in-packet Bloom filter (iBF) to encode the forwarding tree. BloomCasting separates *multicast group management* and *multicast forwarding*.

To join, a host sends a join request (BC_JOIN) towards the source S. Intermediate routers record forwarding information into the packet, thus when the packet reaches S, it will contain a *collecting* iBF for the source-receiver path. By combining together the iBFs for all the receivers, the source will have an iBF encoding for the whole multicast tree. When a host does not wish to receive packets for the group anymore, it sends an authenticated leave message to S. Upon processing this packet, the source will reconstruct the Bloom filter for the group leaving out the recently pruned path. The operation is illustrated on Figure 3.

Data packets are routed using the *forwarding* iBF placed in the BC_FW header. Each intermediate router takes its forwarding decision by querying it with the question: which of my outgoing links are present in the iBF? It then forwards the packet to the corresponding peers. Eventually, the packet reaches all the receivers, following the sequence of routers the BC_JOIN packets traversed, in reverse order.

3.1   Group Membership Management

Group membership management includes the joining, leaving, and maintenance of multicast groups, and this is the main task of the control plane. Along this discussion, we show how multicast trees are encoded into iBFs.

Joining a Group: When a host joins a multicast group, it sends a (BC_JOIN) message towards the source. The packet contains the following information: (S,G) specifying the multicast group and a *collecting* iBF. The latter is used for

Algorithm 1. Adding edge-pair labels (E) and permuting collect and forward iBFs at transit routers.

```
Collect_iBF (C):
    E ← Z_K(S,G,R_p, R_c, R_n);
    C ← C ∨ E;
    C ← Permute_c(C);

Forward_iBF (F):
    foreach outgoing link i do
        F ← Permute_c^{-1}(F);
        E ← Z_K(S,G,R_n, R_c, R_p);
        if E ∧ F = E then
        |   Send F → i;
        end
    end
```

collecting the forwarding information between the source and the receiver. Finally, it also contains a hash chain anchor for future signaling security.

In each router, the next hop for the BC_JOIN message towards S is found from routing information base.[1] As the message travels upstream towards the source, each router records forwarding information into the packet by inserting the edge pair label E into the *collector* iBF. After this, for loop prevention and increased security, it performs a bit permutation on the *collector* iBF. Finally, it selects the next hop upstream towards S. The operation is shown on Algorithm 1. Unlike traditional IP multicast approaches, where the forwarding information is installed in routers on the delivery tree, transit routers do not keep any group-specific state.

Once the BC_JOIN message reaches the source, it contains sufficient information so that the source can send source-routing style packets to the recently joined host. The source stores this information in the Membership Table (MT), as shown in Figure 3. The source can now send packets to the multicast tree by combining iBFs for the group, by bitwise ORing them together.

Leaving a Group: When a receiver wishes to leave the group, it sends a BC_LEAVE towards S, including the next element from the hash chain it used when joining the group. On-path routers forward the packet to S. As no further processing is needed in intermediate routers, unlike pruning packets in IP multicast, BC_LEAVE packets always routed to the source.

S verifies the hash and removes (or de-activates) the entry in the Membership Table. Single message hash authentication, vulnerable to man-in-the-middle attacks, is sufficient, since the hash is only used to verify that the host wishes to leave the group. As a final step, it recomputes the forwarding iBF of the delivery tree. An example of a forwarding iBF is shown in Figure 3 at the separated bottom row of the table.

---

[1] Just like in standardized IP multicast protocols, this forwarding decision can be taken according to the RIB created by BGP or according to the Multicast RIB created by MBGP [8].

Refreshing Membership State: The iBFs in the MT may become stale, either because of changing the key to compute the edge-pair labels or due to route failures. Keys are expected to change periodically (e.g., every few hours) to increase security by excluding brute force attacks [13]. This means that the iBF needs to be recomputed with a new BC_JOIN packet. When making the forwarding decision, during a transition period routers need to compute edge-pair labels for both the old and the new key. If they find that an edge-pair label computed with the old key is present in the iBF, they set a flag in the BC_FW header indicating that the receiver should send a BC_JOIN again, as the iBF will soon become invalid. When a packet is to be forwarded on a failed link, the router sends an error message back to the source.

3.2   Multicast Forwarding

So far, we have discussed how hosts join and leave multicast groups. We now show how data packets are forwarded between the source and the receiver.

As we saw previously, iBFs for each receiver border router are stored separately in the Membership Table. We also saw the basic concept of deriving the forwarding iBF from the MT information; now we extend that with new details.

For each group, the source stores one or more iBF for each next hop router in its BloomCasting Forwarding Table (BFT).[2] In practice, the capacity of a packet-size iBF is limited in order to guarantee a certain false positive performance (practical values suggest around 25 destinations in 800-bit iBFs [25]). In case of large multicast groups, several iBFs are created, one for each partial multicast tree, and duplicate packets are sent to each next hop.

The source creates one copy of the packet for each next hop for (S,G) in the BFT. It creates a BC_FW header, fills it with the corresponding iBF, and sends it to the next hop router.

Each router makes a forwarding decision based on the iBF, as shown in Algorithm 1. First, it applies the reverse permutation function to the iBF, replacing the iBF with the result. Then, it checks for the presence of peer routers by computing one edge-pair label for each potential next hop router R_n, based on the previous and the current router on path R_p and R_c respectively,[3] and on group identity (S,G) found in the IP header as shown in Algorithm 1. In the final step, the router checks whether the iBF contains the edge-pair label, by simple bitwise AND and comparison operations.

The remaining problem is how to compute the dynamic edge-pair labels at core routers at line speed. This can be done by taking the values (S, G, K, Rp, R_c, R_n) and running them through a fast, spreading hash function (cf. e.g. [20,31]). The spreading hash function yields the bit locations for the edge-pair labels. The method can be applied locally at each router, having no impact on the protocol.

---

[2] This improves forwarding performance, as the false positive probability increases with the number of iBF inserted elements.

[3] The router uses the same inputs as in the BC_JOIN. hence the R_p and R_n switch places due to direction change.

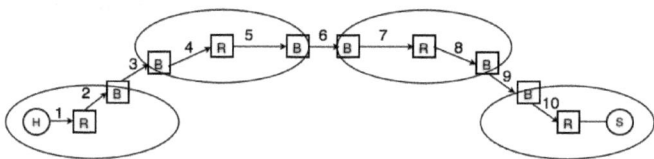

Fig. 4. Protocol messages when joining group (S,G): 1 - IGMP Membership Report or MLD Multicast Listener Report; 2,10 - PIM-SSM JOIN(S,G); 3-9 - BC_JOIN(S,G)

3.3   Connecting Intra-domain Multicast with BloomCasting

BloomCasting can be used to specify the operations between source and receiver ASes.[4] This section discusses how multicast forwarding state is set up inside the domains containing the sender and/or receivers using IP multicast (PIM-SSM deployments) Figure 4 illustrates the protocol messages when a multicast receiver joins a multicast group (S,G).

When a receiver joins (S,G), it signals (1) its interest in its LAN with IGMPv3 or MLDv2 protocols. The Designated Router then sends a PIM-SSM JOIN(S,G) message upstream (2), by looking up the reverse path to S. The message is propagated upstream until a router is found that holds forwarding state for the group or until a border router of the domain is reached (standard PIM-SSM operations). The border routers implement both PIM-SSM and BloomCasting. PIM signaling now terminates. If the border router was not yet a receiver for the group, it creates a BC_JOIN packet and sends it towards S (3-9).

The iBF collection process is otherwise as described in Section 3.1 except each AS is considered to be a singe logical router.

At the other end, the source AS border router receives a BC_JOIN for a group that resides in the local domain and processes it as specified in Section 3.1. If it is not yet a receiver for the group locally, it sends a join packet using PIM-SSM standardized operations (10). The JOIN(S,G) is propagated further upstream towards the source, with standard PIM operations. Eventually, as far as PIM concerned, a domain-local multicast tree will be built with routers representing local receivers and border routers representing subscribers in remote domains.

The data packets are *forwarded* using the domain-local multicast protocol to the border routers in the source AS. The border router creates a single copy for each entry in the BFT, adds the BloomCasting header, and forwards the packets. When an ingress border router receives packet with the BC_FW header, it checks whether it has domain-local receivers and forwards a decapsulated copy using the domain-local multicast protocol. The router also checks whether neighboring domains are included in the iBF and forwards the packet to those domains (using e.g. IP-in-IP, GRE encapsulation, or MPLS paths or trees).

---

[4] An AS is an autonomous system, a network participating in the inter-domain routing protocol (BGP). The source and receiver could also be an area consisting multiple ASes that deploys a shared multicast architecture.

4   Security Techniques in Bloom Filter Based Forwarding

In Section 2, we introduced a threat model for in-packet Bloom filter based forwarding by showing several attacks taking advantage of some forwarding anomalies inherent to Bloom filter based forwarding. Now, we present techniques for solving these forwarding anomalies; then, in Section 5, we evaluate them from security perspective.

Basically, the solutions presented here include pre-processing verification of Bloom filters, and some rules to be followed in the packet forwarding process and during the Bloom filter creation phase.

Limiting the fill factor (ρ_{max}) ensures that the attacker cannot set, e.g., all bits in the Bloom filter to 1, which would equal to every link in the network being included. Before any packet handling operation, routers need to verify the Bloom filter [30], i.e. they need to check for ρ_{max} compliance before attempting to forward the packet. Typically, ρ_{max} is set to ≈ 0.5, which corresponds to the most efficient usage in terms of bits per element per false positive rate.

Cryptographic Bloom filters: Bloom filters for forwarding can be differentiated based on the nature of the link identifiers: (1) link identifiers are common knowledge [25], (2) link identifiers are secret, but static [16], and (3) link identifiers are secret per flow and change periodically with key are computed per incoming/outgoing edge pair instead of per link [13].

Bloom filters gain capabilities [2], when the edge pair label is computed using cryptographically secure hash functions, secret key, and flow information from the packet (e.g., IP 5-tuple, (S, G)). Each link identifier of size m and with k bits set to one (i.e., a one element Bloom filter) can be computed as the output of a function $zF(In, Out, K(t_i), I, p)$. The resulting identifiers become *dynamic* and bound to the In and Out interfaces of each hop i, the time period of a secret key $K(t_i)$, and additionally dependent of packet information like the Flow ID I (e.g., source and group addresses) and an optimization parameter p (cf.Z-formation [13]).

Varying the number of hash bits (k_{var}): This technique deals with the number of ones (k) in the link identifiers set by different routers, and aims to decrease the false positive rate. Assuming that there is a fixed maximum fill factor ρ for iBF, e.g. $\rho = 0.5 + \epsilon$, the average number of false positive in a given router depends on its degree d, the number of hash functions k it uses, and the number of outgoing branches b such that the average number of false positives is $\rho^k \cdot (d - b - 1)$. Hence, we proposed [26] that each router sets k locally such that $\rho^k \cdot d < \alpha$, where $\alpha < 1$ sets the routers preference for the average false positive rate. As routers compute the hash functions for the *collecting* iBF themselves, the number k is purely a local matter. In other words, the number of bits k set to 1 in the link identifiers is not a global parameter, but can be defined per node.

Permutations $P_i(iBF)$: We use per hop bit permutations to prevent loops and flow duplications. A bit permutation is a (pseudo) random rearrangement of the bit array. Each router can use the same bit permutation for all iBFs passing through it making it easy to implement with programmable logic.

First, after passing through the intended path to a router R, the *forwarding* iBF has to match the k hash values that the router added when the *collecting* iBF was forwarded through it. When the iBF is collected, the routers between R and source S change some bits from 0 to 1 and permute the packet. S then combines a set of *collecting* iBFs in to a *forwarding* iBF and the routers between S and R (including R) perform reverse permutations on the iBF. Hence, once the packet arrives in R, the bits that R set to 1 will be in exactly the same positions as they were when the iBF was collected. Since no operation changes a value of a bit from 1 to 0, the matching process works correctly.

Second, if the path taken is different from the one intended for the packet, the iBF should not match the k hash values. Per hop bit permutations enable the iBF itself to carry a "memory" of the path it has traversed [26]. As each router modifies the iBF when forwarding the packet, after passing through two different edges and entering back the initial node, i.e. after a loop, the iBF is changed with a random bit permutation. Hence, it will likely not match the same edge-pair labels again. Each router permutes $P_i(iBF)$ when the iBF is initially collected and then reverse permutes $P_i(iBF)^{-1}$ the iBF when a packet is sent using the iBF.

5   Security Evaluation

We now analyze how BloomCasting mitigates the security threats (described in Section 2) against Bloom filter based multicast forwarding. As mentioned in Section 2.2, we focus on malicious host-initiated attacks. Further architectural considerations w.r.t scalability, bandwidth efficiency, state requirements, control overhead, etc. are out of scope of this evaluation and left for future work.

Table 1 presents an overview of the mapping between the available techniques (Section 4) and the attacks addressed. As can be seen, BloomCasting combines four techniques to prevent the six security threats described in Section 2.2.

Packet storms are prevented with the combination of limiting the maximum fill factor ρ_{max} and the *varying k_{var} technique*. Globally enforced ρ_{max} values enable each router to compute k_{var} locally so that every Bloom filter with a valid fill factor produces, on average, less than 1 false positives. Since the Bloom filters are collected on path with the BC_JOIN packet, it is easy to set k_{var} locally. Additionally, this optimization of k reduces the actual false positive rate [26].

Loops are a serious threat to any network infrastructure. The combination of maximum fill factor ρ and z-Formation makes it difficult for an attacker to construct looping Bloom filters. The first removes the easy attack of just adding bits into the Bloom until every link matches and the z-Formation ensures that guessing the right Bloom filter is difficult (see [13] for details).

To prevent accidental loops, each router performs a bit permutation on the Bloom filter before performing the outport matching – when using the Bloom filter for forwarding (and after matching – when collecting a Bloom filter). If a packet does go through a loop, either because of a false positive or a malicious source, the Bloom filter has been modified with a random permutation (a product of the permutations performed by the set of routers participating in the loop).

Table 1. Mapping of solutions to attacks

Attack - Technique	ρ_{max}	k_{var}	z-F	$P(iBF)$
Packet storms	+	+		
Loops	+		+	+
Flow duplication	+		+	+
Injection	+		+	
Correlation			+	+
Replay			+	

Using permutations ensures a high probability that the packet will not continue looping and that it will not be forwarded to the downstream tree for a
second, or nth time. As an example, the chances of an infinite loop in a three
node loop configuration with $\rho = 0.5$, $k = 6$, and $m = 256$ are in the order of
$O(10^{-12})$. The chances that a packet will be forwarded through the subtree once
are ρ^{κ}, where $\kappa = \sum k_i$ is the sum of all hash functions used in the subtree.

Finally, while the security is not dependent on the secrecy of the permutations
performed in each router, it is dependent on the secrecy of the edge-pair labels.
Consider a *known permutation* attack, in which an attacker knows the network
topology and the permutations used by a set of routers. It can now compute
the cycle sets of the combined permutation and choose a combination that has
approximately the size of the maximum fill factor. However, it does not know
a combination of a Bloom filter and source and group address that will ensure
that the routers on path and in the loop will have edge-pair labels that match
the Bloom filter. The best it can do is vary the group address. In this case, the
probability of success is ρ^{κ}, where κ is the total number of bits that need to be
set on path to the point of loop and in the loop.

Flow duplication: Similarly to loops, flow duplication can be effectively prevented with the combination of restricting fill factor ρ, edge-pair labels, and per
hop bit permutations. The result gives an attacker ρ^{κ} probability of creating a
specific subtree by accident.

Packet injection attacks, correlation attacks, and replay attacks can be efficiently prevented using the z-Formation technique [13]. It uses cryptographically
secure edge-pair labels that are computed based on the flow, and time, and path.
This makes it impossible to share iBFs from different points of network, at different time instants, or to different destinations.

Consequently, the best strategy for a successful *packet injection attack* is reduced to a brute force attack consisting of generating random labels and hoping
that at least one of them reaches the target(s). An attacker needs malformed
iBFs to cause h consecutive false positives to get packets forwarded through a
valid iBF path of length h. The chances of success in one attempt can be ap-
proximated to $p = \rho_{max}^{h \cdot k}$, which is very low for typical configurations (e.g.,
$p = 2^{-36}$ for $h = 4, k = 8, \rho = 0.5$, i.e., over 10^{10} attempts are required for
a $1/2$ probability successful attack). Such brute force attacks can be easily detected, rate limited and pushed back, for instance after the false positive rate

from a given source exceeds some threshold. Additionally, a forged iBF would work through the target path attack as long as the distributed secret K(t) is not renewed.

Source and receiver control: As the group management in BloomCasting is end-to-end, it gives source control over the receivers it accepts. If it wishes to, it can require receiver authentication before adding a receiver into the group. Similarly, multicasting to a receiver requires knowing the iBF that forms the path between source and destination. Since the iBF is cryptographically bound to (S,G), each router's secret key, and the path (via permutations and edge-pair labels), guessing an iBF for a path is difficult, as shown above.

Resource consumption attacks against the memory and processing capacity of routers do not become easier than they are in unicast forwarding. The routers do not need to maintain multicast state and the iBF collection and forwarding processing can be done in line speed in hardware and in parallel for each peer. The multicast source needs to maintain state for receivers. This is a needed feature, since this makes it possible source control over who can and who cannot join the multicast group. Simultaneously, it leaves the source vulnerable to attacker who creates a storm of multicast join packets. A source can use a receiver authentication protocol, which pushes the authentication protocol state to the initiator (e.g., the base exchange of Host Identity Protocol [21] could be used for that purpose) to limit the state requirements to authenticated receivers.

False positive forwarded packets may compromise the *ephemeral secrecy* of the multicast data to non group-members, i.e., some packets may reach unintended destinations. The time- and bit-varying iBFs contribute to spreading false multicasted packets across different links over time, preventing thus a complete reception of a multicast packet flow.[5]

Anonymity of source is not an option in source specific, since the group is identified with combination (S,G) where S is the sender address and G the group address. However, even though the protocol uses source routing, the actual paths, or nodes on path are not revealed to the source and the source can only use the related iBFs in combination with traffic destined to (S,G).

Receivers do not need to reveal their identifies or addresses to the network, or the source – the receiver (IP) address is not necessary in the protocol. The authentication, should the source require it, can be done end-to-end without revealing the identities to the intermediate routers. As the keys used to compute iBFs are changed periodically, correlation attacks between two or more Bloom filters used at different times become impossible. Similarly, since the edge-pair labels are tied to group identifier (S,G), an attacker cannot use a set of iBFs with different group addresses to determine whether the set contains one or more common receivers. These techniques effectively prevent traffic analysis and related vulnerabilities such as clogging attacks (cf. [5]).

---

[5] As assumed in Section 2, *data authenticity* is kept out of scope of the iBF forwarding service and can be provided by orthogonal security policies and group key management techniques (e.g., following the guidelines of [15]).

6   Related Work

Compared with unicast, multicast communication is at a substantially increased risk from specific security threats due to the lack of effective group access control and larger opportunities for link attacks. Over the last decade, much effort has been put in the field of multicast security, see e.g. [6,18,11,15,27].

At the IETF, earlier work has provided a taxonomy of multicast security issues [11] and a framework for secure IP multicast solutions [14] to address the three broad core problem areas identified: (i) fast and efficient source authentication (e.g. [6,17]), (ii) secure and scalable group key management techniques, and (iii) methods to express and implement multicast-specific security policies. Our focus, however, has been on DoS attacks against the network infrastructure.

Service availability attacks due to routing loops and blackholes were discussed in [28]. The proposed solution was the keyed HIP (KHIP) protocol to allow only trusted routers joining the multicast tree. Our aim is a general and open SSM architecture that does not require group access restrictions provided by the infrastructure.

Free Riding Multicast [25] proposes an open any source multicast service in which each link is encoded as a set of hashes from the AS number pair. This leaves the forwarding plane open to a variety of attacks. Odar [29] showed that Bloom filters can be used for anonymous routing in adhoc networks. Limiting fill factor as a security feature in Bloom filter based (unicast) capabilities was first proposed in [30]. LIPSIN [16] uses Bloom filter forwarding plane for publish/subscribe architecture with a separate topology management system that helps to keep the link identifiers secret. However, an attacker can still use target path attacks. Z-formation [13] prevents target path attacks by using edge-pair labels that depend on flow identifier, but is still open to e.g. chain reaction attacks.

Si[3] [1] proposed a secure overlay to solve problems related to secure multicast. While distributed hash tables spread load efficiently across the system, they lack e.g. policy compliant paths and control over who is responsible for particular connection.

7   Conclusions

In this paper, we evaluated the security of Bloom filter based forwarding. False positives inherent to Bloom filters enable a host of attacks on target service and network infrastructure availability. These attacks include chain reaction attacks, which use the Bloom filter properties (e.g. false positives) to ensure that the network forwarding infrastructure multiplies every packet sent using the Bloom filter and targeted attacks in which the attacker enables many nodes to target the same path in the network.

We show that these problems can be solved by the combination of limiting Bloom filter fill factor, both minimum and maximum, using cryptographically computed edge-pair labels in the Bloom filters, varying the number of hash functions locally based on the router degree, and using per hop bit permutations on the Bloom filter.

We also proposed BloomCasting, a secure source-specific multicasting technique based on in-packet Bloom filters. The technique is based on end-to-end signaling of group membership and hop-by-hop collection of the needed Bloom filters. As future work, we intend to study the possibility of collecting multiple paths in advance as a technique for increasing fault tolerance to route failures.

References

1. Adkins, D., Lakshminarayanan, K., Perrig, A., Stoica, I.: Towards a more functional and secure network infrastructure (2003)
2. Anderson, T., Roscoe, T., Wetherall, D.: Preventing Internet denial-of-service with capabilities. ACM SIGCOMM Computer Communication Review 34(1), 44 (2004)
3. Atwood, W., Islam, S., Siami, M.: Authentication and Confidentiality in Protocol Independent Multicast Sparse Mode (PIM-SM) Link-Local Messages. RFC 5796 (Proposed Standard) (March 2010), http://www.ietf.org/rfc/rfc5796.txt
4. Aura, T., Nikander, P.: Stateless Connections. In: Han, Y., Quing, S. (eds.) ICICS 1997. LNCS, vol. 1334, pp. 87–97. Springer, Heidelberg (1997)
5. Back, A., Möller, U., Stiglic, A.: Traffic Analysis Attacks and Trade-Offs in Anonymity Providing Systems. In: Moskowitz, I.S. (ed.) IH 2001. LNCS, vol. 2137, pp. 245–257. Springer, Heidelberg (2001)
6. Ballardie, T., Crowcroft, J.: Multicast-specific security threats and countermeasures. In: SNDSS 1995: Proceedings of the 1995 Symposium on Network and Distributed System Security (SNDSS 1995), p. 2. IEEE Computer Society, Washington, DC (1995)
7. Barbir, A., Murphy, S., Yang, Y.: Generic Threats to Routing Protocols. RFC 4593 (Informational) (October 2006), http://www.ietf.org/rfc/rfc4593.txt
8. Bates, T., Chandra, R., Katz, D., Rekhter, Y.: Multiprotocol Extensions for BGP-4. RFC 4760 (Draft Standard) (January 2007), http://www.ietf.org/rfc/rfc4760.txt
9. Bhattacharyya, S.: An Overview of Source-Specific Multicast (SSM). RFC 3569 (Informational) (July 2003), http://www.ietf.org/rfc/rfc3569.txt
10. Bloom, B.H.: Space/time trade-offs in hash coding with allowable errors. Commun. ACM 13(7), 422–426 (1970)
11. Canetti, R., Pinkas, B.: A taxonomy of multicast security issues. IRTF Internet-Draft (draft-irtf-smug-taxonomy-01) (August 2000)
12. Diot, C., Dabbous, W., Crowcroft, J.: Multipoint communication: A survey of protocols, functions, and mechanisms. IEEE Journal on Selected Areas in Communications 15(3), 277–290 (1997)
13. Esteve, C., Jokela, P., Nikander, P., Särelä, M., Ylitalo, J.: Self-routing Denial-of-Service Resistant Capabilities using In-packet Bloom Filters. In: Proceedings of European Conference on Computer Network Defence, EC2ND (2009)
14. Hardjono, T., Canetti, R., Baugher, M., Dinsmore, P.: Secure ip multicast: Problem areas, framework, and building blocks. IRTF Internet-Draft (draft-irtf-smug-framework-01) (September 2000)
15. Hardjono, T., Weis, B.: The Multicast Group Security Architecture. RFC 3740 (Informational) (March 2004), http://www.ietf.org/rfc/rfc3740.txt
16. Jokela, P., Zahemszky, A., Esteve, C., Arianfar, S., Nikander, P.: LIPSIN: Line speed publish/subscribe inter-networking. In: SIGCOMM (2009)

17. Judge, P., Ammar, M.: Gothic: a group access control architecture for secure multicast and anycast. In: INFOCOM 2002. Twenty-First Annual Joint Conference of the IEEE Computer and Communications Societies. Proceedings. IEEE, vol. 3, pp. 1547–1556 (2002)
18. Judge, P., Ammar, M.: Security issues and solutions in multicast content distribution: A survey. IEEE Network 17, 30–36 (2003)
19. Kleinrock, L., Kamoun, F.: Hierarchical routing for large networks Performance evaluation and optimization. Computer Networks 1(3), 155 (1976/1977)
20. Krawczyk, H.: LFSR-Based Hashing and Authentication. In: Desmedt, Y.G. (ed.) CRYPTO 1994. LNCS, vol. 839, pp. 129–139. Springer, Heidelberg (1994)
21. Moskowitz, R., Nikander, P.: Host Identity Protocol (HIP) Architecture. RFC 4423 (Informational) (May 2006), http://www.ietf.org/rfc/rfc4423.txt
22. Moyer, M., Rao, J., Rohatgi, P.: A survey of security issues in multicast communications. IEEE Network 13(6), 12–23 (1999)
23. Paul, P., Raghavan, S.V.: Survey of multicast routing algorithms and protocols. In: ICCC 2002: Proceedings of the 15th International Conference on Computer Communication, pp. 902–926. International Council for Computer Communication, Washington, DC (2002)
24. Rafaeli, S., Hutchison, D.: A survey of key management for secure group communication. ACM Computing Surveys (CSUR) 35(3), 329 (2003)
25. Ratnasamy, S., Ermolinskiy, A., Shenker, S.: Revisiting IP multicast. ACM SIGCOMM Computer Communication Review 36(4), 26 (2006)
26. Särelä, M., Rothenberg, C.E., Aura, T., Zahemszky, A., Nikander, P., Ott, J.: Forwarding Anomalies in Bloom Filter Based Multicast. Tech. rep., Aalto University (October 2010)
27. Savola, P., Lehtonen, R., Meyer, D.: Protocol Independent Multicast - Sparse Mode (PIM-SM) Multicast Routing Security Issues and Enhancements. RFC 4609 (Informational) (October 2006), http://www.ietf.org/rfc/rfc4609.txt
28. Shields, C., Garcia-Luna-Aceves, J.J.: Khip—a scalable protocol for secure multicast routing. In: SIGCOMM 1999: Proceedings of the Conference on Applications, Technologies, Architectures, and Protocols for Computer Communication, pp. 53–64. ACM, New York (1999)
29. Sy, D., Chen, R., Bao, L.: Odar: On-demand anonymous routing in ad hoc networks. In: Proc. of IEEE Mobile Adhoc and Sensor Systems (MASS), pp. 267–276 (2006)
30. Wolf, T.: A credential-based data path architecture for assurable global networking. In: Proc. of IEEE MILCOM, Orlando, FL (October 2007)
31. Yuksel, K.: Universal hashing for ultra-low-power cryptographic hardware applications. Ph.D. thesis, Citeseer (2004)
32. Zahemszky, A., Jokela, P., Särelä, M., Ruponen, S., Kempf, J., Nikander, P.: MPSS: Multiprotocol Stateless Switching. In: Global Internet Symposium 2010 (2010)

Authentication Session Migration

Sanna Suoranta, Jani Heikkinen, and Pekka Silvekoski

Aalto University, School of Science and Technology, Konemiehentie 2, 02150 Espoo

Abstract. Consumers increasingly access services with different devices such as desktop workstations, notepad computers and mobile phones. When they want to switch to another device while using a service, they have to re-authenticate. If several services and authenticated sessions are open, switching between the devices becomes cumbersome. Single Sign-on (SSO) techniques help to log in to several services but re-authentication is still necessary after changing the device. This clearly violates the goal of seamless mobility that is the target of much recent research. In this paper, we propose and implement migration of authentication session between a desktop computer and a mobile device. The solution is based on transferring the authentication session cookies. We tested the session migration with the OpenID, Shibboleth and CAS single sign-on systems and show that when the authentication cookies are transferred, the service sessions continue seamlessly and do not require re-authentication. The migration requires changes on the client web browsers but they can be implemented as web browser extensions and only minimal configuration changes on server side are sometimes required. The results of our study show that the client-to-client authentication session migration enables easy switching between client devices in online services where the service state is kept in the cloud and the web browser is acting as the user interface.

1   Introduction

During the last ten years, there has been steady increase in the number of web-based applications and cloud services have become widespread. Often, the services require authentication. As the number of applications has increased, the burden of authenticating to each one of these services has become unbearable to the user. Several single sign-on (SSO) techniques have been developed to help users to cope with their accounts in the various services. The problem, however, further aggravated by the fact that people have many devices such as smart phones, laptops, and notepad computers, and they alternate between these devices depending on the context. This context can be determined by several factors, namely the purpose of the use, time, and location. As a result, the number of devices and accessed web-based applications can create a considerable amount of work for a mobile user since there can be a number of sessions on different devices, each of which require separate authentication. In particular, when the user wants to switch to use another of her devices, for example, from a desktop workstation to a notepad computer, she has to re-authenticate. In order to mitigate this problem and to extend SSO to service access from multiple devices, we have developed techniques for authentication session mobility between personal devices.

T. Aura, K. Järvinen, and K. Nyberg (Eds.): NordSec 2010, LNCS 7127, pp. 17–32, 2012.

Different mobility types include mobility of people, services, session state and terminals [7]. All these are necessary for a ubiquitous computing environment. Many solutions and techniques have been developed for terminal mobility, for example, Mobile IP [33] and Session Initiation Protocol (SIP) [40]. Service mobility means mainly consistent network connection establishment — that devices can connect to different kinds of networks seamlessly. In order to provide personal mobility, which means that a user can use any device and switch devices during a task, session mobility or session migration becomes essential. Historically, session migration has meant the migration of processes or virtual machines mainly in homogeneous server farms, and it has been difficult to implement anything similar in heterogeneous client systems. Fortunately, most new services are accessed with web browsers and the session state information is stored in the server or the cloud. Thus, session mobility in many modern services means simply moving the authentication session, which is the only part of the session that has a state stored on the client device.

Web-based applications have the concept of a session for indicating an authenticated user. The session information is typically stored on the server and the client only stores a session identifier in a cookie. When a user returns to the service during the same session, the web server gets the client identity information from the cookie that is delivered together with the service request. Also, many SSO and federated identity management (FIM) techniques, for example, OpenID [35] and Shibboleth [25], use cookies to indicate the authenticated user. In FIM, the service and authentication have been separated to two distinct providers. The user contacts first the service provider, which then redirects the user to a separate identity provider for authentication. When the user has successfully authenticated herself, the identity provider informs the service provider, and the service provider can then decide whether the user has rights to access the service. In the process, an authentication session is created both between the user device and the identity provider and between the user device and the service provider. The user can reuse the authentication session for another service since she has a cookie from the identity provider that shows who she is, or the identity provider remembers that she has already authenticated herself.

In this paper, we implement client-side migration of the authentication sessions. Our goal was to create a system that requires no changes to the identity provider or service provider. In our prototype implementation, the user can continue using a service after transferring the authentication session cookies from one device to another one. We tested our system using the Shibboleth, OpenID and CAS [26] single sign-on mechanisms.

The paper is organized as follows. First, we describe session migration technologies from the literature in Sec. 2. We introduce federated identity management systems and explain how they use cookies in web browsers for sessions in Sec. 3. Then, Sec. 4 and 5 present the design of our solution for client-side migration of authentication session and how we have implemented it on Firefox. In Sec. 6, we discuss how the implementation can be extended to work on other platforms. In Sec. 7, we evaluate the proposed techniques by testing them. In Sec. 8, we discuss what should be done in order to make the session migration work in all browsers and devices and, finally, Sec. 9 concludes the paper.

2   Related Work on Session Migration

Virtual machine process migration was a widely studied subject already as early as in the 1980s. Milojicic et al. [32] survey the most important process migration implementations before year 2000, for example MOSIX [4], Sprite [16], and Mach [1]. They list reasons why these have not gained wide adoption: complexity, costs, non-transparency, homogeneity, lack of applications and infrastructure, and that users did not need the migration. Later, virtual machine process migration has become essential on server side to guarantee higher performance and shorter out-of-service time, to enable load-balancing and to facilitate fault management [12]. For example, Clark et al. [12] describe how to migrate an entire live virtual operating system and all of its applications in Xen virtual machines. Also other virtualized operating systems provide migration. For example, OpenVZ has an extension called CheckPoinTing (CPT) that allows OpenVZ kernel to save a virtual environment and restore it later even on a different host [37], and another Linux based solution, Kernel-based Virtual Machine (KVM) has similar functionality [29]. Mostly virtual operating systems are used on server side for hosting several services on one physical server and for load balancing. Nevertheless, also client side solution exists: MobiDesk virtualizes the user's whole computing session allowing transparent migration of sessions from one computer to another [5].

A whole virtual operating system is easier to migrate than a single application because all memory and state dependencies are handled inside the kernel as one packet. However, moving only application sessions takes less capacity on the communication path and the participating devices may be able to use different operating systems. A stand-alone application is of course easier to move than an application client that communicates with an external service and needs also connection and session state information on the server side. In this paper, we are more interested in the communicating applications. Communication service sessions can be migrated in many ways in different layers of the protocol stack. Some techniques migrate the session directly between two devices, others use proxies where the session is stored during the migration.

Allard et al. [3] have presented a solution for transferring IPsec context using Context Transfer Protocol (CXTP) [31]. The solution is targeted for mobile nodes that move between networks but it works also for switching between devices. The mobile node has a secure connection using IPsec VPN tunnel through an access router with its Mobile IPv6 home agent. In the context transfer, the access router end of the IPsec tunnel is moved to another access router. The IPsec context consists of IP addresses, security parameter indexes that identify the used security associations (SAs), and other SA information telling the used algorithms and modes etc.

On the transport layer, Secure Socket Layer (SSL) [36] and Transport Layer Security (TLS) [14] allow caching of sessions since creation of cryptographic keys can be heavy. Caching is not always enough on the server side where load-balancing is used in addition. Hatsugai et al. [23] present a way for servers to migrate SSL sessions from one server to another one dynamically when the servers form a cluster but their solution is working on the server side and it is not for the client. Koponen et al. [28] extend the TLS protocol so that sessions can survive changing IP addresses, which means that the client can move in the network. Newer transport layer protocols, such as Stream Control Transmission Protocol (SCTP) [48], which is originally designed for transferring telephone signaling messages over IP networks, provides transport layer mobility by multihoming: the connection can have multiple source and destination IP addresses [9].

Many studies present how multimedia sessions or browser based communication sessions can be migrated. Hsieh et al. [24] introduce three approaches for the browser session migration: client-based, server-based and proxy based. Several implementations for these approaches exist. For example, Basto Diniz et al. [15] introduce session management for the ubiquitous medical environment where sessions can be migrated between devices or even suspended by storing them into a server. Cui et al. [13] have developed a middleware solution for user mobility where the client host uses service discovery to locate the services and store state information and handoff manager moves the session when the user changes the device. Bolla et al. [6] approach the problem of multimedia session migration from different starting point: they introduce a Personal Address to identify users and their sessions instead of the network dependent IP addresses. Moreover, many web service solutions are based on SIP. For example, Shacham et al. [42] have created a SIP based session migration for multimedia content. Their solution has two security features: authentication of the device user with a secure token or close proximity, and privacy features where the participants of a communication session can deny session transfer to less trusted devices. Adeyeye et al. [2] present another SIP based solution that allows transferring session data between two web browsers.

RFC3374 [27] lists Authentication, Authorization and Accounting (AAA) information context transfer as one facilitator of seamless IP mobility. For example, Bournelle et al. [8] extend the above mentioned CXTP protocol for transferring network access authentication sessions that use the PANA protocol [19] from one device to another one in order to speed up handover by avoiding re-authentication. Also, Georgiades et al. [20] added AAA context information to Cellular-IP protocol messages in order to improve handover performance.

Nevertheless, many of these above mentioned solutions, especially the AAA context transfer mechanisms, are targeted mainly for device mobility and changing the access network technology or improving server performance, not for application session migration between devices. Nowadays many applications and services works on top of the HTTP protocol to form the communication channel with the client part that uses web browser as user interface. Even though the basic HTTP is stateless, the service can have session state in the server, and the client only has a session identifier in form of a cookie. This means that there is no reason for complex application state transfer between the client devices. Moreover, underlying communication sessions, e.g. TCP connections, can fail and are re-established often. Thus, there is no reason to migrate communication state either. Only authentication session remains to be migrated in the client side.

3   Federated Identity Systems and Web Session Cookies

Web browsers have become the widely used client platform for services on the Internet. Many web services still have their own user account databases and use password-based authentication but new means for identity management are now available. In Federated Identity Management (FIM) systems, the user account management is separated to its own provider: when a user want to authenticate herself to a service, the service provider forwards the request to an identity provider that verifies the user's identification. The core idea of FIM is that the user needs to log in only once in order to use several services and all the services do not need to maintain user account databases. Moreover, some FIM systems allow the user to choose which identity provider they use.

Two common FIM technologies are OpenID [35] and Shibboleth [25]. OpenID is, as its name says, open for anyone to establish their own identity provider, and the OpenID community provides free implementations and instructions for both identity and service providers. The identity verification methods of identity providers vary from strong smart-card-based authentication of legal persons to weak methods where the proof of identity is that the user can receive email using an address. Contrary to the original idea of openness, OpenID allows service providers to choose which identity providers they accept and many organizations that have several online services use OpenID for account management but accept only their own OpenID identity provider.

The other technology mentioned above, Shibboleth, is based on SAML [39] that is also a public standard and free implementations for it are available. Unlike OpenID, SAML requires formal agreements between the participating organizations, which are usually organized as federations. In Finland, the institutions of higher education have formed a federation called HAKA [18] where the universities can provide common services using their own user accounts for access management. The HAKA federation provides schemas and instructions for both the identity and service providers. Fig. 1 depicts how a service authenticates a user with the help of an identity provider in Shibboleth. The user first opens the webpage of the service. Her connection is redirected to the identity provider. If the service accepts several IdPs, a list is provided for the user before the redirection. The IdP authenticates the user and redirects the connection back to the service provider with information that the authentication was successful. Then, the service can decide if the authenticated user has right to use the service or not.

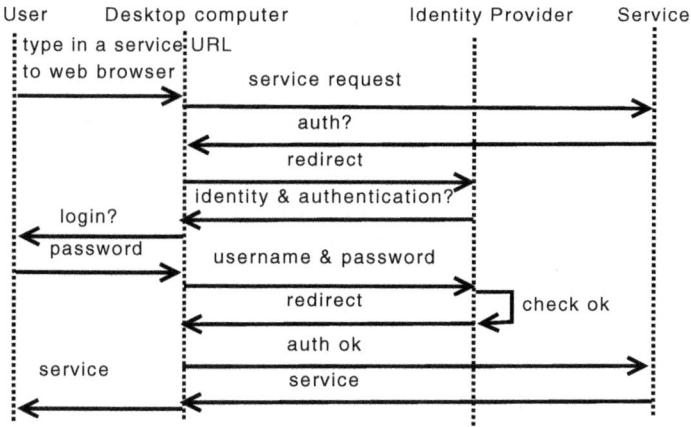

Fig. 1. Shibboleth authentication

In its basic form, an HTTP session is stateless and can consist of many short TCP connections [17]. A web server handles the stateful sessions by sending cookies to the client side web browsers. Samar [41] presents three approaches for cookie based SSO systems: centralized cookie server, decentralized cookie server and centralized cookie login server. In centralized SSO, for example, authentication is done by a centralized entity that gives cookies to services telling the state of the user [10].

Both OpenID and Shibboleth use cookies for storing the authentication session with the identity provider and also possibly for storing the session with service provider. In OpenID, an authentication session is formed between the client and identity provider. Service providers do not necessarily have a session with the client at all. The user must always type in the OpenID identifier since the service providers do not even know if the user is already authenticated to some identity provider. Shibboleth client, on the other hand, creates sessions with both identity and service providers and both of them send their own cookies to the client side. A third cookie maybe created when the user has chosen an identity provider for a service. This means that the user does not need to identify herself while re-authenticating to the service since the service provider knows, based on the cookie, with which identity provider to check that the user still has an active authentication session. The cookies are local to the browser at the client device and neither OpenID nor Shibboleth has any support for sessions that involve multiple client devices or browsers.

4   Design

In this paper, our goal is to design and implement a system that allows the user to switch between devices while using a service that requires authentication and uses single sign-on. Overall, the implementation of SSO migration consists of cookie extraction, creating cookie file, transfer between the devices, importing the cookie and opening the web browser using the same webpage where the user was before the migration. In this section, we describe in detail how all these parts were designed. Silvekoski [46] gives an even more detailed description.

Fig. 2 depicts how a Shibboleth authentication session is migrated from a desktop computer to an Internet tablet device in our implementation. First, the user starts the migration by choosing it from the web browser menu. This starts a browser extension that first extracts the Shibboleth IdP and service cookies and then transfers them to the target device. The target device opens a web browser with the URL of the service that the user was accessing. Since the authentication cookies have been transferred from the other device, the user does not need to re-authenticate and can continue using the service with the mobile device browser. The migration works similarly in the other direction, when moving the session from the mobile device to the desktop computer.

In some cases, however, the service cookies cannot be transferred. If the transfer at the service cookies fails or the service provider does not, for any reason, accept them, the authentication session transfer still succeeds but another step is needed. When a web browser is opened on the target device after the cookie migration, the service redirects the connection to the identity provider. Since the user is already authenticated, the identity provider does not ask her password again. It redirects the connection back to the service provider with the user authentication information.

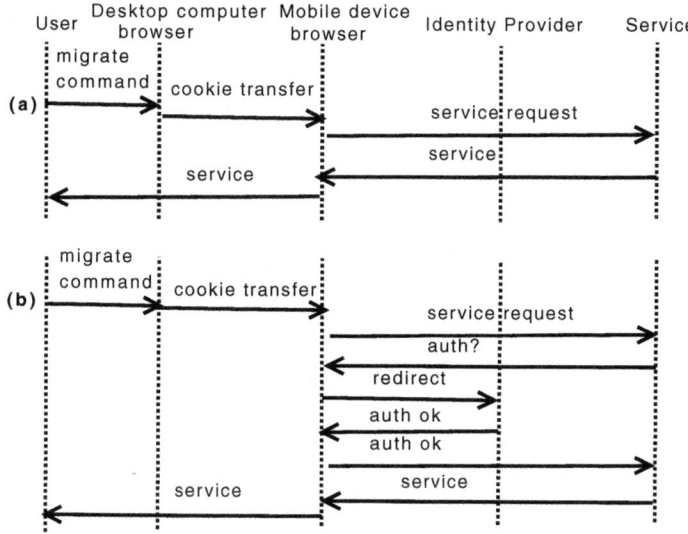

Fig. 2. Authentication session migration with (a) all cookies (b) only authentication cookies

As described above, many SSO systems use cookies to store information about sessions in the client-side web browsers. The session information tells, for example, which user has logged in to the service and how long the session is valid. Moving the cookie from one device and web browser to another one should migrate the session since all the client-side session information is stored in the cookie. Next, we present the design of our cookie based session migration for single sign-on.

Migrating the SSO session requires three steps: extracting the cookies from the original device and web browser, transferring the cookies from the original device to the target device, and importing them into the target device browser. Fig. 3 depicts the SSO cookie migration. When the user chooses to migrate the session, a browser extension first extracts the cookies from the browser and writes them into a cookie file. Then the browser extension starts a transfer module and gives it the location of the cookie file and the URL of the current page on the browser that tells the service location. The transfer module creates a connection to transfer module on the target device and sends the cookie file and URL over to it. The transfer module on the target device imports the cookie into the web browser and starts the browser with the given URL. The migration works similarly both ways between the two devices.

The method for extracting and importing the cookies depends on how they are stored on the original and target device and which web browsers are used. Either the browser or the operating system handles the cookies, but usually an interface for cookie management is offered. The extraction application fetches the cookie information, stores it into a file, and passes the file to the transfer module. Usually, SSO uses session cookies which are stored in the memory rather than on the disk. For this reason, the cookies cannot be simple read from a file and an API for accessing them is needed. If the browser manages the cookies, the extraction is done with a browser extension. Otherwise, the

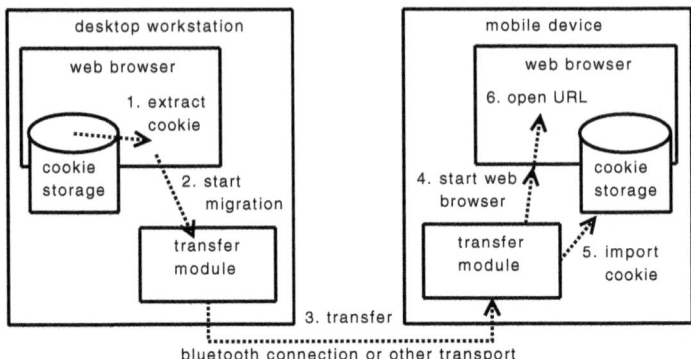

Fig. 3. Shibboleth authentication

operating system provides the cookie information but also a browser extension is needed since that allows the user to start the migration and gives the URL of the current page.

The cookies are transferred between devices in files. If the cookies are stored in the memory, the cookie extractor creates a file and stores the cookie information into it in the format in which they were stored in the memory. SSO cookies are encrypted and thus the exact byte values are essential so that the cookie data does not change. However, it is not always necessary to transfer all cookie data, just the name, value, domain and path must be transferred. The cookie domain and path tell the owner of the cookie, namely the service, whereas name and value give the purpose of the cookie and session data. The cookie information is stored in a file where each cookie is four lines long with following content: name, value, domain and path. Several cookies can be stored into one file.

The transfer module takes care of moving the cookie file from the original device to the target device. It has two behaviors: a client that sends the cookie from the original device and a server that receives the cookie on the target device. In our implementation, when the user wants to migrate her session, she starts the transfer server on the target device and clicks a start button in a menu of the web browser on the original device. The target device shows a dialog that tells where the connection is coming from so that the user can be sure the cookies are coming from the correct original device. In addition to the cookie, also the URL of the current page on the web browser is sent. The transfer client reads the cookie file, establish a connection with the transfer server that waits for the connections on the target device, and transfers the cookie and URL over to it. After successful copying the cookie to the target device, the transfer client removes it from the original device. Otherwise, the session might remain open on the original device, and this might confuse some services. Also, ending the session on the target device does not remove the cookie on the original device but only on the target device and the session might accidentally stay open even when the user thinks she has logged out and closed the browser. On the target device, the corresponding transfer server receives the cookie file, stores it, and starts the local web browser with the URL it received. After the transfer, also the transfer server closes itself. In future implementations, the transfer module could always run as a daemon process, which would slightly simplify the user experience. Next, we describe the implementation in more detail.

5   Firefox Implementation

The SSO technologies chosen for the implementation were Shibboleth and OpenID. Both of these are freely available open source systems and thus easy to take into use. Shibboleth is used in Finnish universities and there are several services available. All students and staff members have their own user accounts. OpenID has several identity providers and services available on the Internet. We chose to use Mozilla Firefox on the desktop computer running Windows XP operating system and Fennec on the Nokia N810 Internet Tablet running Maemo OS. The Fennec browser was a beta, which caused some problems that we describe later.

We used Bluetooth for transferring the cookies. It provides encrypted connections between the devices and the devices are identified with their unique addresses. The devices can be found using Bluetooth service discovery. If the connecting device is unknown, the user is asked to approve the connection. The devices can also be paired to remember each other. Bluetooth is designed for personal area connections and transferring data between one user's devices, which means that the pairing usually needs to be only once for new devices. Bluetooth has built-in encryption and its security is generally considered adequate [22]. We used the Python language to implement the transfer module that receives the connection at the target device since the only Java edition, Java micro edition (JME), that support Bluetooth, does not work on N810.

Both of the used web browsers save the session cookies in the memory of the device but offer a possibility to fetch the cookies using scripting. Moreover, same extensions such as the cookie handling extension work on both Firefox and Fennec since both are Mozilla-based web browsers. The extensions are cross-platform component object model (XPCOM) components than can use cross-platform libraries. Mozilla extensions can be done with JavaScript. We used nsICookie [43], nsICookieManager [44], nsIFile [34] and nsIProcess [45] interfaces and components. The first difference between the browsers is that Fennec does not have drop down menus. Thus, the user starts the migration by choosing it from Firefox drop-down menu on the desktop computer or by clicking a button in the Fennec menubar on the mobile device.

First, in the authentication session migration, nsICookieManager is used to extract the cookie data from the web browser memory. The cookies are in nsICookie format as UTF-8 text, which consists of the cookie name, value, host and path, and additional information. In the extraction process, all cookies in the browser memory are enumerated and the needed SSO cookies are chosen based on their name. Neither of our example FIM systems, OpenID and Shibboleth, has strict instructions for naming the cookies. OpenID uses usually a combination of the identity provider name and openid tags, for example _exampleidp_openid. Shibboleth names usually the service session with _shibsession_ and application code and the authentication session with _idp_session but both of these can be changed using system attributes. The cookie names also depend on the used authentication method in Shibboleth. The recognized cookies are stored in a file in the root directory of the browser extension using the nsIFile interface and the UTF-8 encoding.

For transferring the cookies, nsIProcess starts the python application for Bluetooth and gives it the location of the cookie file and the current URL of the web browser. We used an external Python library called PyBluez [21] for the Bluetooth operations.

It works both on Windows XP and Maemo, so that the same code can be used on both devices. Since cookies are small text files, we used the Bluetooth RFCOMM serial port profile (SPP) to transfer them. First, the Bluetooth client starts the device and service discovery. Of course, the Bluetooth server on the target device must be already waiting for the connections. The client asks the user if the correct target device is found by showing a dialog that gives the device identifiers of discovered devices. The dialog is done with native graphical library of N810, GTK+, since it was harder to find a browser-integrated UI library that works on the internet tablet. When the target device has been selected, the client opens the connection and transfers the cookie information file as a string. Before client closes, it deletes the cookie from the original device using nsICookieManager.

On the target device, the transfer server module receives the message. It stores the URL and writes the cookie into a file. Then, it starts the web browser that uses nsIFile to read the cookie and nsICookieManager to import it into the browser memory. When the authentication session is migrated from a mobile device to the desktop computer, the Firefox web browser is started on the desktop computer with the Python web browser library. In the other direction, this could not be done since Fennec is a new browser still under development. As an intermediate solution, we started the Fennec browser with the subprocess command in Maemo by executing a shell script and the user must browse to the right page herself. Next, we discuss how to extend the same process to work in other web browsers and devices.

6   Porting to Other Browsers and Operating Systems

The way the cookies are stored depends on the device, operating system and web browser. In addition, there are two kinds of cookies, session and persistent cookies, whose storage differs. For example, both the identity and service cookies are session cookies in Shibboleth but the "Where are you from" (WAYF) cookie that allows user to store chosen identity provider into the web browser is a persistent cookie. Different web browsers on different platform handle the cookies in their own way. Usually, persistent cookies are stored in the file system while session cookies exist only in the browser memory. Therefore, accessing the cookies differs between devices and browsers. In order to migrate the authentication session, full access to session cookies is necessary since the cookies must be extracted from the web browser on the original device and entered to the web browser on the target device.

Table 1. The session cookie handling in different browsers

Web browser	Accessing cookies in memory	File for cookies	Storage format
Internet Explorer	not possible	in separate files	text
Mozilla Firefox	user side scripting	cookie.sqlite	sqlite
Opera	manually	cookie4.dat	Opera's own format

Table 1 summarizes the handling of cookies on different browsers. In Windows environment, persistent cookies are stored in the file system and the session cookies in the device memory in many popular web browsers, namely Internet Explorer (IE), Mozilla Firefox, and Opera. The location and format of the stored persistent cookies differs between browsers. IE stores the persistent cookies into separate files in its cookie directory but it does not give developers opportunities to manipulate the session cookies in the device memory. Mozilla Firefox offers wide possibilities to extend the browser, and one existing extension offers programmers full control of the stored cookies. Opera offers an editor to the user for manipulating both session and persistent cookies manually but only persistent cookies can be extracted. Thus, the user must first change a session cookie into a persistent one before it can be transferred, and scripting cannot do this. In Mac OS, cookies are handled differently: the operating system offers an HTTP package that handles all the cookies and offers the possibility to add and manipulate cookies freely.

Mobile devices are even more heterogeneous with respect to their operating systems and browsers. A browser that works on all mobile operating systems does not exist, and even all programming languages are not available on mobile devices. Many popular browsers have their own mobile version that has a lighter graphical user interface than the desktop computer version. For example, of the Mozilla based browser, MicroB works on the Nokia Maemo operating system and Fennec has a beta for Nokia N810 and an alpha version for Window mobile. Most Firefox extensions should work on Fennec. Opera Mini, on the other hand, has a completely different approach to mobile browsing: it uses a proxy that compresses and preprocesses the web pages for the device, and the proxy handles also the cookies. Moreover, the operating system handles the cookies for the mobile version of Apple Safari that works on the IPhone. Similarly, the Symbian OS handles the HTTP connections and cookies for Browser, which is the mobile version of Safari on Symbian operating systems.

7   Experimental Evaluation

For testing the authentication session migration, we performed three experiments using different SSO technologies. First, we tested OpenID authentication session migration with Livejournal [30] as the service provider since it accepts other OpenID identity providers than its own. We used claimID [11] as the OpenID identity provider since it allows creating new accounts easily. Migrating the session cookie named _claimid_openid migrates the authentication session into the target device where the user could continue using the service. OpenID service provider differ in the ways the cookies are implemented and, in order to migrate Livejournal SP, two cookies were needed: ljloggedin and ljmastersession. We cannot be sure if we migrated also other information than the authentication session with these two cookies. In Livejournal, the user can choose whether the service provider will check that the client IP address for the session remains constant. Insisting that the IP address does not change prevented the session migration as was expected since the devices have the different IP addresses.

The second test was done using Shibboleth, which is used to authenticate users at our university. Thus, we had one identity provider, the university, and we tried several different services. Unfortunately, many of the services required that the connections are from the same IP address, which prevents the session migration. The address is stored in the cookie and it cannot be changed. Since we did not have possibility to reconfigure the services, we tested the migration only with those providers that allowed the client to change its IP address. For them, the migration works fine with the Shibboleth SSO.

In addition to the two federated solutions, we tested another centralized authentication mechanism that is used in social media services in the OtaSizzle project [47] at the university. These services use the Central Authentication Service (CAS) [26] to authenticate users, and the experiments showed that transferring its cookies successfully migrates the authentication session. The service session could be continued after migration without re-authentication.

Our main goal was to create system where authentication session can be migrated from one device to another in a way that re-authentication is not necessary and no or minimal modifications for the server side are required. Of course, the session migration should be faster and require less input from the user than re-authentication. Moreover, the user should be able to continue her browser session from the same URL and logical state on the target platform.

From the session migration point of view, our prototype fulfills the requirements. Transferring the authentication session cookies were enough and no additional information was required for the session migration on the tested services. Migration of cookies on the client side did not require changes on server side. OpenID worked directly with its default settings. Shibboleth, which has replay attack prevention on by default, did not work since it checks that also the authentication session cookies come from the same IP address. This means that service providers should be configured not to check the IP address in order to allow user to migrate the authentication between her devices. This configuration enables also mobile computers to continue their sessions after moving between access networks.

From the usability point of view, the migration is faster than typing the passwords on the mobile device. However, the Bluetooth device discovery sometimes took a long time. For example, Windows repeated the service discovery of PyBluez devices four times in order to be sure that all devices were found. To speed up the discovery, the searching for services can be restricted to already paired devices. The other requirement, that the user can continue from the same URL and state of the service, is usually met since web browsers can be started with a command line or shell script with the starting URL as a parameter. In our prototype implementation, the continuing on the same location worked only when the session was migrated from mobile device to a desktop computer, not vice versa, since the Fennec browser used on mobile device was only a beta version and did not have the required feature of starting on the given URL. This will be easily fixed when the browser becomes more complete.

Our main goal was to move only the authentication session, not the whole user session, because the user session is maintained by the web server, and by the cloud services in the future, and only the authentication session binds the user connection to the services on the client side. From the server point of view, the migration is tantamount to the client moving to a different IP address and the user pressing the refresh button on the browser.

8 Discussion

In our tests, we showed that transferring the authentication session cookies migrates the authentication session and, in most cases, the entire user session between devices. In order to take the authentication session migration into wider use, following steps are required:

- Standardization of the API for accessing authentication cookies in web browsers,
- Standardization of the naming of the authentication cookies in SSO systems,
- Recommendation not to bind the cookies to IP addresses but to use some other replay attack protection technology,
- Defining standard ways to transmit the cookies over Bluetooth, IP and other channels, and
- Definition of a cookie file format for cookie transfer.

Technically these changes are fairly easy to do, as shown is this paper, but the hard part is the interoperability between many devices and browsers. Thus, standardization is needed.

The methods for *accessing cookies* differ between web browsers and devices as described in Sec. 6. Nowadays, accessing the session cookies is not always possible at all or requires actions from the user. In order to enable universal authentication session migration, the session cookies must be available through an API in all operating systems and web browsers. Then, the migration extension can extract the cookies for transfer.

Naming cookies in a standard way in SSO specifications helps identifying them for the migration. The FIM specifications should give stricter guidelines for naming the cookies.

The IP address of the client is often stored in the cookies to prevent connections from other client hosts than the original one. This is a historical feature to prevent sniffing of the authentication cookies in services that do not use SSL/TLS to protect the cookies. In such services, the cookies may be transferred as plain text. An attacker can record the cookie and send it to a server pretending to be the original communication partner and thus hijack the connection [38]. The service provider mitigated this threat by accepting cookies only from the current IP address of the user. In OpenID, the administrator of the identity provider must take the protection into use. Shibboleth, on the other hand, checks by default that, when the connection is redirected from the service provider to the identity provider and back, the IP address of the client remains the same, and that the client sends the cookies always from the same IP address during the following session. Session migration requires such controls to be disabled. Some other means to prevent replay attacks with stolen cookies should be used. For example, SSL/TLS with client certificates prevents the attack.

A secure connection for the cookie transfer between the user's devices must be easy to take into use. We used Bluetooth that provides easy way to securely pair the devices, but the devices offer many other possibilities. For example, a mobile devices could use a WLAN connection in peer-to-peer mode to connect to other devices without external gateways, or the connection could be created through the Internet using an access point. WLAN has its own security mechanism called Wi-Fi Protected Access (WPA). An Internet proxy could also be used to deliver the cookies and the connections from the two devices to the proxy protected with TLS. For authentication session migration, creating a secure connection must be easy and not to require active participation from the user after the initial setup. The device discovery and verifying the connection parties must happen transparently after the user initiates the session transfer. In this respect, our current implementation needs to be developed further: the user should not need to start the migration on both devices on every migration but only to pair the devices on the first connection.

Cookie transfer file format is the last important part of the migration. The devices may use different encoding for files and text but the cookie information must not change during the transmission or when storing it to the target browser. Cookies often contain special characters, and thus using the same encoding for the information on the original device and on the target device is important.

9   Conclusion

In this paper, we have experimented with authentication session migration based on the transfer of client-side cookies. Many web services use cookies for recognizing the users and for storing information about the service state. Also, the Shibboleth, OpenID and CAS SSO technologies use cookies to tell that a user has already authenticated herself. Moving the cookies that the identity provider created for the user enables her to continue using the service with another device without re-authentication.

The session transfer does not require any changes on server side if the authentication session cookies can be identified by standard names on the client side and the server is not configured to use IP-address-based replay attack protection. Our current implementation relies on Bluetooth device pairing for secure transfer of the session state and shows a dialog to the user for choosing the target device before migrating the authentication session cookies. We had minor performance problems with the Bluetooth service discovery when the devices were not continually connected but otherwise the migration was fast enough to be used regularly.

Client-side session migration works well in a situation where the only party that knows which services and which identity providers are in use is the client. A drawback of the client side implementation is that all different browsers on different devices and platforms need their own extensions since the cookies are handled very differently in these. Solving this problem requires standardization of some SSO features that have currently been left as configuration and implementation options. In the future, online services increasingly are such that the service state is kept in the cloud and the web browser is acting as the user interface, and only the authentication binds the service session to a device or a operating system. Based on the results of this paper, we believe that client-to-client session migration for such services is easy to implement and should become a regular feature of web browsers and SSO services.

References

1. Accetta, M., Baron, R., Bolosky, W., Golub, D., Rashid, R., Tevanian, A., Young, M.: Mach: A new kernel foundation for UNIX development. In: Proceedings of the Summer USENIX Conference (1986)

2. Adeyeye, M., Ventura, N.: A sip-based web client for http session mobility and multimedia services. Computer Communications 33(8) (2010)
3. Allard, F., Bonnin, J.M.: An application of the context transfer protocol: IPsec in a IPv6 mobility environment. International Journal of Communication Networks and Distributed Systems 1(1) (2008)
4. Barak, A., Laden, O., Yarom, Y.: The NOW MOSIX and its preemptive process migration scheme. Bulletin of the IEEE Technical Committee on Operating Systems and Application Environments 7(2), 5–11 (1995)
5. Baratto, R.A., Potter, S., Su, G., Nieh, J.: Mobidesk: mobile virtual desktop computing. In: MobiCom 2004: Proceedings of the 10th Annual International Conference on Mobile Computing and Networking (2004)
6. Bolla, R., Rapuzzi, R., Repetto, M., Barsocchi, P., Chessa, S., Lenzi, S.: Automatic multimedia session migration by means of a context-aware mobility framework. In: Mobility 2009, The 6th International Conference on Mobile Technology, Application & Systems (2009)
7. Bolla, R., Rapuzzi, R., Repetto, M.: Handling mobility over the network. In: CFI 2009: Proceedings of the 4th International Conference on Future Internet Technologies (2009)
8. Bournelle, J., Laurent-Maknavicius, M., Tschofenig, H., Mghazli, Y.E.: Handover-aware access control mechanism: CTP for PANA. Universal Multiservice Networks (2004)
9. Budzisz, L., Ferrús, R., Brunstrom, A., Grinnemo, K.J., Fracchia, R., Galante, G., Casadevall, F.: Towards transport-layer mobility: Evolution of SCTP multihoming. Computer Communications 31(5) (March 2008)
10. Chalandar, M.E., Darvish, P., Rahmani, A.M.: A centralized cookie-based single sign-on in distributed systems. In: ITI 5th International Conference on Information and Communications Technology (ICICT 2007), pp. 163–165 (2007)
11. claimID.com, Inc: claimID (2010), http://claimid.com (referred 2.8.2010)
12. Clark, C., Fraser, K., Hand, S., Hansen, J.G., Jul, E., Limpach, C., Pratt, I., Warfield, A.: Live migration of virtual machines. In: NSDI 2005: 2nd Symposium on Networked Systems Desgin and Implementation. USENIX Association (2005)
13. Cui, Y., Nahrstedt, K., Xu, D.: Seamless user-level handoff in ubiquitous multimedia service delivery. Multimedia Tools and Applications 22(2) (February 2004)
14. Dierks, T., Rescorla, E.: The transport layer security (TLS) protocol version 1.1. RFC 4346, IETF (April 2006)
15. Diniz, J.R.B., Ferraz, C.A.G., Melo, H.: An architecture of services for session management and contents adaptation in ubiquitous medical environments. In: SAC 2008: Proceedings of the 2008 ACM Symposium on Applied Computing (2008)
16. Douglis, F.: Process migration in the Sprite operating system. In: Proceedings of the 7th International Conference on Distributed Computing Systems, pp. 18–25 (1987)
17. Fielding, R., Gettys, J., Mogul, J., Frystyk, H., Masinter, L., Leach, P., Berners-Lee, T.: Hypertext transfer protocol – http/1.1. RFC 2616, IETF (June 1999)
18. Finnish IT center for science (CSC): HAKA federation, http://www.csc.fi/english/institutions/haka (referred 10.2.2010)
19. Forsberg, D., Ohba, Y., Patil, B., Tschofenig, H., Yesig, A.: Protocol for carrying authentication for network access (PANA). RFC 5191, IETF (May 2008)
20. Georgiades, M., Akhtar, N., Politis, C., Tafazolli, R.: Enhancing mobility management protocols to minimise AAA impact on handoff performance. Computer Communications 30, 608–628 (2007)
21. Google: Pybluez (bluetooth library for python), http//code.google.com/p/pybluez/ (referred 15.12.2009)
22. Hager, C., Midkiff, S.: An analysis of bluetooth security vulnerabilities. In: Proceedings of IEEE Wireless Communications and Networking (WCNC 2003) (March 2003)

23. Hatsugai, R., Saito, T.: Load-balancing SSL cluster using session migration. In: AINA 2007: Proceedings of the 21st International Conference on Advanced Networking and Applications. IEEE Computer Society (May 2007)
24. Hsieh, M., Wang, T., Sai, C., Tseng, C.: Stateful session handoff for mobile www. Information Sciences 176(9), 1241–1265 (2006)
25. Internet2: Shibboleth (2006), http://shibboleth.internet2.edu/ (referred 5.9.2006)
26. Jasig: Central authentication service (CAS), http://www.jasig.org/cas (ref. 15.1.2009)
27. Kempf, J.: Problem description: Reasons for performing context transfers between nodes in an IP access network. RFC 3374, IETF (September 2002)
28. Koponen, T., Eronen, P., Särelä, M.: Esilient connections for SSH and TLS. In: USENIX Annual Technical Conference (2006)
29. KVM: Kvm migration, http://www.linux-kvm.org/page/Migration (referred 27.7.2010)
30. Livejournal: Livejournal, http://www.livejournal.com (referred 16.1.2010)
31. Loughney, J., Nakhjiri, M., Perkins, C., Koodli, R.: Context transfer protocol (CXTP). RFC 4067, IETF (July 2005)
32. Milojicic, D.S., Douglis, F., Paindaveine, Y., Wheeler, R., Zhou, S.: Process migration. ACM Compuring Surveys 32(3), 241–299 (2000)
33. Montenegro, G., Roberts, P., Patil, B.: IP routing for wireless/mobile hosts (mobileip) (concluded ietf working group) (August 2001), http://datatracker.ietf.org/wg/mobileip/charter/ (referred 26.7.2010)
34. Morgan, P.: nsIFile (mozilla extension reference), http://developer.mozilla.org/en/nsIFile (referred 15.12.2009)
35. OpenID.net: Openid.net (2008), http://openid.net/
36. OpenSSL: Openssl project (2005), http://www.openssl.org/ (referred 17.10.2008)
37. OpenVZ: Checkpointing and live migration (September 6, 2007), http://wiki.openvz.org/Checkpointing_and_live_migration (referred 27.7.2010)
38. Park, J.S., Sandhu, R.: Secure cookies on the web. IEEE Internet Computing 4(4), 36–44 (2000)
39. Ragouzis, N., Hughes, J., Philpott, R., Maler, E., Madsen, P., Scavo, T.: Security assertion markup language (saml) v2.0 technical overview. Tech. rep., OASIS (February 2007)
40. Rosenberg, J., Schulzrinne, H., Camarillo, G., Johnston, A., Sparks, J.P.R., Handley, M., Schooler, E.: Sip: Session initiation protocol. RFC 3261, IETF (2002)
41. Samar, V.: Single sign-on using cookies for web applications. In: Proceedings of IEEE 8th International Workshop on Enabling Technologies: Infrastructure for Collaborative Enterprises (WET ICE 1999), pp. 158–163 (June 1999)
42. Shacham, R., Schulzrinne, H., Thakolsri, S., Kellerer, W.: Ubiquitous device personalization and use: The next generation of IP multimedia communications. Transactions on Multimedia Computing, Communications, and Applications (TOMCCAP) 3(2) (May 2007)
43. Shepherd, E.: nsICookie (mozilla extension reference), http://developer.mozilla.org/en/nsICookie (referred 15.12.2009)
44. Shepherd, E.: nsICookieManager (mozilla extension reference), http://developer.mozilla.org/en/nsICookieManager (referred 26.7.2010)
45. Shepherd, E., Smedberg, B.: nsIProcess (mozilla extension reference) (May 2009), http://developer.mozilla.org/en/nsIProcess (referred 15.12.2009)
46. Silvekoski, P.: Client-side migration of authentication session. Master's thesis, Aalto University School of Science and Technology (2010)
47. Sizzlelab.org: Otasizzle (April 2010), http://sizl.org/ (referred 28.7.2010)
48. Stewart, R.: Stream control transmission protocol. RFC 4960, IETF (September 2007)

Mitigation of Unsolicited Traffic across Domains with Host Identities and Puzzles

Miika Komu[1], Sasu Tarkoma[2], and Andrey Lukyanenko[1]

[1] Aalto University
[2] University of Helsinki

Abstract. In this paper, we present a general host identity-based technique for mitigating unsolicited traffic across different domains. We propose to tackle unwanted traffic by using a cross-layer technique based on the Host Identity Protocol (HIP). HIP authenticates traffic between two communicating end-points and its computational puzzle introduces a cost to misbehaving hosts. We present a theoretical framework for investigating scalability and effectiveness of the proposal, and also describe practical experiences with a HIP implementation. We focus on email spam prevention as our use case and how to integrate HIP into SMTP server software. The analytical investigation indicates that this mechanism may be used to effectively throttle spam by selecting a reasonably complex puzzle.

1 Introduction

One challenge with the current Internet architecture is that it costs very little to send packets. Indeed, many proposals attempt to introduce a cost to unwanted messages and sessions in order to cripple spammers' and malicious entities' ability to send unsolicited traffic. From the network administration viewpoint, spam and DoS traffic comes in two flavors, *inbound* and *outbound* traffic. Inbound traffic originates from a foreign network and outbound traffic is sent to a foreign network. Typically, spam and packet floods originate from networks infested with zombie machines. A *zombie* machine is a host that has been taken over by spammers or persons working for spammers, e.g., using Trojans or viruses.

We address the problem of unsolicited network traffic. We use two properties unique to the *Host Identity Protocol (HIP)* protocol: First, hosts are authenticated with their public keys which can be used for identifying well-behaving SMTP servers. Second, a computational puzzle introduces a cost to misbehaving hosts. Our approach has a *cross-layer* nature because a lower-layer security protocol is used to the benefit of higher-layer protocols.

2 Host Identity Protocol

The Host Identity Protocol (HIP) [9] addresses mobility, multi-homing, and security issues in the current Internet architecture. HIP requires a new layer in

T. Aura, K. Järvinen, and K. Nyberg (Eds.): NordSec 2010, LNCS 7127, pp. 33–48, 2012.

the networking stack, logically located between the network and transport layers, and provides a new, cryptographic namespace. HIP is based on *identifier-locator split* which separates the *identifier* and *locator* of an Internet host. The identifier uniquely names the host in a cryptographic namespace, and the locator defines a topological location of the node. Communication end points are identified using public cryptographic keys instead of IP addresses. The public keys used for HIP are called *Host Identifiers (HIs)* and each host generates at least one HI for itself.

The HIs can be published as separate HIP-specific records in the DNS [11]. Legacy applications can use HIP transparently without any changes. Typically, the application calls the system resolver to query the DNS to map the host name to its corresponding address. If a HIP record for the host name does not exist, the resolver returns a routable IPv4 or IPv6 address. Otherwise, the resolver returns a Host Identifier fitted into an IPv4 or IPv6 address. *Local-Scope Identifier (LSI)* is a virtual IPv4 address assigned locally by the host and it refers to the corresponding HI. *Host Identity Tag (HIT)* is an IPv6 address derived directly from the HI by hashing and concatenation. An LSI is valid only in the local context of the host whereas a HIT is statistically globally unique.

When an application uses HIP-based identifiers for transport-layer communications, the underlying HIP layer is invoked to authenticate the communication end-points. This process is called the *base exchange*, during which the end points authenticate to each other using their public keys. The host starting the base exchange, the initiator, is typically a client, and the other host, the responder, is typically a server. During the base exchange, the initiator has to use a number of CPU cycles to solve a computational puzzle. The responder can increase the computational difficulty of the puzzle to throttle new incoming HIP sessions. Upon successful completion, both end-hosts create a session state called *HIP association*.

The base exchange negotiates an end-to-end tunnel to encapsulate the consecutive transport-layer traffic between the two communicating end-hosts. The tunnel is required because routers would otherwise discard traffic using virtual, non-routable identifiers. Optionally, the tunnel also protects transport-layer traffic using a shared key generated during the base exchange. By default, the tunnel is based on IPsec [7] but S-RTP [14] can be used as well. It should be noted that a single tunnel can encompass multiple transport-layer connections.

With HIP, transport-layer connections become more resilient against IP address changes because the application and transport layers are bound to the location-independent virtual identifiers, HITs or LSIs. The HIP layer handles IP-address changes transparently from the upper layer using the *UPDATE* procedure [10]. In the first step of the procedure, the end host sends all of its locators to its connected peers. Then, the peers initiate so called *return routability test* to protect against packet-replay attacks, i.e., to make sure that the peer locator is correct. In the test, each node sends a nonce addressed to each of the received peer locators. The peer completes the test by signing each nonce and echoing it back to the corresponding peer. Only after the routability test is successfully completed, the peer can start using the locator for HIP-related communications.

HIP sessions can be closed using the *CLOSE* [9] mechanism. It is consist of two packets, in which one of the peer sends a CLOSE message to the other, which then acknowledges the operation using CLOSE-ACK. After this, all state is removed and the tunnel is torn down on both sides.

HIP employs *rendezvous servers* [5] to address the *double jump* problem. This occurs when two connected HIP hosts lose contact with each other when they are relocated simultaneously to new networks. The rendezvous server has a stable IP address and offers a stable contact point for the end hosts to reach each other.

The computational puzzles of HIP [1] play a major role in this paper and have been investigated by others as well. Beal et al. [3] developed a mathematical model to evaluate the usefulness of the HIP puzzle under steady-state DDoS attacks. They also stated that the difficulty of the DoS-protection puzzle should not be too high because otherwise an attacker can just choose a cheaper method such as simple flooding of the network. Tritilanunt et al. [13] explored HIP puzzles further with multiple adversary models and variable difficulties. They also noticed that solving of HIP puzzles can be distributed and a non-distributable puzzle algorithm would provide more resilience against DDoS. Our work differs from Beal et al. and Tritilanunt et al. because our use case is spam rather than DDoS and our approach is based on cross-layer integration.

3   System Model

The basic idea is to assign each node in the network with an identity based on a public key. The hosts may generate their private keys by themselves, or a third party can assign them. Computational puzzles are a well-known technique for spam prevention [4,2,6] but are typically used on a per message basis. In our case, puzzles are applied to each pair of Host Identifiers. The difficulty of the puzzle is varied based on the amount of unwanted traffic encountered.

Our example use case for the technique is spam prevention. Typical spam prevention techniques are applied in a sequence starting from black, white or gray listing techniques and sender identification, and ending in content filtering. Our approach involves a similar sequence of spam testing but relies on the identity of the sender rather than its IP address.

3.1   Basic Architecture for Spam Mitigation

In the email systems deployed in the Internet, there are *outbound email servers* which are used for sending email using SMTP. Typically, the users access them either directly or indirectly with a web-based email client. Usually users are authenticated to these services with user names and passwords. In many cases, direct access to outbound SMTP servers is restricted to the local network as a countermeasure against spam. However, spam is still a nuisance and there are networks which still allow sending of spam. In this paper, we use the term *spam relay* for a malign or compromised outbound email server that allows sending spam, and the term *legitimate relay* for a well-behaving outbound email server.

Correspondingly, *inbound email servers* process incoming emails arriving from outbound emails servers. Users access these servers either indirectly via web interfaces or directly with protocols such as POP or IMAP. Typically, the inbound email server tags or drops spam messages and also the email client of the user filters spam messages.

Our idea in a nutshell is to require a HIP session with an SMTP server before it will deliver any email. The sender has to solve a computational puzzle from the server to establish the session. If the sender sends spam, the server ends the HIP session after a certain spam threshold is met. To continue sending spam, the sender has to create a new session, but this time it will receive a more difficult puzzle from the server.

The proposed architecture follows the existing SMTP architecture but requires some changes. First, the inbound and outbound SMTP servers have to be HIP capable. Second, we assume the spam filter of the inbound server is modified to control the puzzle difficulty. Third, we assume the inbound SMTP servers publish their Host Identifiers in the DNS.

3.2   Deployment Considerations

A practical limitation in our approach is that HIP itself is not widely deployed. Even though we compare the HIP-based approach to the current situation later in this paper, the benefits of our design can be harnessed to their full extent only when HIP, or a similar protocol, has been deployed more widely in the Internet. Alternatively, our design could be applied to some other system with built-in HIP support such as HIP-enabled P2P-SIP [8].

We assume that Host Identities are published in the DNS which requires some additional configuration of the DNS and also SMTP servers. However, based on our operational experience with HIP, this can be accomplished in a backward-compatible way and also deployed incrementally. First, the DNS records do not interfere with HIP-incapable legacy hosts because the records are new records and thus not utilized by the legacy hosts at all. Second, *bind*, a popular DNS server software, does not require any modifications to its sources in order to support DNS records for HIP. Third, SMTP servers can utilize a local DNS proxy [12] to support transparent lookup of HIP records from the DNS.

3.3   Pushing Puzzles to Spam Relays

We considered two implementation alternatives for pushing puzzle computation cost to spam relays. In the first alternative, the UPDATE messages could be used to request a solution to a new puzzle. However, this is unsupported by the current HIP standards at the moment. In the second alternative, which was chosen for the implementation, inbound servers emulate puzzle renewal by terminating the underlying HIP session. The termination is necessary because current HIP specifications allow puzzles only in the initial handshake. When the spam relay reconnects using HIP, a more difficult puzzle will be issued by the server.

3.4   Re-generating a Host Identity

One obvious way to circumvent the proposed mechanism is to change to a new Host Identity after the server closes the connection and increases the puzzle difficulty. Fortunately, creating Host Identities is comparable in cost to solving puzzles, which can discourage rapid identity changes. In addition, non-zero puzzle computation time in the initial session further discourages creation of new identities.

3.5   Switching Identities

It is reasonable to expect that a server relaying spam is able to generate new host identities. Let C_K denote a key-pair generation time and C_N the cost of making the public key and the corresponding IP address available in a lookup service. We expect a spam relay to reuse its current identity as long as the following equation holds:

$$C_j < C_K + C_N + C_0, \tag{1}$$

where C_j is the puzzle computation time of the jth connection attempt. In other words, the spam relay continuously evaluates whether or not to switch to a new identity. If the next puzzle cost is greater than the initial cost, the spam relay has motivation to switch the identity. We note that the spam relay may devise an optimal strategy if the cost distribution is known.

When the puzzle cost is static, there is no incentive for the spam relay to change its identity unless blacklisted because the cost would be greater due to the C_K and C_N terms. For a dynamic cost, the spam relay is expected to change identities when the cost of a new identity and a new connection is less than maintaining the current identity and existing connection. For a DNS-based solution, the C_N term has a high value because DNS updates are slow to take effect.

Our proposed approach addresses identity-switching attacks using three basic mechanisms. First, a node must authenticate itself. This means that the node must be able to verify its identity using the corresponding private key. This does not prevent the node from using multiple identities or changing its identity, but ensures that the key pair exists. Second, a node must solve a computational puzzle before any messages are transported.

Third, a level of control is introduced by the logically centralized lookup service. The DNS maps host names to identities and IP addresses. A node must have a record in the lookup service. The limitation of this approach that control is introduced after something bad (e.g. spam) has already happened. The bad reputation of malicious nodes can be spread with, for example, DNSBL lookups performed by SMTP servers.

Nevertheless, identity switching could used to reduce the proposed system and, therefore, we have taken it into account in the cost model analysis of the next section.

4 Cost Model

In this section, we present an analytical cost model for the proposed identity-based unsolicited traffic prevention mechanism. We analyze the performance of the proposed mechanism when a number of legitimate senders and spam relays send email to an inbound SMTP server. It should be noted that our model excludes puzzle delegation in the case of multiple consecutive relays because it is not advocated by the HIP specifications.

4.1 Preliminaries

Let us consider a set of N_L legitimate email relays and N_S spam relays. Each legitimate relay sends messages at the rate of λ_L messages per second and each spam relay at λ_S. We assume that the inbound email server has a spam filtering component. It has a false negative of probability α, which refers to undetected spam. Thus, $(1-\alpha)$ gives the probability for detecting a spam message. The filter has also a false positive of probability β, which denotes good emails classified as spam. Even though the inbound server could reject or contain the spam, we assume the server just tags the message as spam and passes it forward.

An inbound SMTP server has a spam threshold κ given as the number of forwarded spam messages before it closes the corresponding HIP session. After the session is closed, the outbound email relay has to reopen it. Let the number of reopened sessions be ξ in case of spam relays, and η in case of legitimate email relays. The base exchange has an associated processing cost for the SMTP source, T_{BE}, given in seconds. This processing cost includes also the time spent in solving the puzzle. Let T_M denote the forwarding cost of a message. The finite time interval T, for which we inspect the system, is expressed in seconds.

4.2 Cost Model

To demonstrate scalability, we derive the equation for the load of the inbound SMTP server with and without HIP. The server load is determined by the number of HIP sessions at the server and the number of email messages forwarded. Without HIP, the email processing cost in seconds at the server is

$$R_N = T \cdot T_M \cdot (N_L \cdot \lambda_L + N_S \cdot \lambda_S). \tag{2}$$

In case of HIP, let us define the accumulated puzzle computation time function $G(\xi) = \sum_{i=0}^{\xi} C_i$. First, we consider the case with constant puzzle computation time that is independent of number of session resets, i.e. $C_1 = C_2 = \ldots C_N = T_{BE}$, and $G(\xi) = \xi \cdot T_{BE}$.

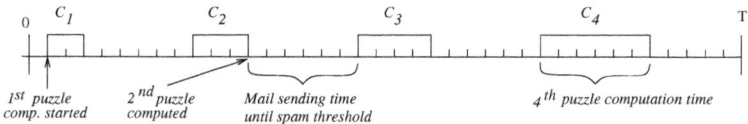

Fig. 1. Division of system inspection time (T) into puzzle re-computation and mail delivery stages with different puzzle computation times c_i, where i is the number of session resets. All $C_i = T_{BE}$ if the puzzle computation time is constant.

Next, we derive the number of HIP sessions due to session resets caused by spam under the condition of identical puzzle computation time. The following equation presents the number of session resets for a single spam relay:

$$\xi = \frac{(T - T_{BE} \cdot \xi)\lambda_S(1 - \alpha)}{\kappa} \tag{3}$$

From equation 3, we can deduce that

$$\xi = \frac{T \cdot \lambda_S \cdot (1 - \alpha)}{\kappa + \lambda_S \cdot (1 - \alpha) \cdot T_{BE}}. \tag{4}$$

The equation for the number of HIP sessions η needed by the legitimate SMTP relays is similar to equation 4, but the false positive rate β is used instead of $(1 - \alpha)$, and correspondingly λ_L is used instead of λ_S. We assume that legitimate relays do not send significant amount of spam so that only false positives need to be considered. The cost to a paying customer is given by η, and ξ is the cost to a spam relay. Given a small false positive probability, η is small. Therefore, the mechanism is not harmful to paying customers.

Next, we derive the equation describing the HIP load of the inbound server R_H consisting of both legitimate and spam messages:

$$R_H = N_L \cdot (\eta \cdot T_{BE} + T \cdot \lambda_L \cdot T_M) + N_S \cdot (\xi \cdot T_{BE} + T_S \cdot \lambda_S \cdot T_M), \tag{5}$$

The equation can be simplified by substituting the total time used for sending spam messages T_S with $T - T_{BE} \cdot \xi$ and by applying equation 2:

$$R_H = R_N - T_M \cdot T_{BE} \cdot (\lambda_S \cdot N_S \cdot \xi) + T_{BE} \cdot (N_L \cdot \eta + N_S \cdot \xi) \tag{6}$$

We assume β is small and, therefore, we used T instead of $T - T_{BE} \cdot \eta$ (with η denoting the number of session resets for a legitimate host). To evaluate the effectiveness of the HIP-based solution against a solution without HIP, we define ratio φ as:

$$\varphi = \frac{R_H}{R_N}. \tag{7}$$

Now, consider the case when puzzle computation time is not constant, but rather a function of the number of session attempts. This has to be reflected in equation 4, which becomes

$$\kappa \cdot \xi + G(\xi)\lambda_S(1 - \alpha) - T \cdot \lambda_S(1 - \alpha) = 0. \tag{8}$$

The equation can be solved using numerical iteration.

4.3 A Comparison of HIP with Constant Puzzle Cost to the Scenario without HIP

For numerical examples, we use HIP base exchange measurements obtained from an experimental setup described further in Section 5. We plot the ratio of non-HIP versus HIP approaches φ shown in equation 7. The HIP base exchange with a 10-bit puzzle was measured to take 0.215 s of HIP responder's time and 0.216 s for the initiator. We note that our analysis excludes the impact of parallel network and host processing. The email forwarding overhead without HIP is set to 0.01 seconds. We assume that the false negative probability of the server is 1/3 and the false positive probability is $1/10^4$. In other words, 2/3 of spam messages will be correctly detected as spam, and good messages are rarely classified as spam. Let N_L be 10^4, N_S be 100, $\lambda_L = 1/360$, and $\lambda_S = 10$. The time-period T for the analysis is 24 hours.

Figure 2 presents the ratio of HIP versus non-HIP computational cost as a function of the puzzle computation time. Both x and y axes are logarithmic. Ratio in the figures denotes φ, the ratio of the HIP and non-HIP capable mechanisms. The point at which the HIP mechanism has less overhead is approximately at 2 seconds. This means that the proposed HIP mechanism becomes superior to the constant non-HIP benchmark case with an 2-second or greater puzzle computation time. Naturally, this point depends on the selection of the values for the parameters.

As the spam relay sending rate increases, the HIP spam prevention mechanism becomes considerably better than the non-HIP benchmark case. With low spam rates, HIP sessions are reset seldomly and spam flows mostly through. When the spam rate increases, the spam relay spends more time on puzzle computation and the spam forwarding rate decreases. Then, the performance of the proposed HIP mechanism improves in comparison to the non-HIP benchmark case.

4.4 A Comparison of HIP with Exponential Puzzle Cost the Scenario without HIP

We also analyze the scenario where the puzzle cost grows exponentially for each new session. The parameters are the same as before, but the computation time of the puzzle grows exponentially with the puzzle difficulty. Moreover, we introduce a *cut-off point* after which the puzzle difficulty does not increase anymore. After the number of sessions reaches the cut-off point, the computation time of the puzzle (and the number of bits) remains at the current level. As an example, given a cut-off point of 23 and an initial puzzle size of 20 bits for the first throttled session, spam relays experience puzzle sizes {20, 21, 22, 23, 23, ... } as they reconnect.

Figure 3 presents the effect of the exponential base exchange time with a varying cut-off point. The y axis is logarithmic. The figure shows that the proposed mechanism performs considerably better than the non-HIP benchmark with a cut-off point of 22 or greater.

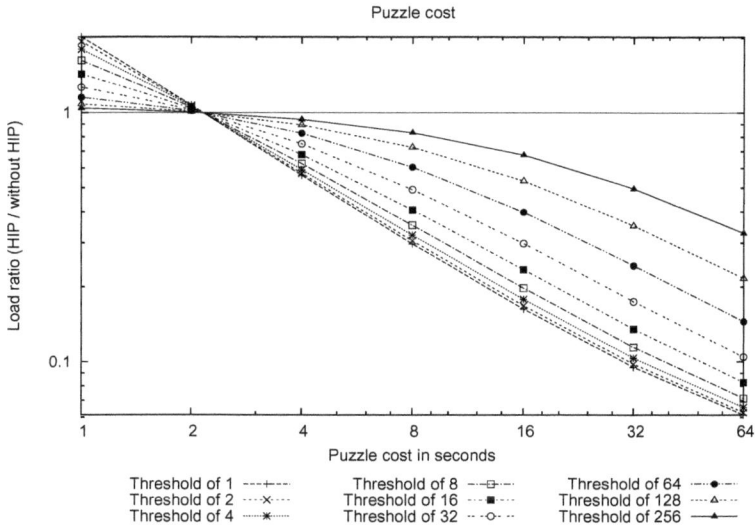

Fig. 2. Fixed-cost puzzles with different spam threshold κ

Now, we have compared HIP with both constant and variable-sized puzzles to the benchmark scenario without HIP. In the next sections, we focus on the identity-switching attacks (without cut-off points) against the proposed HIP-based architecture.

4.5   Optimal Strategies for a Spam Relay

Directly from equation 8, we know that

$$\xi \cdot \frac{\kappa}{\lambda_S \cdot (1 - \alpha)} + G(\xi) = T. \tag{9}$$

This means that, for the entire time during which a server relays spam, it splits its performance into ξ steps (one step is one session reset). To contact the inbound server, the spam relay spends $G(\xi)$ time for all puzzle computations, and during every step it sends exactly κ messages and each step consumes $\frac{\kappa}{\lambda_S(1-\alpha)}$ time.

The inbound server chooses the form of the function G, while a spam relay selects the number of session resets to tolerate, ξ. Here, we consider first a naive strategy for the spam relay. It chooses G based on the number of messages to send and does not try to whitewash its own history at the inbound server (i.e. by changing its identity according to equation 1). Under such an assumption, the spam relay has to optimize (maximize) a function of the following form:

$$p_Z \cdot \kappa \cdot \xi - c_Z \cdot G(\xi), \tag{10}$$

where p_Z is the profit for one delivered message and c_Z is the payment for the puzzle computation time. The strategy for the spam relay is to select

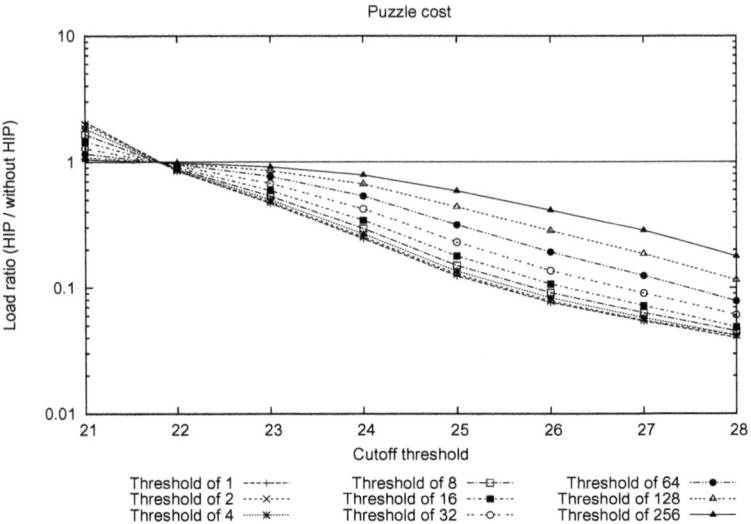

Fig. 3. Variable-sized puzzles with initial puzzle size of 20 and different cut-off points

the number of rounds for which it would like to send κ-sets of messages and the number of rounds to recompute puzzles. Let this value be ξ.

Note that if puzzle difficulty is constant (i.e. $G(\xi) = T_{BE} \cdot \xi$), then solution is one of the boundary cases

$$\xi = \begin{cases} 0, & \text{if } p_Z \kappa \le c_Z \cdot T_{BE}, \\ \infty, & \text{if } p_Z \kappa > c_Z \cdot T_{BE}, \end{cases} \tag{11}$$

More important is the case when the puzzle computation time is changing. Let the puzzle complexity growth be exponential compared to the increase of puzzle difficulty. Consider that the puzzle computation time on every reset has an exponential form of $C_i = aq^i + b$, then by definition

$$G(\xi) = \sum_{i=0}^{\xi} (aq^i + b) = a\frac{q^{\xi+1} - 1}{q - 1} + b = \frac{aq}{q - 1} q^\xi + b - \frac{a}{q - 1}. \tag{12}$$

Let us generalize this function as $G(\xi) = kg^\xi + s$, where g is an exponential growth parameter, s is initial shift, and k is the coefficient.

Now, a spam relay has to maximize the function

$$p_Z \cdot \xi \cdot \kappa - c_Z \cdot (k \cdot g^\xi + s). \tag{13}$$

Let us find the points where the derivative of this function with respect to ξ is zero:

$$p_Z \cdot \kappa - c_Z \cdot k \cdot \ln g \cdot g^\xi = 0. \tag{14}$$

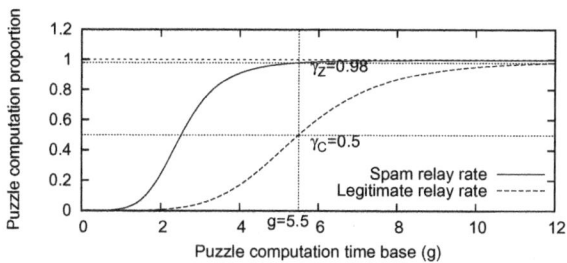

Fig. 4. An example plot to illustrate the proportion of time used by a legitimate and spam relay for puzzle computation

Thus, the maximum point is

$$\xi^* = \log_g \frac{p_Z \cdot \kappa}{c_Z \cdot k \cdot \ln g}. \tag{15}$$

4.6 Optimal Strategies for an Inbound Server

The previous section suggests an optimal strategy for a spam relay under the assumption that there is a payment involved in sending of spam. Otherwise, infinite number of messages would be the optimal strategy for the spam relay. In this section, we have a look at the situation from the view point of an inbound server.

First of all, the main goal for the inbound server is to slow down the flood of spam. It may be formulated in terms of the portion of time which spam relays spend for the puzzle computation time, compared to the overall time. Here, we assume that the inbound relay knows the number of HIP session resets during which spammer reuses its current identity according to equation 1. As previously, let it be ξ. To process ξ resets, a spam relay has to waste $G(\xi)$ of its own time for puzzle computation. The overall time, which it may use for message delivery, we also define as a function of ξ. Thus, the definition of the overall time follows from equation 9

$$T(\xi) = \xi \frac{\kappa}{d} + G(\xi), \tag{16}$$

where d is equal to $\lambda_Z(1 - \alpha)$ in case of a spam relay, and is equal to $\lambda_C \beta$ in case of a legitimate email relay. We assume that an inbound server classifies (or receives classification) with relatively good accuracy and, hence, $1 - \alpha$ is considerably higher than β.

Then, the proportion of time used for puzzle computation by spam relays (on left side) and legitimate email relays (on the right side) can be calculated as

$$\frac{G(\xi)}{G(\xi) + \frac{\kappa \cdot \xi}{\lambda_Z \cdot (1-\alpha)}}, \qquad \frac{G(\xi)}{G(\xi) + \frac{\kappa \cdot \xi}{\lambda_C \cdot \beta}}. \tag{17}$$

The inbound server has control over variables k, g, s of function $G(\xi) = kg^\xi + s$. For simplicity, let k and s be constants because the most relevant variable is the growth base g for the puzzle computation time. The values grow as a function of the parameter g. The function results in values ranging from 0 to 1, where 0 means that the time spent for the puzzle computation is negligible, while 1 means that the puzzle computation takes all of the time.

For the functions (17), the objective of the inbound server is to maximize the time spam relays spend on computing puzzles. Correspondingly, the inbound server should minimize this time for legitimate relays. These are somewhat contradictory conditions because $\alpha < 1$ and $\beta > 0$. Therefore, punishment for possible spam relays affects also legitimate relays.

To overcome this dilemma, we introduce a new constant γ: $0 \leq \gamma \leq 1$, which we select as the maximum value for the possibly legitimate client computation rate, i.e.

$$\frac{G(\xi)}{G(\xi) + \frac{\kappa \cdot \xi}{\lambda_C \cdot \beta}} \leq \gamma, \tag{18}$$

where γ defines the portion of the overall time which a possibly legitimate client spends for puzzle computations. From the inequality 18 it follows, that

$$g \leq \left(\frac{\gamma \cdot (\kappa \cdot \xi + s \cdot \lambda_C \cdot \beta)}{k \cdot \lambda_C \cdot \beta \cdot (1 - \gamma)} \right)^{\frac{1}{\xi}}. \tag{19}$$

On the other hand, the inbound server should maximize puzzle computation rate for possible spam relays (the left function in equation 17, which grows exponentially towards 1 as a function of g). The optimal strategy for the server is

$$g^* = \left(\frac{\gamma \cdot (\kappa \cdot \xi + s \cdot \lambda_C \cdot \beta)}{k \cdot \lambda_C \cdot \beta \cdot (1 - \gamma)} \right)^{\frac{1}{\xi}}. \tag{20}$$

The optimal strategy both for a spam relay, $\xi^*(g)$, as shown in equation 15, and for an inbound server, $g^*(\xi)$, as shown in equation 20, results in an equilibrium point (ξ^*, g^*) in terms of game theory.

The optimal strategies are illustrated in figure 4. For the legitimate relay, the bound for the computation rate is fixed as $\gamma_C = 0.5$ The set of parameters is assigned as $\alpha = 0.5$, $\beta = 0.01$, $\kappa = 100$, $\lambda_C = \lambda_Z = 10$, and we assume that the number of session resets is 5 ($\xi = 5$). Under such parameters, the legitimate relay has $g \approx 5.5$. The resulting puzzle computation for a possible spam relay is $\gamma_Z = 0.98$. In other words, the spam relay spends 0.98 of its time for puzzle computations whereas the legitimate relay spends half of its time. As g grows, both parties are eventually spending all of their time for puzzle computation. Thus, it is a local policy for the inbound server to decide a "good" value for g in terms of how much legitimate servers can be throttled with puzzles. For low spam rates, the value can be small but, with high spam rates, the server may increase the value at the cost of throttling also legitimate relay servers.

5   Experimental Evaluation

In this section, we describe how we integrated puzzle control to an inbound SMTP server and its spam filtering system. We show some measurements with variable-sized puzzles and compare this against identity-generation costs to give some engineering guidance against identity-switching attacks. The source code for HIP for Linux and the spam extensions are available as open source [1]. It should be noted that evaluation the mathematical models presented in section 4 e.g. with network simulators is future work.

5.1   Setup

The experimented environment consisted of two low-end commodity computers with the Linux Debian distribution and HIP for Linux (HIPL) [12] implementation. One computer served as a sending SMTP relay (1.60GHz Pentium M) and the other represented a receiving SMTP server (Pentium 4 CPU 3.00GHz). The receiving server detects the spam messages and closes the HIP session when a threshold is reached for the session. The inbound server was configured not to reject any email. We were mostly interested in software changes required to deploy HIP in SMTP servers and in the effects of increasing the puzzle size.

5.2   Results

We implemented the spam throttling mechanism successfully by using unmodified sendmail. We turned on the IPv6 option in the configuration of sendmail in order to use HITs.

The receiving SMTP server was equipped with a modified version of *SpamAssassin Milter*. The changes were straightforward to implement. The milter increased the puzzle size by one for every κ spam message detected and closed the HIP session to induce a new base exchange. The puzzle computation time grew exponentially with the size of the puzzle and the spam sender was throttled, as expected, by the mechanism.

We faced some implementation challenges during the experimentation. Firstly, sendmail queues the email messages and this makes it difficult to provide measurements from the spam filtering process itself. Secondly, if the session with the SMTP server is lost temporary, for example, because the HIP association are is closed, e-mails can accumulate in the queue for an extended time. Thirdly, when sending excessive amounts of email, the built-in connection throttling mechanism in sendmail takes over and queues the emails for long periods. However, sendmail's queuing process was robust and eventually emptied the queue successfully.

One challenge with proof-of-work techniques is that there are many different devices on the network and their computing capabilities vary. By default, the puzzle difficulty is zero in HIPL. A puzzle with difficulty of 25 bits took 12.4 s on

---

[1] https://launchpad.net/hipl/

average on the low-end machine used in the performance tests. The time was 4.4 seconds on a more recent CPU (Intel Core 2, 2.3 Mhz) on a single CPU core. The puzzle algorithm used in HIP does not prevent parallel computation. Thus, the computation time could be decreased by fully utilizing multi-core architectures.

For identity changing attacks, the strategy should also take into account the public key algorithm. RSA keys can be created faster than DSA keys with a corresponding size. As a consequence, the responder should give initiators that use RSA public keys more difficult puzzles than initiators with DSA keys. Further, it should be noted that creation of insecure, albeit perfectly valid keys, can be faster than creation of secure ones.

Figures 5(a) and 5(b) contrast secure key-pair generation time (horizontal lines) with puzzle solving time (vertical lines). It should be noticed that the y-axis is logarithmic. From the figures, it can be observed that the puzzling solving time is, as expected, exponential with the number of bits used in the puzzle difficulty. The standard deviation grows as puzzle difficulty is increased. In addition, the time to generate DSA key-pairs is considerably higher than RSA. On the average, the creation of a 2048-bit DSA key pair took 6.46 seconds and this was equal to the solving time of a 24-bit puzzle. With RSA, creation of a 2048-bit key pair took 0.72 seconds which corresponded to a 21-bit puzzle. This indicates that the key-generation algorithm and key length need to be taken into account when deciding the initial puzzle size to discourage identity-switching attacks.

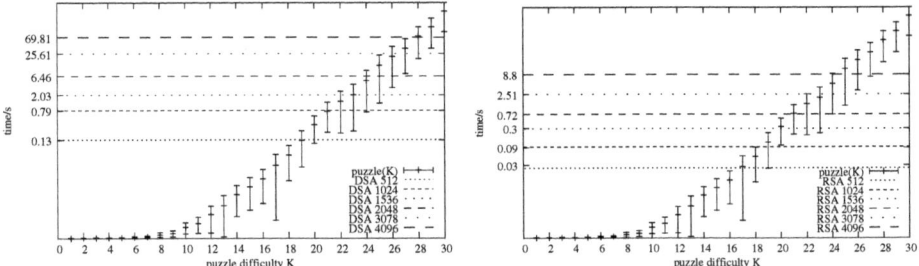

(a) Puzzle solving vs. DSA key generation   (b) Puzzle solving vs. RSA key generation

Fig. 5. Puzzle computation time results

6   Conclusions

In this paper, we proposed a cross-layer identity solution for mitigating unsolicited traffic between administrative domains. The proposed architecture primarily concentrates on inbound session control but is applicable also to the outbound direction as well. As an example application of the system, we focused on email spam prevention.

The Host Identity Protocol introduces a public key for the hosts. They key can be used for identifying well-behaving SMTP servers. The proposed approach introduces a cost to sending spam using the computational puzzles in HIP. Large-scale changes to the SMTP architecture are not required because HIP is backwards compatible. However, a practical limitation of the approach is that it requires wide-scale adoption of HIP as a signaling protocol and requires integration of HIP puzzle control to inbound email servers.

We presented a formal cost model that considered static and exponential base exchange puzzle costs. The analytical investigation indicates that the proposed spam prevention mechanism is able to mitigate unwanted traffic given a set of reasonable parameters. We used parameter values based on experimental results for server-side cost of HIP and the puzzle computation time. A spam mitigation approach based on HIP puzzles caused less load at the email server than an approach that was not using HIP.

The exponential cost of the puzzle introduces more work for email servers relaying spam. However, it also results in an incentive for the spammer to switch its identity when it is throttled with more difficult computational puzzles. We identified this as a potential weakness of the proposed system and analyzed this from the viewpoint of the spammer and the email server. As a theoretical result, we provided a method for the server to choose an optimal strategy against identity switching. When choosing a strategy, it should be noted that increasing puzzle costs for spammers also increase costs for legitimate hosts.

We implemented a simple prototype of the system based on a popular email server, sendmail. We integrated throttling support for HIP puzzles with minimal changes to SpamAssassin, a popular spam filtering software. We reported the practical experiences of running such a system and showed real-world measurements with HIP puzzles.

While the simple prototype was a success, we observed that the use of computational puzzles with email relays is challenging. Malicious hosts can overwhelm and exhaust the resources of a relay unless preventive measures are taken. Potential solutions to this include refusal to solve large puzzles for hosts, message rejection, and blacklisting. More work with simulation or larger test beds is needed to establish the efficacy of the proposed cross-layer system and to validate our mathematical models.

Acknowledgements. We would like to thank the following people for providing valuable feedback for this paper: Jaakko Kangasharju, Teemu Koponen, Kristian Slavov, Antti Järvinen, Oleg Ponomarev, Andrei Gurtov and Tuomas Aura. This work was supported by Tekes InfraHIP project and the Academy of Finland, grant numbers 135230, 122329 and 135230.

References

1. Aura, T., Nikander, P., Leiwo, J.: Dos-Resistant Authentication with Client Puzzles. In: Christianson, B., Crispo, B., Malcolm, J.A., Roe, M. (eds.) Security Protocols 2000. LNCS, vol. 2133, pp. 170–177. Springer, Heidelberg (2001)

2. Back, A.: Hashcash (May 1997), http://www.cypherspace.org/hashcash/
3. Beal, J., Shepard, T.: Deamplification of DoS Attacks via Puzzles (October 2004), http://web.mit.edu/jakebeal/www/Unpublished/puzzle.pdf
4. Dwork, C., Naor, M.: Pricing via Processing or Combatting Junk Mail. In: Brickell, E.F. (ed.) CRYPTO 1992. LNCS, vol. 740, pp. 139–147. Springer, Heidelberg (1993)
5. Eggert, L., Laganier, J.: Host Identity Protocol (HIP) Rendezvous Extension. IETF (April 2008), Experimental RFC
6. Goodman, J., Rounthwaite, R.: SmartProof. Microsoft (2005), http://research.microsoft.com/en-us/um/people/joshuago/smartproof.pdf
7. Jokela, P., Moskowitz, R., Nikander, P.: RFC5202: Using the Encapsulating Security Payload (ESP) Transport Format with the Host Identity Protocol (HIP) Internet Engineering Task Force (April 2008), http://www.ietf.org/rfc/rfc5202.txt
8. Keränen, A., Camarillo, G., Mäenpää, J.: Host Identity Protocol-Based Overlay Networking Environment (HIP BONE) Instance Specification for REsource LOcation And Discovery (RELOAD). Internet Engineering Task Force (July 2010) (internet draft, work in progress)
9. Moskowitz, R., Nikander, P., Jokela, P., Henderson, T.: RFC5201: Host Identity Protocol. Internet Engineering Task Force (April 2008); Experimental RFC
10. Nikander, P., Henderson, T., Vogt, C., Arkko, J.: End-Host Mobility and Multihoming with the Host Identity Protocol. Internet Engineering Task Force (April 2008); Experimental RFC
11. Nikander, P., Laganier, J.: Host Identity Protocol (HIP) Domain Name System (DNS) Extension. IETF (April 2008); Experimental RFC
12. Pathak, A., Komu, M., Gurtov, A.: Host Identity Protocol for Linux. Linux Journal (November 2009), http://www.linuxjournal.com/article/9129
13. Tritilanunt, S., Boyd, C., Foo, E., Nieto, J.M.G.: Examining the DoS Resistance of HIP. In: Meersman, R., Tari, Z., Herrero, P. (eds.) OTM 2006 Workshops. LNCS, vol. 4277, pp. 616–625. Springer, Heidelberg (2006)
14. Tschofenig, H., Shanmugam, M., Muenz, F.: Using SRTP transport format with HIP. Internet Engineering Task Force (August 2006); expired Internet draft

Experimental Analysis of the Femtocell Location Verification Techniques

Ravishankar Borgaonkar, Kevin Redon, and Jean-Pierre Seifert

Security in Telecommunications
Technische Universität Berlin and Deutsche Telekom Laboratories
10587, Berlin, Germany
{ravii,kredon,jpseifert}@sec.t-labs.tu-berlin.de

Abstract. Mobile network operators are adapting femtocells in order to simplify their network architecture for increased performance and greater revenue opportunities. While emerging as a new low-cost technology which assures best connectivity, it has also introduced a range of new potential risks for the mobile network operators. Here we study the risks associated with the location verification techniques of femtocells. First we state the goals of location verification and describe techniques implemented in the existing femtocells. We demonstrate how location locking techniques can be defeated by using modern attack vectors against the location verification methods. Our experimental result suggest that location security methods are insufficient to avoid femtocell's misuse. An attacker can operates the femtocell from an unregistered location, thereby creating problems for various important services such as for assisting emergency call services, for following licensed spectrum rules, for Lawful interception services, and for the commercial purposes.

Keywords: Femtocell, HNB, Security, Location.

1 Introduction

Femtocell is a emerging technology which enhances third generation (3G) coverage and provides assurance of best connectivity in the 3G telecommunication networks. It acts as an access point that securely connect standard mobile stations to the mobile network operator's core network using an existing wired broadband connection. For mobile service operators key benefits are increase in network capacity, lowers capital cost and expands revenue opportunities. For users it assures increase in indoor coverage, higher rate of data transfer, high quality voice and higher multimedia experience. A femtocell can be deployed in a licensed spectrum owned by a mobile network operator and in the users premises, for example home, office and enterprise.

The femtocell security is divided into two parts: the device authentication and the encryption of the calls and control information transferred across the untrusted backhaul connection between the femtocell and the femtocell gateway. Even though the femtocell supports the necessary security features that a base

T. Aura, K. Järvinen, and K. Nyberg (Eds.): NordSec 2010, LNCS 7127, pp. 49–54, 2012.

station provides; in particular which are mutual authentication, encryption and integrity over the wireless link, there are still two issues. First is use of an existing wired broadband connection as backhaul is a challenge, as the provider of the backhaul is not necessarily the same as the provider of femtocell. Secondly, security of the femtocell device is vital and different from the standard base station. Adversaries can get the physical access to a device due to its low cost and easy availability in the market. These two issues suggest that the femtocells may become an attractive target for the attackers.

Main aim of our study is to analyze the risk associated with the femtocell security. Our study finds that the femtocells, which are currently deployed in the market, are insecure and do not follow the security requirements mentioned by the 3GPP standard. In this paper, we experimentally evaluate various security aspects, in particular, the location verification techniques used in the device. We examine and show that the location verification techniques are inadequate to block the use of femtocell, if it is operating at an unregistered location and at unlicensed frequency spectrum.

The rest of the paper is organized as follows. Section 2 describes security architecture of femtocell. Section 3 explains goals of location locking methods of the femtocell. Femtocell location tracking methods and various attacking vectors are presented in Section 4. Conclusions and discussions are presented in Section 5. Note that the Home NodeB (HNB) is the 3GPP standard name of the femtocell and we will use the HNB in the following sections.

2   HNB Security Architecture

The HNB is installed in the users' premises and its traffic is tunneled via public Internet (wired broadband) connection. Hence for the mobile network operator, it is important to ensure that HNB protects the communication over the insecure public Internet, and over the air-link between itself and the mobile device. Main components of the HNB security architecture and their roles are described as follows [3,1]:

HNB Device- The main function of the HNB is to act as a small base station. The HNB connects the UE via its radio interface to the mobile service operator's core network. It transmits the UE data by establishing a secure IPsec [4] ESP tunnel with the SeGW over an insecure backhaul link (broadband Internet connection).

SeGW - The SeGW acts as a border gateway of the operator's core network. First, it mutually authenticates and registers the HNB to establish a secure IPsec tunnel, and then forwards all the signaling and the user data to the operator's core network. Mutual authentication can be performed using certificates. The interface between the SeGW and the operator's core network is considered to be secured.

HNB Management System (HMS) - The HNB Management System is a management server, and responsible for the configuration and the provisioning of the user data according to the operator's policy. It can be functioned to provide the required software updates on the HNB and can be located inside the operator's core network.

AAA Server and HSS - The subscription data and authentication information is stored in the HSS. The AAA server authenticates the hosting party (the HNB) by accessing the authentication information from the HSS. Both the AAA server and the HSS are deployed in the operator's core network.

HNB GW - The HNB gateway performs the access control for the non-CSG (Closed Subscriber Group) capable UE attempting to access a HNB. The SeGW can be integrated with a HNB-GW, and if not integrated then, the interface between SeGW and HNB-GW may be protected using NDS/IP (Network Domain Security/IP network layer security) [5] .

UE- The UE is a standard user equipment that supports the 3G (UMTS) communication. It connects to the HNB over-the-air using a 3G AKA (Authentication and Key Agreement) procedure.

3   Goals of the Location Locking Methods

It is important for the operator to ensure that the HNB operates at the given location and satisfy various requirements such as security, regulatory, and operational requirements [2]. The HNB can only provide reliable and accurate home address information if the users keep them in their assigned and registered location. However, it is possible for users to move the HNB when traveling, intending to continue using free roaming service anywhere they go. This could led to a verity of problems for the operator. Hence the operator has to lock the HNB to a specific location for the following reasons: a) to provide the users location for emergency calls, b) to ensure that the HNB is operating in a country in which it has a network operation, c) to provide real-time lawful interception data to the government agencies.

4   Location Locking Methods and Attacks

In this section, we describe location locking techniques implemented in the HNBs. Then we present various attack vectors to beat these location locking methods. Note that without opening the HNB box and with no physical tampering, we were able to bypass the location locking methods. We performed experimental analysis of the location locking techniques in a Faraday Cage. Different attacks on the location based techniques were performed in the cage only. Though the attacks we described below are performed on the two HNB, it may affect other HNBs which are deployed currently.

The HMS registers and verifies location information of the HNB. First the operator registers and fix the HNB location information in the server called Access point Home Register (AHR). After the initial registration process, the operator obtains the location information of the HNB and compares it with the corresponding information stored in the AHR. The main parameters used for identifying the HNB location information are a) IP address of the broadband access device, b) information of the surrounding macro-cells ,and c) information received from the GPS device attached to the HNB or the UE. In this section, we explain these location locking mechanisms deployed in the HNB system architecture [3]. They are as follows:

4.1   IP Address of the Broadband Access Device

The HNB gets an IP address when connected to the devices which provides the broadband access such as a DSL modem or a home router. The operator can locate the HNB by its assigned IP address and by the location information related to IP address which is stored in the server (AHR). When the HNB is placed behind NAT (Network Address Translator), STUN protocol is used to determine its IP address. The HNB operator can request the geographic location information based on the IP address to the interface defined by the NASS (Network Attachment Subsystem) standard [6].

Attack Vectors

The virtual private network (VPN) can be used to impersonate the IP address of the legitimate HNB. A VPN emulates a private IP network over the public Internet infrastructure [7]. The VPN technology can be used to connect remotely to the a LAN (Local Area Network) (where the HNB in installed and registered) and thus the HNB can obtain a local IP address. Thus VPN can be used to impersonate the IP address of the legitimate HNB and the use of IP address for location authentication is not considered reliable.

There may be a situation in which the 3G or 2G signals are not be available in the home In addition, not all the HNB devices are equipped with the GPS receivers. In these circumstances, the operator has two parameters to authenticate the HNB location: IP address and the information received from the UE. However it is obvious that if there are no 2G or 3G signals in the area, the HNB can not receive any information from the UE. For the attack, we use a VPN to replay the HNB's IP address. We placed the HNB to an unregistered location and established a VPN tunnel to the LAN at the HNB's registered location. We were able connect the HNB to the SeGW with the registered IP address. We were able to operate the HNB in a normal mode from an unregistered location.

4.2   Information of Neighboring Macro-cells

The HNB can receive neighboring macro-cells information such as PLMN ID (Public Land Mobile Network Identity), LAI (Location Area Identity) or Cell ID. It contains a hardware chip to scan PLMN ID and cell ID. In this method, first ,the HNB scans the neighboring macro-cells information in a receiver mode when it powered on and sends this scanned information to the AHR (Home Register of HNB). The AHR role is to store this information along with the registration message requests to the appropriate HNB profiles. Most of the electronic devices including the HNB use a 2G receiver hardware to scan the neighboring macro-cell information because 3G signals are weak inside the house.

Attack Vectors

In this scenario, the operator can fetch and use neighboring micro-cell information to perform location authentication of the HNB device. As discussed earlier in Section 4.1, the adversary can use a VPN connection to emulate the IP address. However, in order to operate the HNB with the given regulations, the attacker still needs to block or simulate neighboring micro-cell information. This can be done in two ways. An attacker can use a 2G signal jammer device. The 2G jammer devices blocks any nearby 2G network signals without interrupting other electronic devices. We analyzed a few HNB devices and found that most of the devices use a 2G receiver hardware to record neighboring micro-cell information. Hence it is possible to block nearby 2G network signals using such jammers without interrupting the 3G network signals of the HNB.

In other way, the attacker can use a nanoBTS [9] and openBSC package to replay the neighboring micro-cell information. The nanoBTS picocells are small 2G (GSM) base-stations that use the A-bis interface. They can be connected to the openBSC with A-bis over IP interface [10]. The adversary can configure the nanoBTS to transmit the recorded (registered) micro-cell information. In this way, the attacker can show that the HNB is operating at the given and registered location by providing the legitimate micro-cell information. We examined this attack using a nanoBTS and were able to provide required information to the HNB for location authentication.

4.3   UE Information

The UE position can be useful to verify the HNB location, provided that it is equipped with the GPS (Global Positioning System) feature. In addition, the UE can send its location information using available micro-cells or GPS data to the AHR via the HNB.

4.4   GPS Information

The location information can be obtained using an A-GPS receiver unit built inside the HNB. A-GPS (Assisted GPS) is a system used to improve the start-up performance of a GPS satellite-based positioning system [8]. The HNB can receive the location information from the A-GPS unit and deliver it to the home registration server for the verification. However, it is important to install the HNB in a location where it can receive the GNSS (Global Navigation Satellite Systems) satellites signals.

Attack Vectors

Use of GPS as a geolocation technology is ineffective since the HNBs are installed in the home and GNSS signals are weak inside the house. However some mobile network operators suggest to use an additional antenna to improve the signal strength. The attacking vectors against this mechanism includes jammers, an attenuation methods, and GPS generators devices. An attacker can use of GPS jammers. These low cost jammers are commercially available in the market and could be positioned in the vicinity of HNB antenna. This attack could be arguable due to legal issues in using the jammer. In an attenuation method, the attacker can wrap the HNB in layers of aluminum foil to create a Faraday cage like environment and blocks the GPS signals. The GPS generators are the devices used by GPS manufactures for the research and development. It can transmit the recorded timing signals and orbital data. The attacker can use such devices to spoof the HNB. The method in which the HNB receive location information from the UE is not reliable, since in the UE may not have inbuilt GPS feature and not receive 3G or 2G signals.

5   Discussion and Conclusion

In this paper, we practically analyzed and showed that the location verification techniques used in the femtocells that are built and deployed today are insufficient to avoid its misuse. Our results reveals that the femtocell location can be spoofed by an adversary which could have impact on the emergency services, on the lawful interception procedure, and on the operators regulations. An adversary may move femtocells for avoiding expensive roaming calls while traveling and for hiding his location from government agencies. Our study suggest that most of the femtocells deployed today are vulnerable against the modern location attack vectors. Hence new additional location locking mechanisms are needed to improve the overall femtocell security architecture.

References

1. 3GPP, Security of Home Node B (HNB) / Home evolved Node B (HeNB), TS 33.320, V9.1.0 (April 2010), http://www.3gpp.org
2. 3GPP Technical Specification Group Service and System Aspect, Security of H(e)NB, TR 33.820, V8.3.0 (December 2009)
3. 3GPP TR 33.820 V8.3.0: Technical Specification Group Service and System Aspects; Security of H(e)NB; (Release 8)
4. Kent, S., Atkinson, R.: [RFC 2406]: IP Encapsulating Security Payload (ESP), http://www.ietf.org/rfc/rfc2406.txt
5. 3GPP TS 33.210: Network Domain Security (NDS); IP network layer security (IP)
6. ETSI ES 282 004 V1.1.1 Telecommunications and Internet Converged Services and Protocols for Advanced Networking (TISPAN); NGN functional architecture; Network Attachment Sub-System(NASS) (2006)
7. Gleeson, A., Lin, A., Heinanen, J., Armitage, G., Malis, A.: [RFC 2685]: A framework for IP Based Virtual Private Networks
8. Djuknic, G.M., Richton, R.E.: Geolocation and Assisted GPS. IEEE Computer 34, 123–125 (2001)
9. The nanoBTS: small GSM base stations, http://www.ipaccess.com
10. OpenBSC, http://openbsc.gnumonks.org/trac/wiki/nanoBTS

"Why Wasn't I Notified?":
Information Security Incident Reporting Demystified

Erka Koivunen

Finnish Communications Regulatory Authority, CERT-FI, Itämerenkatu 3 A, FI-00180,
Helsinki, Finland
Erka.Koivunen@ficora.fi

Abstract. An information security incident, if successfully discovered and reported, initiates a distributed response process that activates a diverse collection of independent actors. Public officials, network service providers, information security companies, research organisations, and volunteers from all over the world can be involved; often without the participants realising whom they are working with. The cooperation is based on mostly informal bilateral arrangements and is aided by mutual trust accumulated over course of time. Each participant wants to limit their involvement and typically only assumes responsibility on their own actions. Information suggesting that third parties would be affected may or may not be followed up. The result is an unplanned mesh of bilateral information sharing and a formation of an ad-hoc network of partial stakeholders. No single entity exercises total control over the process, which makes it inherently uncontrollable and its results difficult to anticipate. This contrasts with the information security standards, where the process is expected to be well defined and under the control of a clearly stated leadership. The study suggests that internet-connected organisations should adopt a rather agnostic approach to information security incident reporting.

Keywords: Information security, network security, CSIRT, CERT, incident reporting, IODEF, security breach, network attack, abuse, computer break-in, event monitoring, intrusion detection, IDS, takedown notice, RFC, ISO/IEC.

1 Introduction

Network and security incidents are situations where effects harmful to security have manifested or have had potential to manifest in the networks or networked information systems. Each day, the home computers of thousands of private individuals become infected with mass-spreading malware and business servers are brought down to a halt by denial of service attacks initiated by criminals on the other side of the world. Unfavourable conditions such as software errors open up exploitable vulnerabilities, making the task of defending the information processing systems a game of cat and mouse. The incidents deprive people of their right to confidentiality, integrity, and availability of information processing services.

Most information security standards would agree that preventive security controls should be reserved a central role in preventing the incidents from taking place in the

T. Aura, K. Järvinen, and K. Nyberg (Eds.): NordSec 2010, LNCS 7127, pp. 55–70, 2012.

first place. The basic rationale being that controls employed to protect the intended target or some other entity on the attack path would successfully repel the attack attempts.

Merely applying preventive measures to protect information security is not sufficient, however. The highly distributed and uncontrollable nature of the internet makes it virtually impossible to anticipate the attacks beforehand, let alone to prevent attacks from taking place altogether. While it is advisable to continue investing in preventive measures, experience has shown that there is an ever-greater demand for efficient after-the-fact handling of computer security incidents. It turns out that while the art of incident handling suffers from many process deficiencies, it still somehow yields excellent results. This study examines the incident reporting mechanisms and incident handling cooperation of Computer Security Incident Response Teams (CSIRT).

2   Methodology

In the study, an effort was made to outline the differences between the literate approach and the practice as observed through real-life incidents. A preconceived notion was that there already are well-defined processes in the literary, but that they were not followed in the practice. The implications of the differences between the theory and the practice are being discussed throughout this paper.

2.1   Outlining the Disconnect between the Theory and the Practice

For the theoretical foundations of this study, a selection of normative literature and security standards was examined in search of guidance on how incidents should be discovered and how information about the incidents should find their way to the affected parties. Most notably, information security standards from Internet Engineering Task Force (IETF) and International standardisation body ISO/IEC were studied.

The literary view of incident discovery and reporting was then contrasted with empirical evidence on how past incidents were being handled in the practice. The real-life incidents were obtained from the archives of the Finnish national computer security incident response team CERT-FI.

2.2   Linear Model of the Incident Reporting Process

To facilitate the comparison of theory and practice, a linear model of the incident reporting and handling process was devised, as shown in Fig. 1, below. The first four phases of the process were identified to be the most interesting to this study as they involve information gathering and data exchange. They were assumed prerequisites to a successful incident response in the latter stages of the process. The last three phases deal with actions taken after the information about an incident has already reached the subjects and are thus out of scope of this study.

The four phases of interest – namely, incident discovery, identification of points of contacts, exchange of incident data, and means to validate the reports – were then examined separately.

Fig. 1. Linear model of the incident reporting and handling process. The four leftmost phases are considered specific to the incident reporting and information exchange and thus of interest to this study.

2.3   Cases of Real-Life Incidents

The real-life incidents were selected to represent typical scenarios in which information about an incident is passed between various participants of the incident response process. The incidents were analysed using a combination of three methods.

	Discoverers	Incident reporting clearing-house	National CERT	ISP	ISP	ISP
	Anonymous discoverers	Incident Repository (identity withheld)	CERT-FI	Elisa	Netsonic, Mediateam	Auria, Elisa
Report received from	-	Anonymous Discoverers	Incident Repository	CERT-FI	CERT-FI	?
Incident ID	-	-	[FICORA #295909]	#69327, #69328,	?	?
Associated IDs	-	-	-	[FICORA #295909]	[FICORA #295909]	?
Next-in-line incident handling contacts	Incident Repository	CERT-FI	Elisa, Netsonic, Mediateam, Auria	customer	customer	?
Recorded incident status	-	-	resolved, site assumed taken offline	?	?	?
Date discovered (in UTC)	2009-08-16 12:54	2009-08-16 12:54	2009-08-17 09:31	2009-08-18 05:11	2009-08-18 05:11	?
Resolved (in UTC)	-	-	2009-08-21 05:25	?	?	before 2009-09-18 05:05
Persistence	-	-		?	?	?
Network info resolved	URL	URL, IP, ASN, AS name	Multiresolver tests[a]	?	?	?
Evidence inherited from	-	Anonymous Discoverers	Incident Repository	CERT-FI	CERT-FI	?
Evidence secured	-	malware sample	connectivity test	?	?	?
Actions taken	discover, share	receive, share, archive	receive, verify, analyse, send takedown request, archive	issue take-down	issue take-down	?

Fig. 2. A data accumulation map of an incident with a CERT-FI issued identifier [FICORA #295909]. Data in the green cells indicate that material has been verified either from the CERT-FI archives or from other sources. Empty cells indicate that information has not been collected, whereas red cells indicate that the value is not known. Cells in amber contain speculative information by the author.

First, the cases were transcribed to a narrative form. The focus was put in the journey the reports make while on their way from the discoverer to those with a need to know. The reporting sources, various intermediaries, and the affected parties were identified where possible. The narratives were – besides being entertaining reading – vital to the understanding of the incidents and how they were handled. The raw material obtained from CERT-FI was often unorganised and at times hard to follow. Furthermore, the material in the CERT-FI archives mostly focused on the actions taken by CERT-FI and gave a limited view on the actions performed by others. To overcome this, the narratives were augmented with external material where appropriate. However, a deliberate decision was made to limit to public sources only.

Next, based on the narratives, a data accumulation map similar to one displayed in Fig. 2, above, was populated, where the process participants were grouped with respect to their role in the process, and the data in the reports was sorted in terms of data accumulation and exchange. Participants were observed to receive data from others, some of introduced new and lost some data and eventually passed a subset of their data on to the next participants. This test was especially suited for examining process deficiencies by identifying parties that were not being informed or were only given partial information.

Lastly, an attempt to establish a graphical representation of the process flow was made as depicted in Fig. 3, below. A tool of choice for the study was GraphingWiki [19], mostly because CERT-FI is already conducting experiments in using wiki in the daily analytical work. It was discovered that the graphs illustrate the valuable role of report-handling intermediaries and helps to bring to light process dead ends.

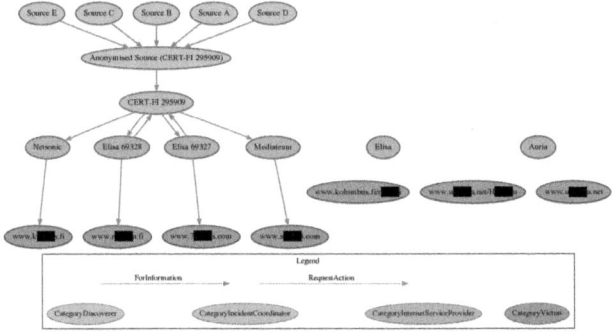

Fig. 3. A process flow graph of the incident [FICORA #295909]. The uppermost circles represent the discoverers of the incidents. The reports are then passed to a set of intermediaries until finally the affected victims are reached. In this case, three out of seven victims never received a notification. Information indicating the identities of the victims has been withheld.

3   Theory and Practice of the Incident Reporting Process

We will now examine the four phases of the incident reporting process in more detail and seek to contrast the theoretical foundations with the real-life incident handling practices.

3.1   Incident Discovery

A traditional source of incident discoveries in information and communications (ICT) systems is local event monitoring. Albeit often neglected in practice, anomalous event monitoring is well understood in the standards literature. Already over 20 years ago a document called Orange Book [17] recognised event monitoring as an essential feature of a secure information system. A similar requirement can be found in practically all normative documents, ranging from functional auditing requirements described in Common Criteria [12] to ISO/IEC information security standards [28], [29] and the Finnish Act on the Protection of Privacy in Electronic Communications [23]. As ISO/IEC 27002:2005 puts it:

"Systems should be monitored and information security events should be recorded. Operator logs and fault logging should be used to ensure information system problems are identified." [29]

Naturally, an ICT system can only log events that take place within its own domain of control. File system events are local to the computer attached to the data storage and firewalls only register communications whose paths cross its network interfaces. Local event logging completely misses incidents that take place in remote systems, thus giving no early warning about impending attacks that may exploit similar vulnerabilities existing in the local systems. Local event logging also loses track of incidents once the focus of the attacker's actions has shifted to other systems. This is especially true in cases where information stolen from one system is being spread or exploited in other systems. This appears to be an important limitation of the event-monitoring paradigm, further underlined by real life experiences.

A striking commonality between the incidents examined for this study is that none of the victims of the security breaches seemed to have discovered the incidents on their own. Clues from external reporters in one form or another were required either to set the wheels of incident response in motion or at least to complement the victim's limited view of the incident's true scope.

This is an important revelation; the notion that an external entity would be able to detect incidents appears to be foreign to information security standards and regulation. Yet, victims of many internet threats are among the last ones to learn about the information security incidents affecting them.

During the study, three mechanisms were identified through which security breaches in a networked system can be brought to the attention of the affected organisation. They are illustrated in Fig. 4, below. The leftmost portion in the picture represents the local event-monitoring paradigm endorsed by standards such as ISO/IEC 27002:2005. However, there exist neither standards nor regulatory requirements that would encourage organisations to take into account the remaining two scenarios in the Fig. 4. The middle of the picture depicts a situation where signs of known attack patterns are searched in the local ICT systems. The right side is about collaboration with external observers and information exchange about incidents discovered elsewhere.

In the lack of standards, practical approaches have emerged. Most organisations already employ anti-virus products, intrusion detection systems (IDS), security information and event management systems (SIEM) and other content inspection technologies to protect their ICT infrastructure from malicious software and attack attempts. Arguably, signature-based and heuristic attack detection tools can be categorised under the middle portion of Fig. 4.

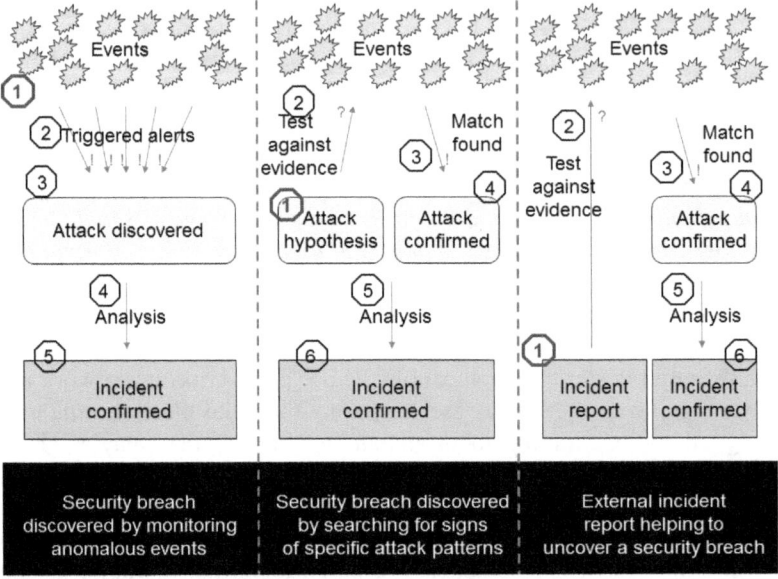

Fig. 4. Three routes via which security breaches in a networked system can be discovered by an affected organisation. The entry points for the incident response process are highlighted in red.

Even when not directly observable by monitoring the event flow, some attacks can still be detectable through various side channels. For example, a networked IT system that all of the sudden slows down or becomes unresponsive may be experiencing a denial of service condition caused by a resource exhaustion attack. In many practical incidents, the initial discovery can be attributed to observant administrators familiar with the system having an intangible feeling of "things not being as they should." While these weak signals contain little information that would help put a finger on the problem, they may be the result of complex holistic analysis of a subconscious sort – something the automated anomaly detection systems still cannot fully replicate. These manifestations of systems administration prowess can also be categorised under the middle portion of Fig. 4.

The rightmost portion of Fig. 4, on the other hand, involves sharing specific and actionable information about on-going incidents with external parties. These would include approaches manifested by The ShadowServer Foundation and Team Cymru. Over the years, both have evolved into globally significant clearing-houses for incident reports. While many security researchers limit themselves to merely analysing large volumes of incident reports obtained through a variety of log submission channels, Shadowserver and Team Cymru rather tasks themselves into finding suitable recipients with a means to help in solving the incidents. In a concrete way, they help bridge the gap between casual observers and the victims.

Automated reporting tools, such as CERT-FI Autoreporter [26] and Abuse Helper [1], aim to automate the process further. Example would be an arrangement where data related to Finnish networks is first acquired from the Shadowserver and then redistributed to the Finnish network administrators through the Autoreporter by CERT-FI. Lately, this has enabled CERT-FI to send hundreds of thousands of incident reports annually as compared to number of cases counted in hundreds before the adoption of the tool. Additionally, most reports are handled by automated means by the ISPs, thus reducing the time between the attack discovery and successful incident remediation. It turns out; a seemingly accidental chain of voluntary incident reporters can after all be herded towards a common goal in an effort to better the chances of matching the incident-related data with the victims.

3.2   Identifying Points of Contacts

As hinted in the previous section, the discoverer of the incident may have no practical way to inform the victims. Probably one of the most straightforward – and probably one of the most neglected – recommendations to overcome this problem comes from the United States National Institute of Standards and Technology (NIST) whose incident-handling manual [38] recommends:

"Organizations should publish a phone number and e-mail address that outside parties can use to report such incidents."

Some of the earlier attempts to solve the problem of identifying points of contacts for incident response in the internet are to be found in Request for Comment (RFC) series of documents. Starting from most recent published in the year 2000, the RFCs most relevant for our purpose are 3013 *Recommended Internet Service Provider Security Services and Procedures* [30], 2350 *Expectations for Computer Security Incident Response* [5], 2196 *Site Security Handbook* [25], 2142 *Mailbox Names for Common Services, Roles and Functions* [15] and 1281 *Guidelines for the Secure Operation of the Internet* [34]. In practice, the recommendations are partly out-dated and are not uniformly followed.

Regional internet registries (RIRs) oversee the allocation of IP addresses and autonomous system numbers. There are five RIRs, each responsible for a certain region of the world, namely RIPE NCC, ARIN, LACNIC, APNIC, and AfriNIC. Currently, the RIRs are in the process of creating public registries of incident response contacts within their allocated IP networks. [13], [2], [32], [31] Similar idea was adopted by Finland in 2005 when a regulation issued by Finnish Communications Regulatory Authority (FICORA) came into force. It requires the Finnish network owners to document their abuse handling contacts in WHOIS. [22] However, these only affect the IP and AS number allocations, not domain name holders.

Over the years, CSIRTs have grown to accept that it is not always possible for them to find the ultimate report recipient on their own. Instead, the CSIRTs employ various methods that help identify the next-in-line incident handlers that can be of help by passing the report on to a next intermediary contact. It is hoped that after repeated passes, the report will eventually reach recipients with means to resolve the incident. The next-in-line handlers are identified by enumerating DNS names and network addresses, analysing network topology, and utilising geolocation services.

A recent study conducted by the Finnish Communications Regulatory Authority (FICORA) charted the services, organisation, and mandate among 11 European national and governmental CERTs. [8] One of the major findings of the study is summarised as follows:

"The CSIRT needs to have a clearly defined point of contact that interfaces the team with the outside world." [7]

The European Commission has identified national CSIRTs as key players in incident response coordination and has set a goal to establish CSIRTs in every European Union member state. [11]

CSIRTs themselves have long ago recognised the need for identifying and maintaining a list of authoritative peer contacts. Several initiatives have been introduced by organisations such as European Network and Information Security Agency (ENISA) [21], CERT/CC [10], Forum of Incident Response and Security Teams (FIRST) [24], Trusted Introducer (TI) [40], the European Government CERTs Group (EGC) [20] and Asia Pacific Computer Emergency Response Team (APCERT) [4].

Outside the standardisation and regulatory realms, the G8 countries have facilitated an International CIIP Directory [9], a collection of government-appointed contact points in the field of critical information infrastructure protection. The directory has since evolved and nowadays includes official contact information on 16 different topics from nearly 30 countries. The directory is compiled by the British Centre for the Protection of National Infrastructure (CPNI) and is promoted by the Meridian process. The document has not been made available to the public. Another somewhat similarly titled publication, the CIIP Handbook [6] compiled by ETH of Switzerland, however, is publicly available.

3.3   Information Exchange

The study found that RFCs of most relevance to incident data exchange are 5070 *The Incident Object Description Exchange Format* [16] and its predecessor 3067 [3].

Somewhat surprisingly, RFCs prior to the 21st century – namely 2350 and 2196 – were rather vague on the data formats. This suggests that automating the processing of incident reporting is a relatively new idea. Up until recent years, it was expected that communications would take place between human handlers. A machine-readable data format was not formulated until the Trans-European Research and Education Networking Association (TERENA) proposed an XML-based scheme:

"The Incident Object Description and Exchange Format (IODEF) is a format for Computer Security Incident Response Teams (CSIRTs) to exchange operational and statistical incident information among themselves, their constituency, and their collaborators." [14]

In a presentation [18] during the FIRST Conference in 2009, Till Dörges brought together a comprehensive listing of data expression and exchange standards in the technical information security field. According to Dörges' assessment, the key standards associated with incident handling are IODEF, Abuse Reporting Format (ARF) [39], and – to a certain extent – Common Event Expression (CEE) by MITRE [33]. Of these, however, only IODEF is of interest to this study. CEE defines taxonomy of expressing events in logs, and ARF is limited to registering complaints regarding unsolicited bulk e-mail. Both are relatively new and their adoption remains to be seen. IODEF on the other hand appears to be mature and already has applications in practical settings.

IODEF enjoys all the benefits and power of XML data formats. The data can be parsed using standard libraries without having to go through pain of writing dedicated software to interpret the incoming data. Human-readable presentation of the data can be treated separate from the actual data contents. The data can be exchanged on practically any type of transport such as e-mail or http. The schema can also be tailored to suit the needs of individual applications without having to invent altogether new data formats.

While the majority of incidents handled by CERT-FI are still being handled using human-readable data formats, new tools are built to support IODEF from the beginning. Autoreporter supports IODEF as an alternative form of representing the data. Abuse Helper, whose development is still under way, sees IODEF as a key component in inter-organisational data exchange. Understanding the current state of play, the Abuse Helper project crew has acknowledged that in order for the tool to be useful in practical settings, it has to provide support for legacy data formats, too. Also worth remembering is that even the RFC authors remind that merely agreeing on data formats is not sufficient to eliminate the human intervention. [16]

3.4   Report Validation

At this point, the incident has already been discovered, the recipients have been identified, and information has been sent. Now, according to the documentation, we only need to validate the data in the report or find a way to satisfy that the reporter is known and trustworthy.

In order to validate the accuracy of the report, the recipient should be provided either with enough information to reconstruct the incident or pointers to additional information obtainable by the recipient. For instance, anti-virus vendors have a convention where malware samples are packaged inside a zip archive with the word "infected" as password. Due to CSIRTs having close relationship with anti-virus research community, they have too adopted the convention.

The cases in Section 4.1 exhibit practical solutions to the problem of providing the recipient with just the right amount of incident related information. For example, a German incident-handling clearing-house CLEAN MX sends brief e-mail notifications to the abuse helpdesks and instead of charging up the letter with technical evidence, they provide pointers to a searchable database where additional material can be found. Meanwhile, familiar and trusted reporters need to pass only minimal amount of information. A case in point is the trust relationship between F-Secure and CERT-FI: most of the time, the anti-virus analysts simply pass notifications no longer than single line to the national incident response team for further processing.

On the standards front, IODEF defines an optional method of submitting incident descriptions, impact assessments, and even event logs:

"The EventData class can be thought of as a container for the properties of an event in an incident. These properties include: the hosts involved, impact of the incident activity on the hosts, forensic logs, etc." [16]

Situations are bound to surface, where it is not possible to provide proof along with the report. If crucial incident details are left out, that leaves the receiving party with a dilemma. The options are to either blindly follow the reporter's request and risk falling into hoax or to put the report aside until additional proof is presented. The decision is made easier if the reporter has previously proven to be trustworthy. The recipient may then decide to extend the trust to this new piece of information. This kind of trust is easy to exploit for nefarious purposes, however, if the report's contents cannot be verifiably linked to the trusted reporter.

One method of establishing the report's authenticity would be to sign the message digitally with a method that lets the recipient validate the origins to a known – possibly trusted – party. RFC 2350 [5] suggests that each incident response handler employ at least Pretty Good Privacy (PGP) for encryption and message authentication. Most CERTs follow this advice. For instance, FIRST requires that a team aspiring to become a member must support PGP:

"To be a member in FIRST, a CSIRT must maintain and use PGP encryption. Encryption keys must be distributed to all parties that will use it." [36]

The Trusted Introducer program recognised PGP as a *de-facto* standard. [37] The EGC and APCERT follow similar conduct in recommending the use of PGP in both encrypting sensitive e-mail communication and signing content. Other methods for authentication include S/MIME, extranet websites attributable to the reporter, and out-of-band communications channels.

During the study, the reporter identification problem turned out to be more multifaceted than first anticipated. It was originally assumed that the challenge was to positively identify the reporter. Instead, examination of the cases showed there was considerable demand for the incident discoverers to retain their anonymity. In addition, according to CERT-FI's experience, the ultimate recipients are sometimes best being kept secret from the reporters. Recognising this, a special breed of incident-reporting clearing-houses has emerged to solve the anonymising challenge. The clearing-houses accept incident reports from a network of volunteers, repackage them with the reporters' identities masked and forward the material to the owners of the affected networks. There are several advantages to this approach. It effectively limits individual discoverer's responsibility. The clearing-house utilises a large number of discoverers instead of having to build a monitoring capability of its own. The network owners only need to learn to trust a limited number of incident-reporting clearing-houses. Finally, over the time, the clearing-houses accumulate a useful database of historical incidents. Conversely, the ISPs and the CSIRTs are in a good position to shield the recipients' identities from being disclosed to the reporters.

Lastly, the reporter may want to be able to follow up with the reports and validate that the information has been sent to the correct place. In the absence of normative references, a novel categorisation scheme was devised for the purpose of this study. In According to the categorisation, the reporter may choose from three options to track the subsequent progress of the incident.

Opportunistic reporters submit the material in blind and generally expect neither acknowledgements nor additional information in return. The reporter regards the case resolved and moves on to conduct other business as soon as the report has been sent.

Iterative reporters accept the fact that some of the recipients are interested in learning additional details while some may never return a call. In the iterative approach, the initial contact only serves as a trigger after which additional material can be requested and exchanged.

Active reporters assume ownership of the incident for as long as they can find other responsible handlers to take over. Should the case exhibit signs of stalling, an active reporter can take corrective measures to escalate it or otherwise circumvent obstacles.

The real-life incidents examined exhibited all three incident-reporting strategies. Each appeared to produce results if used in favourable circumstances. The study was not able to devise a methodological way to distinguish which approach would yield the best results in given situation.

4   Case Summaries

For the purpose of this study, six real-life incidents were examined in detail using material obtained under special permission from the CERT-FI incident archives. The inherently non-public material was augmented with information found in public sources.

Four of the cases involved compromised web servers that had subsequently been turned into malware distribution platforms or phishing sites. To the knowledge of CERT-FI, these were isolated incidents and were handled in routine fashion. The remaining two incidents required more coordination and their handling lasted for an extended period of time. One was a distributed denial of service attack directed to an insurance company and the other involved a series of web server breaches that lead to a disclosure of 78.000 user names and passwords. Remarkably, both were followed by a successful law enforcement operation and the perpetrators were eventually tried in court.

4.1   Compromised Web Servers

Incidents involving compromised web servers are almost a daily routine for CERT-FI. Despite of that, each of the four cases examined was handled in a slightly different manner. In each case, CERT-FI was involved in different role – this turned out to play an important role in deciding the choice of actions to take. In addition, the route via which reports passed through the contact network was not directly transferable from case to case.

In each case, the initial incident discovery was not only attributable to source other than the original attack target but also to a party with no apparent dealings with the compromised party. Hence, one or more intermediaries were needed to deliver the information within reach of parties with better means to resolve the issues. Interestingly, in each case, not all affected parties were included in the information sharing. Chances are that they never came to discover that they had been affected by an information security incident.

Someone Else's Problem. In the first case examined, a web server in Finland had been broken into and a lookalike page portraying to be an online banking service had been inserted onto the server. The compromised server belonged to a small Finnish non-profit organisation. Over a hundred similar phishing cases were registered with CERT-FI in 2009. This particular incident has been assigned an identifier [FICORA #309474] by CERT-FI.

CERT-FI received the report from a commercial German incident clearing-house CLEAN MX. The identity of the original discoverer was withheld by the clearing-house. Instead, a compelling set of evidence supporting the incident report was provided. Although the material received by CERT-FI was actionable, no action to resolve the incident was taken. CERT-FI was able to satisfactorily verify that a copy of the report had been delivered to the security team of the responsible network.

Interestingly, in the material examined, there was nothing to suggest that the foreign bank was contacted or its affected customers identified.

Assuming Responsibility of Someone Else's Problem. In a second case, identified [FICORA #308909], a compromised server in Finland had been turned into malware distribution platform. As with previous case, CLEAN MX was involved and CERT-FI received an informational copy of the report. This time, however, action was needed to inform the network provider about additional findings uncovered by CERT-FI. CERT-FI sent the additional material to the upstream network connection provider. Based on the material available, it is not clear why the actual hosting provider was not contacted. This may have been either an oversight or – with the benefit of hindsight – an effort to put pressure onto the hosting provider. In any case, shortly after escalating the incident to the upstream operator, the material was removed from the server.

Enforcing the Chain of Trust. In this case, six servers in Finland had been compromised and turned into malware distributing platforms. CERT-FI received information from a clearing-house that has expressed a wish to remain unidentified. The identities of the original discoverers were unknown to CERT-FI. Due to previous engagements and mutual agreements, the reports were considered trustworthy and CERT-FI proceeded to inform the ISPs about incidents. Only four ISPs out of six acknowledged that they had responded to the report. The incident id was [FICORA #295909].

Informing a Foreign Victim. As part of their routine job, analysts at an internet security company F-Secure had been reverse-engineering malware samples. Among other things, they had been able to extract addresses of the web sites containing additional malware. These addresses were passed on to CERT-FI who then opened an incident ticket [FICORA #307761] and proceeded to contact the

ISP in the United States. Upon receiving acknowledgement from the reputable US business, CERT-FI closed the case. Performing extra checks was not deemed necessary.

4.2   Data Breach

In late 2007, a young Finnish male in his teens broke into at least ten web sites and stole their user databases. He then proceeded to publish the credentials along with the passwords – 78,000 altogether – with an apparent intention to create havoc among the users. The incident with a ticket identifier [CERT-FI: 36789] was discovered by several private citizens independently. Figuring out, which services the credentials had been stolen from required some investigation and limiting collateral damage was seen a priority by CERT-FI.

After some guesswork, the compromised systems were identified and their owners contacted. Information acquired from their administrators helped establish the chain of events and that all compromised systems had been identified. Within a week, the police proceeded to successfully arrest the perpetrator. He was eventually tried in court. [35]

CERT-FI never contacted the end users whose passwords had been leaked. Most were informed in some way by their administrators or they found out about the incident thanks to the widespread media coverage.

4.3   Denial of Service Attack

The websites of three Estonian companies began experiencing symptoms of denial of service attacks in the summer of 2006. One of the targets was a subsidiary to a company based in Finland, which automatically made the incident interesting to CERT-FI. A ticket with an id of [CERT-FI: 19608] was issued. It was soon discovered that the attack traffic came from thousands of compromised computers all over the world.

During the investigation, it was discovered that several versions of a specialised autonomously propagating malware had been issued by an unknown author. The malware contained no command and control structure and would hence continue the attack perpetually. In fact, the attack is still on going at the time of collecting material for this study. The malware author was subsequently arrested and tried [27] but even he is unable to cancel his creations. According to the telecommunications provider, after four years, roughly 99 % of the incoming traffic to the web servers is still considered generated by the attack and is filtered out before it reaches the servers.

5   Conclusion

In this study, a review of normative literature was combined with an examination of real-life incident cases. This was done in an effort to produce an informed opinion about the state of play in the field of network and information security incident reporting. The purpose was to find how far apart the two worlds are from each other.

5.1   Incidents Can Be Detected by Outside Parties

The cases examined for this study helped underline the fact that there is a discontinuation in the way incidents are being discovered and whom they target. The victims are often among the last ones to learn about incidents affecting them, while at the same time perfect strangers can detect them without an effort. This underlines the importance of an agnostic approach to the sources of incident reports. Refusal to accept incident reports from the so-called outsiders causes an organisation to miss important information about its own security weaknesses.

5.2   Finding Correct Incident Reporting Contacts Is Challenging

Internet registries have only recently discovered that they could have a role to play in helping people determine who is responsible for handling information security breaches in various parts of the internet. It is rather remarkable that this has not happened earlier, as the delay has helped produce black spots in the internet where malicious activities go often unnoticed for long periods of time. Incident-reporting clearing-houses are invaluable as they perform the task that otherwise would belong to nobody. That is, they help the incident discoverers in getting the message to the victims.

5.3   Incident Reporting Not Fully Understood in Standards Literature

The standards have yet to discover the importance of complementing local event monitoring with reports received from external sources. The notion of having to base security procedures partly on data from unknown sources fits rather poorly with the control-driven worldview of standardisation. The study found ISO/IEC 27002 and IETF RFC 5070 to be the prime examples of standards with a say in incident response and reporting. The ISO standard describes the management system-level requirements and justification for incident response and the RFC provides a way to automate the processing and exchange of incident-related data.

5.4   Automation Not Fully Exploited in Incident Reporting

The everyday business of incident reporting and handling takedown requests still largely relies on human-to-human e-mail correspondence. The current automated tools are reduced to producing human-readable reports in an automated fashion and parsing incoming human-readable material. Existing standards for automating the whole exchange of incident-related material are heavily underused. Due to the holistic nature of the incident response process, there is continued need for human supervision. The challenge is to support the iterative information exchange and ad-hoc communications paths.

References

1. AbuseHelper project pages, `http://code.google.com/p/abusehelper/`
2. American Registry for Internet Numbers ARIN: Introduction to ARIN's database, `https://www.arin.net/knowledge/database.html#abusepoc`
3. Arvidsson, J., Cormack, A., Demchenko, Y., Meijer, J.: TERENA's Incident Object Description and Exchange Format Requirements (RFC 3067). Internet Engineering Task Force (2001)
4. Asia Pacific Computer Emergency Response Team, Member Teams, `http://www.apcert.org/about/structure/members.html`
5. Brownlee, N., Guttman, E.: Expectations for Computer Security Incident Response (RFC 2350, BCP 21). Internet Engineering Task Force (1998)
6. Brunner, E., Suter, M.: International CIIP Handbook 2008/2009, An Inventory of 25 National and 7 International Critical Information Infrastructure Protection Policies. Center for Security Studies, ETH Zurich, Switzerland (2008)
7. Bryk, H.: National and Government CSIRTs in Europe, Study Conducted by CERT-FI. Finnish Communications Regulatory Authority, Helsinki, Finland (2009)
8. Bryk, H.: A study among certain European computer security incident response teams and application of good practices in Finnish Communication Regulatory Authority. Helsinki University of Technology, Espoo, Finland (2008)
9. Centre for the Protection of National Infrastructure, International CIIP Directory, Issue 21 (2009) (unpublished)
10. CERT Coordination Center, CSIRTs with National Responsibility, `http://www.cert.org/csirts/national/`
11. Commission to the European Communities: Communication from the Commission to the European Parliament, the Council, the European Economic and Social Committee and the Committee of the Regions on Critical Information Infrastructure Protection - Protecting Europe from large scale cyber-attacks and disruptions: enhancing preparedness, security and resilience, COM (2009) 149 final. Brussels (2009)
12. Common Criteria for Information Technology Security Evaluation: Part 2: Security functional components. Version 3.1, Revision 3, Final (2009)
13. Cormack, A., Stikvoort, D., Woeber, W., Robachevsky, A.: IRT Object in the RIPE Database, ripe-254 (2002)
14. Cover, R. (ed.): Incident Object Description and Exchange Format (IODEF), `http://xml.coverpages.org/iodef.html`
15. Crocker, S.: Mailbox Names for Common Services, Roles and Functions (RFC 2142). Internet Engineering Task Force (1997)
16. Danyliw, R., Meijer, J., Demchenko, Y.: The Incident Object Description Exchange Format (RFC 5070), Internet Engineering Task Force (2007)
17. DoD 5200.28-STD: Department of Defense Trusted Computer Security Evaluation Criteria. National Computer Security Center (1985)
18. Dörges, T.: Information Security Exchange Formats and Standards. Slides for the presentation held during FIRST 2009 Conference in Kyoto (2009)
19. Eronen, J., Röning, J.: Graphingwiki - a Semantic Wiki extension for visualising and inferring protocol dependency. Paper presented in the First Workshop on Semantic Wikis "SemWiki 2006 - From Wiki to Semantics," co-Located with the 3rd Annual European Semantic Web Conference (ESWC), Budva, Montenegro, June11-14 (2006)
20. European Government CERTs Group, EGC Emergency Contact Information (unpublished)

21. European Network and Information Security Agency: Inventory of CERT activities in Europe,
    `http://www.enisa.europa.eu/act/cert/background/inv/files/`
    `inventory-of-cert-activities-in-europe`
22. Finnish Communications Regulatory Authority: On information security and functionality of Internet access services, Regulation 13 A/2008 M. Finnish Communication Regulatory authority, Helsinki, Finland (2008)
23. Finnish Parliament: Act on the Protection of Privacy in Electronic Communications 516/2004, Edita Publishing Oy, Helsinki, Finland (2004)
24. Forum of Incident Response and Security Teams, Alphabetical list of FIRST Members, http://www.first.org/members/teams/
25. Fraser, B.: Site Security Handbook (RFC 2196). Internet Engineering Task Force (1997)
26. Grenman, T.: Autoreporter – Keeping the Finnish Network Space Secure. Finnish Communications Regulatory Authority, CERT-FI, Helsinki, Finland (2009)
27. Harju Maakohus (Harju District Court): Court decision in criminal case 1-09-3476(07221000080), judge Julia Vernikova, Tallinn (2010); (only available in Estonian)
28. ISO/IEC 27001:2005(E): Information technology. Security techniques. Information security management systems. Requirements. International standard, First edition (2005)
29. ISO/IEC 27002:2005(E): Information technology — Security techniques — Code of practice for information security management. International standard, First edition (2005)
30. Killalea, T.: Recommended Internet Service Provider Security Services and Procedures (RFC 3013, BCP 46). Internet Engineering Task Force (2000)
31. Knecht, T.: Abuse contact information (prop-079-v003),
    `http://www.apnic.net/policy/proposals/prop-079`
32. Latin American and Caribbean Internet Addresses Registry LACNIC: Allocation of Autonomous System Numbers (ASN), LACNIC Policy Manual (v1.3 - 07/11/2009),
    `http://lacnic.net/en/politicas/manual4.html`
33. MITRE Corporation, Common Event Expression, `http://cee.mitre.org/`
34. Pethia, R., Crocker, S., Fraser, B.: Guidelines for the Secure Operation of the Internet (RFC 1281). Internet Engineering Task Force (1991)
35. Porvoo magistrate's court: Decision 09/863 in criminal case R 09/446 (2009) (only available in Finnish)
36. Ruefle, R., Rajnovic, D.: FIRST Site Visit Requirements and Assessment, version 1.0. Forum of Incident Response and Security Teams (2006)
37. S-Cure: Trusted Introducer for CSIRTs in Europe, Appendix B: Information Template for "accredited" CSIRTs, version 4.0. Trusted Introducer (2009)
38. Scarfone, K., Grance, T., Masone, K.: Computer Security Incident Handling Guide - Recommendations of the National Institute of Standards and Technology, NIST Special Publication 800-61, Revision 1. National Institute of Standards and Technology (2008)
39. Shafranovich, Y., Levine, J., Kucherawy, M.: An Extensible Format for Email Feedback Reports, Internet-Draft version 4. MARF Working Group (2010)
40. Trusted Introducer, Team Info, Listed Teams by Name,
    `https://www.trusted-introducer.org/teams/alpha_LICSA.html`

Use of Ratings from Personalized Communities for Trustworthy Application Installation

Pern Hui Chia[1], Andreas P. Heiner[2], and N. Asokan[2]

[1] Q2S* NTNU, Trondheim, Norway
[2] Nokia Research Centre, Helsinki, Finland
chia@q2s.ntnu.no, {andreas.heiner,n.asokan}@nokia.com

Abstract. The problem of identifying inappropriate software is a daunting one for ordinary users. The two currently prevalent methods are intrinsically centralized: certification of "good" software by platform vendors and flagging of "bad" software by antivirus vendors or other global entities. However, because appropriateness has cultural and social dimensions, centralized means of signaling appropriateness is ineffective and can lead to habituation (user clicking-through warnings) or disputes (users discovering that certified software is inappropriate).

In this work, we look at the possibility of relying on inputs from personalized communities (consisting of friends and experts whom individual users trust) to avoid installing inappropriate software. Drawing from theories, we developed a set of design guidelines for a trustworthy application installation process. We had an initial validation of the guidelines through an online survey; we verified the high relevance of information from a personalized community and found strong user motivation to protect friends and family members when know of digital risks. We designed and implemented a prototype system on the Nokia N810 tablet. In addition to showing risk signals from personalized community prominently, our prototype installer deters unsafe actions by slowing the user down with habituation-breaking mechanisms. We conducted also a hands-on evaluation and verified the strength of opinion communicated through friends over opinion by online community members.

Keywords: Usable security, User-centered design, Risk signaling.

1 Introduction

The versatility of mobile devices paves the way for a large array of novel applications; mobile devices today contain ever more sensitive information such as medical data, user location and financial credentials. As device manufacturers open up the mobile

---

* Centre of Quantifiable Quality of Service in Communication Systems (Q2S), Centre of Excellence appointed by the Research Council of Norway, is funded by the Research Council, Norwegian Uni. of Science and Technology (NTNU) and UNINETT.
http://www.q2s.ntnu.no

T. Aura, K. Järvinen, and K. Nyberg (Eds.): NordSec 2010, LNCS 7127, pp. 71–88, 2012.

platforms to encourage third party software development, applications from different sources are becoming available. Some of these applications, although not malicious, are inappropriate in the sense that they can cause harm (e.g., loss of privacy) or offense (e.g., culturally or religiously-insensitive content) to some users. The appropriateness of FlexiSpy – one of several commercial applications intended to spy on the activities of the user of a mobile phone – has been contentious. Mobile applications with potentially inappropriate content are becoming publicly available[1].

The bar for developing "applications" is also being lowered drastically. One can now develop simple applications for mobile devices by using only scripting languages (e.g., using JavaScript+HTML+CSS for Palm webOS [27]), or even without much programming experience using online tools (e.g., OviAppWizard [28] and AppWizard [29]). These applications are unlikely to be malicious (as they don't do too much) but we can expect a flood of applications from a larger variety of originators which increases the chance of a given application offending a certain group of users.

1.1   What Is Inappropriate Software?

StopBadware.org [30] defines badware as software that fundamentally disregards a user's choice about how his or her computer or network connection will be used. In addition to software with malicious intent, the definition covers bad practices, such as installing additional unexpected software, hiding details from users, and incomprehensible End User License Agreement (EULA) that hinder an informed consent. Our understanding of "inappropriate software" is close to this notion of badware. In addition to maliciousness and disregard of user-choice, we consider software appropriateness to cover also the cultural and social dimensions.

1.2   Software Certification and Its Limitations

A dominant approach for reducing the risk of malicious software on mobile platforms (e.g., Symbian, BlackBerry, J2ME and Android) is to rely on software certification and platform security. *Software certification* (e.g., Java Verified Program [31] and Symbian Signed [32]) is usually subject to software testing conducted by an authorized third party using publicly available criteria. But testing typically focuses only on technical compliance such as proper usage of system resources, proper application start/stop behavior and support for complete un-installation. *Platform security* (e.g., Symbian OS Platform Security [10] and Java Security Architecture [8]) refers to the isolation and access control features of the operating system or runtime. Ideally, software certification and platform security are used in tandem: an application is granted the privileges it requires if it is signed by a party trusted by the device platform. However, certification does not guarantee software security. It also does not consider the social and cultural aspects of software appropriateness.

Uncertified Software: The Risk of Habituation. Many application installers (in mobile or desktop environment) resort to displaying warning and disclaimer notices to

---

[1] A search using the keyword 'entertainment' in the iTunes Appstore returns a number of applications with potentially mature content.

signal risks when software to be installed is not certified. Visual difference when installing certified and non-certified software is often low; the text is also typically uninformative (see Figure 1). Providing system-generated notifications to which user attends to maintain security is the practice of "security by admonition" [26]. Besides degrading user experience, such notices lead to a high rate of false-positives causing many users to habitually click-through them. Click-through behavior is further entrenched when warnings equating "uncertified software" as possibly "harmful" may contradict other signals a user receives. An example of this is the installation of Gmail application (Figure 2a); the installer warns that it is 'untrusted' and 'maybe harmful' since it is not certified. A user, who trusts Google and who has just downloaded the application from Google's website will ignore and click-through the warning.

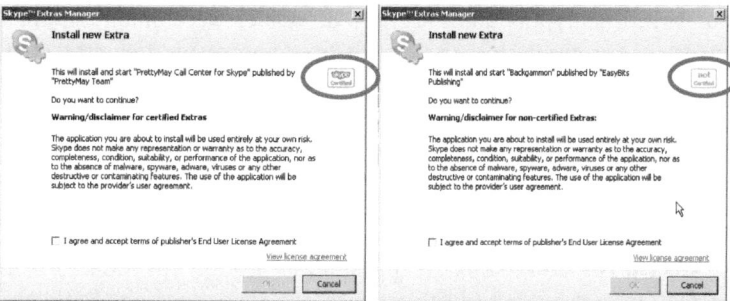

Fig. 1. The Skype PC version has a list of 'featured extras' that include both Skype-certified and non-certified plugins. The visual difference when installing the two types is only the color of certification label (light-blue vs. soft-yellow).

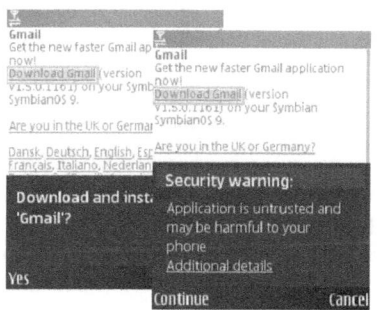
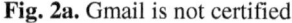
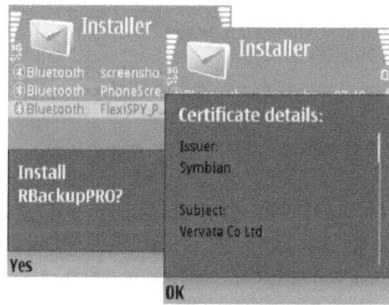

Fig. 2a. Gmail is not certified   **Fig. 2b.** FlexiSpy is certified [33]

Certified Software: The Risk of Centralized Judgment. On the other hand, software certified by a central authority may be perceived as inappropriate by some communities. An example of this is FlexiSpy – advertised as a tool to monitor the work force and protect the children and is available on most mobile platforms. The application has a number of characteristics that can be construed inappropriate: it spies on user activities (call, SMS, email, location), is invisible in the application list, uses a deceptive name (RBackupPro) and allows the device to be controlled remotely. F-Secure flagged it as spyware that may be used for malicious purposes illegally [33] but as FlexiSpy fulfills the certification criteria, it is Symbian certified. In other words, a user is given a warning (Figure 2a) when he tries to install Gmail although he may likely trust it, whereas FlexiSpy can be installed without warnings (Figure 2b) even though he may belong to the group of people who consider it inappropriate.

On iPhone, Apple decides which 3rd party applications can be distributed through the iTunes Appstore; we regard this as a scheme of implicit certification. Apple has also the means to activate a "kill-switch" to disable applications that may have been "inadvertently" distributed and later deemed "inappropriate by Apple". Apple's review criteria are, however, not publicly available. This has resulted in outcomes that are contested by developers and the Electronic Frontiers Foundation [34]. South Park, Eucalyptus and the Stern.de reader were among applications that were deemed "inappropriate by Apple" but later approved after protests [34]. Such contentions exemplify that centralized judgment can hardly cater for the value systems of different users.

1.3   Our Contribution

- We derived a set of design guidelines, grounded in cognitive and information flow theories, for a trustworthy software installation process (Section 2). Although we focus on mobile devices here in this paper, the guidelines are applicable to other platforms (e.g., desktop, Facebook) where installation by end-users can take place.
- We surveyed for the behaviors during installation, and we found high relevance of information from friends/family and user motivation to protect them. (Section 3)
- We built and evaluated a prototype system (Section 4 & 5). Although we could not test the efficacy of our prototype against habituation, we verified that opinion by friend is of higher impact than that of by online community through the user study.

2   Designing a Trustworthy Installation Process

We consider that *a trustworthy installation process* to be one that helps users to avoid installing inappropriate application. Besides providing risk signals that are perceived reliable and relevant, the installer should take into account of the risk of habituation, which undermines the efficacy of many security mechanisms involving end-users.

2.1   Cognition during Application Installation

In the conventional installation task flow, as a user defines his expectation or desired software functionality (for a task at hand), he starts by searching for an application in the application market or on the web that meets his requirements. When such an application is found (and downloaded), the user will have to perform some "post-selection" actions such as accepting security-related conditions and configuration options before he is able to use it (objective attained). These "post-selection" steps are nearly always made without the user paying attention to what is asked. Habituation to click-through this "post-selection" phase could be attributed to current design of installation that lacks understanding for user's cognition.

To develop guidelines that take into account of user's cognition, we draw on the *dual processing theory* [12] in cognitive science, which identifies two main types of cognitive processes: *controlled* and *automated* processes.

Controlled processes are goal-directed; a user defines an objective and plans a path that (in his opinion) will lead to the objective. At certain points, the user will make an appreciation of the current context in order to decide on the next best-move in achieving his end goal. This process is highly dynamic and requires logical thinking. For these reasons, one can execute only one controlled process at a time. Appreciation of the current context and decision for a course of action, over time, can be based on superficial comparison of contexts. This leads to faster decision making [7,12]. Despite a potential high degree of *automation in decision making*, it remains a controlled process as one will always have to compare between multiple contexts.

Automated processes such as habits, on the other hand, pose little to no cognitive load. *Habits* develop from deliberate into thoughtless actions towards a goal. If the context for an action is nearly identical over a series of performances, the action becomes mentally associated with the context; observing the context is enough to trigger the action [1,17]. The simpler a task, the more frequently it is executed and the higher similarity in context, the stronger a habit can become. New information that invalidates the initial conditions (which led to an action or habit) will go unnoticed.

The difference between *habits* (automated) and *automation in decision making* (controlled) lies in the constancy of the context. Habits are developed if the context is (nearly) always the same. With the latter, context varies between a number of states with reasonable likelihood, thus requiring a controlled process of context comparison.

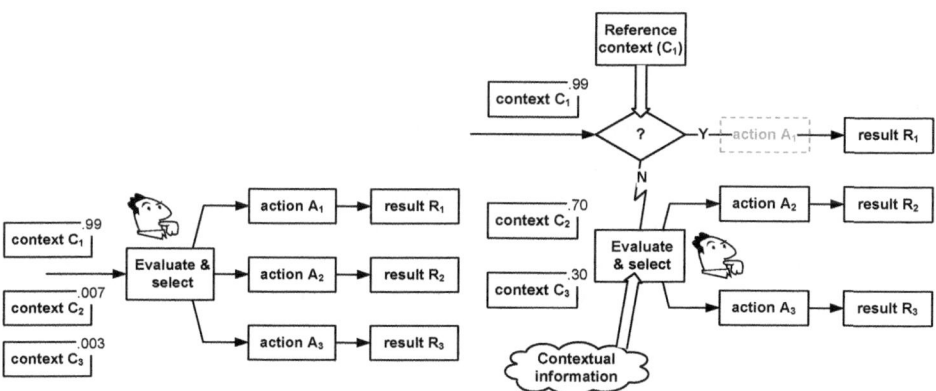

Fig. 3. (Left) A constant context results in habitual behavior. (Right) Using the attention capture process with the dominant context as reference prevents this.

The constant context (lack of context-sensitive information) during installation makes the action of confirmation a habit. This is exemplified in Figure 3 (left); the context of a normal installation flow (C1) demands the decision of action A1 (install) that results in R1. An abnormal context (C2) should lead to R2 (installation aborted). But as context C1 occurs much more often (denoted with probability .99) than context C2, user will over time expect context C1 and habitually selects action A1. This is more likely if there is no clear visual difference between the contexts (e.g., Figure 1). Furthermore, from a user perspective, the choice (install or abort) is asked after the last conscious step of *having decided* to download and install a particular application. Users also rarely face immediate consequence for installing inappropriate software.

We argue that habituation can be avoided by eliminating the need for user action in the normal and frequent context (an easy target of habituation) altogether. Depicted in Figure 3 (right), context C1 can be taken as reference context with an implied action A1. User can then be made aware of the deviation from this reference context through *attention capture* – the process of making a user aware of a change in environment that (may) require the user to attend to a new task [15]. A predominant view is that attention capture is an automated, stimulus-driven process modulated by the current controlled task [18]. The cognitive load required for the current task, as well as the strength and the relevance of the stimulus to the current task, affect the likelihood that a person will act on the stimulus. Thus, in addition to *visual salience*, the *relevance* and *strength of a warning (risk signal)* are paramount to ensure that users will take note of and evaluate the warning, during the installation process.

2.2   Information Flow and Risk Signaling

Software warnings (risk signals) have conventionally been communicated to users in a hypodermic-needle manner by expert entities (e.g., antivirus vendors). These risk signals are designed against malware and do not cover for aspects such as the respect for user choice and the social/cultural factors of software appropriateness.

In search of risk signals that are relevant and of high impact, we refer to the *two-step flow theory* [13] – the founding work of innovation diffusion theory – which describes how communication can be more effective through a network of people (rather than through the hypodermic-needle fashion). Central to the theory are the information brokers (originally known as opinion leaders in [13]) who are not necessarily the most knowledgeable but are nevertheless skillful in interconnecting people [3]. Information brokers guide the information flow from sources into separate groups (first step) given incentives such as early information access and social capital [3]. When information gets into a particular group, competition among group members can serve to encourage each other to improve own knowledge and exchange opinions, which constitutes the second step of information flow [3]. Social media such as Twitter and Facebook are successful examples that have harnessed the power of social networks for effective communication. Use of social networks for provisioning or relaying of risk signals is, however, still an early concept.

PhishTank [35] and Web of Trust (WOT) [35] are systems that employ "wisdom of crowds" (using a global community, *not* personalized network) to improve web security. PhishTank solicits reports and votes against phish-sites, while WOT collects public opinions on the trustworthiness, vendor-reliability, child-safety and privacy-handling of websites. Both systems aggregate user ratings into global (rather than personalized) values. Such global values can, however, be susceptible to exploitation. Moore and Clayton [16] argued that as participation in PhishTank follows a power-law distribution, its results can be easily influenced by the few highly active users[2].

Prior work has pointed to the advantages of using inputs from personalized networks instead of the global community. Against phishing, Camp advocated for the use of social networks to generate risk signals that are trustworthy as the incentive to cheat is low among members who share (long-term) social ties [4]. Inputs from social networks can also be verified through offline relationship, allowing incompetent or dishonest sources to be removed [4]. Personified risks are also perceived greater than anonymous risks [22]; this may help to mitigate the psychological bias (known as valence effect) in which people overestimate favorable events for themselves. Inputs from social networks are also socially and culturally relevant.

2.3   Design Guidelines

To sum up, we consider that a trustworthy installation process should:

- **Avoid requiring user actions that can be easily habituated.** User actions in a normal and frequent context could be made implicit and complemented with an attention capture mechanism to signal any deviation from this context.
- **Employ signals that are visually salient, relevant and of high impact.** Signals should cover both the objective and subjective factors of software appropriateness.
- **Incorporate mechanisms to gather and utilize feedbacks from user's personalized community.** In this work, we refer a *personalized community* to *friends* and *experts* whom individual users trust in providing valuable inputs about software appropriateness. *Experts* could be vendors or gurus who are knowledgeable in the technical evaluation of software. A list of reputable experts can be set for all users by default. Meanwhile, *Friends* refer to ones whom users have personal contacts with and whom could help by sharing personal experience about applications or relaying information. Here, we hypothesize that risk signals from the personalized community can be more effective (due to their relevance and trustworthiness) than that of from global community. We verified the relevance and strength of inputs from friends in our survey (Section 3) and user study (Section 5).

3   Web-Based Survey

We conducted an online survey to identify the installation behaviors and to evaluate the potentials of a personalized community in providing relevant and helpful signals.

---

[2] We note that this may be not too serious as determining whether a website is a phishing site (similar to whether an application is malicious) is usually objective. But judging if a website is trustworthy (with WOT, similar to evaluating the subjective factors of software appropriateness) can be contentious and prone to dishonest behavior (e.g., Sybil attack [5]).

Recruitment and Demographics. We recruited our participants mainly from universities. We put up posters around popular campus areas. Emails were also sent to colleagues in other universities with the request to take part and to the forward the invitation to their contacts. Throughout the recruitment and responding process, we referred our survey as a study on user behaviors during installation using the title: "A Survey on Software Installation". Considerations were taken to avoid priming of secure behaviors. The reward for participation was to receive a cinema ticket on a lucky draw basis. Winners who do not reside in the Nordic region were rewarded with a souvenir-book. The lucky draw was made a few weeks after the data collection.

The survey was open for participation for 3 weeks. In total, 120 participants took part in the survey. Participants who did not complete all questions, or whose total response time was unrealistically low (<10 minutes) were excluded. The final population consists of 106 subjects (36% females). 12% have a PhD degree, 42% have a Master degree while 28% have a Bachelor degree. 61% have a background in IT or engineering (power, electrical, mechanical, etc.) while 39% have a non-technical background (see Table 1). Subjects took 15 minutes on average to complete the survey, which was structured into 12 questions with 105 items in total. We mostly used a 4-point Likert scale on the perceived importance of an element and the likelihood or frequency of performing an action.

Table 1. Demographics of survey participants   **Table 2.** When know of digital risks

Education/work background		Age group	
IT or Engineering	61%	18-24	15%
Business / Finance	12%	25-29	41%
Science / Math	8%	30-39	32%
Arts & Social Science	10%	40-49	11%
Others	9%	50+	1%

User would always / often inform	
friends or family	62 %
members of online community	15 %
expert individuals	14 %
expert organizations	8 %
antivirus software company	6 %

Results. We present a few interesting findings that we obtained. Finding-1 concerns the behaviors during installation while the others demonstrate the potentials of ratings from a personalized community. The percentage values were computed after reducing the responses from 4-point Likert scales into nominal levels of important/not, likely/not, or usually/seldom.

i. **Information during installation is mostly ignored.** 83%, 90% and 75% of the subjects reported that they seldom read the EULA, privacy policy and disclaimer notices respectively during the installation process. Similarly, 78% of the subjects seldom check for digital signatures (or software certificates), nor abort installation when they are absent. Only 30% usually abort installation given warnings from the installer. However, 69% usually abort installation if unnecessary personal questions were asked. 76% usually abort installation if warned by antivirus software, while 53% usually abort installation in the presence of advertisement pop-ups.

ii. **Security vendors, experts and friends are important sources for information on digital risks.** About 90% of the subjects reported that antivirus software is an important source of information about digital risks (e.g., harmful or inappropriate software/services). Expert organizations and individuals also scored high (75%). Undeniably, security vendors and experts are the most important sources of information on digital risks. The survey gave further interesting results. 65% of the subjects regarded the first-hand experience by friends and family members as important. In comparison, fewer subjects (50%) considered the experience from members of an online community to be important. This difference was statistically significant (p<.01, Chi-square). This suggests that users regard inputs from friends and family members to be more relevant than that of from an online community.

iii. **When users know about digital risks, they are motivated to inform friends or family rather than the online community.** 60% reported that they could usually find security-related information by themselves. However, only 34% have been asked by friends or family members on whether software is trustworthy or appropriate. This could be due to the lack of existing system to share their opinions about software with his friends or family members. Indeed, we find that motivation to inform friends or family members about digital risks is high. 62% of the subjects would inform them about digital risks. Comparatively, only 15% were motivated to inform the online community (see Table 2). The difference was statistically significant (p<.0001). This suggests that users have more motivation to protect his friends than members of online community. This supports the feasibility of a rating system based on personalized communities over the global-community compatriot.

iv. **Users consider reviews from trusted sources to be helpful.** With considerations to the limited screen size of mobile devices, 80% regarded reviews from trusted sources to be important/helpful information during software installation.

Limitation and Discussion. We note that the education level of the participants was high, and 61% of the subjects have a background in IT or engineering. Yet, even though we might expect the subjects to be more aware of digital risks, there is an evident 'click-through' behavior. Excluding those with an IT/Engineering background, slightly fewer subjects (51%) could usually find security-related information themselves. However, the key results remain unchanged: 66% regarded friends as important source of risk information; 60% would inform friends or family when know about digital risks (compared to only 12% would inform such risks to an online community); 72% perceived reviews and ratings from trusted sources to be important/helpful information during software installation.

4   System Architecture and Prototype

Two important components in our architecture are: (i) *software repository*, which maintains a list of applications available for installation and a software catalog (containing metadata such as price, author, description and keywords); (ii) *rendezvous server*, which issues identity certificates and manages the user database, social graph and application reviews. To use the prototype installer (developed on the Nokia N810 tablet), a user must first register and obtain his credentials at the rendezvous server. Thereafter, the user can add friends and experts whom he trusts into his personalized community, and share software reviews with them, using the prototype. Sharing is done through the rendezvous server, Bluetooth or email. Software reviews are digitally signed and verified on the prototype to ensure authenticity and integrity.

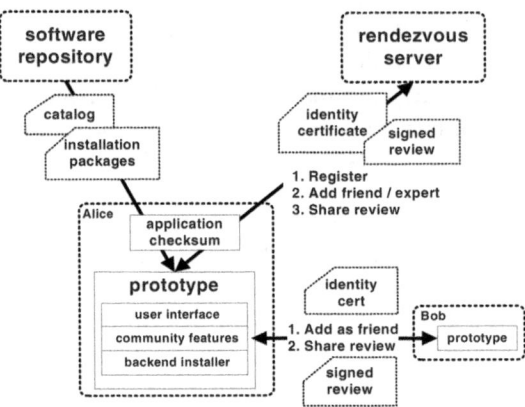

Fig. 4. System Architecture. The prototype was implemented on the Nokia N810 tablet, while a rendezvous server was setup on an Ubuntu desktop. The prototype interacts with conventional software repositories to obtain application catalog and installation packages.

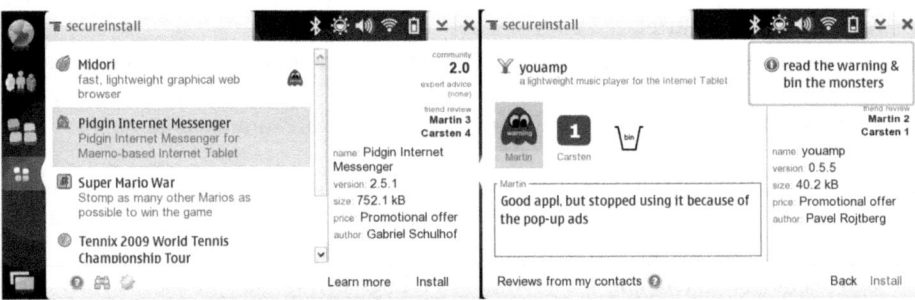

Fig. 5. Prototype. (Left) The front-page shows an application list with basic description on the right panel. (Right) The experimental 'bin-the-monster' mechanism: user clicks on a monster to read the negative review; he has to drag it into the bin if he chooses to disregard the review. (Note that the reviews and ratings were artificially generated for evaluation purposes only)

The installation task flow was redesigned. When a user defines his requirements and searches for suitable applications (using some keywords), our prototype displays a list of related software (Figure 5, left). The right panel shows basic information of a selected application, while detailed reviews from user's personalized community can be accessed by clicking on the "learn more" button. The "install" button will install an application without further prompting (if it has not been 'flagged' as potentially inappropriate by the user's personalized community). This removes user actions (in the post-selection phase of conventional task flow) that are prone to habituation.

For an application that has received *negative reviews* (i.e. flagged by the personalized community), a risk signal is shown prominently to catch the user's attention. To reflect the personal/social dimension of the warning, we chose a non-conventional risk symbol: a Pacman-like monster. Warning triangles and stop signs may signal that it is an "objective" opinion by some authorities.

The symbol is shown for flagged applications only; salience is increased by not showing positive cues. It is placed at the same level as the application name, and is enlarged when the application is highlighted. If the user decides to install an application that has been flagged, he is redirected to the review-page (Figure 5, right) where he has to read the detailed reviews. Textual review improves the relevance of a risk signal as user can appreciate what is said better than numerical values [20]. Negative reviews are framed in red (bottom-up salience). To mitigate a potential click-through when attending to the negative reviews, we experimented with two habituation-breaking tasks (to improve the efficacy of attention-capture):

- Delay: User has to read every negative review by clicking on each of the monsters with some time interval. When clicked, a monster will disappear into an icon with numerical rating only after a few seconds, before the next review can be read.
- Bin-the-monster: As before, but the monster only disappears when it is dragged into the bin. User cannot install until all monsters have been binned (Figure 5).

5   User Evaluation

We conducted a hands-on evaluation and investigated the strength of opinion given by friends compared to opinion given by online community members.

Recruitment and Demographics. Participants were mainly recruited from universities. We distributed recruitment notes around popular campus areas especially in the social science and science/math faculties. A web-form was also created to allow subjects to sign-up online. Participants of our survey were especially encouraged to take part if they reside in the Nordics; they were directed to the signup form upon completing the survey. Each participant was rewarded with two cinema tickets. There were in total 20 participants (7 females) consisting of students, researchers and a few working adults. 6 participants came from an IT background. The remaining subjects comprised of 6 mechanical, electrical or power engineering students, 4 science/math graduates, 3 art/design graduates, and 1 psychology undergraduate.

Experimental Setting. We specified 4 testing days and arranged with the participants a suitable session of an hour each. Individual participants were invited to our premises where the study took place. Each session was preceded with a brief interview. The main task was structured into four evaluation scenarios. In the end, we asked for the overall experience with our prototype before a final debrief.

In the brief interview, we asked if a subject has encountered situations where he had difficulties or doubts in determining the appropriateness of certain software; all subjects responded that they had been in such situations before. We then requested the subject to write down the names of two friends whose opinions could be useful in these situations. We then keyed in these two names into our prototype system.

We gave the subject a script containing the description of the initial setting and the four evaluation scenarios (denoted as S1, S2, S3 and S4). The initial setting depicts a situation where there was a special offer on 4 applications which the subject would have to decide if he would like to buy and install. The special offer was meant to provide motivation to buy/install the applications in the evaluation scenarios. Two games, a browser and a media player (denoted as A1, A2, A3 and A4) were selected such that the likelihood of subjects having prior experience with them was low.

Having understood the initial setting, the subject was required to decide if he would buy/install a specific application in each evaluation scenario based on some basic description (application name, file size, name of developer, a short text provided by developer) and software reviews provided by online community members as well as the two friends mentioned during the brief interview.

Four negative reviews were scripted to signal a mild level of inappropriateness. They concerned advertisement pop-ups, pornographic content, program crashes (data loss) and suspicious elements. A set of positive reviews were also scripted. Each application was associated with a fixed pair of negative and positive reviews.

The evaluation scenarios were designed to present to the subject, positive and negative reviews from either friends or online community, as described in Table 3 (left). We assigned the applications (A1, A2, A3 and A4) to the four scenarios in a rotating manner. Specifically, subject-1 would decide whether to buy/install applications A1, A2, A3 and A4, while subject-2 go through applications A2, A3, A4 and A1 in the fixed order of scenarios (from S1 to S2, S3 and finally S4). Rotating the applications in this manner avoided the potential bias due to the characteristics of individual applications and their fixed pair of positive/negative reviews.

Table 3. (Left) The 4 evaluation scenarios. (Right) Installation ratio in each scenario

		Install	Didn't Install
S1	No reviews from online community nor friends were provided	13	7
S2	Negative reviews were given by online community but friends gave positive reviews	10	10
S3	Positive reviews were given by online community but friends gave negative reviews	4	16
S4	Same as S3; the "bin-the-monster" mechanism was activated. After noting down the installation decision, subject was required to try installing the application (regardless of his decision) to experience the habituation-breaking interaction.	7	13

The subject was required to write down his decision to whether buy/install in each scenario and the reason on the evaluation script. In scenario S3, we asked for feedbacks on the use a Pacman-like monster as risk symbol. In scenario S4, we asked for experience with the "bin-the-monster" habituation-breaking mechanism. We used a 5-point Likert scale in both tasks.

Upon completing the four evaluation scenarios, we asked the subject his overall experience in using our prototype system in the form of descriptive feedback and a 5-point Likert scale (from terrible to great-idea). In the debrief, we informed the subject that all applications used were in reality good software available for the N810 tablet; all ratings and reviews had been scripted for experimental purposes only.

Results. Installation count in each evaluation scenario is shown in Table 3 (right). In S1, without any software reviews, 65% of the subjects went ahead to buy/install an application. The installation ratio decreased slightly (from 65% to 50%) in scenario S2 but dropped drastically (to 20%) in S3. Using the installation ratios, we evaluated the T1, T2 and T3 tests with the respective null hypothesis NH3, NH4 and NH5:

(T1) NH1: Negative community review does not overrule positive review by friend

(T2) NH2: Negative review by friend does not overrule positive community review

(T3) NH3: Overall strength of review by friend is not stronger than that of community review

Installation ratio in S1 served as the baseline of T1 and T2 tests (i.e. T1 compared the ratio in S2 to S1, while T2 compared the ratio in S3 to S1). Meanwhile, T3 was performed by comparing the ratio in S3 to S2. The hypothesis tests were evaluated using (one-tailed) Chi-square (good-of-fit) and binomial exact test. We favor results from binomial test as Chi-square statistics works better with a larger sample size.

Table 4. Results of hypothesis testing

	Chi-square	Binomial	Result
T1	$p = .080$	$p = .122$	NH1 cannot be rejected
T2	$p < .001$	$p < .001$	NH2 is strongly rejected
T3	$p = .004$	$p = .006$	NH3 is strongly rejected

We could not reject NH1 in T1. Although users reacted to negative reviews from online community members (resulting in a slightly smaller installation ratio in S2), the effect was not statistically significant. While we believe that users tend to react more towards negative reviews; warnings by online community members do not overrule positive feedbacks given by friends.

With T2, it was evident that negative reviews provided by friends overruled positive reviews by online community members. This was significant at 0.1% level.

The large ratio difference (30%) between S3 and S2 suggested the higher impact of information from friends. We evaluated this in T3. The overall strength of reviews by friends is stronger than reviews by online community members (significant at 1% level). The strength of (risk) signals communicated via friends should be exploited to mitigate click-through and careless behaviors during software installation.

We observed that the installation ratio in S4 (35%) was higher than in S3 (20%). We tested if the "bin-the-monster" mechanism had inadvertently reduced the effectiveness of risk signaling, and found that the effect was significant at 10% level. With our experimental "bin-the-monster" mechanism, a bin was shown after some delay when user clicked on a monster. However, the sudden appearance of the bin might have that caused subjects to prioritize binning the monster over reading the review. As it might not be obvious that the monster could be binned, we tried to assist the users by showing a hint (Figure 5, bottom). The short hint ("read the review and bin the monsters") might have been also construed as an instruction (or suggestive that it was ok to install) rather than to encourage a conscious decision. Our experimental 'bin-the-monster' mechanism was not a very successful one. An improved design could be to display the bin constantly to avoid a sudden appearance. The hint would need to be rephrased. A more direct association between the monster and review may also be helpful. For example, when user drags a monster into the bin, the corresponding review should be dragged together to signal that he is disregarding a review from his personalized community.

Table 5. On using Pacman-like monster as risk symbol

	μ	σ²
Monster draws attention	4.3	.69
Monster gives clear message	2.8	1.3
Monster gives warning	3.8	1.1
Prefer monster over ⚠	3.2	1.1
Prefer monster over 🛑	3.4	1.1

1=strongly disagree, 5=strongly agree

Table 6. Overall user experience

	μ	σ²
Experience with habituation-breaking	3.5	1.5
Experience with social rating integrated with software installation	4.4	.61

1=terrible, 5=great idea

The reactions to the use of the monster as risk symbol were mixed (Table 5). While most subjects agreed that it drew attention (salient), a few noted that they did not get a clear message of risk/warning. Subjects remained neutral on preferring the monster over the conventional "stop" and "exclamation-mark" symbols. We interpret these as using a new risk symbol would demand extra effort in educating the users.

Experience with the experimental "bin-the-monster" habituation-breaking mechanism was diverse (Table 6). Some liked it and found it interesting, while a few found such mechanism unnecessary. We note that habituation-breaking mechanisms are designed to trade off some level of convenience for safer user actions, and may be hard to satisfy all users. Feedback on social rating (for software appropriateness) integrated with the installation process was, on the other hand, very positive. This suggests that it could be a useful feature on mobile devices (or other computing environments that involve installation of third party applications by ordinary users).

Limitation and Discussion. There are two weaknesses with regard to our user study. We note that the T3 test might have an order-bias as subjects were always required to complete scenario S2 before proceeding to S3. We should have mitigated this by randomizing the order of test scenarios.

We note that also the initial setting of "software offer" to provide subjects with motivation might not be very realistic. An alternative setting is to have the subjects to decide whether to buy/install an application on behalf of someone whom they care. However, we think that both settings have limitations that are hard to avoid in a laboratory testing. We could create a sense of realistic risks, for example by informing the subjects that they would be required to login to his email/bank account using the test device after the study. Yet, we thought that this was not too relevant as we did not require the subjects to evaluate whether to install software that are potentially harmful; our study concerned only applications that may be mildly inappropriate.

Summary of Findings

- Opinions by friends are stronger than that of by online community; warnings by friends overruled positive feedbacks by online community, but not vice-versa
- The experimental "bin-the-monster" mechanism needs to be improved; designing and evaluating an effective habituation-breaking mechanism remain as interesting research problems
- The response towards habituation-breaking mechanisms and a new risk symbol was mixed; yet, majority was very positive with the idea of integrated social rating

6   Related Work

It is well-known by now that improving only the visual salience of risk signals is not enough to ensure secure user behaviors. Studies [23,24] have shown the inefficacy of security toolbars and site-authentication images, which mainly rely on an improved risk salience. Brustoloni and Villamarin-Salomon [2] suggested using polymorphic dialogs (that will vary the order of decision options) to capture user attention and break habituation. They advocated also the use of audited dialogs that would keep track of user decisions to hold them accountable for irresponsible actions. However, subjects regarded audit dialogs as intrusive; audited dialogs also did not assist users to make better decisions. In addition to improving the visual salience (through a better interface design), our work here increased the relevance of risk signals by employing inputs from user's personalized community.

Compared to FireFox's approach of making potentially unsafe actions (e.g., browsing a site with invalid certificate) more difficult to slow-down the users, our experimental habituation-breaking mechanisms (albeit need further improvements) are complemented with context-relevant information from personalized communities, that is absent in FireFox.

Related to software installation is the study by Good et.al. [9] which found that displaying a short summary (especially right-after the normal EULA notice) can effectively reduce the installation of unwanted applications. Yan et.al. concluded that visualizing the reputation and a personalized trust value for applications can be a helpful feature on mobile devices [25]. These studies highlighted the importance of timely signals. Our work integrated risk signals from personalized communities with the installation process. This integration was very well received in our user study.

Our idea of the personalized community is similar to NetTrust's [4] which employs personalized rating against the threat of phishing. NetTrust employs implicit inputs of browsing and bookmarking history of friends, as well as, explicit recommendations from third parties like banks and Google. Continuing from the initial work in [11,5], in this paper, we have provided supports for the use of inputs from personalized communities, based on theories, a survey and a hands-on study on a prototype system.

7   Discussion and Future Work

Use of inputs from personalized communities is not without several shortcomings. We outline several challenges along with the potential mitigation strategies worth of future investigation.

Reliability. Inputs provided by user's personalized community may not be always correct. Information from technical sources may also be misinterpreted when guided through ordinary users. These issues can be mitigated by making the evaluation process more structured. For example, an evaluation can be divided into several aspects of software appropriateness rather than a single overall rating.

Coverage. Although users are likely to encounter similar applications with (some of) his friends in practice, undeniably ordinary users will have limited exposure and resources to identity all possible inappropriate applications. This is why we have included the notion of *expert users* (whom individual users trust) into the structure of a personalized community. A list of experts can be set by default (for all users) to deliver critical risk information. We could also extend our work to compute or infer recommendations for specific applications when there is no direct input from the personalized community. We note that there is much to learn from the field of recommender systems. However, this should be done with care so that the high relevance and strength of risk signals, as perceived by users, do not diminish.

Scalability. Software features such as usable contact and review sharing, re-usability of reviews (across mobile platforms) as well as robust handling of software versions would be helpful to scale our implementation. Rather than building a system of social networks from scratch, we plan to merge the prototype with existing services (such as Facebook) that are now seamlessly integrated with smart phones.

Incentives. Like any community-based systems, there are challenges in initiating and sustaining user efforts. An important future work is thus to design an incentive scheme that would encourage active user participation. Here, we note that in contrast to a "crowds" system (i.e. one that employs a global community, such as PhishTank and WOT) where the success of the system is a public good, our work can benefit from unselfish behaviors among members in the personalized community. Indeed, we have seen strong motivation to protect friends and family members in our survey.

8   Conclusions

We developed a set of design guidelines grounded on theories for a trustworthy software installation process. Through a survey, we verified the high relevance of inputs from a personalized community and user motivation to protect friends and family. We implemented a prototype system with contact management and reviews sharing capabilities as well as a redesigned installation task-flow. Our user evaluation confirmed the strength of information communicated through friends, while the idea of integrated ratings from a personalized community during application installation was very well-received.

There may be some challenges that need to be addressed in future work; given the high relevance and strength of inputs from known sources, we show in this paper, the potentials of relying on personalized communities to evaluate software appropriateness and to mitigate the problem of click-through habituation during installation.

References

1. Aarts, H., Dijksterhuis, A.: Habits as Knowledge structures: Automaticity in goal directed behavior. Journal of Personality and Social Psychology 78(1), 53–63 (2000)
2. Brustoloni, J.C., Villamarin-Salomon, R.: Improving security decisions with polymorphic and audited dialogs. In: Proc. SOUPS 2007 (2007)
3. Burt, R.S.: The social capital of opinion leaders. Annals of the American Academy of Political and Social Science: The Social Diffusion of Ideas and Things 566, 37–54 (1999)
4. Camp, J.L.: Reliable, usable signaling to defeat masquerade attacks. In: Proc. WEIS 2006 (2006)
5. Chia, P.H.: Secure software installation via social rating, Masters Thesis, Helsinki University of Technology (TKK) and Royal Institute of Technology (KTH)
6. Douceur, J.R.: The sybil attack. In: Proc. IPTPS 2001(2001)
7. Frederick, S.: Automated Choice Heuristics. In: Gilovich, T., Griffin, D., Kahneman, D. (eds.) Heuristics and Biases. Cambridge University Press (2002)
8. Gong, L., Ellison, G., Dageforde, M.: Inside Java 2 Platform Security: Architecture, API Design, and Implementation. Addison Wesley (2003)
9. Good, N.S., Grossklags, J., Mulligan, D.K., Konstan, J.A.: Noticing notice: a large-scale experiment on the timing of software license agreements. In: Proc. CHI 2007 (2007)
10. Heath, C.: Symbian OS Platform Security. John Wiley & Sons (2006)
11. Heiner, A.P., Asokan, N.: Secure software installation in a mobile environment (poster). In: Proc. SOUPS 2007 (2007)
12. Kahneman, D.: Maps of Bounded Rationality: Psychology for Behavioral Economics. The American Economic Review 93(5), 1449–1475 (2003)
13. Lazarsfeld, P., Berelson, B., Gaudet, H.: The people's choice (1944)
14. Lyn Bartram, L., Ware, C., Calvert, T.: Moving Icons: Moving icons: detection, distraction and task. In: Hirose, M. (ed.) Proc. INTERACT 2001 (2001)
15. María Ruz, M., Lupiáñez, J.: A review of attentional capture: On its automaticity and sensitivity to endogenous control. Psicológica 23, 283–309 (2002)
16. Moore, T., Clayton, R.C.: Evaluating the Wisdom of Crowds in Assessing Phishing Websites. In: Tsudik, G. (ed.) FC 2008. LNCS, vol. 5143, pp. 16–30. Springer, Heidelberg (2008)

17. Neal, D.T., Wood, W., Quinn, J.M.: Habits: A repeat performance. Current Directions in Psychological Science 15, 198–202 (2006)
18. Peters, R.J., Itti, L.: Beyond bottom-up: Incorporating task-dependent influences into a computational model of spatial attention. In: Proc. CVPR 2007 (2007)
19. Rogers, E.: Diffusion of innovation, 5th edn. Free Press (2003) ISBN: 978-0743222099
20. Rubinstein, J.S., Meyer, D.E., Evans, J.E.: Executive Control of Cognitive Processes in Task Switching. Journal of Experimental Psychology: Human Perception and Performance 27(4), 763–797 (2001)
21. Schneider, W., Chein, J.M.: Controlled and automatic processing: behavior, theory, and biological mechanisms. Cognitive Science 27, 525–559 (2003)
22. Schneier, B.: The psychology of security (2008),
    `http://www.schneier.com/essay-155.html`
23. Schechter, S.E., Dhamija, R., Ozment, A., Fischer, I.: The emperor's new security indicators. In: Proc. S&P 2007 (2007)
24. Wu, M., Miller, R.C., Garfinkel, S.L.: Do security toolbars actually prevent phishing attacks? In: Proc. CHI 2006 (2006)
25. Yan, Z., Liu, C., Niemi, V., Yu, G.: Trust Indication's Influence on Mobile Application Usage, NRC Technical Report (2009),
    `http://research.nokia.com/files/NRCTR2009004.pdf`
26. Yee, K.-P.: Aligning security and usability. IEEE Security and Privacy 2(5), 48–55 (2004)
27. Developing applications for Palm webOS using HTML, CSS and JavaScript,
    `http://developer.palm.com/index.php?option=com`
    `_content&view=article&id=1603&Itemid=43`
28. OviAppWizard for Symbian, `http://oviappwizard.com`
29. AppWizard for iPhone, `http://www.appwizard.com/`
30. StopBadware, `http://www.stopbadware.org/`
31. Java Verified Program, `http://javaverified.com/`
32. Symbian Signed, `https://www.symbiansigned.com/app/page`
33. F-Secure identified FlexiSpy as a spyware,
    `http://www.f-secure.com/sw-desc/`
    `spyware_symbos_flexispy_f.shtml`
34. Objections towards iTunes Appstore approval process,
    `http://news.cnet.com/8301-13506_3-10317057-17.html`,
    `http://www.eff.org/deeplinks/2009/06/oh-come-apple-reject`,
    `http://www.eff.org/deeplinks/2009/05/apple-says-public-do`,
    `http://www.eff.org/deeplinks/2009/02/`
    `south-park-iphone-app-denied`,
    `http://www.thelocal.de/society/20091125-23501.html`
35. PhishTank, `http://www.phishtank.com`
36. Web of Trust, `http://www.mywot.com`

Practical Private Information Aggregation in Large Networks

Gunnar Kreitz, Mads Dam, and Douglas Wikström

KTH—Royal Institute of Technology
Stockholm
Sweden

Abstract. Emerging approaches to network monitoring involve large numbers of agents collaborating to produce performance or security related statistics on huge, partial mesh networks. The aggregation process often involves security or business-critical information which network providers are generally unwilling to share without strong privacy protection. We present efficient and scalable protocols for privately computing a large range of aggregation functions based on addition, disjunction, and max/min. For addition, we give a protocol that is information-theoretically secure against a passive adversary, and which requires only one additional round compared to non-private protocols for computing sums. For disjunctions, we present both a computationally secure, and an information-theoretically secure solution. The latter uses a general composition approach which executes the sum protocol together with a standard multi-party protocol for a complete subgraph of "trusted servers". This can be used, for instance, when a large network can be partitioned into a smaller number of provider domains.

Keywords: Multi-party computation, Private aggregation, Partial mesh network.

1 Introduction

With the continuous increase of network complexity and attacker sophistication, the subject of network and security monitoring becomes increasingly important. Traditionally, organizations have performed network and security monitoring based only on data they can collect themselves. One of the reasons for this is a reluctance to share traffic data and security logs between organizations, as such data is sensitive.

There is much to be gained from collaboration in security monitoring. Attacks range from being targeted at specific individuals or organizations, to global scale attacks such as botnets. Naturally, the response measures depend on the type of attack. The same situation applies to network monitoring, where the complexity of networks, and large amount of applications can make it difficult to distinguish between local and global disruptions with access only to local data.

A natural path towards a solution is to use multi-party computation (MPC) techniques, which have been long studied within the field of cryptography. The

T. Aura, K. Järvinen, and K. Nyberg (Eds.): NordSec 2010, LNCS 7127, pp. 89–103, 2012.

goal of MPC is to allow a group of mutually distrusting parties to jointly evaluate a function of their private inputs, while leaking nothing but what can be
deduced from the output of the function. Furthermore, protocols built on MPC
techniques are generally secure, even if several parties (up to a fraction of the
parties involved in the computation) collude to break the privacy of the other
participants.

The traditional setting of MPC is one where the number of parties is relatively
small and the network is assumed to be full mesh. Sadly, this precludes the
immediate application of such techniques in the large, partial mesh networks
which are prevalent today.

Recent approaches to monitoring in large networks employ an in-network
paradigm [1] whereby monitoring is performed collaboratively by the network
nodes themselves, using algorithms based on spanning trees [26,11] or gossip-
ing [24,22]. For these applications, scalability is often taken to mean sub-linear
growth in resource consumption growth in the size of the network.

Towards a general solution to the problem of collaborative network and security monitoring we present in this paper efficient protocols for computing sum,
max, disjunction, and thresholds in partial mesh networks. These operations are
sufficient to implement many of the aggregates of interest in monitoring. Our
protocols are efficient, both in terms of message and computational overhead.

We focus in this paper on passive, "honest-but-curious" adversaries whereby
attackers are bound to follow the protocol but may collude to learn information about the honest parties' inputs. This is much simpler than the active
attack model also considered in multi-party computation and often leads to
more efficient protocols. However, it is also a reasonable and attractive model
in many practical situations where e.g. side conditions related to traffic observations and arguments of utility can be appealed to to ensure protocol behavior is
adhered to.

The security of MPC protocols is commonly characterized by the size of col-
lusions they remain secure against. Such thresholds become less meaningful for
protocols, such as ours, which can be used on arbitrary networks. Thus, we analyze security in terms of tolerable adversary structures in the sense of Hirt and
Maurer [20], and describe the tolerable structures in terms of graph theoretical
properties of the network on which the protocol is executed.

As the need for monitoring is common to many areas, and our protocols are
efficient, we believe there is a wide range of applications. We give a few examples
of possible applications to set some context for the work.

Example 1 (Collaborative Security Monitoring). The need to aggregate security
log information as part of general intelligence gathering is widely acknowledged,
cf. [29]. The importance of collaboration is further emphasized by services such
as Internet Storm Centre's `www.dshield.org`, where firewall logs can be shared,
and aggregate statistics are collected.

Network providers and supervisors have strong interest in accurate security
log aggregates, as this will allow more precise estimations of the global security situation, in order to take countermeasures and improve operations. There

are, however, important privacy concerns, as log data, even in sanitized form, can reveal significant amounts of critical information concerning internal business and network operations. Previous work has explored techniques such as log anonymization and randomized alert routing to deal with this problem [29,25]. We argue that private aggregation techniques can be used in this scenario to produce practical security aggregates with strong privacy guarantees in near real time.

One application would be to collect aggregate packet- or flow counts to various destination ports. Due to the computational efficiency of our protocols, they could be run directly on network devices such as routers, and without the need to trust a third party.

Example 2 (Anonymous and robust peer-to-peer networks). Consider a peer-to-peer network for anonymous publication and retrieval of files where the network acts as a distributed storage. In this scenario, it could be of interest to compute the number of copies of a file to discover if further duplication of that file is needed, something that could be done by a private computation of a sum. It may also be useful to be able to query for availability of a file without learning any other information than if the file exists in the network or not, which would correspond to a private computation of disjunction.

Another application within the realm of peer-to-peer networking would be to implement monitoring of the overlay to enhance quality and research. This could be useful both for overlays with strict anonymity requirements, but also for more traditional file-sharing applications where individual users may still be hesitant to share information on e.g. the amount of data they've uploaded.

Example 3 (Joint control of SCADA systems). A research topic of growing importance is the security of Supervisory Control and Data Acquisition (SCADA) systems, e.g. systems controlling criticial infrastructure such as the electrical grid. Many different entities are involved in running the electrical grid, and they must co-operate to ensure production and consumption is balanced throughout the grid. However, many of the entities are direct competitors, which can prevent collaboration that would involve sharing of business-sensitive data.

Our protocols could be applied to monitor aggregate power flows over various areas of the grid, which is a summation. They could also be applied to compute the disjunction of alert statuses at operators. Then, if one operator has some form of disruptions, other operators would automatically be put on alert and be prepared in case the failure condition affects other parts of the grid. This would decrease the risk of cascading failures by giving early warnings to other operators, without sharing detailed information on the reliability of any individial operator.

We believe that in the scenarios presented above, the assumption of a passive adversary could be reasonable. For network monitoring, there is little to be gained for the participants in disrupting the computation of the aggregated information. In the P2P scenario, attacking monitoring is likely to be uninteresting, but searches and functions ensuring replication may be suitable candidates for protocols with stronger security properties, depending on the nature of the network.

In the SCADA scenario, in addition to the small gains from actively manipulating the computations, it's possible that legislation would demand that data was retained for auditing, thus increasing the risk involved in cheating.

1.1   Our Contributions

Firstly, we give a protocol for summation, where we perform a single round of communication to achieve privacy, and then reduce the problem to non-private summation. A single group element is sent in each direction over every link in this extra round. The protocol is similar to a protocol by Chor and Kushilevitz [10], but adapted to a partial mesh network, and with a precise characterization of tolerable adversary structures. It is also similar to the dining cryptographers networks proposed by Chaum [9] which is essentially the same protocol but applied to provide sender untraceability.

Secondly, we present a computationally secure protocol for computing disjunction, based on homomorphic cryptosystem, such as El Gamal [15]. The protocol requires two rounds of communication and then uses a non-private protocol for summation. Computationally, it requires a small number of encryptions and decryptions per neighbor.

We also give a composition structure where the information-theoretically secure protocol for summation is composed with a standard protocol for computing some other function. We show that this can be used for several standard functions in network management, such as disjunction, min/max, or threshold detection. For this composition, there needs to be a complete subgraph K of the network such that no union of two sets from the adversary structure contains K. This is a reasonable assumption in many network monitoring applications where the members of K represent trusted servers appointed by a disjoint collection of network providers. This is similar to the use of trusted aggregation servers in [5,13,7]. The composition essentially performs an efficient and secure "aggregation" of all inputs to some smaller subset of parties who can then run a more expensive protocol with stricter connectivity requirements.

1.2   Related Work

There are general results [18,3] showing that every computable function can be privately evaluated in a multi-party setting, but the protocols involved require a full mesh network between the parties and can be prohibitively expensive to execute.

There are many specialized protocols for computing specific functions in the literature, that are more efficient than the general constructions. Examples of such protocols include an information-theoretically secure protocol for summation by Chor and Kushilevitz [10], and computationally secure protocols for disjunction and maximum by Brandt [6], which uses the homomorphic El Gamal cryptosystem as a building block. While such protocols are more efficient than the general solutions, they are still not scalable in the sense of the previous section. Just sending one message between every pair of parties forces each party to process too many messages.

In most of the works on multi-party computation, the parties are connected in a full mesh network. An article by Franklin and Yung [14] describes how to emulate the missing private channels between parties, and using their construction, protocols built for full mesh networks may also be run on arbitrary networks. However, this emulation can be very expensive, and may not always be possible, depending on what parties an adversary can corrupt.

There has also been research exploring how the network connectivity affects what functions can be computed with information-theoretical privacy. There are results due to Bläser et al. [4] and Beimel [2] categorizing the functions that can be computed on 1-connected networks.

The Dining Cryptographers problem, and its solution were discussed by Chaum [9]. They study the problem of creating a channel such that the sender of messages is untraceable and their suggested protocol is similar to our protocol for summation.

A technique that can be applied to sidestep the connectivity and performance issues of traditional MPC solutions is to aggregate data to a small set of semi-trusted nodes, who can then perform the computation. As these servers are few, it is more feasible to connect them with a full mesh network. Examples of such schemes include Sharemind [5], SEPIA [7], and a system by Duan and Canny [13]. These are similar to the protocols we present in Section 5, with a difference being that our protocols perform aggregation while collecting information from the nodes, thus decreasing the load on the servers performing the computation, but limiting what can be computed.

A number of authors propose additive secret sharing to secure information aggregation in large networks or databases. Privacy schemes similar to the sum protocol used here have been explored in the area of sensor networks and data mining [28,19]. In fact, a very large range of algorithms used in data mining and machine learning, including all algorithms in the statistical query framework [23], can be expressed in a form compatible with additive secret sharing. Several authors have investigated secure aggregation schemes for the case of a centralized aggregator node (cf. [21,27]). A solution with better scalability properties is proposed by Chan et al. [8]. There, an additive tree-based aggregation framework is augmented by hash signatures and authenticated broadcast to ensure that, assuming the underlying aggregation tree is already secured, an attacker is unable to induce an honest participant to accept an aggregate which could not be obtained by direct injection of some private data value at the attacking node. Other recent work with similar scope uses Flajolet-Martin sketches for secure counting and random sampling [16].

1.3   Organization of This Paper

We begin by presenting the security and computational model and various definitions in Section 2. We then proceed to outline and prove properties of the protocol for computing sums in Section 3. Then, we give a computationally secure protocol for computing disjunctions in Section 4. We then show a composition structure where the protocol for summation is composed with standard protocols to compute for instance disjunction in Section 5.

2   Model and Definitions

We consider multi-party computation (MPC) protocols for n parties, $P_1, \ldots, P_n$, and denote the set of all parties by $\mathcal{P}$. Each party P_i holds a private input, x_i, and the vector of all inputs is denoted x. The network is modeled as an undirected graph $\mathcal{G} = (\mathcal{P}, \mathcal{E})$ where messages can only be sent between adjacent parties.

For a graph $\mathcal{G} = (\mathcal{P}, \mathcal{E})$, we say that $\mathcal{G}$ is *disconnected* if there exists a pair of vertices such that there is no path between them. For a set of vertices $X \subseteq \mathcal{P}$, we denote by $\mathcal{G} - X$ the subgraph of $\mathcal{G}$ induced by the set of vertices $\mathcal{P} \backslash X$. In other words, $\mathcal{G} - X$ is the graph obtained by deleting all vertices in X and their incident edges from $\mathcal{G}$.

Definition 1 (Separator, set of vertices). *Given a graph $\mathcal{G} = (\mathcal{P}, \mathcal{E})$, a set of vertices $X \subseteq \mathcal{P}$ is called a* separator *of $\mathcal{G}$ if the graph $\mathcal{G} - X$ is disconnected.*

2.1   Adversary Structures

The most common adversary considered in the MPC literature is a threshold adversary corrupting up to a threshold of the parties. More generally, we can allow an adversary corrupting some subset of parties as specified by an *adversary structure* [20].

An adversary structure $\mathcal{Z}$ over $\mathcal{P}$ is a subset of the power set of $\mathcal{P}$, containing all possible sets of parties which an adversary may corrupt. We require that an adversary structure is monotone, i.e., it is closed under taking subsets.

Definition 2 (Separator, adversary structure). *In a network $\mathcal{G} = (\mathcal{P}, \mathcal{E})$, an adversary structure $\mathcal{Z}$ is called a* separator *of $\mathcal{G}$ if some element in $\mathcal{Z}$ is a separator of $\mathcal{G}$.*

From the monotonicity of $\mathcal{Z}$, it follows that if $\mathcal{Z}$ is not a separator of $\mathcal{G}$, then no matter what subset in $\mathcal{Z}$ the adversary chooses to corrupt, every corrupted party will have at least one honest neighbor. More precisely, for every set $C \in \mathcal{Z}$ it must be the case that every party $P \in C$ has at least one neighbor who is not in C. This observation is important for the proof of security of the computationally private protocol for disjunction given in Section 4.

2.2   Security Definition

The security definition of a multi-party computation says that the adversary should not learn anything from the protocol execution except what it can deduce from its inputs and the output of the function the protocol computes.

In the security analysis of our protocols, we only consider passive (*honest-but-curious*), static adversaries in a network with private and reliable channels. The protocols in Sections 3 and 5 are information-theoretically private, and the protocol in Section 4 is computationally private.

We consider information about the network the protocol is executed on to be public knowledge. Our protocols do not depend on honest parties knowing the network structure, but neither do anything to hide that information from the adversary.

We refer to [3,17] for details on security definitions for information-theoretical and computational security of multi-party computation.

2.3   Homomorphic Cryptosystems

A cryptosystem $\mathsf{CS} = (\mathsf{Gen}, \mathsf{E}, \mathsf{D})$ is said to be homomorphic if the following holds.

- Each public key pk output by Gen defines groups of messages, randomness, and ciphertexts, denoted $\mathcal{M}_{pk}$, $\mathcal{R}_{pk}$, $\mathcal{C}_{pk}$ respectively, for which the group operations are efficiently computable.
- For every public key pk, every messages $m_1, m_2 \in \mathcal{M}_{pk}$, and every $r_1, r_2 \in \mathcal{R}_{pk}$: $\mathsf{E}_{pk}(m_1, r_1)\mathsf{E}_{pk}(m_2, r_2) = \mathsf{E}_{pk}(m_1 + m_2, r_1 + r_2)$.

It is convenient in our applications to use additive notation for both the group of messages and the group of randomness. However, we do not require that the cryptosystem is "additively homomorphic", e.g., that $\mathcal{M}_{pk} = \mathbb{Z}_m$ for some from integer m. Thus, any homomorphic cryptosystem with sufficiently large message space suffices, e.g., El Gamal. We remark that we do not use the fact that the cryptosystem is homomorphic over the randomness.

3   Computing Sums

We present an information-theoretically secure protocol for computing sums over a finite Abelian group. The protocol is similar to a protocol by Chor and Kushilevitz [10], but adapted to arbitrary networks, and with a precise characterization of tolerable adversary structures. It is also similar to a protocol by Chaum [9], with the difference that we explicitly create shared random secrets by a straightfoward technique and use the protocol for summation rather than sender-untraceability.

When computing sums, privacy comes cheap. We can take any non-private protocol for sums, $\texttt{NonPrivateSum}(x_1, \ldots, x_n)$, and augment it with a single additional round to turn it into a private protocol. The protocol admits all adversary structures $\mathcal{Z}$ which do not separate the network $\mathcal{G}$. This requirement on the adversary structure is necessary in the information-theoretical setting.

Protocol 1 (Sum). In the protocol for computing $\sum_{i=1}^{n} x_i$ over an Abelian group $\mathcal{M}$, on the network $\mathcal{G} = (\mathcal{P}, \mathcal{E})$, $P_i \in \mathcal{P}$ proceeds as follows:

1. For each neighbor P_j, pick $r_{i,j} \in \mathcal{M}$ randomly and send it to P_j.
2. Wait for $r_{j,i}$ from each neighbor P_j.
3. Compute $s_i = x_i - \sum_{(P_i, P_j) \in \mathcal{E}} r_{i,j} + \sum_{(P_i, P_j) \in \mathcal{E}} r_{j,i}$.
4. Output NonPrivateSum($s_1, \ldots, s_n$).

We begin by observing that the protocol correctly computes the sum of the inputs x_i. For every value $r_{i,j}$ sent in step 1 of the protocol, that value is added to s_j and subtracted from s_i, so all $r_{i,j}$ cancel when summing the s_i.

We now show that the protocol is information-theoretically private with respect to passive, static adversaries. We do this by showing that for any non-separating collusion, the remaining s_i values are uniformly random, conditioned on $\sum_{i=1}^{n} s_i = \sum_{i=1}^{n} x_i$.

Theorem 1. *Protocol 1 is information-theoretically private to a passive and static adversary if the adversary structure $\mathcal{Z}$ does not separate the network $\mathcal{G} = (\mathcal{P}, \mathcal{E})$.*

To prove the theorem, we begin by stating a lemma from which the theorem follows immediately.

Lemma 1. *Consider executions of Protocol 1 on a network $\mathcal{G} = (\mathcal{P}, \mathcal{E})$ where: the output $\sum_{i=1}^{n} x_i$, a non-separating collusion $\mathcal{C}$, and the inputs x_i and communication $r_{i,j}, r_{j,i}, s_i$ for $P_i \in \mathcal{C}$ are fixed. For such executions the remaining values s_i for $P_i \in \mathcal{P} \backslash \mathcal{C}$ are uniformly random, conditioned on $\sum_{i=1}^{n} s_i = \sum_{i=1}^{n} x_i$.*

Proof (Theorem 1). The values $r_{i,j}$ sent in the first round are independent of the input. By Lemma 1, for any fixed input and random tapes of a non-separating collusion, and fixed output of the protocol, the remaining messages have the same distribution. □

Proof (Lemma 1). Consider two vectors $s = (s_1, \ldots, s_n)$, $s' = (s'_1, \ldots, s'_n)$, and two vectors of inputs $x = (x_1, \ldots, x_n), x' = (x'_1, \ldots, x'_n)$ such that $\sum_{i=1}^{n} x_i = \sum_{i=1}^{n} x'_i = \sum_{i=1}^{n} s_i = \sum_{i=1}^{n} s'_i$, and $s_i = s'_i, x_i = x'_i$ for all $P_i \in \mathcal{C}$.

Let R denote an $n \times n$ matrix of $r_{i,j}$, where $r_{i,j} = 0$ if (P_i, P_j) is not an edge in $\mathcal{G}$. Define $s(x, R)$ to be the vector of s_i values sent in the protocol when executed on input x with random values R. The value at the ith position of $s(x, R)$ is denoted by $s_i(x, R)$.

We show that the probability of s being sent on input x is equal to the probability of s' being sent on input x'. This is done by, for any tuple of vectors s, s', x, x' constructing a bijective function $f(R)$ such that if $s = s(x, R)$ then $s' = s(x', f(R))$. The function $f(R)$ has the form $f(R) = R + R'$ for an $n \times n$ matrix $R' = (r'_{i,j})_{i,j}$. Furthermore, $r'_{i,j} = 0$ if $P_i \in \mathcal{C}$ or $P_j \in \mathcal{C}$.

We note that $s = s(x, R)$ holds iff R is such that for each P_i we have $s_i - x_i = \sum_{j=1}^{n} r_{j,i} - r_{i,j}$. Thus, for R' we need precisely that for each P_i we have

$$\sum_{j=1}^{n} (r'_{j,i} - r'_{i,j}) = (s'_i - x'_i) - (s_i - x_i). \tag{1}$$

Since $\mathcal{C}$ is not a separator, there exists a directed spanning tree T that spans the honest parties, $\mathcal{P} \backslash \mathcal{C}$. Let $r'_{i,j} = 0$ if (P_i, P_j) is not an edge in T. We can now fill in R' iteratively during a postorder traversal of T. When a non-root P_i is visited, only $r'_{j,i}$ for its parent P_j is still undefined on the ith row and column of R', and its value is determined by Equation 1.

When the root is visited, R' is completely filled in and we know that Equation 1 holds for all other parties. Consider the sum of Equation 1 over all parties. The left hand side satisfies $\sum_{i=1}^{n} \sum_{j=1}^{n} (r'_{j,i} - r'_{i,j}) = 0$. The right hand side also satisfies $\sum_{i=1}^{n} (s'_i - x'_i) - (s_i - x_i) = 0$ since $\sum_{i=1}^{n} x_i = \sum_{i=1}^{n} x'_i = \sum_{i=1}^{n} s_i = \sum_{i=1}^{n} s'_i$. Since Equation 1 holds for all parties except for the root, it must also hold for the root. □

We would like to remark that the proof of Lemma 1 does not make use of the monotonicity of the adversary structure $\mathcal{Z}$. Thus, if we allow non-monotone adversary structures (for instance, if parties 1 and 2 must always be corrupted jointly), the protocol is still private given that $\mathcal{Z}$ does not separate the network $\mathcal{G}$.

It is intuitively clear that sums cannot be privately computed if $\mathcal{Z}$ separates the network, and this is indeed the case. In [2], Beimel gives a characterization of the functions that can be privately computed in non-2-connected networks, with an adversary structure consisting of all singleton sets, and shows that sums cannot be computed in that setting. Any information-theoretically private protocol computing sums tolerating $\mathcal{Z}$ separating the network can be turned into a protocol violating the bounds given in [2] by standard simulation techniques, and cannot exist.

4 A Computationally Secure Protocol for Disjunction

We now consider the problem of computing the disjunction of all parties' inputs, and present a computationally secure protocol, requiring two rounds of communication and an execution of non-private protocol for summation.

As a building block, we need a cryptosystem $\mathsf{CS} = (\mathsf{Gen}, \mathsf{E}, \mathsf{D})$ that is homomorphic. We further need that the group of messages $\mathcal{M}_{pk}$ is the same group for all keys generated with the same security parameter, κ. For notational convenience, we denote this group $\mathcal{M}$. We require the cryptosystem to have IND-CPA security, i.e., resistance to chosen-plaintext attacks. We relax the correctness requirements slightly, and allow our protocol to incorrectly output `false` with negligible probability $2^{-\kappa}$.

In this protocol, we construct a linear secret sharing of a group element which is zero if all the parties' inputs are `false`, and a uniformly random group element otherwise. The protocol then proceeds by opening the share, which is done by (non-private) summation.

Conceptually, each party contributes either a zero or a random group element, depending on its input. However, it is important that a party does not know the group element representing its own input, as this would allow it to recognize if it was the only party with input `true`. In order to achieve this, we apply homomorphic encryption to allow its neighbors to jointly select how its input is represented.

If the security requirements are relaxed slightly, and it is acceptable that the adversary can learn if any other parties had input `true`, then Protocol 1 can be used instead (with each party herself choosing 0 or a random element as her input).

For ease of notation, we identify `false` with 0, and `true` with 1. In the description of the protocol, we abuse notation slightly and multiply a value by a party's input as a shorthand for including or excluding terms of a sum.

Protocol 2 (Disjunction). In the protocol for computing $\mathtt{Or}(x_1, \ldots, x_n)$, where $x_i \in \{0, 1\}$, on the network $\mathcal{G} = (\mathcal{P}, \mathcal{E})$, based on a homomorphic cryptosystem $\mathsf{CS} = (\mathsf{Gen}, \mathsf{E}, \mathsf{D})$, $P_i \in \mathcal{P}$ proceeds as follows:

1. Generate a key-pair $(pk_i, sk_i) \leftarrow \mathsf{Gen}(1^\kappa)$.
2. For each neighbor P_j, pick a random element $a_{i,j} \in \mathcal{M}$, and send $pk_i, c_{i,j} = \mathsf{E}_{pk_i}(a_{i,j})$ to P_j.
3. Upon receiving $pk_j, c_{j,i}$ from P_j, pick a random $r_{i,j} \in \mathcal{M}$, and send $c'_{i,j} = \mathsf{E}_{pk_j}(r_{i,j}) + x_i c_{j,i}$ to P_j.
4. Wait for $c'_{j,i}$ to be received from every neighbor P_j, and then compute $s_i = \sum_{(P_i, P_j) \in \mathcal{E}} (\mathsf{D}_{sk_i}(c'_{j,i}) - r_{i,j})$
5. Compute $\mathtt{NonPrivateSum}(s_1, \ldots, s_n)$ and output 0 if the sum is the identity, and 1 otherwise.

The protocol is efficient, both in terms of computational resources and communication. Each party needs to perform two encryptions, one decryption and one ciphertext multiplication per neighbor. The first encryption does not depend on the input, and can be performed off-line. The communication overhead of the protocol is two rounds, in addition to performing a (non-private) summation.

Theorem 2. *Protocol 2 for computing the disjunction of n bits on a network $\mathcal{G} = (\mathcal{P}, \mathcal{E})$, gives the correct output if it is `false`, and gives an incorrect output with probability $2^{-\kappa}$ when the correct output is `true`.*

Proof. Consider the sum

$$\sum_{i=1}^{n} s_i = \sum_{i=1}^{n} \sum_{(P_i, P_j) \in \mathcal{E}} (x_j a_{i,j} + r_{j,i} - r_{i,j}) = \sum_{(P_i, P_j) \in \mathcal{E}} x_j a_{i,j} .$$

If all x_j are 0, clearly the sum is 0. Otherwise, it is a sum of uniformly random group elements, and thus has uniformly random distribution. In particular, with probability $1 - 2^{-\kappa}$ it is non-zero. □

4.1 Privacy

Theorem 3. *If the cryptosystem* CS *is (t, ϵ)-IND-CPA secure, then no adversary running in time $t - t'$, for a small t', can violate the privacy of Protocol 2 with advantage more than $\frac{n^2}{4}\epsilon$.*

The proof of Theorem 3 begins like the proof of Theorem 1 with a combinatorial lemma similar to Lemma 1, essentially saying that unless the adversary learns something about the values $a_{i,j}$ from seeing them encrypted, it cannot violate the privacy of Protocol 2. Given the lemma, we apply a hybrid argument to prove the security of the protocol.

Lemma 2. *Consider executions of Protocol 2 on a connected network $\mathcal{G} = (\mathcal{P}, \mathcal{E})$ with input x such that $x_i =$ true for at least one P_i, and where a collusion $\mathcal{C} \in \mathcal{Z}$ from a non-separating adversary structure $\mathcal{Z}$, and communication $a_{i,j}, r_{i,j}, r_{j,i}, s_i$ for $P_i \in \mathcal{C}$ is fixed. For such executions, the values s_i for $P_i \in \mathcal{P}\backslash\mathcal{C}$ have a uniform and independent distribution.*

Proof (Theorem 3). We begin with the observation that if all the parties have input false, then the protocol behaves exactly as Protocol 1 with zeroes as inputs and by Lemma 1, then the honest parties' s_i will be uniformly random conditioned on $\sum_{i=1}^{n} s_i = 0$.

First, consider the case where the inputs of all corrupted parties are false. In this case, a simulator that independently samples the pk_i, $c_{i,j}$, $r_{i,j}$ and s_i included in the adversary's view, conditioned only on $\sum_{i=1}^{n} s_i = 0$ if the output is false, or $\sum_{i=1}^{n} s_i \neq 0$ otherwise perfectly simulates the protocol to the adversary, by the previous observation and Lemma 2. Thus, in this case, the adversary cannot violate the privacy of the protocol.

Now, consider the case when at least one of the corrupted parties has input true. We begin by constructing a simulator S_0 that randomly selects inputs and $a_{i,j}$ for all honest parties, conditioned on the output matching the output it should simulate. It then follows the protocol to simulate the adversary's view.

We now construct hybrid simulators, S_k, working like S_0 but replacing the first k ciphertexts $c_{i,j}$ in the adversary's view by random ciphertexts. It follows from the (t, ϵ)-IND-CPA security of $\mathsf{E}_{pk_i}(x)$ that no adversary running in time $t - t'$, for some small t' required to run the simulator S_k, can distinguish between the views simulated by S_k and S_{k-1}.

Assume that the adversary's view includes T ciphertexts $c_{i,j}$, so the view simulated by S_T contains no information on the $a_{i,j}$ sent by honest nodes to corrupted nodes. There can be at most $(n/2)^2$ edges between honest and corrupted nodes, so $T \leq n^2/4$. By Lemma 2, the distribution of simulated $r_{i,j}$ and s_i values is exactly the same as in a real execution, so the view simulated by S_T contains no information on the honest parties inputs. □

Proof (Lemma 2). Consider the following mental experiment, where we modify an execution of the protocol in two steps.

MODIFICATION 1. For each neighbor P_j of P_i we subtract $x_i c_{j,i}$ from $c'_{i,j}$ in Step 3 of the protocol and add $x_i a_{j,i}$ to s_i in Step 4 of the protocol. It is easy to see that this does not change the distribution of either s_i or $\mathsf{D}_{sk_i}(c'_{i,j})$ for any neighbor P_j.

MODIFICATION 2. Remove all encryptions and decryptions. This transforms Steps 3-5 of the protocol into an execution of Protocol 1, where P_i holds the input $\sum_{j=1}^{n} x_i a_{j,i}$.

From Lemma 1 we conclude that with the two modifications, the s_i are independently distributed conditioned on $\sum_{i=1}^{n} s_i = \sum_{i=1}^{n} \sum_{j=1}^{n} x_i a_{j,i}$, but the right side of this equation is randomly distributed when some $x_i = 1$ and $a_{i,j}$ for some neighbor P_j is randomly distributed. From the conditions of the lemma, we know there is at least one P_i such that $x_i = 1$, and from the monotonicity of $\mathcal{Z}$ and that it is non-separating, we know that every party has an honest neighbor. Thus, the s_i are uniformly and independently distributed. This concludes the proof.   □

4.2 Computing the Maximum

In the setting with passive adversaries, it is easy to construct a protocol for computing the maximum by repetition and parallel composition of a protocol for disjunctions.

Assume the inputs are integers of ℓ bits. We can then compute the disjunction of the most significant bits of all parties' inputs, which is also the most significant bit of the maximum of the inputs. We then proceed to the next most significant bit. When a party learns that its input is smaller than the maximum (its input was 0 and the output was 1), it participates with input 0 in the remaining protocol executions.

Several bits can be handled in parallel to reduce the number of rounds at the cost of more protocol executions. To find the maximum of k bits, one can run $2^k - 1$ parallel disjunction computations, where the parties set their inputs based on if their k most significant bits represent an integer greater or equal to $2^k - 1, 2^k - 2, \ldots, 1$, respectively. Thus, to find the maximum of ℓ-bit integers, one can run $\lceil \ell/k \rceil$ rounds of protocols for disjunction, with $2^k - 1$ protocol executions in each round.

5   General Composition

Many functions can be computed as a function of the sum of inputs of the parties. Examples include disjunction, counting and threshold functions. In this context, a threshold function is a function returning `true` if the sum of inputs exceeds some threshold and `false` otherwise.

We can combine our Protocol 1 with standard protocols (which assume full mesh communications) to construct information-theoretically secure protocols for computing such functions. The benefit of this approach is that information-theoretical security is achieved in a partial mesh network while maintaining efficiency. Another approach would have been to simulate the missing edges (e.g., with the techniques from [14]) and then immediately using standard protocol, but this approach is generally more expensive in terms of communication.

By this composition, we essentially run a cheap protocol to "accumulate" the inputs of most parties and then let some small subset of parties run a more expensive protocol and jointly act as a trusted party. This can be useful when performing computations with a large number of parties where some subset can be trusted not to collude with each other. This can be compared to the trusted servers in [5,13,7].

Executing the standard protocol requires a complete network, so this construction is only applicable when $\mathcal{G}$ contains a subgraph K that is complete. Furthermore, tolerable adversary structures $\mathcal{Z}$ are those that do not separate the graph, and which, restricted to K, are tolerable by the standard protocol being used. For most protocols, the requirement will be that no two subsets in $\mathcal{Z}$ cover K, or using notation from [20], the predicate $Q^{(2)}(\mathcal{Z}|_K, K)$ must hold.

Protocol 1 constructs a secret sharing of the sum of the parties inputs and then opens it. When we adapt the protocol for composition, we only construct the secret sharing, and accumulate the sum (still shared) in the nodes in K.

As an example, we give an information-theoretically secure protocol for disjunction. Here, we let each party input 0 or 1 (for `false` and `true`) and then use a protocol by Damgård et al. [12] for comparison.

Protocol 3 (Disjunction). In the protocol for computing $\text{Or}(x_1, \ldots, x_n)$ where $x_i \in \{0,1\}$ on the network $\mathcal{G} = (\mathcal{P}, \mathcal{E})$ with a set $K \subseteq \mathcal{P}$ of designated parties, $P_i \in \mathcal{P}$ proceeds as follows:

1. For each neighbor P_j, pick $r_{i,j} \in \mathbb{Z}_p$ randomly and send it to P_j.
2. Wait for $r_{j,i}$ from each neighbor P_j.
3. Compute $s_i = x_i - \sum_{(P_i,P_j)\in\mathcal{E}} r_{i,j} + \sum_{(P_i,P_j)\in\mathcal{E}} r_{j,i}$.
4. Compute $s = \sum_{P_j \notin K} s_j$ using `NonPrivateSum`.
5. If in K, execute comparison protocol from [12] to test if $s + \sum_{P_j \in K} s_j = 0$.

Theorem 4. *Protocol 3 is information-theoretically private to a passive and static adversary if the adversary structure $\mathcal{Z}$ does not separate the network $\mathcal{G} = (\mathcal{P}, \mathcal{E})$ and there is a complete subgraph $K \subseteq \mathcal{G}$ such that no two sets in $\mathcal{Z}$ cover K.*

Proof. The values $r_{i,j}$ are independent of the input. By the restriction on $\mathcal{Z}$ there must be at least one party in K not corrupted by the adversary. By Lemma 1 we know that the s_i values input to `NonPrivateSum` are uniform and independent. Thus, the adversary gains no information from these, and by the composition theorem [17, Theorem 7.5.7], we conclude that the protocol is private. $\square$

6   Conclusion

In this paper we have given efficient protocols for privately evaluating summation and disjunction on any network topology. The ability to privately evaluate these two basic primitives have applications in several widely varying contexts. As the most expensive part of our protocols is the task of non-private summation, privacy comes very cheaply.

We believe that the question of which functions can be efficiently privately evaluated in arbitrary network topologies is an interesting topic for further study.

References

1. The FP7 4WARD project, http://www.4ward-project.eu/
2. Beimel, A.: On private computation in incomplete networks. Distributed Computing 19(3), 237–252 (2007)
3. Ben-Or, M., Goldwasser, S., Wigderson, A.: Completeness theorems for non-cryptographic fault-tolerant distributed computation (extended abstract). In: STOC, pp. 1–10. ACM (1988)
4. Bläser, M., Jakoby, A., Liskiewicz, M., Manthey, B.: Private computation: k-connected versus 1-connected networks. J. Cryptology 19(3), 341–357 (2006)
5. Bogdanov, D., Laur, S., Willemson, J.: Sharemind: A Framework for Fast Privacy-Preserving Computations. In: Jajodia, S., López, J. (eds.) ESORICS 2008. LNCS, vol. 5283, pp. 192–206. Springer, Heidelberg (2008)
6. Brandt, F.: Efficient Cryptographic Protocol Design Based on Distributed El Gamal Encryption. In: Won, D.H., Kim, S. (eds.) ICISC 2005. LNCS, vol. 3935, pp. 32–47. Springer, Heidelberg (2006)
7. Burkhart, M., Strasser, M., Many, D., Dimitropoulos, X.: SEPIA: Privacy-preserving aggregation of multi-domain network events and statistics. In: 19th USENIX Security Symposium, Washington, DC, USA (August 2010)
8. Chan, H., Perrig, A., Song, D.X.: Secure hierarchical in-network aggregation in sensor networks. In: Juels, A., Wright, R.N., di Vimercati, S.D.C. (eds.) ACM Conference on Computer and Communications Security, pp. 278–287. ACM (2006)
9. Chaum, D.: The dining cryptographers problem: Unconditional sender and recipient untraceability. J. Cryptology 1(1), 65–75 (1988)
10. Chor, B., Kushilevitz, E.: A communication-privacy tradeoff for modular addition. Inf. Process. Lett. 45(4), 205–210 (1993)
11. Dam, M., Stadler, R.: A generic protocol for network state aggregation. In: Proc. Radiovetenskap Och Kommunikation, RVK (2005)
12. Damgård, I., Fitzi, M., Kiltz, E., Nielsen, J.B., Toft, T.: Unconditionally Secure Constant-Rounds Multi-Party Computation for Equality, Comparison, Bits and Exponentiation. In: Halevi, S., Rabin, T. (eds.) TCC 2006. LNCS, vol. 3876, pp. 285–304. Springer, Heidelberg (2006)
13. Duan, Y., Canny, J.F.: Practical private computation and zero-knowledge tools for privacy-preserving distributed data mining. In: SDM, pp. 265–276. SIAM (2008)
14. Franklin, M.K., Yung, M.: Secure hypergraphs: Privacy from partial broadcast. SIAM J. Discrete Math. 18(3), 437–450 (2004)
15. El Gamal, T.: A public key cryptosystem and a signature scheme based on discrete logarithms. IEEE Transactions on Information Theory 31(4), 469–472 (1985)

16. Garofalakis, M.N., Hellerstein, J.M., Maniatis, P.: Proof sketches: Verifiable in-network aggregation. In: ICDE, pp. 996–1005. IEEE (2007)
17. Oded, G.: Foundations of Cryptography. Basic Applications, vol. 2. Cambridge University Press, New York (2004)
18. Goldreich, O., Micali, S., Wigderson, A.: How to play any mental game or a completeness theorem for protocols with honest majority. In: STOC, pp. 218–229. ACM (1987)
19. He, W., Liu, X., Nguyen, H., Nahrstedt, K., Abdelzaher, T.F.: PDA: Privacy-preserving data aggregation in wireless sensor networks. In: INFOCOM, pp. 2045–2053. IEEE (2007)
20. Hirt, M., Maurer, U.M.: Player simulation and general adversary structures in perfect multiparty computation. J. Cryptology 13(1), 31–60 (2000)
21. Hu, L., Evans, D.: Secure aggregation for wireless networks. In: Workshop on Security and Assurance in Ad hoc Networks, p. 384. IEEE Computer Society (2003)
22. Jelasity, M., Montresor, A., Babaoglu, Ö.: Gossip-based aggregation in large dynamic networks. ACM Trans. Comput. Syst. 23(3), 219–252 (2005)
23. Kearns, M.J.: Efficient noise-tolerant learning from statistical queries. In: STOC, pp. 392–401 (1993)
24. Kempe, D., Dobra, A., Gehrke, J.: Gossip-based computation of aggregate information. In: FOCS, pp. 482–491. IEEE Computer Society (2003)
25. Lincoln, P., Porras, P.A., Shmatikov, V.: Privacy-preserving sharing and correlation of security alerts. In: USENIX Security Symposium, pp. 239–254. USENIX (2004)
26. Madden, S., Franklin, M.J., Hellerstein, J.M., Hong, W.: TAG: A tiny aggregation service for ad-hoc sensor networks. In: OSDI (2002)
27. Przydatek, B., Song, D.X., Perrig, A.: SIA: secure information aggregation in sensor networks. In: Akyildiz, I.F., Estrin, D., Culler, D.E., Srivastava, M.B. (eds.) SenSys, pp. 255–265. ACM (2003)
28. Roughan, M., Zhang, Y.: Secure distributed data-mining and its application to large-scale network measurements. SIGCOMM Comput. Commun. Rev. 36(1), 7–14 (2006)
29. Slagell, A.J., Yurcik, W.: Sharing computer network logs for security and privacy: A motivation for new methodologies of anonymization. CoRR, cs.CR/0409005 (2004)

Tracking Malicious Hosts on a 10Gbps Backbone Link⋆

Magnus Almgren and Wolfgang John

Computer Science and Engineering
Chalmers University of Technology, Sweden
`first.lastname@chalmers.se`

Abstract. We use anonymized flow data collected from a 10Gbps backbone link to discover and analyze malicious flow patterns. Even though such data may be rather difficult to interpret, we show how to *bootstrap* our analysis with a *set of malicious hosts* to discover more obscure patterns. Our analysis spans from simple attribute aggregates (such as top IP and port numbers) to advanced *temporal analysis of communication patterns* between normal and malicious hosts. For example, we found some complex communication patterns that possibly lasted for over a week. Furthermore, several malicious hosts were active over the whole data collection period, despite being blacklisted. We also discuss the problems of working with anonymized data. Given that this type of privacy-sensitive backbone data would not be available for analysis without proper anonymization, we show that it can still offer many novel insights, valuable for both network researchers and practitioners.

Keywords: Network Security, Malicious Traffic, Internet Backbone.

1 Introduction

The amount of Internet malware in circulation has increased and is forecasted to increase even further [1]. Also the types of attacks have changed over time and are today very different from the ones seen a decade ago. From being a way to gain esoteric prestige, the attacks nowadays are connected to organized crime [2]. It is important to understand how prevalent malicious code is, how it spreads, how many "normal" users are infected, and what happens when one is infected.

There are several orthogonal methods to find partial answers to these questions. For example, companies or other large organizations can analyze the traffic in their networks. In these settings, especially given the fact that the organization has a budget for security incident investigation, there often exists a security policy with enforcement. That is, as certain security mechanisms are used the data from such organizations will only show a subset of possible security incidents.

Antivirus companies [3,4], with their software ubiquitously deployed on many computers around the world, can also collect certain data from their customers to analyze larger trends. However, some information is sensitive to export from the client and the

---

⋆ This work is supported by the Swedish Civil Contingencies Agency (MSB) and SUNET. The research leading to these results has received funding from the European Union Seventh Framework Programme (FP7/2007-2013) under grant agreement n° 257007.

T. Aura, K. Järvinen, and K. Nyberg (Eds.): NordSec 2010, LNCS 7127, pp. 104–120, 2012.

data are again skewed; they come from computers where security mechanisms have been installed and where the owners (presumably) are security conscious.

Large networks of honeypots [5,6] offer invaluable insights into malware behavior but again the data are biased as these are not regular computers with regular users. Given their specialized nature, it is also expected that other hosts on the network have a higher-than-average security protection; the administrators that spend time to install and monitor a honeypot usually also invest time into other (simpler) security mechanisms. Similar reasoning goes for DShield/SANS' aggregated data [7,8].

In our work, we analyze traffic from the backbone of the Swedish University Network SUNET. This is a high-level cross-section of traffic from a very large domain, giving us an aggregated view of a very large number of hosts containing both security-conscious users (i.e., researchers in security) as well as less sophisticated users (students using the computer as a means to an end). By analyzing such traffic, we hope to gain a different, and potentially more general, view of current malware behavior than the approaches described above. However, we acknowledge that our cross section of users is also skewed, albeit in a different way than above. SUNET mainly provides high-speed Internet access to academic institutions in Sweden, meaning that a majority of the users are either students or other people connected to academic institutions or research environments, but there are also other types of users such as museums and some government agencies.

Our analysis of malicious behavior and the corresponding collection is focused on *anonymized flows* (i.e. summaries of packet streams between communication endpoints) and not full packet payload. The advantages include a more manageable amount of data that are less privacy-invasive than a full packet payload capture. The disadvantages include no ground truth and a limited ability to further refine or validate our results. Even though anonymized flow data may stymie some type of analysis, we show that such data can still be used to discover typical *malicious flow patterns* that we then investigate in detail. We consider our results here as a survey with possibilities of future extensions, both when it comes to the extent of the data analyzed and the methods used.

The rest of the paper is organized as follows. In Section 2 we describe the collection of traffic and explain the type of data available for analysis. In Section 3, we describe the general characteristics of this data. We then outline the problem of finding malicious behavior in Section 4 and formally describe the assumptions and requirements we need for the analysis of malicious flows. In Section 5, we analyze the behavior of malicious hosts. In Section 6, we describe related work. The paper is concluded in Section 7.

2   Description of the Data Collection

2.1   Measurement Setup

We collected backbone traffic on an OC-192 (10Gbps) link in the core-backbone of SUNET, the Swedish University Network. Its current version, *OptoSUNET*, is a star structure over leased fiber, with a central exchange point in Stockholm. OptoSUNET connects all SUNET customers redundantly to a core network in Stockholm, as depicted

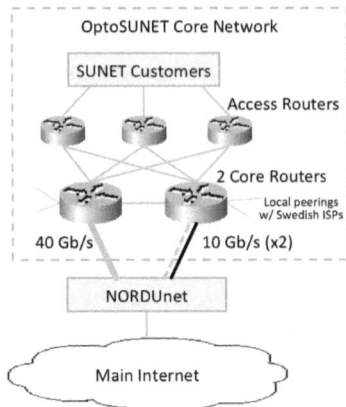

Fig. 1. OptoSUNET core topology. All SUNET customers are via access routers connected to two core routers. The SUNET core routers have local peering with Swedish ISPs, and are connected to the international commodity Internet via NORDUnet. SUNET is connected to NORDUnet via three links: a 40Gbps link and two 10Gbps links. Our measurement equipment collects data on the first of the two 10Gbps links (black) between SUNET and NORDUnet.

in Figure 1. Traffic routed to the international commodity Internet is carried on three links between SUNET and NORDUnet, where NORDUnet peers with Tier-1 backbone providers, large CDNs (Content Distribution Networks) and other academic networks. We used an existing 10Gbps measurement infrastructure [9] to collect traffic on one of the 10Gbps links between SUNET and NORDUnet, indicated in black color in Figure 1.

Our measurement hardware includes two measurement nodes on site and one additional processing platform at our university. At the core network in Stockholm, we apply optical splitters to tap the two OC-192 links, one for each direction. The splitters are attached to the measurement nodes on-site, which also preprocess the traces, including prefix-preserving IP address anonymization [10]. We always collected network data simultaneously for both directions. For the final analysis, we transferred anonymized network flows to the processing platform at Chalmers University.

2.2   Description of the Collected Data: Unidirectional Flows

We ran our data collection every week for 24 hours with *crl_flow* of the CoralReef Suite [11]. We define flows by the unidirectional sequence of packets sharing a 5-tuple of {sourceIP,destinationIP,sPort,dPort,proto}. Flows are then further discriminated by a 5-minute timeout interval, i.e., two packets sharing the same tuple belong to the same flow if their timestamps are within the given interval. A sample flow summary of crl_flow with anonymized IP addresses is shown in Table 1. Flow summaries include the identifying 5-tuple, where the *proto* represents transport protocol numbers as assigned by IANA, such as 6 for TCP, 17 for UDP and 1 for ICMP. Note that in the case of ICMP the port fields contain the type and code, respectively. Other meaningful fields are *pkts* and *bytes*, containing the number of packets and bytes seen within the flow interval; and *firstTS* and *latestTS*, representing POSIX timestamps of the first and last captured packet in a flow, respectively. Note that we do not normally see any TCP/IP header information apart from the ports and timestamps described above.

Table 1. Two lines describing the flow output from CoralReef (IP addresses anonymized)

sourceIP	destinationIP	proto	ok	sport	dport	pkts	bytes	flows	firstTS	latestTS
192.168.52.11	74.125.43.147	6	1	445	3995	3	120	1	t_0^1	t_n^1
192.168.10.69	74.125.43.101	1	1	3	1	1	56	1	t_0^2	t_n^2

2.3 Measurement Bias and Errors

According to SNMP statistics [12], the applied load-balancing mechanisms by SUNET assigned about 30% of all inbound but only 15% of the outbound traffic volume to the 10Gbps link measured, and the rest to the alternative links. This type of sampling bias is hard to quantify, since the routing policies are outside our control and differ for incoming and outgoing traffic. They may also change without our knowledge.

The routing of the outgoing traffic is decided by the organization the traffic is originating from, meaning that different rules govern different parts of the "inside" network. We have observed that we are blind to outgoing traffic from some IPs, for some hosts we only see a subset of their traffic and for yet others, we may detect all traffic.

The policy for incoming traffic is slightly more uniform, but still complex due to the setup of different peering points and agreements, introducing e.g. hot potato routing effects. In general, we see a subset of all traffic, depending on routing decisions based on a three-tuple of {sourceIP, sPort, destinationIP} for TCP/UDP flows. Traffic from some peering points are not visible at all at our measurement point.

There are also a few caveats of the experimental hardware setup. Even though we normally had no traffic loss within collection periods, there were two exceptions. Firstly, the measurement cards can sometimes loose synchronization with the OC-192 PoS framing, so we proactively restarted the collection in 3h periods, leading to missing packets in the second between such data collection periods. Secondly, there were four short, but immense traffic surges, where traffic was increasing from the normal rate of $<200k$ to $>400k$ packets per second. During these surges, our nodes could not keep up with the speed and dropped packets, which was logged by the measurement cards.

Finally, the measurements were done over an operational large network, meaning that parameters change over the course of the data collection. For example, on April 22, we saw a spike of traffic over the outgoing link we were monitoring, as one of the alternative routes was down for a short period of time. It is important to understand the limitations of the experiment setup for correct analysis of the data. We can reason about data we captured, but we need to be careful when interpreting missing data; a flow may be missing because it was never sent but it may also be missing because it was routed around our measuring point.

3   Overall Data Characteristics

In this section, we describe the overall data characteristics of the captured flows. Table 2 shows traffic statistics of the collection days used for this study.[1] The first observation is that we see many more incoming than outgoing flows, mainly due to the load-balancing mechanisms we explained in Section 2.3.

For the incoming traffic, the transport protocol breakdown in terms of flow numbers was about 42% TCP, 56% UDP, and 2% ICMP, while the outgoing link showed a slightly different protocol ratio with 28% TCP, 69% UDP, and 3% ICMP.[2] The number of flows changed over the data collection period but the traffic mix was relatively constant with two exceptions, April 8 and May 6. On these two days, we observed a larger number of flows due to major events involving a single host inside SUNET. This particular host was the target of a large number of connections from a widely scattered IP range via known IRC port numbers within short time periods. We see many incoming 1-pkt flows with 40 Bytes (probably RST packets), but also a substantial number of established connections involving exchange of small data portions. We suspect that this host was sending out *Botnet Command & Control* (C&C) traffic, where we see only the return traffic of the botnet zombies all over the world. Thus, we observe that malicious activity may even leave a footprint in large aggregates as the ones shown in Table 2.

Table 2. A summary over the collection days and the corresponding traffic characteristics. The values in parenthesis in the columns for *Flows* and *Bytes* show the percentage of the traffic for TCP, UDP and ICMP respectively. Data for all days are captured in 2010 with a duration of 24h.

	Incoming Link			Outgoing Link		
Date	# Pkts / 10^9	# Flows / 10^8	# Bytes / 10^{12}	# Pkts / 10^9	# Flows / 10^8	# Bytes / 10^{12}
April 01	8.38	2.33 (39/59/2)	5.74 (83/17/0)	3.95	1.20 (27/70/3)	3.21 (58/41/0)
April 08	11.4	3.11 (48/50/2)	8.42 (85/15/0)	5.44	1.54 (27/70/3)	3.93 (52/47/0)
April 15	10.4	2.79 (40/58/2)	7.80 (84/16/0)	3.89	0.96 (28/69/3)	2.98 (54/45/0)
April 22	11.7	2.91 (41/57/2)	9.41 (87/12/0)	3.95	1.09 (29/69/2)	3.31 (61/38/0)
April 29	10.4	2.73 (41/58/2)	7.76 (86/13/0)	3.38	0.95 (30/68/2)	2.77 (57/43/0)
May 06	9.46	3.14 (46/52/2)	6.75 (84/16/0)	4.23	1.16 (30/67/2)	3.62 (58/41/0)

Similarly, we can consider the protocol mix based on the number of bytes transferred. As can be seen, there was much more traffic sent over TCP than over UDP even though the number of flows of UDP exceeded the number of flows for TCP. Surprisingly, the UDP traffic accounted for as much as 43% of the outgoing traffic.

In Table 3, we show how many unique IP addresses we saw on the links on the first collection day. Note that the destination address space for the incoming link is represented by the source address space on the outgoing link, due the opposing directions of the unidirectional links. Even though part of the difference between the address spaces observed can be explained by routing differences, there is a factor of 41 between the observed IPs inside SUNET between the two directions. We know from previous

---

[1] Note that our data include a substantial portion of incoming flows on UDP port 53, due to a RIPE DNS server located inside SUNET, serving over 400 zones. Traffic from and to port 53 on this server cannot be considered native SUNET traffic and we filtered it out for this study.

[2] Other protocols in the order of 0.1% are excluded. The values are often rounded to the nearest percent, and the sum is sometimes not exactly 100% (as in Table 2).

Table 3. Unique hosts during the data collection 2010-04-01

	Inside SUNET	Outside SUNET
Incoming Link	Destination IPs 970,149	Source IPs 24,587,096
Outgoing Link	Source IPs 23,600	Destination IPs 18,780,894

measurements that scanning operations, even though often unanswered from hosts inside SUNET, inflate the number of incoming destinations [13], and for that reason we have not done any closer analysis of such behavior on the data presented here.

Table 4. The number of unique source IP addresses found in the traffic on the *outgoing* link

Date	April 1	April 8	April 15	April 22	April 29	May 6
Unique IP:s	23,600	26,398	12,223	76,143	12,218	12,603

In Table 4, we show the number of unique source IP addresses seen on the outgoing link. There are two artifacts we would like to highlight. First, on April 22 we see many more source hosts. During a short period this day, one of the alternative routing links was down and more traffic was routed over the link we measure. By roughly excluding the 20 minutes the link was down, we have 16,823 unique sources, an *estimate* more similar in size to the other collection days.The other artifact is that onward from April 15 we see only about half of the sources, maybe because of a new routing policy. We briefly investigated how many of the sources on the outgoing link were also present in the data collected on the incoming link. Given the asymmetry of Table 3, one would expect a majority of the source IPs on the outgoing link also be present as destinations on the incoming link. In the data of April 1, it is 97.24%, confirming our expectations.

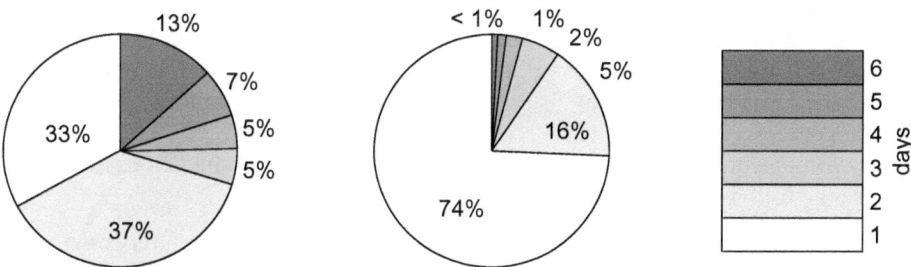

Fig. 2. The figure shows how many days a particular host is active. The pie chart to the left shows hosts inside SUNET (source IP addresses) while the pie chart to the right shows hosts outside SUNET (destination addresses). The figure is based on data collected on the *outgoing* link.

We also investigated how long we could detect traffic from a particular IP address. For example, an IP address may become unused with DHCP, a host may be removed from the network, or the routing policy is changed. In Figure 2, we have included two pie charts that show how many collection days a typical IP address was active. The chart on the left represents hosts inside SUNET while the one on the right represents hosts outside SUNET. Note we use the *estimate* for April 22, where the 20 minutes of exceptional traffic is excluded as described above.

Among hosts inside SUNET, we have found that a majority are only active on one or two data collection days even though 13% seem to be reoccurring every single data collection day. In our data, most hosts outside SUNET are also only visible a single day and there are very few hosts that reoccur over time.

4   Finding Malicious Hosts

We are interested in finding and analyzing typical *malicious flow patterns*. However, we face several problems when determining whether a host is malicious. First, its status can mostly only be determined in relation to a local security policy of allowed behavior. Transmission of data from a system, e.g., might be very permissible at some sites (research centers sharing results) but very suspicious at other sites (government agency analyzing pre-election numbers) where it could indicate exfiltration attacks. As we have a bird's view over the network, we cannot make subjective judgment calls. However, certain behavior, such as spreading malware, is quite universally seen as malicious.

Second, as we only see flow information, it is difficult to verify our suspicions of a host's malicious status. Through statistical analysis of the anonymized flow data we can determine whether a host is behaving strangely compared to the mean, but we cannot directly verify its status. For example, Google's servers are an example of beneficial hosts that would stand out in such an analysis unless accounted for.

However, others have the ability to more closely analyze payload, through, for example, the analysis of malware collected in a honeypot. Several organizations make a list of known malicious hosts available to the community. For our purposes, we use the lists published from DShield and SRI Malware Threat Center to create a large set of possible malicious hosts. They provide non-obfuscated IP addresses, which we anonymized [10] similarly to the IP addresses in our flow data (cf. Section 2). More specifically, we use DShield's recommended block list [14], with 20 subnets and the *Most Aggressive Malware Attack Source and Filters* [15] and *Most Prolific BotNet Command and Control Servers and Filters* [16], 30 day lists, from SRI. The latter two contain about 400-500 hosts together.

We leverage these host classifications to create a set of known malicious hosts, $\mathcal{M}^F$. We use the following definition for malicious hosts and flows.

Definition of a malicious host. A host, x, visible in our traffic capture, is defined as being *malicious*, if $x \in \mathcal{M}^F$. All such hosts are added to the *malicious set, $\mathcal{M}$*.

Definition of a malicious flow. A flow, f, with endpoints f_s and f_d is defined as being *malicious*, if either $f_s \in \mathcal{M}$ or $f_d \in \mathcal{M}$.

We usually downloaded the external malicious host lists in conjunction to the general data collection, and then aggregated them ($\mathcal{M}^F$). Note that we never reclassified these hosts; if they have been deemed to be malicious at one point during the data collection period, they were malicious the whole period. We chose this policy for its simplicity, and given the relatively short time span of the collection period, we do not find this to be a problem. The original data may also lag slightly in time (a host is only discovered as malicious after a series of activities), and by treating it as malicious the whole time we do not miss any of its initial behavior.

The set $\mathcal{M}^F$ contains 25,900 potential hosts, where we on average saw activity from about 5.0% of these hosts in the outgoing traffic and 4.6% of these hosts in the incoming traffic. The sets have about 30% overlap, i.e. of the malicious hosts seen on the outgoing link only 30% of the same sources were also present on the incoming link the same collection date. We would like to emphasize that no hosts inside SUNET belonged to $\mathcal{M}$. The hosts in this set were thus all outside SUNET.

The resulting list of malicious hosts allows us to find *malicious flow patterns* that in turn can be used for a larger analysis on a wider set of hosts. Also, concentrating on the hosts in the malicious group facilitates the analysis as it is easier to find patterns in this smaller subset. Certain attack patterns, such as denial-of-service attacks, cause by their very nature a very large footprint on the flow data and can easily be found (see for example [17]). However, we are also interested in behavior that is not so large scale, and that is part of the reason why we bootstrap our analysis with the *malicious set $\mathcal{M}$*.

Finally, our set of malicious hosts is quite restrictive, e.g. a host needs to display quite aberrant traffic to be on the block list from DShield. There are probably many other hosts that are malicious but are not in our malicious set, as e.g. the IRC C&C server described in Section 3. Thus, we expect that certain patterns found for the malicious hosts will also be applicable to some, what might seem to be, *normal hosts*.

5   Analysis of Malicious Host Behavior

We use the set of *Malicious Hosts*, $\mathcal{M}$, defined in Section 4, to discriminate normal flows from malicious ones. We divide the analysis into two parts. First, we look at overall characteristics of the malicious flows and discuss large malicious footprints. We then describe two particular patterns found by analyzing the traffic flows to malicious hosts on the *outgoing* link.

5.1   Characteristics of Malicious Flows

In Table 5, we show the average fraction of malicious flows, i.e. the number of malicious flows divided by all flows averaged over the data collection period. We note that for incoming traffic, we seem to have more malicious flows over TCP while for outgoing traffic, ICMP flows are dominating. We can explain this fact by previous observations on data from an older generation of SUNET[3] showing that the majority of anomalies (including unsolicited network scanning) originates outside SUNET, i.e. on the main Internet [13]. Table 5 once more confirms these earlier observations with higher numbers of incoming TCP flows, many of them probably SYN probing attempts.

Since possible responses to such unsolicited probes are important to understand for the following analysis, we briefly outline them here. Basically, we can differentiate between four scenarios following incoming SYN probings or connection attempts: *i)*

---

[3] GigaSUNET, a ring architecture, was in 2007 replaced by OptoSUNET, a star architecture.

Table 5. Average fraction of malicious flows per protocol

	Incoming Link	Outgoing Link
TCP	0.35%	0.05%
ICMP	0.02%	0.16%
UDP	0.04%	0.01%

replied by SYN/ACK packets,[4] i.e. connection establishment (which should be rather rare for unsolicited scanning events); *ii)* unreplied, e.g. by firewalls; *iii)* replied with a RST response from host sockets;[5] and finally *iv)* replied with *type 3 (net/host/port unreachable)* ICMP messages from network or end nodes.

Discussion: The larger number of outbound malicious ICMP flows is likely to be an artifact of the unbalance caused by incoming unsolicited TCP probes. In fact, 75% of the outgoing malicious ICMP flows are of *type 3 – destination unreachable*, which is an overrepresentation compared to around 50% *type 3* messages when analyzing all flows.

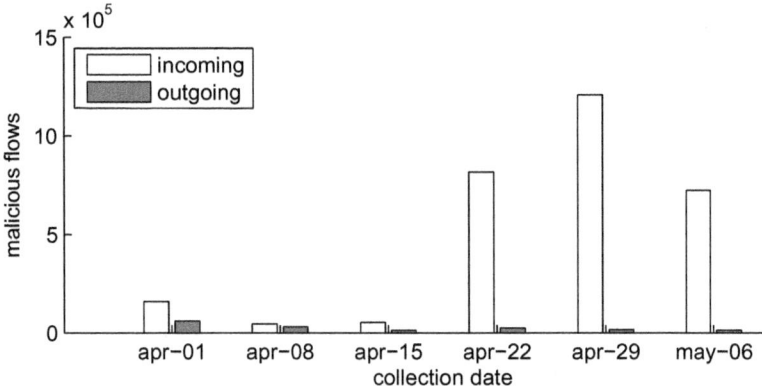

Fig. 3. The figure shows the number of malicious flows detected each data collection day

Incoming Malicious Traffic: The High-Hitters

In Figure 3, we show the number of *malicious flows* for each data collection day. In general, we observe more incoming than outgoing malicious traffic. We can also see an inflation of incoming malicious flows by a factor of 15–25 on the last three days. This increase stems from a very small number of IPs responsible for the majority of malicious flows. In the following, we define *high-hitters* as source IPs outside SUNET responsible for more than $4k$ malicious incoming flows during one day. Disregarding the high-hitters further discussed below, we found a quite stable amount of incoming malicious traffic during all days, consisting of between $25k$–$35k$ flows stemming from between 1,108 and 1,349 malicious hosts per day.

---

[4] SYN/ACK packets are typically larger than 40 Bytes, i.e. 20B IP header, 20B TCP header, up to 20B TCP options header, no payload.

[5] RST packets are normally exactly 40B, i.e. 20B IP header, 20B TCP header, no payload.

On April 1, we observe one high-hitter, responsible for 83% of the incoming malicious flows on this day. This host sent UDP packets to $132k$ different hosts inside SUNET on port 1434 with 404-Byte-sized packets during a period of 21 hours. The port number and packet size suggests that this host tried to spread the *Sapphire worm* [18].

In the data from April 8 and 15, we observe one high-hitter that was at both dates responsible for about 33% of incoming malicious flows, a rather moderate traffic density compared to high-hitters found other days. Flows from this host (to 40 hosts inside SUNET) were probably DNS responses, since they came from UDP port 53 with packet sizes of typical DNS answers (around 120 Bytes) and there were corresponding DNS queries (around 70 Bytes) from a few SUNET hosts found on the *outgoing link*. We suspect that this host might have been involved in some sort of *DNS poisoning attack* [19].

On April 22, we observe as many as five high-hitters, responsible for 97% of incoming malicious traffic. Three of these high-hitters (generating 44%, 10% and 10% of the flows, respectively) attempted to connect and login at large IP address ranges of up to $300k$ hosts via either SSH (TCP port 22) or VNC (TCP port 5900) during a couple of hours. The remaining two high-hitters (22% and 11%) also talked to large IP ranges (around $60k$ hosts) without fixed destination port numbers, but rather with fixed TCP source ports of 31414 and 1723, respectively. This would indicate that we actually observe return-traffic from SUNET to these hosts on these port numbers, but we have to further investigate this behavior for its significance.

On April 29, there were three high-hitters, together responsible for 97% of the incoming malicious flows. The main host (59%) was active during the entire 24 hour period and connected to $107k$ hosts on five different proxy port numbers (e.g. TCP 8080, 3128, 1080, 9415) from port 6000, which is a scanning behavior also observed elsewhere [20]. The other two high-hitters (23% and 15%) showed similar behavior to the two unexplained high-hitters on April 22, with random destination port numbers but fixed source ports of 14700 and again 31414.

On May 6, there was only one high-hitter, responsible for 96% of all incoming malicious flows. This host was scanning on TCP port 1433 (MSSQL), which is known for many vulnerabilities. Interestingly, this scanner also used a single source port number of 6000, and is from the same \24 network as the main high-hitter on April 29.

Discussion: The data basically include a quite constant level of *background radiation*, as also observed elsewhere [21,22]. However, at the same time we observe *transient high-hitters* with varying traffic density. These outstanding, special events complicate determination of *regular traffic patterns* and highlight the importance of longitudinal measurements spanning time, allowing us to differentiate between the transient high-hitter traffic from the constant background radiation in our analysis.

5.2   The Ubiquitous Malicious Hosts

We also decided to investigate how long the malicious hosts were active and the behavior of the most active hosts. We used $\mathcal{M}_{out}$, i.e. the set of all visible malicious host found in the outgoing traffic. We then counted how many collection days these malicious hosts could be found (see Figure 4). As can be seen, a majority of the hosts were only visible a single day during the collection period. A little more than 20% were visible for two days, and only about 3% were visible all collection days. This should be compared with the pie chart to the right in Figure 2.

Discussion: The behavior of the malicious hosts was different from the behavior of all hosts (cf. Figure 2). For example, there were more malicious hosts active all six data collection days, as compared to all hosts. However, we believe this may be an artifact of using a predefined malicious set, i.e., for a host to be blacklisted it must exhibit malicious behavior over a period of time.

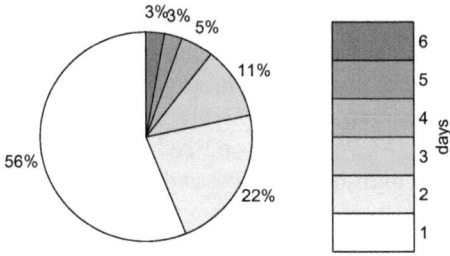

Fig. 4. The number of days the malicious hosts were active in the *outgoing* traffic

Below we further investigate the traffic flows for the malicious hosts that were present all six data collection days. Even though they only made up 3% of all the malicious hosts we detected, they still stand for 26% of the malicious traffic we found on the outgoing link. We concentrate on the two most prolific hosts and their traffic pattern over TCP, below referred to as *host-A* and *host-B*. As these flows are outgoing, the flows originated at an internal host (marked as source in the packet). Either the traffic is in *response* to earlier connection attempts by the malicious host or it is *unsolicited traffic* sent directly to the malicious host. We believe the pattern for *host-A* described below is of the former type, while the patterns seen concerning *host-B* is of the latter type.

Massive Connection Attempts: The Scanner

Host-A was the most active ubiquitous host in terms of number of flows over TCP, being part of 3,593 flows over the whole collection period with 2,904 distinct hosts inside SUNET. Many of these hosts inside SUNET were clustered into portions of \24 subnets, and there were usually only 1–2 flows between two distinct end points. Most of the flows (94%) were directed towards destination port 6000 on *host-A*.

For example, from the subnet with the most TCP flows toward *host-A*, we found flows from 123 distinct hosts. Looking in detail at the flows, there was exactly a single packet from each host to *host-A* of the form:

```
srcSubNet.host:2967 host-A:6000 packets:1 Bytes:40
```

Clearly, this is a RST packet in response to a scan. This particular scanning technique, using port 6000, has also been seen elsewhere [20] even though the tool behind it is not completely understood. We also saw this kind of behavior among the high-hitters on the *incoming* link (see Section 5.1).

It is particularly interesting that *host-A* probed different services over the collection period. A majority of the captured flows came from April 1 (69%), where *host-A* probed port 2967 (from 6000). Similarly, on April 8, port 2967 was probed. On April 15, we see the first sign of a new target; 51% of the captured flows were the result of a scan to port 2967 but 39% also targeted port 135, 6% port 1617, and, finally, 4% port 3230. On April 22 the shift was larger still; 21% targeted port 2967 while 79% targeted port 135. On April 29, we can only see a single connection: one RST flow from source 2967 to destination port 6000. On May 5, the malicious host was again more active. At this particular day, only a single connection went from 2967 to destination port 6000, while 99% instead involved port 135. Thus, the potentially vulnerable target port shifted over the collection period, where first port 2967 and in the end only port 135 was probed.

Table 6. Pattern for a possible secondary return and infection

src	dst	sport	dport	pkts	bytes	date	time
src_1	host-A	2967	6000	1	60	2010-04-22	04:09:16
src_1	host-A	2967	1143	927	48,212	2010-04-22	04:09:21

The second interesting observation of *host-A*'s behavior is the following; the malicious host immediately tried to connect (and infect?) hosts that seemed to have the appropriate service running. As we said above, most of the traffic was actually a single packet with size 40, i.e. a RST packet. What is interesting is when the SUNET host replied with other packet sizes. In Table 6, we list one such example taken from the data captured on April 22. The first flow summarizes the probing attempt by *host-A* but the response we see is *not* the typical RST packet, i.e. the connection seemed to be accepted.[6] Within 5s, *host-A* returned and opened a connection to the SUNET host and then data were actually exchanged, possibly being malicious code. We see similar behavior on all days; if the first attempt did not elicit a RST packet, there was a follow-up flow in almost all cases. For example, on April 1, there was a new flow, on average within 12s, in 25 of the 27 cases where the SUNET host replied with a packet of size 44.[7] This tells us something about the scanning software. In the first pass, it tries to connect from a standard port and it probably blasts out packets. If the service is not refused, it returns within 10–12s and reconnects through other ports.

Discussion: Summarizing the behavior of *host-A*, we first see that the scanner remains constant over the data collection period despite it being blacklisted. Apparently, the owner did not feel it is worth changing the IP address (because few home users use blacklists?). Second, *host-A* was actively monitored and supervised as we can see from its shifting probing profile over the collection period. Third, the return after a successful probe happened within seconds, either for further data collection or an infection attempt. As future work, it would be interesting to monitor these possibly infected SUNET hosts for their post-infection behavior.

---

[6] Note that SYN/ACK responses are, due to TCP option headers, typically larger than 40 Bytes.
[7] The missing two cases may be an effect of the routing bias explained in Section 2.3.

Temporal Patterns: Connecting to the Malicious Server

Host-B was the second most active malicious host that was also present on all connection days. We found 972 flows involving this host coming from 27 distinct sources in the outgoing data. These flows do not seem to be part of a scan; for many of these outgoing flows, a few packets were sent from a non-privileged port from the host inside SUNET to a few very specific ports on the malicious host. We did not at all see similar scanning behavior as with *host-A*. Interestingly enough though, these flows to *host-B* sometimes seemed to follow *temporal patterns*.

We analyzed the traffic patterns based on their time properties from four of the hosts inside SUNET communicating with *host-B*, shown in Figure 5. Each subgraph (with one exception) shows all flows between a single host inside SUNET to a specific destination port on *host-B*. The connection index n in the graph represents flow n (ordered chronologically), which is then plotted at $(t_n - t_{n-1}, n)$. That is, the x axes represent the time differences between two consecutive flows, while the y axes simply index the flows ordered by time. Let us look at each of the subplots separately. We order them from top to bottom, left to right, according to the number in parenthesis in the figure text along the x axes.

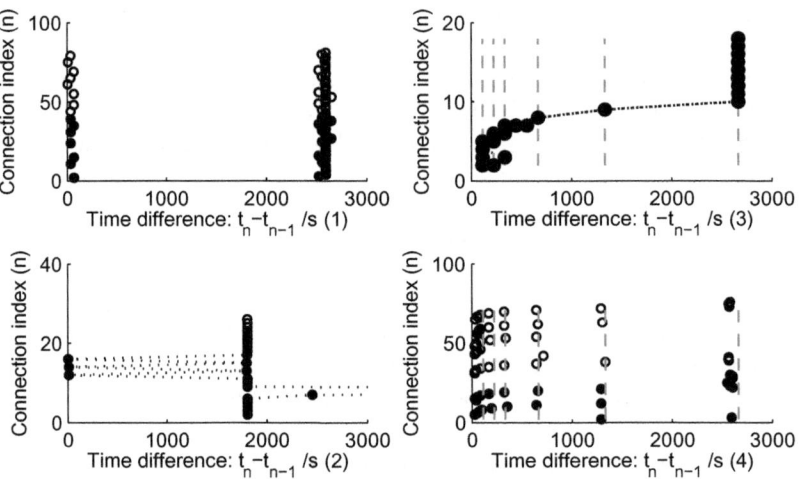

Fig. 5. The figure shows temporal communication patterns to the malicious *host-B*

In Subplot 1 in Figure 5, we show one of the time patterns we found. Here, the source host connected to *host-B*, port 6969, about once every 43min. Now and then, such a connection was immediately followed by another flow (i.e. through a new source port on the host inside SUNET), probably a reconnect after a failed first attempt. This particular pattern existed over two collection dates, where the flows from the second day is marked with unfilled markers.

Similarly, in Subplot 2, we found a consistent pattern but with a period of 30min instead of 43min as in Subplot 1. In this graph, we have also added dotted lines between two consecutive connections to make the connection pattern more visible. The SUNET host connected to *host-B*, port 8000, about every 30min with a few exceptions. Three times, the "ordinary" connection was immediately followed by a new connection. Two times[8] the reconnections took more than 30min to establish. Again, the pattern lasted over two collection dates spaced a week apart, and the flows from the second day are marked with unfilled markers.

Discussion: The patterns seen for the hosts in Subplot 1 and 2 imply relatively simple programming, i.e. a regular refresh or a keep-alive signal. The hosts inside SUNET may contain malware, meaning that these patterns would indicate an attempt to "call home" by the malware to the blacklisted *host-B*. However, sometimes other services are also running on the malicious hosts and the seen pattern could be the result of a more regular service. Especially interesting is the pattern length; interpolating, it would seem that the keep-alive signal was present over a week.

In Subplot 3 we can see a complex back-off pattern with $t_1 = 111s$, $t_2 = 222s$, $t_3 = 333s$, $t_4 = 666s$, $t_5 = 1,332s$, $t_6 = 2,664s$, i.e. $t_n = \sum_{i=1}^{n-1} t_i$ for $n > 2$. The vertical dotted lines are added at these *anchor times* for ease of reading the figure. The source tried to connect to *host-B* with a total of about 16–17 distinct flows, with about 3–4 connections spaced 111s apart. The following connection then came after $222s$ followed by one at $333s$, $666s$, $1,332s$, and finally about nine flows spaced $2,664s$ apart. What makes this particular pattern stand out, apart from its complexity, is that the source connected to *host-B* on several distinct ports (6969, 8000, 8080), always following the exact same pattern, seldom being off even a full second from the *anchor times* described above. Moreover, this very same host also tried to connect to *six* other hosts, using the exact same connection pattern but with different destination ports (80, 2710, 6997, 6969, 9999, 60500). Thus, in total the host exhibited the very same pattern in *twelve* distinct cases and they have all been superimposed in Subplot 3. Even though Subplot 3 in reality contains 12 graphs, we can see that the pattern in each of these graphs is so similar to the others that each individual point is plotted on top of another and it is easy to distinguish the overall structure. There are a few errant points in the beginning but towards the end the sequence is stabilized. Most of the flows that make up this pattern, contained three packets with a total of 152 Bytes. These 12 patterns appeared within four minutes of each other, which might indicate a common event triggering their initialization. They may also have contained more points than shown in the graph, but any subsequent point is beyond our 24h data collection period.

Finally, in Subplot 4 we show a similar pattern to that found in Subplot 3. We could only find the single host in Subplot 3 with a back-off pattern within a second of the *anchor times*. However, we found a few other instances where the pattern is somewhat similar. One such example is shown in Subplot 4, where we again show flows from a subsequent collection day with unfilled markers. In contrast to Subplot 3 (where 12 similar patterns are superimposed), Subplot 4 contains a single pattern, i.e. one host that used different source ports to connect to the same destination port (8080) on *host-B*. In contrast to the patterns in Subplot 3, we can see that this host was repeating the pattern over and over again, lasting over a week, i.e. two data collection dates.

---

[8] In Subplot 2 we have one outlier at about 38,293s that is not shown (the dotted lines hint to its existence). In Subplot 4, we have five outliers not visible in the graph.

Discussion: The time properties for these two hosts represent a more complex program-ming logic, implying that the programmer chose this particular algorithm for a reason. As discussed above, these patterns could indicate an attempt to "call home" by the mal-ware but it could also be part of a more regular service.[9] The patterns were probably triggered by some event, as all 12 occur within four minutes of each other. Given the exact nature of the pattern displayed by the host in Subplot 3, we have described it at several mailing lists but without conclusive responses as most people suggested a full packet capture for further analysis – which is not possible for us due to privacy con-cerns. We have also been unable to find other hosts within our data that follow such an exact pattern as displayed by this host. This means that regardless of the pattern being the result of a regular program or malware, it is not widespread.

6   Related Work

As already outlined, malicious traffic can be studied by several orthogonal methods, such as *distributed sensors*, *honeypot networks*, *network telescopes/darknets*, and *large-scale passive measurements*. The relation of the first two methods to our work has al-ready been discussed in Section 1. They introduce a serious bias, as the users obviously care about security, and they are not very suitable for analysis of *real* user responses.

Given that *network telescopes* monitor large, unused IP address spaces, they see traffic that by its very nature should not exist [23]. Even though network telescopes have been used for extensive studies of worm outbreaks [24] and for general characterization of background radiation [25,26], they are only traffic sinks and do not respond genuinely to incoming traffic.

Our approach, passive measurements on large-scale links, is generally viewed as the best way to study Internet traffic, as it includes real behavioral responses from a diverse user population. Others made use of observations of connection properties to study general characteristics of scanning traffic both on campus links [21] and backbone links [27]. Also one of the authors of this paper previously quantified unsolicited traffic by simple heuristic methods utilizing connection patterns [17,22]. Malicious traffic (i.e. scanning and DDoS attacks) was observed to be the main reason for short, unidirec-tional one-way flows on both campus and backbone links [28]. Rehák et al. [29] uses NetFlow data to fine-tune an Intrusion Detection System (IDS) by periodical insertion of challenges (or fault injections).

In contrast, in this paper we have observed and analyzed traffic patterns of malicious hosts, describing their changing behavior over the data collection period. Behavioral analysis of malware is also possible by reverse engineering [30], and we consider such approaches complementary to ours; reverse engineering requires a significant effort but may yield an exact analysis of the malware in question but with our measurements a wide range of behavioral patterns can directly be observed. Furthermore, reverse engineering can never directly answer certain questions, such as how widespread a certain malware is, but this is a property we can measure.

---

[9] For example, one of the destination ports found (6969) may be associated with bittorrent.

7 Discussions and Conclusions

We have shown that we can use anonymized flow data to discover and analyze malicious flow patterns, a result useful for network researchers and practitioners interested in security related topics such as intrusion detection. Some attacks leave such a big footprint that they are visible even in summaries of large traffic aggregates, as the C&C server described in Section 3. To detect more obscure patterns, though, we bootstrapped our analysis with a predefined set of malicious hosts, and analyzed their behavior from a large-scale perspective based on Internet backbone data. Each finding is *discussed* in detail within the paper. For example, we showed the need for longer-time measurements to be able to separate the *transient high-hitters* from the background traffic. Despite being blacklisted, we found some malicious hosts that stayed active over the whole measurement period. One of these hosts seems to automatically scan and possibly infect vulnerable hosts within seconds, but is most likely under active human supervision as its scanning profile shifted over time. In contrast to many previous measurement methods, we went beyond the analysis of simpler attribute aggregates (such as top source port, etc.) to also include a *temporal analysis of communication patterns*, originating from hosts within SUNET to a malicious host. We found both simple refresh logic and complex back-off patterns, sometimes lasting over a week. The latter patterns are not easy to discover because they do not leave large footprints in traditional traffic summaries.

Summarizing, there are disadvantages with using anonymized flow data in that it is rather difficult to both interpret the data and to validate the result. However, such data would otherwise not be available for analysis and they can still offer many valuable insights, not possible with complementary methods. The findings in this paper are just the first look at the data, which we are still expanding by regular weekly measurements (ongoing since April 2010). By improving the selection of the malicious hosts, both by using collected information from locally installed honeypots with access to full payload and a more automatic classification of hosts and malicious traffic [31], we expect more detailed and conclusive results in the future.

References

1. Corrons, L.: Computer Threat Trend Forecast for 2010,
   http://pandalabs.pandasecurity.com/
   computer-threat-trend-forecast-for-2010/ (December 2009)
2. Mueller III, R.S.: Major Executive Speeches, RSA Cyber Security Conference (2010),
   http://www.fbi.gov/pressrel/speeches/mueller030410.htm
3. Symantec, AntiVirus, Anti-Spyware, Enpoint Security (2010),
   http://www.symantec.com
4. McAfee, Antivirus, IPS, Firewall, Web Security (2010), http://www.mcafee.com
5. The Honeynet Project, Honeynet Project Blog (2010), http://www.honeynet.org
6. NoAH, European Network of Affined Honeypots (2010), http://www.fp6-noah.org
7. DShield, Cooperative Network Security Community - Internet Security (2010),
   http://www.dshield.com
8. SANS, Internet Storm Center (2010), http://isc.sans.edu
9. John, W.: Characterization and Classification of Internet Backbone Traffic. Chalmers University of Technology, Doctoral Thesis (2010) ISBN 978-91-7385-363-7

10. Fan, J., Xu, J., Ammar, M., Moon, S.: Prefix-Preserving IP Address Anonymization: Measurement-Based Security Evaluation and a New Cryptography-Based Scheme. Computer Networks 46(2) (2004)
11. Moore, D., Keys, K., Koga, R., Lagache, E., Claffy, K.: The CoralReef Software Suite as a Tool for System and Network Administrators. In: USENIX LISA (2001)
12. OptoSUNET, Core Map,
    `http://stats.sunet.se/stat-q/load-map/`
    `optosunet-core,,traffic,peak`
13. John, W., Tafvelin, S.: Differences between in- and outbound Internet Backbone Traffic. In: TERENA Networking Conference, TNC (2007)
14. DShield, Recommended block list (2010), `http://www.dshield.org/block.txt`
15. SRI International Malware Threat Center, Most aggressive malware attack source and filters (2010), `http://mtc.sri.com/live_data/attackers/`
16. SRI International Malware Threat Center, Most prolific botnet command and control servers and filters (2010), `http://mtc.sri.com/live_data/cc_servers/`
17. John, W., Tafvelin, S.: Heuristics to Classify Internet Backbone Traffic based on Connection Patterns. In: Int. Conference on Information Networking, ICOIN (2008)
18. Moore, D., Paxson, V., Savage, S., Shannon, C., Staniford, S., Weaver, N.: The Spread of the Sapphire/Slammer Worm. CAIDA, Tech.Rep. (2003)
19. Friedl, S.: An Illustrated Guide to the Kaminsky DNS Vulnerability (2008),
    `http://www.unixwiz.net/techtips/iguide-kaminsky-dns-vuln.html`
20. White, G.N.: What's up with all the port scanning using TCP/6000 as a source port? (2010),
    `http://isc.sans.edu/diary.html?storyid=7924`
21. Allman, M., Paxson, V., Terrell, J.: A Brief History of Scanning. In: Internet Measurement Conference, IMC (2007)
22. John, W., Tafvelin, S., Olovsson, T.: Trends and Differences in Connection-Behavior within Classes of Internet Backbone Traffic. In: Claypool, M., Uhlig, S. (eds.) PAM 2008. LNCS, vol. 4979, pp. 192–201. Springer, Heidelberg (2008)
23. Moore, D., Shannon, C., Voelker, G., Savage, S.: Network Telescopes. CAIDA, Tech.Rep. (2004)
24. CAIDA, Research:Security (2010),
    `http://www.caida.org/research/security/#PreviousMalware`
25. Pang, R., Yegneswaran, V., Barford, P., Paxson, V., Peterson, L.: Characteristics of Internet Background Radiation. In: Internet Measurement Conference, IMC (2004)
26. Bailey, M., Cooke, E., Jahanian, F., Nazario, J., Watson, D., et al.: The Internet Motion Sensor: A Distributed Blackhole Monitoring System. In: SNDSS (2005)
27. Sridharan, A., Ye, T., Bhattacharyya, S.: Connectionless Port Scan Detection on the Backbone. In: IPCCC (2006)
28. Lee, D., Brownlee, N.: Passive Measurement of One-way and Two-way Flow Lifetimes. ACM SIGCOMM Comp. Comm. Rev. 37(3) (2007)
29. Rehák, M., Staab, E., Fusenig, V., Pĕchouček, M., Grill, M., Stiborek, J., Bartoš, K., Engel, T.: Runtime Monitoring and Dynamic Reconfiguration for Intrusion Detection Systems. In: Balzarotti, D. (ed.) RAID 2009. LNCS, vol. 5758, pp. 61–80. Springer, Heidelberg (2009)
30. Porras, P., Saidi, H., Yegneswaran, V.: An Analysis of Conficker's Logic and Rendezvous Points. Computer Science Laboratory, SRI International, Tech.Rep. (2009)
31. Almgren, M., Jonsson, E.: Using Active Learning in Intrusion Detection. In: 17th IEEE Computer Security Foundations Workshop, CSFW 2004 (2004)

Service Users' Requirements for Tools to Support Effective On-line Privacy and Consent Practices

Elahe Kani-Zabihi and Lizzie Coles-Kemp

Information Security Group, Royal Holloway University of London,
Egham, Surrey, TW20 0EX, UK
{Elahe.Kani,Lizzie.Coles-Kemp}@rhul.ac.uk

Abstract. The work presented in this paper explores how privacy dialogues within an on-line service might be constructed by conducting field experiments those identify privacy practices used when engaging with on-line services and elicit service user requirements for privacy dialogues. The findings are considered against the established design principles for general CRM dialogue design such as: frequency, initiation, signalling, service provider disclosure and richness [1] as well as privacy specific design principles including: transparency, service user disclosure and the agreement of privacy norms and rules [12].

Keywords: Service User, Service Provider, Privacy, Privacy Policy, User agreements, Consent, Privacy and Consent Technology.

1   Introduction

The work presented in this paper is part of a project entitled Visualisation and Other Methods of Expression (VOME) whose main objective is to develop methods of expressing privacy that enable a wider range of privacy concerns to be articulated and offer a broader variety of privacy protection responses. The original premise on which the project is based stated as: "Many users cannot and do not engage sufficiently with issues of privacy and consent in their interactions with ICT. Consequently they are not able to adequately assess the risks they run and organisations cannot develop services which adequately address users' privacy and consent needs". In the first year of the project, three academic teams worked together to produce a baseline of privacy concerns and practices when using on-line services. As part of this work an on-line survey was carried out [7] which incorporated Buchanan et al.'s scale for measuring privacy practices [8]. Buchanan et al. developed and validated Internet-administered scales measuring privacy-related attitudes and behaviours. In the case of privacy-related practices, they identified two distinct groups of actions people may take to protect their on-line privacy. The first group can be categorised as General Caution and contains common sense steps that people take. The second group, known as Technical Protection of privacy, requires a specific level of technical competency and involves sophisticated use of hardware

T. Aura, K. Järvinen, and K. Nyberg (Eds.): NordSec 2010, LNCS 7127, pp. 121–135, 2012.

and software as tools for safeguarding privacy. While everyone can engage to some extent in General Caution to protect their on-line privacy, a higher level of technical knowledge is necessary for Technical Protection.

In-line with Solove's perspective [16] of privacy as a facet of relationships, one of the conclusions of the baseline work was that privacy is enmeshed in the relationships that are being developed and maintained on-line. The baseline work also concluded that privacy is a collection of issues rather than a single issue or problem and the type of relationship in which privacy is situated, influences the foregrounding and back grounding of privacy issues. Research participants demonstrated that they select privacy protection practices in line with the privacy issues that are fore grounded.

The focus of the work presented in this paper is a closer exploration of the type of privacy practices invoked by on-line service users and the contexts in which these privacy practices are invoked. In the discussion section we evaluate how privacy and consent dialogue services might be designed in order to enable a more effective selection of privacy practices.

1.1   The Privacy Dialogue

At present, on-line service users are often obliged to reveal their personal information to have access to on-line services. Service users have no control of how their personal information is preserved and used. Privacy is regarded by on-line service providers as both an aspect of governance [11, 12] and an aspect of customer relationship management [9, 2].   One of the purposes of customer relationship management (CRM) is to build trust between the service user and service provider and one of the trust building mechanisms is the use of dialogue between service users and service providers [10].

Best practice [9, 11, 12] encourages on-line service providers to use privacy policies and statements. Privacy trust marks are used to communicate service provider commitment to privacy. There is also strong encouragement to make privacy enhancing technologies (PETs) available to provide service users with the means to respond to any remaining privacy concerns. However, it is noticeable that there is scant provision for dialogue on privacy issues within the on-line service. Our previous research shows that service users often reach out for dialogue opportunities with the service provider when deciding on the appropriate privacy practices when using on-line services [2].

We have learnt that having better understanding of user behaviours and needs would enable system designers to appreciate what end users feel about using their systems and what changes would be needed to meet their needs [17]. The work presented in this paper explores how privacy dialogues within an on-line service might be constructed by conducting field experiments that identify privacy practices used when engaging with on-line services and elicit service user requirements for privacy dialogues.

2   Positioning of Our Work

When positioning our work, we use the following types of literature as a basis for our study: privacy protection practice literature and dialogue system literature

2.1   Privacy Protection Practice Literature

There is a substantial body of research [3] which considers privacy protection in terms of accessing online services. Although we agree that users should be protected from revealing unnecessary personal information, we argue that users must first be informed of privacy risks and should be guided during online registration process.

Therefore, we undertook a user study to identify requirements for developing such an information system. Our work is in-line with McDonald & Cranor [5] and McDonald & Cranor [6]. McDonald & Cranor [5] conducted an online study of 212 participants to measure time taken to read online privacy policies. Participants were presented with one of six different policies of varying lengths. They discovered it takes 244 hours per year for each person to read privacy policies, which is an average of 40 minutes a day. Hence, they estimated if all American Internet users were to annually read the online privacy policies, they will spend about 54 billion hours reading privacy policies. Moreover, McDonald & Cranor [6] performed a series of in-depth interviews with 14 participants on one subject of Internet advertising. In this study participants raised their privacy concerns without any prompting about privacy. It was discovered that many of the participants had poor understanding of third party cookies and believed that their actions online are anonymous unless they are logged into a website. We enhance these works by asking users what are their concerns with regards to online privacy statements and how they wish to be informed of them.

Tsai et al. [14] reported that providing accessible "privacy risk information" reduces the information asymmetry gap between service users and service providers. Such accessible information results in a consistent use of online services where service users feel service providers protect their privacy. Therefore, in terms of providing more information about online privacy, in our study we will question service users of their expectations from service providers.

2.2   Dialogue System Literature

When considering the design of dialogue in a system, much can be drawn from the socio-technical perspective. In order to resolve issues of mistrust, unfairness and unjustness, socio-technical design looks to optimise community performance in the system design. Community performance can be defined as the ability of a community to reach its goals. Privacy could be considered as one of the community performance characteristics. The belief of socio-technical designers is that by achieving an acceptable balance of these community characteristics trust is augmented between the different members of the community. In an on-line system, community performance is negotiated using a variety of on and off-line techniques, all of which use dialogue and communication. In today's on-line systems, there is little provision for tools which support on-line dialogues and therefore, the more complex the relationship, the more likely the negotiation is to take place off-line. This results in increased costs of on-line service delivery [4].

When designing on-line tools to support privacy dialogues, it is important to consider the established design principles dialogue in the CRM literature. These principles include: frequency (the timing of dialogue communication, frequency of messages), initiation (the manner of initiation and the method of initiation), signaling (the type and method of signaling), service provider disclosure (the types of disclosures that service providers need to make in order to establish credibility and trustworthiness) and richness (the layers of communication necessary for customer confidence where communication layers may be both on and off-line) [1]. When considering the nature of richness, Whitworth [13] makes the point that, in addition to layers of communication, richness also specifies how much meaning is communicated at each layer, confidentiality controls, extendibility bounded by security. Daft, R.L. et al [15] define richness as the "capacity of the media to facilitate shared meaning." In addition to these general dialogue requirements, consideration also has to be given to the requirements specified in privacy guidance literature. These include: transparency, service user disclosure and the agreement of privacy norms and rules [12].

3   Research Method

We undertook a fieldwork to understand service users' expectations and preferences of privacy dialogues when interacting with on-line services. Unlike a survey approach to privacy research, this method assesses service user expectations and preferences at the point of service use, not as part of a reflective study. This "in service use" approach was selected in order to try and more closely understand the subtleties and nuances of privacy practice and the points at which service users reach for a dialogue with service providers. For the purpose of our fieldwork, we situated our study in the context of the service user-service provider relationship and we focused on the service registration and purchasing aspects of on-line service engagement.

There was a need to investigate the service users' perceptions of having dialogues about their privacy with service provider. Hence a pilot study was deployed. Accordingly three participants (users), all women aged 32 to 41, volunteered to take part in our study. In this study, service users were asked to perform tasks using current online services. Since the objective was to find out users' views therefore both the following implicit and explicit methods for collecting data were employed:

— Observation – Users' behaviour during their interaction with user interfaces were observed and recorded. We needed to observe users' reaction at the point of registration.
— Task based questionnaire – There was a need to elicit users' opinions after completing their tasks. Quantitative data (close-ended questions) was used to

obtain an average of users' overall perceptions of the current privacy and consent dialogues. Qualitative data in terms of open ended questions were used so that users could freely express their views.

— Interview – Users were interviewed to expand our understanding of their perceptions. Following the university's policy, we asked each participant to read and sign a consent form to give authorisation to researchers for audio recording the interview session.

The emphasis in this approach is on situated research at the time of service use. Therefore, in the first part of the research activity, participants were observed completing the following tasks:

Task 1. Register with one of the following services which you have not been registered with before.

Task 2. Search for your subject/product.

Task 3. Save it or Add to the Shopping Basket.

Task 4. Leave your comment and feedback about the product.

It was explained to service users that they would not be judged on how fast or efficiently they performed the tasks, and the purpose of the exercise was to study the service provider's website. All participants were observed by the same single person, who recorded their action and their achievement.

The second part of the study involved participants replying to a questionnaire soliciting their views on privacy and consent. Accordingly, we administered a questionnaire soliciting both qualitative and quantitative data, via the use of both closed (Table 1) and open-ended questions (Table 2).

In the first part of the questionnaire, mainly focusing on privacy practices, we asked users whether they have read the privacy policy page (Table 1, Q1) and also whether they agreed with the 'terms and conditions' of the website (Table 1, Q2).

McDonald & Cranor [5] stated that "companies collect personally identifiable information that website visitors are not always comfortable sharing". Hence we questioned our participants whether they revealed their personal information willingly (Table 1, Q3). Moreover, in order to find out if participants are comfortable with revealing their identity we asked if they register with the website with their real personal information (Table 1, Q4).

Q5 contained a set of 14 statements (focusing on privacy practice and also dialogue) on which the participant expressed their opinion on a five-point scale (strongly agree, agree, neutral, disagree, and strongly disagree). The aim of these questions was to understand whether users have privacy concerns when it comes to registering with online service providers (the context of this study) and if they feel the need for dialogue.

In the second part of the questionnaire we used privacy perception and dialogue questions to solicit users' requirements for privacy and consent using online services (Table 2). Therefore we asked participants to reply to open-ended questions. Participants were free to give their comments on whether they trust a service provider with their personal information (Q6); how can a service provider assure their privacy (Q7 & Q8); how can a service provider communicate with them (Q9); and finally how should they be informed of privacy policies (Q10). One researcher was present to make sure all participants understand terminologies used in the questionnaire and also the purpose of each task given to them.

Table 1. Privacy and Consent questions – part 1

Q1. Did you read the privacy policy page?

Q2. Did you agree with the terms and conditions page?

Q3. Did you feel you were forced to give out your personal information in order to use the service?

Q4. Did you register with the website with your real personal information?

Q5. Privacy and Consent statements:
1. I wish I could communicate with the service provider about giving my personal information to them.
2. The service provider will not sell my information to a third party.
3. I feel confident in leaving comments on this website.
4. It was better if I could speak to someone on the phone about their services.
5. I can't rely on this website to keep my information secure.
6. I know the service provider will use my information for advertising.
7. There was enough information on the website to make it trustworthy.
8. I will provide them with more personal information if it is necessary.
9. I feel confident to register with this service online rather than filling a paper form.
10. I don't think the information they wanted was really private.
11. I don't mind if my information is passed to another company for commercial purposes.
12. The service provider explained why they need my personal information.
13. The service provider must give me assurance that my information is safe and confidential.
14. If I don't trust the service provider I will give fake personal information to use their services.

Table 2. Privacy and Consent questions – part 2

Q6. Did you trust the service provider with your personal information?

Q7. How can a service provider show you that they are trustworthy with keeping your personal information?

Q8. What expectations do you have about the safety of your personal information?

Q9. How would you like to communicate with the service provider about your privacy? Think of different ways which would have been helpful to support your interaction with the service.

Q10. How do you think the service provider should have informed you of their privacy policy?

The third part of the study involved a semi-structured interview with each participant. The questions asked in the interview followed on from the questionnaire. The aim of the interview questions was to further explore the participants' views and obtain a deeper understanding of possible dialogue system requirements. Following on from Q5 (Table 1), to find out whether users were comfortable revealing their personal information, we asked:

    1.   Do you think the service provider was reliable?

Furthermore, in line with Q9 and Q10 (Table 1), we opened the discussion on 'privacy dialogue' by asking the following questions:

    2.   How do you think the service provider should communicate with you to gain your trust?

    3.   Do you think there was enough information for you to be confident using the website? If not, why?

The above interview questions also helped the researcher to clarify and interpret responses in the questionnaire. The pilot study helped us to better understand privacy practices and the general need for dialogues when selecting practices. In the pilot study, each participant indicated different points in the registration process when they would have liked further assurances from the service provider and when they would have liked to raise concerns as well as gather further information. The feedback clearly indicated that there is a need for three types of privacy dialogue where service users can a) request information b) raise queries and concerns c) contest the privacy stance of a service provider. We explored these findings further in the study presented in this section.

3.1   User Study – UK Online Centres

Following the approach trialled in the pilot study, we conducted a user study aiming at a wider audience. We recruited our participants through six UK online centres.

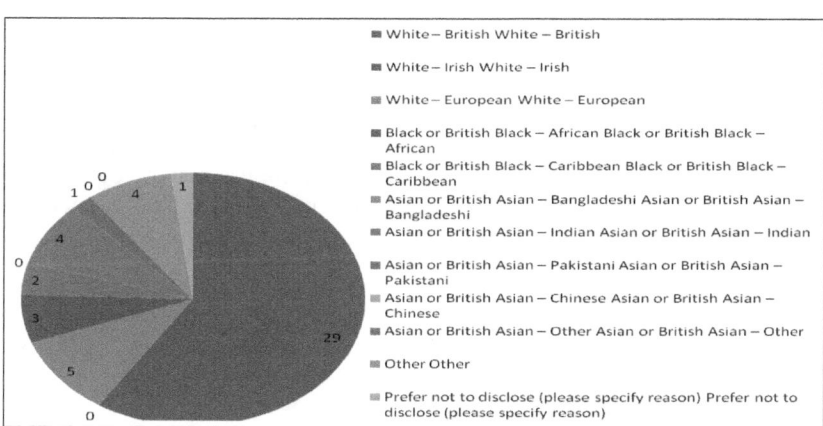

Fig. 1. Participants' ethnicity

All participants (all Internet users at the centre) were recruited by the Centre Manger. Each participant was offered a shopping voucher as a reward for their contribution to the research. We were interested in a wide range of Internet users. Accordingly, 49 users

(31 female and 18 male) aged between 15 and 60 years old from a diverse ethnic background (Figure 1) participated in our study. The same research process was followed, as described in section 3. In addition, we asked further questions on trust, consent negotiation and dialogue design. Trust is an important factor when a service user determines how much information to disclose to a service provider and is a key part of relationship building. Therefore, much focus was given to the nature of trust between service user and service provider. In order to open our discussion on trust we asked:

1. Do you think the service provider was trustworthy?

Furthermore, in our pilot study we learned that users trust brand names. We needed to understand if this is true for our wider audience. Hence, we also asked:

2. Do you trust brand names? Why?
3. How do you think a service provider should build your trust?

Following the findings from the pilot study, in order to learn what the best practice for obtaining consent is, we asked:

4. What would make online consent easier? Do you prefer to be informed in more detail or to have it in a "visual" style?

Finally, as we described in section 2.2, to learn more about participants' views on general CRM dialogue design principles, we asked:

5. Do you think it is important to have a relationship with the service provider? What sort of relationship is appropriate?
6. How much frequency of interaction do you think is necessary to obtain a good relationship with the service provider? Would that affect your trust in them?

The result of these interviews is given in next section (4.3).

4   Results

As explained in 3.1, in the first part of our study, participants were asked to interact with current service providers with whom they have not previously registered. Figure 2 shows the registration break-down. One participant refused to register with any online services but agreed to complete the relevant questions in the questionnaire and participate in our interview.

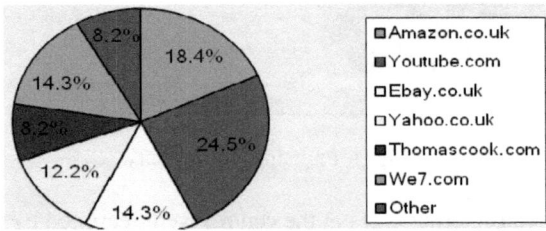

Fig. 2. Online services, registered by participants

4.1   Privacy Practice

The researcher noted that only 2 out of 48 users read privacy policy/users' terms and condition pages. As to be expected when answering Q1 (Did you read privacy statements?) 64% (n=31) of users said "yes" and 91% (n=44) said they have agreed and accepted them. This indicates that often users believe that they have read and understood privacy statements when in fact they are unaware of the contents. In our interview, users commented privacy statements are "too long". One user stated: "...we are in a very fast modern world now and people want things to be done in a flash...". Moreover, users commented these statements are often displayed in "small letters" which is difficult to read; have too much "legal jargon". Some users claimed they know the content and avoid reading them.

This is in-line with [6] the empirical study, which reported that users are unaware how their data is collected and used. Furthermore, the majority (48%, n = 22) of users disagreed (n = 15 'Disagree' and n = 7 'Strongly disagree') when responding to Q3 (I feel I was forced to give out my personal information?) whereas 35% (n=17) of users remained neutral (Figure 3). Therefore, users have willingly revealed their personal information without the knowledge of how this information will be used by the service providers. However, not all users have given their real details as 31% (n = 15) of users registered with false information (Q4) which clearly indicates that they have concerns in giving their identity away.

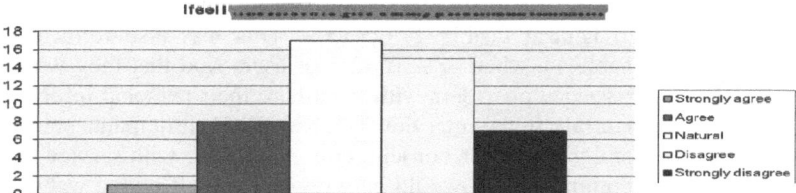

Fig. 3. Users' opinion on revealing their personal information

In terms of privacy practice in the context of service registration, these results indicate that a substantial number of service users are not fully aware of on-line privacy risks but often choose to "circumvent" any lack of knowledge by withholding personal information.

Furthermore, in an open-ended question we asked whether participants trusted the service provider with their personal information (Q6). Hence 62% (n=30) said yes, and some users gave their reason as:

- The service provider is a well known organization;
- Their privacy policy assured us that our personal information is safe;
- They only asked for users' address;
- Not many personal details where requested;
- They have a privacy policy.

37% (n=18) of users stated that they distrust the service provider. Here are some feedbacks given as why:

- There is always a chance that they will give it away;
- It is not clear to me how they will use my information;
- I feel uncomfortable with them;
- It was easy to register on their site, so anyone can get access to their website;
- I have a bad experience from past that my information were sold to a third party without my consent;
- The privacy statements given in small print so I had insufficient time to read it.

The responses given from both groups of users indicate that privacy statements can have a positive effect on users' trust if this information is understandable for users. This further strengthens the argument that it is necessary to explore not only what messages are communicated but the richness and the frequency of the signalling. The responses to "why service providers might be distrusted" show that different service users have different communication requirements. This leads to the consideration of a configurable dialogue system which has tuneable parameters not only for signal content but also for signal format.

4.2   Privacy Dialogue

The majority of participants (68%, n=33) have agreed service providers must give them assurance that their personal information is safe and confidential whereas 8 participants remained neutral (Table 1, Q5.13).   This was also reflected in their responses to Q5.1 (Table 1), when 48% (n=23) of users said that they would like to have a dialogue with service providers with regards to their personal information and 31% (n=15) stayed neutral. In the interview we learned all participants believed when it comes to privacy and giving their consent, communicating with service provider is essential. One user commented: "I would only register myself with a website if there is a contact telephone number and an address, so that I can call and speak to someone".

Furthermore, 70% (n=34) of users agreed with Q5.4 (it was better if they could speak to someone on the phone about their services). This indicates that although users feel the need to communicate with service providers, they prefer if this can be done via an online channel. Moreover, only 31% of users agreed that the service providers have explained to them why they need users' details (Q5.12). In addition, only 35% (n=17) of users believe there was enough information on the websites to make them trustworthy (with keeping their personal information confidential). One conclusion can be drawn here is that the lack of communication between service users and service providers has caused an issue of trust where, only 37% (n=18) of participants said they will trust the service provider and avoid using fake details at registration process (Q5.14). Moreover, only 35% (n=17) of participants said they can rely on service providers to keep their information secure (Q5.5).

In terms of dialogue design, these results indicate dissatisfaction with existing communication methods. On the subject of privacy it suggests that signalling needs to be clearer in privacy statements. Signaling also needs to clearer and more readily identifiable when communicating the degree to which personal data is protected by service providers. Attention needs to be paid to the richness of the signalling, with a significant proportion wanting a combination of on-line messaging and initial contact by telephone. The importance of signalling and the need for a configurable dialogue system is demonstrated by the comments given from users in answering Q7 (How can a service provider show you that they are trustworthy with keeping your personal information?) The following list is typical examples of what users (3 users skipped the question) said with regards to trusting the service providers: 69% (n = 32) of users said "I will trust a service provider if they:"

- promise they will not sell my personal information.
- give me some genuine information of who they are.
- give me some form of agreement.
- can prove my information is safe.
- have a clear privacy policy that my information is safe.
- show me that they are aware of Data Protection Act.
- show me that they are trustworthy.

The above feedbacks provided by users clearly suggest that users need some form of communication to acknowledge them of their privacy e.g. policy on data confidentiality. Moreover, common feedbacks given from 13% (n = 6) of users who said "I never trust service providers because:"

- they will pass my information to a third party.
- several news reports that service providers sell our personal information.
- they ask for too much personal information.

The remaining of 19% (n = 9) of users said "I don't really mind because:"

- I avoid giving personal information.
- they ask for basic information which I don't mind.
- I never register with service providers who ask a lot.

Furthermore, on-line privacy was an important requirement for the participants and is clearly a privacy practice of choice. Therefore, 35 participants (some participants elected not to respond to the question) suggested various ways that they think service provider should inform them of their privacy (Q10):

- Email (n = 10);
- Pop-up messages (n = 1);
- An screen displaying the privacy policy before registration (n = 19);
- Sending a hard copy of signed agreements for both sides (n = 3);
- Sending text messages (n = 1);
- Contacting users (n = 1).

Hence, to analyze the above request from users, we believe that all are feasible as an approach to online privacy messaging. Consequently, in answering the above question two participants commented:

User 1: "I have never experienced web communication where one has the option to revert to telephone or email (at the time). Clearly even now it would help if at the registration process there were some explanations".

User 2: "I think it's outrageous that the privacy policy is this lengthy document and normally given to you at the end of an equally lengthy registration process - it's obvious that nobody is going to read it. Also, it is written in a legal jargon that most of the time leaves scope for varied interpretation. If service providers are serious about building up trust with clients in this area, privacy policy should be explained at the beginning of the registration process in a short and accessible form, and its practical implications should be brought to clients' attention".

In order to find out how signalling might be implemented, we asked the participants: How would you like to communicate with the service provider about your privacy? (Q9) In response to this 36 users stated:

- To chat with someone online (n = 6);
- Face to face (n = 2);
- Via a contact telephone number (n = 12);
- Email (n = 13);
- Confirmation letter (n = 3);

Therefore, we suggest further research is needed to see whether a pattern can be identified in terms of the type of signalling that is required and whether combinations of signals (richness) are more appropriate for some privacy issues than others.

4.3   User Preference for Online Privacy and Consent

Finally in the last part of the study we interviewed each participant. We have grouped participant responses into five sections: frequency, initiation, service provider disclosure, signalling and richness (Table 3). As mentioned earlier (section 2.2), these are the established design principles for general CRM dialogue design which should be considered when designing on-line tools to support privacy. Thus, as far as frequency requirements are concerned, users indicated that, they are interested to receive frequent useful information upon their request. This highlights that users want to be in control of the frequency of interactions between them and service providers. Users' responses regarding signalling and richness were more about receiving valuable information about the services and the presentation of information about privacy on their websites. Therefore, they were concerned about seeing feedback given by other users; receiving updated information on terms and conditions; and also contact details for reaching service providers offline. All participants in interviews confess that they avoid reading privacy policy and users' terms and conditions pages for a common reason: it's too long; fonts are small and not easy to follow; it is full of legal jargon; and it was ambiguous on the webpage. Hence, for service providers to be able to gain users' trust, they should communicate information on privacy openly and clearly. This more detailed feedback from the interviews enables us to construct requirements for the content of privacy signals, the format and the possible combinations of signals. In response to the question on: How do users think the service provider should build their trust; users indicated that, they would trust a service provider who can show their openness and trustworthy to its users; has a secure website only accessible to valid users; communicates with users on a regular basis; avoids sending advertisement against users' will; provides secure transactions; easy to use services; and is registered with the data protection act.

Table 3. Users' preferences

Users' preferences: Online Service Provider should...	
Frequency	• Provide frequent useful information requested by users. • Allow users to make decision on the frequency of interactions.
Initiation	• Provide a secure online service accessible to valid users. • Provide enough information about who they are. • Provide enough information to users to establish the relationship in future. • Avoid requesting personal information other than necessary.
Signaling & Richness	• Update users of new changes in their terms and conditions. • Display comments and feedback given by their current users. • Display easy to read information on their services. • Provide contact details where they can be reached offline. • Allow users to make decision on how they will maintain their relationship with the service provider. • Provide information about users' privacy in an accessible form. • Provide useful privacy policy/users' terms and conditions page by presenting in a: • language understandable by all type of users; • concise page; • readable font size • noticeable location
Service Provider disclosure	• Provide a hard copy privacy contract between them and their users. • Specify the reason for requesting personal information. • Provide feedback given by other organisation about them. • Include Data Protection Act information. • Provide information on their implemented security system.

Users start to indicate the importance of service provider disclosure when building trust. In addition to trust in the service provider as an organization, participants also emphasise the need for a trusted, secure platform. Therefore, honesty is an important aspect of trust building in the relationship and security is an important aspect of trust building in the architecture. Users' responses with regards to their preference for giving their online consent were that, online consent forms should be displayed in simple and clear language. They also indicated that service providers should make sure users have understood the content. Hence, users indicate the importance of dialogue and the need for service providers to check understanding or provide a means for service users to check understanding.

5   Conclusion

This paper has explored users' requirements and preferences for online privacy and consent. These findings show that dialogues are needed in order to ensure more effective privacy practice. Not only is it necessary to break down the information contained in privacy agreements into shorter, clearer signals but consideration also needs to be given to the frequency and richness of the signals. In addition to communicating the privacy policy contents, privacy risks also need to be communicated. As a service user's privacy stance adjusts over time, the dialogue system needs to be configurable. Service providers need to consider how they are going to convey an honest position on privacy and service users need be able to contest that position. Furthermore in our interview, users responded there should be a frequency of interaction between them and service providers. This indicates that closed questions should be used to further identify the role frequency plays in a dialogue system. Lab experiments could also be constructed for this purpose. It can be argued that the dialogue system as a whole contributes to transparency of a service provider's privacy practices. However, further work needs to be done to pinpoint methods that accurately provide transparency of service provider privacy practices to the service user. Further work is also needed to explore privacy practices and the need for dialogue in other on-line relationships and in other contexts. This will help develop a more complete requirement specification and a deeper understanding of the types of privacy practices which need to be developed.

Acknowledgements. We are grateful to all 52 participants who took part in this study. This work was supported by the Technology Strategy Board; the Engineering and Physical Sciences Research Council and the Economic and Social Research Council [grant number EP/G00255/X].

References

[1] Leuthesser, L., Kohli, A.K.: Relational Behaviour in Business Markets Implications for Relationship Management. Journal of Business Research 34, 221–233 (1995)
[2] Coles-Kemp, L., Kani-Zabihi, E.: On-line Privacy and Consent: A Dialogue, Not a Monologue. In: NSPW, Concord, MA (2010)
[3] Ardagna, C.A., Di Vimercati, S.D.C., Neven, G., Paraboschi, S., Preiss, F.S., Samarati, P., Verdicchio, M.: Enabling Privacy-Preserving Credential-Based Access Control with XACML and SAML. In: 10th IEEE International Conference on Computer and Information Technology, p. 1090. IEEE Computer Society, Bradford (2010)

[4] Bogdanovic, D., Crawford, C., Coles-Kemp, L.: The need for enhanced privacy and consent dialogues. Information Security Technical Report 14(3), 167–172 (2009)

[5] McDonald, A.M., Cranor, L.F.: The cost of reading privacy policies. ISJLP 4, 543–897 (2009)

[6] McDonald, A.M., Cranor, L.F.: An Empirical Study of How People Perceive Online Behavioral Advertising. CyLab, p. 2 (2009)

[7] Coles-Kemp, L., Lai, Y., Ford, M.: Privacy: Contemporary Developments in Users' Attitudes and Behaviours (2009),
http://www.vome.org.uk/index.php/publications/

[8] Buchanan, T., Reips, U.-D., Paine, C., Joinson, A.N.: Development of measures of online privacy concern and protection for use on the Internet. Journal of the American Society for Information Science and Technology 58(2), 157–165 (2007)

[9] Horn, D., Feinberg, R., Salvendy, G.: Determinant Elements of Customer Relationshjp Management in e-Business. Behaviour and Information Technology 24(2) (2005)

[10] Bruhn, M., Grund, M.: Theory, Development and Implementation of National Customer Satisfaction Indices: The Swiss Index of Customer Satisfaction (SWICS). Total Quality Management 11(7) (2000)

[11] A Joint Report of the Information and Privacy Commissioner of Ontario and the Canadian Marketing Association (2004), Incorporating Privacy into Marketing and Customer Relationship Management,
http://www.ipc.on.ca/images/Resources/priv-mkt.pdf
(last accessed August 5, 2010)

[12] Information Commissioner's Office (2008) Privacy by Design,
http://www.ico.gov.uk/upload/documents/pdb_report_html/
index.html (last accessed August 5, 2010)

[13] Whitworth, B.: The Social Requirements of Technical Systems. In: Whitworth, B., de, M. (eds.) Socio-Technical Design and Social Networking Systems, pp. 1–22 (2009)

[14] Tsai, J., Egelman, S., Cranor, L., Acquisti, A.: The effect of online privacy information on purchasing behaviour: An experimental study. In: The 6th Workshop on the Economics of Information Security (WEIS), Citeseer (2008)

[15] Daft, R.L., Lengel, R.H., Trevino, L.K.: Message Equivocality, Media Selection, and Manager Performance: Implications for Information Systems. MIS Quarterly 11(3), 355–366 (1987)

[16] Solove, D.J.: Understanding Privacy. Harvard University Press (2008)

[17] Kani-Zabihi, E., Ghinea, G., Chen, S.: User perceptions of online public library catalogues. International Journal of Information Management 28, 492–502 (2008)

Analyzing Characteristic Host Access Patterns for Re-identification of Web User Sessions

Dominik Herrmann, Christoph Gerber, Christian Banse, and Hannes Federrath

Research Group Security in Distributed Systems
Department of Informatics
University of Hamburg, 22527 Hamburg, Germany
`lastname@informatik.uni-hamburg.de`

Abstract. An attacker, who is able to observe a web user over a long period of time, learns a lot about his interests. It may be difficult to track users with regularly changing IP addresses, though. We show how patterns mined from web traffic can be used to re-identify a majority of users, i. e. link multiple sessions of them. We implement the web user re-identification attack using a Multinomial Naïve Bayes classifier and evaluate it using a real-world dataset from 28 users. Our evaluation setup complies with the limited knowledge of an attacker on a malicious web proxy server, who is only able to observe the host names visited by its users. The results suggest that consecutive sessions can be linked with high probability for session durations from 5 minutes to 48 hours and that user profiles degrade only slowly over time. We also propose basic countermeasures and evaluate their efficacy.

1 Introduction

With the continuing dissemination of the World Wide Web we are increasingly living our lives online. The websites that are retrieved by an individual reflect – at least to some degree – his or her interests, habits and social network. The URL of some pages may even disclose the user's identity. If one is able to observe a substantial portion of the web traffic of a user over some period of time, he will learn many private details about this user. Many users are willing to trust their ISP, who can trivially intercept all traffic from a dial-up account and attribute it to the respective customer. Malicious observers or other third-party service providers are not supposed to be able to compile profiles that contain users' interests together with their identity, though. Third parties that can easily obtain users' web traffic include open proxy servers, free WiFi hotspots as well as single-hop anonymisation services like Anonymizer.com or the recently launched IPREDator.se. As web browsers usually issue a DNS query before the requested page can be retrieved, the providers of public DNS servers such as OpenDNS or the recently launched Google Public DNS[1] are also part of this group.

---

[1] See `http://www.opendns.com/` and `http://code.google.com/speed/public-dns/`

T. Aura, K. Järvinen, and K. Nyberg (Eds.): NordSec 2010, LNCS 7127, pp. 136–154, 2012.

A malicious observer can group all requests originating from a single source IP address and (assuming exactly one user per address) attribute all of them to a (now pseudonymous) single user. Clearly, in this scenario the attacker's capability to track a user over time mainly depends on the lifetime of the user's IP address. While it is straightforward to track users with static IP addresss, *re-identifying* users with dynamically assigned, frequently changing IP addresses is more challenging. The *web user re-identification attack* addresses this challenge.

In this paper we examine to which extent a passive observer can link the web sessions of a given user solely based on a record of his past activities on the web. Recently, privacy concerns have raised interest in such *re-identification* problems [25]. The first stepping stone for long-term tracking attacks of web users is linking two or multiple *surfing sessions* of individuals, which we address in this paper. In the long run we are interested in a realistic threat assessment of such linkage attacks in real-world environments. Note that we do not examine how to recover the true identity of a web user based on their browsing behaviour in this paper, though. Previous work, e. g. an analysis of the AOL search logs, has shown that at least some users tend to disclose their identity via entering uniquely personally identifying information in web forms or search engines [3]. The more sessions of one user an attacker can link, the more he will learn about his interests and personality – and thus the more likely he will be able to uncover the real-world identity of the user.

For the purpose of our evaluation we model a surfing session to consist of the access frequencies of all hosts a user visits in a certain time window. We will use machine learning techniques to link multiple sessions and analyse how effective a malicious observer (or a third party mentioned above) can re-identify web users. Without loss of generality, we will describe the attack from the perspective of a malicious web proxy server.

Contribution Firstly, we demonstrate that Internet users exhibit characteristic web browsing behaviour that can be exploited for linkage attacks. Our evaluation on a privacy-preservingly collected real-world dataset demonstrates that even an attacker with limited power can exploit characteristic behaviour to re-identify a majority of users on a session-to-session basis. Contrary to previous work, i. e. re-identifying users in 802.11 networks [28], which relies on numerous properties of network traffic, our attack solely utilises destination host access frequencies. Another novelty of our work is the transformation of the raw access frequency vectors to counter the effects of the power-law distribution on access frequencies and a thorough evaluation taking into account the attacker's viewpoint. While previous work operated on monthly traffic aggregates [18] and destination IP addresses, we evaluate our approach for shorter sessions (between 5 minutes and 48 hours) and only rely on host (DNS) names. Furthermore, we discuss and evaluate countermeasures that degrade the effectivity of the attack.

This paper is structured as follows: After reviewing related work in Section 2, we briefly present the data mining techniques used for our attack in Section 3. We continue with our data acquisition methodology in Section 4 before we describe our evaluation methodology and results in Section 5. We present countermeasures in Section 6 and discuss the results in Section 7 before concluding the paper in Section 8.

2 Related Work

Closely related to our work are Kumpost's publications [16,17,18], which describe a large-scale study on NetFlow traffic logs. His ultimate goal and approach is quite similar to ours: finding out whether it is possible to pinpoint individual users among others due to their characteristic behaviour in the past. He devises a classifier that compares behavioral vectors of users with a similarity measure based on cosine similarity and shows that inverse document frequencies (IDF) can improve re-identification accuracy. His study differs from ours in several ways, though: Kumpost operates on monthly aggregates of the access frequencies of hosts; on the contrary, we adopt an attacker's point of view and track users on a smaller scale and for shorter timeframes. Furthermore, while Kumpost operates on network traces, we work with a pseudonymized web proxy dataset specifically collected for this purpose. Finally, Kumpost only describes the actual attack, whereas we also discuss and evaluate countermeasures.

Yang's publications [27,36] and especially [35] are also related to our study. Yang studies to which extent samples of 2 to 100 web users can be re-identified with profiling and classification methods from a dataset containing 50,000 users in total. As Yang's focus is the utility of web user profiles for fraud detection and other applications in e-commerce, she does not tackle the problem from our *attacker's view*. To some degree her methodology is comparable to our *simulations*, but there are some differences, which are of relevance for our purpose. For instance, while we concentrate on training sets of size 1, her evaluation focuses on the improvements obtained by the use of multiple labelled training instances (up to 100), which are usually difficult to obtain for the type of attacker we have in mind. Another difference stems from the selection of training and test instances: while Yang selects training and test instances with an arbitrary temporal offset, we explicitly evaluate the influence of the temporal offset between them in order to analyse profile degradation over time.

Also related is the work of Pang et al., which studies an attacker who aims to re-identify users in 802.11 wireless networks [28]. Pang considers a number of properties of network traffic to link multiple sessions of users – even if ephemeral, pseudonymous MAC addresses are used. While they do look at exploiting destination addresses for their linkability attack, their focus lies on characteristics of 802.11 devices such as SSID probes, the size of broadcast packets and MAC protocol fields. Their methodology, which relies on the Jaccard index and a Naïve Bayes classifier with Gaussian kernel density estimation, differs from ours considerably, though.

Data mining techniques have been applied to attack users' privacy in many related user re-identification and de-anonymization studies ([31,15,20,5,23] and most recently [11,34]) and for attacks on anonymized traffic logs [29,9,8]. Web usage mining (cf. [30,6,14,24]) is also a related area of work.

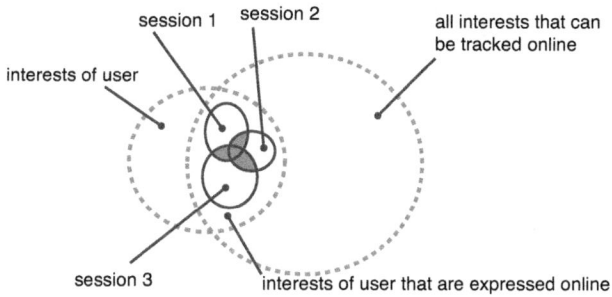

Fig. 1. Venn diagram representation of the web user re-identification problem

3   Re-identification Methodology

In the following sections we will present our methodology. We assume that most users exhibit at least some part of their interests online, and that they are reflected by the websites they access in a particular surfing session (cf. Fig. 1). Our re-identification attack works on the intersection of two or more sessions of a user. In an ideal world the intersections of one user will not substantially overlap with the intersections of other users as they have a differing set of interests.

Both, term frequencies [37] and host access frequencies [1,4,10], have shown to obey Zipf's law: there is a small number of attributes (terms or hosts) that is part of almost all instances (documents or sessions) and always occurs in large frequencies. As a consequence we conjecture that text mining and web user re-identification can be tackled with similar techniques. Therefore, we model instances using the *vector space model* [2,21,33]. For our analysis, we apply the Multinomial Naïve Bayes classifier, an off-the-shelf text mining technique, and various transformations, which have proven effective for text mining problems, to the input data.

3.1   Modelling the Web User Re-identification Problem

Our analysis relies on a basic model that captures users' surfing habits. With this model we can reduce the web user re-identification attack to a data mining *classification problem* [33], which can be tackled with various supervised learning methods. We consider each *surfing session* of a user to be an *instance* of a *class* $c_i \in C$, i.e. each class represents all surfing sessions of a specific user. Each instance consists of the web browsing requests sent by a user's machine during one surfing session. From each HTTP request we only use the destination host name (e. g. *www.google.com*).[2] We disregard port, path, filename and other features. Instead of a binary encoding of the fact whether some *host* (e. g. *www.google.com*) has been accessed or not, we take into account the *number of*

---

[2] Accesses to various sub-domains are not merged, i. e. *www.site.com*, *site.com* and *www1.site.com* are treated as different hosts.

requests to each host within a session to model usage intensity. The order of requests as well as timing information is neglected in our basic model, as we do not expect the behaviour of most users to show significant patterns in those dimensions. There are certainly more sophisticated models conceivable, which may take into account such characteristics.

Note that previous studies [16,17,18] have not relied on host names, but on IP adddresses. While it is certainly possible to carry out the attack with IP addresses only, we deem IP addresses not as suitable as host names: firstly, the IP address of a web server may be subject to frequent changes, secondly, some web sites may use multiple IPs for load distribution and thirdly, virtual hosts may serve multiple different web sites from the same IP address. The instances will reflect user interests more closely, if destination host names are used instead of IP addresses. This is straightforward for the kind of attacker we have in mind, i. e. the provider of a HTTP proxy.

Each instance consists of a multiset $(x_1^{f_{x_1}}, x_2^{f_{x_2}}, \ldots, x_m^{f_{x_m}})$ containing all the hosts x_j and their respective access frequencies $f_{x_j} \in \mathbb{N}_0$ for a given user and session. From the multisets, we obtain *attribute vectors* $\boldsymbol{x} = \mathbf{f} = (f_{x_1}, f_{x_2}, \ldots, f_{x_m})$ for all visited hosts m that are present in the dataset. Even for rather small user groups, those vectors become very sparse as the number of distinct websites increases rapidly.

The re-identification attack consists of two stages. Firstly, the attacker has to obtain a set of k *training instances* $I_{\text{train}} = \{(\boldsymbol{x}_1, c_1), \ldots, (\boldsymbol{x}_k, c_n)\}$; $c_i \in C$; $k \geq n$; $n \leq |C|$ that he labels with class information.[3] Afterwards, he will use a *classifier* to predict the class, i. e. the user, of a number of *test instances* in order to establish a mapping between the sessions contained in the test instances and the sessions within the training instances.

3.2   Multinomial Naïve Bayes (MNB)

The Multinomial Naïve Bayes (MNB) classifier is a well known method for text mining tasks [33]. The choice of the MNB classifier is motivated by the fact that attributes in natural language models and in our model, which relies on host access frequencies, both are distributed according to a power-law, i. e. their frequency distribution is heavy-tailed.

Although Naïve Bayes and related probabilistic classifiers naïvely assume independence of attributes (which is often not the case for real-world problems), they have been applied to many privacy-related classification attacks with great success. Of particular interest for our analysis is the application to traffic analysis problems (cf. [12,38,22,32]) and to website fingerprinting [19,13] in previous

---

[3] The *class labels* may either be actual real names of the users, in case the attacker already knows them for the training instances or can deduce them using context information. Alternatively, the attacker can use arbitrarily chosen user IDs, i. e. pseudonyms, in case he does not know the real identities of the respective users during the training stage yet. Later on he can substitute the pseudonyms with real-world identifiers, once users have revealed (parts of) their identity by their online activities (which is not within the scope of this paper).

works. We apply the MNB classifier to the host access frequencies within individual user sessions. Given m unique hosts, the classifier evaluates the probability that a given instance $\mathbf{f}$ belongs to some class c_i as:

$$P(\mathbf{f}|c_i) \sim \prod_{j=1}^{m} P(X = x_j|c_i)^{f_{x_j}}$$

The resulting probability is proportional to the product of $P(X = x_j|c_i)$, which is the probability that a certain host x_j is drawn from the aggregated multiset of all host accesses of the training instances of class c_i. The individual probabilities contribute f_{x_j} times to the result, where f_{x_j} is the number of accesses to host x_j in the test instance at hand. In other words: the more often the dominant hosts of the test instance $\mathbf{f}$ appear in the training instances of class c_i, the more likely does instance $\mathbf{f}$ belong to class c_i. The classifier will select the class c_i for with the highest value $P(\mathbf{f}|c_i)$ is observed. For a more formal coverage of the MNB classifier refer to a recent text book by Manning et al. [21].

3.3   Vector Transformations

There are several transformations that – if applied to the raw attribute vectors – have shown to improve the accuracy of classifiers on text mining problems. We will analyse to what extent web user re-identification attacks benefit from them.

TF Transformation.   Extremely high frequencies of a small number of attributes can overshadow the contribution of the remaining features, which makes it difficult for the classifier to distinguish between instances of different classes. A frequently mentioned solution is to apply a sublinear transformation to the raw occurence frequencies: $\mathbf{f}^*_{x_j} = \log(1 + \mathbf{f}_{x_j})$, the so-called *term frequency (TF) transformation* (cf. [33] for details).

IDF Transformation.   Using raw vectors all attributes (host frequencies) contribute equally to the resulting vector, regardless of their *relevance*. Popular hosts that are part of a vast majority of instances do not confer much information about a class, though. This problem can be alleviated using the *inverse document frequency (IDF) transformation*: given n training instances the occurrence frequencies f_{x_j} are transformed using the *document frequency* df_x, i.e. the number of instances that contain term x: $f^*_{x_j} = f_{x_j} \cdot \log \frac{n}{\mathrm{df}_{x_j}}$. The application of both of the aforementioned transformations is referred to as *TF-IDF transformation* [33].

Cosine Normalisation (N).   Results from empirical research have shown that the accuracy of many classifiers and information retrieval algorithms can be greatly improved by normalizing the lengths of all instance vectors [21, p. 128]. This is usually achieved by applying cosine normalisation, i.e. all frequencies are divided by the Euclidean length of the raw vector: $f^{\mathrm{norm}}_{x_j} = \frac{f^*_{x_j}}{\|(f^*_{x_1}, \dots, f^*_{x_m})\|}$. While it stands to reason that cosine normalization is reasonable for text documents, its utility for the web user re-identification problem may seem counterintuitive at first sight: the total number of requests of a session seems to be a promising feature for differentiation, after all.

Table 1. Properties of our proxy user linkability dataset

Duration in days	57
Number of HTTP requests	2,684,736
Number of unique destination hosts	25,124
Transmitted data volume in GiB	110.74

4   Data Acquisition

In this section we will outline our data acquisition methodology and present the dataset used for the evaluation of the user re-identification attack. To collect web surfing data, we recorded the web traffic of 28 web users at the university of Regensburg (cf. Table 1 for descriptive statistics of the dataset).

Our participants installed a proxy server (a slightly modified version of Privoxy[4]), which recorded all of their HTTP traffic, on their local client machines. We provided a convenient obfuscation and submission tool that enabled users to anonymize log files on their machines before uploading them to a central server for later collection. The tool labelled the logs with a static user-specific pseudonym (e. g. *RQFSPJ75*) and obscured the requested URLs (see below). To conceal the IP addresses of our participants, we made sure that the log files themselves did not contain any source IP addresses and encouraged the participants to upload their logs using an anonymization service like JonDonym or Tor.[5]

The requested URLs were split into multiple components (scheme, host, port, path) before hostnames and paths were obfuscated using a salted hash-function. The salt value was hard-wired in the obfuscation tool and ensured that there would be a consistent mapping between host names and hash values for all users. The hash function was repeatedly applied to discourage dictionary attacks during the study. Once the study was completed we deleted all references to the salt in order to reduce the risk of dictionary attacks in the future. Our participants were satisfied with the basic level of protection offered by our URL pseudonymization scheme. Even the technically savvy ones, who were familiar with signature and fingerprinting attacks on such log files (cf. [7,15]), were willing to accept the remaining risks.

While our user group is rather small and certainly biased to some degree, our user profiles also have some advantage in comparison to profiles compiled from passively collected flow traces of a large network segment like used by Kumpost [17]: Firstly, the user group is quite homogeneous and shares common interests (24 out of 28 participants are undergraduate or postgraduate students with high affinity towards information technology); this may also be the case in reality for users who share the same proxy server. Secondly, we know as a ground truth that all HTTP requests submitted by a user (i. e. labelled with his pseudonym)

---

[4] Available for download at `http://www.privoxy.org/`
[5] Available for download at `http://www.jondonym.com/` and
`http://torproject.org/`

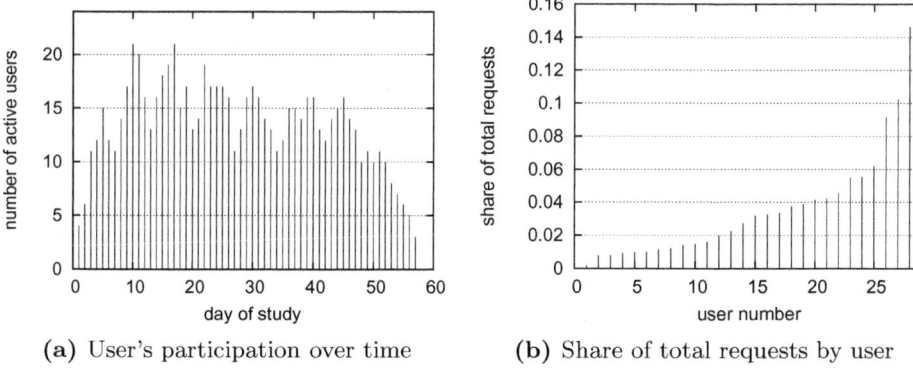

(a) User's participation over time

(b) Share of total requests by user

Fig. 2. Overview of dataset used for evaluation

originate from exactly one individual[6], while passively collected profiles may be subject to unobservable influences such as multiple people sharing one IP address or sudden changes in the IP address assignment of a user. Finally, our user profiles are mostly comprised of requests issued via the user's web browser: only 14 % of the participants chose to submit *all* HTTP requests of their machines.

Fig. 2 shows the participation of users over the course of the study as well as the amount of HTTP requests contributed by the individual users. The number of users contributing data on a given day varies between 3 and 22. 15 users or more contributed on at least 50 % of the days, with contributions ranging from 10 to 57 days. The number of HTTP requests submitted by the individual users varies considerably: the 50 % most active users contribute 80 % of the requests, with the most active user contributing 14.6 % of the total number of requests. Note that we will disregard any context information as well as timing information and activity patterns regarding to specific weekdays in this paper. Instead, we will only consider the access frequencies of the destination servers to assess the effectiveness of our web user re-identification attack.

5   Evaluation Methodology and Results

In this section we evaluate the user re-identification attack using our dataset. The evaluation consists of two parts, which allow us to analyse different aspects. In the first part, which we call the *attacker's view*, we merge all the log files of our participants (maintaining the exact timing of the requests). This allows us to evaluate the feasibility of the user re-identification attack if all participants had used a malicious *central proxy server* for our study. The second part consists of *simulations* which analyse the impact of various parameters on the effectiveness of the attack using random samples of our dataset.

---

[6] This claim is substantiated by the results of an anonymous questionnaire we requested the participants to fill out.

Table 2. Evaluation of predictions from an attacker's point of view for user u (with class c_u) with training instances $x_.^t$ and test instances $x_.^{t+1}$. TP/FP/TN/FN conditions are shown for clarity; cases are sorted according to their evaluation: *correct* $(1,2)$, *wrong-detectable* $(3,4)$ and *wrong-undetectable* $(5,6)$.

(1)	TP:1 FP:0 TN:0 FN:0	u contributed on days t and $t+1$; user's instance x_u was correctly assigned to c_u; attacker can track u
(2)	TP:0 FP:0 TN:1 FN:0	u contributed on day t only; no instance was incorrectly assigned to c_u
(3)	TP:0 FP>1 TN:0 FN:1	u contributed on both days, but x_u^{t+1} was not assigned to c_u; multiple instances $x_v; v \neq u$ were assigned to c_u
(4)	TP:1 FP>0 TN:0 FN:0	u contributed on both days; x_u^{t+1} was assigned to c_u; at least one instance $x_v; v \neq u$ was assigned to c_u
(5)	TP:0 FP:0 TN:0 FN:1	u contributed on both days; but no instance was assigned to c_u at all; attacker believes there is no x_u^{t+1} and loses track of u; attacker confuses this prediction with (2)
(6)	TP:0 FP:1 TN:0 FN:0	u contributed on both days, but x_u^{t+1} was not assigned to c_u; one instance $x_v; v \neq u$ was assigned to c_u; attacker confuses v with u; attacker confuses this prediction with (1)

5.1 Attacker's View

We start out with an attacker on a proxy server who exploits characteristic surfing patterns to re-identify individual users on consecutive days, i.e. we consider sessions with a duration of 24 hours (we study other session times and non-consecutive sessions in Section 5.2).

Therefore, we assume that on one day t the attacker decides to track a specific user u^t from now on (e.g. due to a intriguing request of that user). The attacker chooses u from the set of all users U^t who are present on day t. For the attack he sets up a classifier with $|U^t|$ classes c (one for each user), and trains the classifier with the available instances x^t of all users from U^t (one instance per user). On the next day, the attacker tries to find the instance x_u^{t+1}, i.e. all the instances that are predicted to belong to class c_u are of interest. Ideally, only the correct instance x_u^{t+1} will be assigned to c_u.

Due to the peculiarities of the attacker's view there are more than the four canonical evaluation results (true positives, false positives, true negatives and false negatives) [33]. Table 2 contains an overview of our more differentiated evaluation scheme. The prediction of the classifier can either be *correct* $(1,2)$, *wrong-detectable* $(3,4)$ or *wrong-undetectable* $(5,6)$.

Evaluation Results. We iterate over all days and users and evaluate the prediction of the MNB classifier for the transformations presented in Section 3.3.

Table 3. Classification accuracy for attacker's view (AV) and simulation (SIM), i. e. the proportion of user sessions for which the classifier correctly and unambiguously predicted the correct class (1) or correctly predicted that the user did not participate on the second day (2).

	none	N	IDF	IDFN	TF	TFN	TFIDF	TFIDFN
(AV)	60.5 %	62.9 %	65.0 %	62.8 %	56.0 %	**73.1 %**	66.1 %	72.8 %
(SIM)	55.5 %	56.2 %	65.0 %	60.2 %	53.3 %	77.1 %	68.5 %	**80.1 %**

Each prediction is evaluated independently, i. e. the conceived attacker is stateless and does not change his behaviour based on the predictions on previous days. For each experiment we report the overall *classification accuracy*, i. e. the proportion of correct predictions (1, 2). An overall comparison of the various transformations is shown in the (AV) row in Table 3. Cosine normalisation (N) increases the accuracy of the classifier significantly when applied in combination with one of the other transformations. The TFN transformation leads to the highest number of correct predictions: 73.1% of all day-to-day links were correctly established, i. e. user u was either re-identified unambiguously (1) or the classifier correctly reported that u was not present on day $t + 1$ any more (2). Note that the utility of the IDF transformation is rather limited in the attacker's view scenario. This counterintuitive finding can be explained by the relatively small number of only 765 predictions in the attacker's view scenario.

While already this basic attack achieves respectable results, there is certainly room for improvements. We present only one of them here: *learning*. We have found that the accuracy of the classifier can be increased considerably, if the attacker is not stateless, but is allowed to "learn", i. e. he can add already predicted instances x_u^{t+1} to the set of training instances for user u, if the prediction *appears* to be correct (1,6). In the case of the MNB classifier and the TFN transformation, the proportion of *correct* decisions (accuracy) increased from 73.1 % to 77.6 %, the proportion of *detectable errors* decreased from 14.5% to 12.5 % and the proportion of *undetectable errors* decreased from 12.4 % to 9.8 %.

5.2   Simulations

The results obtained from the *attacker's view* experiments indicate that a central proxy can carry out the web user re-identification attack for small user groups like ours. Due to its dynamic nature, i. e. not all users having participated on all days (cf. Fig. 2a), the *attacker's view* is not very suitable for analysing influence factors that determine the effectiveness of the attack, though. Thus, we will resort to simulations, in which we set up well-defined and balanced scenarios, to gain further insights.

Each simulation experiment works on a random sample of training and test instances drawn from the whole dataset. For each user 10 pairs of training and testing sessions are drawn for each experiment (iterations). The properties of the pairs are controlled by a number of parameters. Only one parameter is varied in each experiment to analyse its influence. The varied parameters are:

- session duration in minutes (default: 1440, i. e. 1 day),
- number of simultaneous users (default: 28),
- offset between the last training session and the test session (default: the session duration, i. e. adjacent sessions) and
- number of consecutive training instances (default: 1).

The default setup simulates all 28 users concurrently surfing on 10 days (iterations), i. e. for each iteration there are 28 training sessions (1 for each user), each one capturing all requests of the user within one day. Training and test sessions are *not* drawn independently, though: for each user the random session selection process prefers training sessions, which have a (chronologically) immediately succeeding session for the respective user. The succeeding session will then be selected as the test session. This ensures that the parameter "offset between the last training and the test session" equals the session duration for all users. The classifier will be trained with the training sessions (which may in fact come from different days in our real-world dataset) and will have to make a prediction for each of the 28 test sessions. This training and prediction will be repeated for the 10 randomly drawn session pairs (iterations).

The simulation results are obtained by repeating each experiment 25 times and taking the average of the obtained accuracy. This approach incorporates a large proportion of the dataset in each experiment: the classifier makes $25 \cdot 10 \cdot 28 = 7000$ predictions per simulation experiment. The results for the application of the various text mining transformations are shown in the (SIM) row of Table 3. The TFIDFN transformation achieves slightly better results than the TFN transformation here. The results of all of the following simulations were obtained using the TFN transformation, though, which has lower computational costs and still offers comparable accuracy.

Evaluation Results. The results of the simulations are summarized in Fig. 3 for various session durations. Fig. 3a shows that the accuracy of the classifier decreases once session durations become shorter than one day (1440 minutes), which we found is due to the smaller amount of distinct sites and issued requests visited within them. Thus, the information amount available to the classifier decreases. The accuracy increases once again for short sessions below 30 minutes. This is partly due to users' activites spanning session boundaries, which increases the linkability of two adjacent sessions. Furthermore, accuracy increases with decreasing numbers of concurrent users (Fig. 3b), which explains the higher accuracy of the classifier for the attacker's view scenario.

Fig. 3c shows that the quality of the user profiles deteriorates only moderately over time. The waveform patterns in the plot for session durations of 1 and 3 hours have a periodicity of 24 hours. Thus, it is easier to link two sessions of a user if they are obtained at the same *time of day* on different days. Apparently, our users exhibit different behaviour at different times during the day.

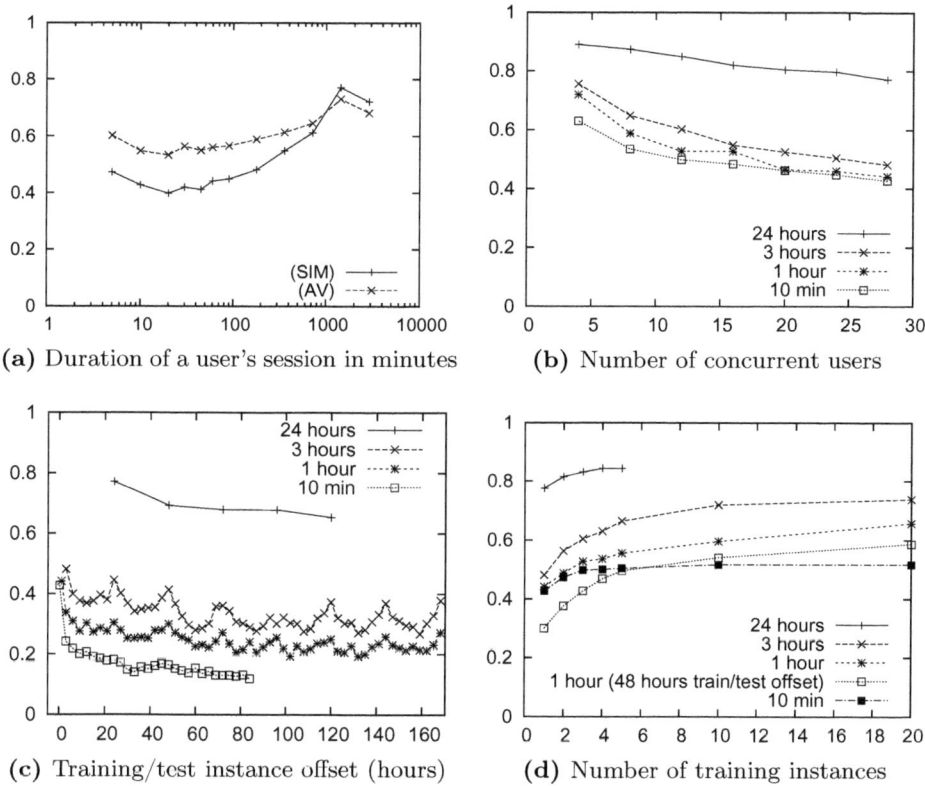

(a) Duration of a user's session in minutes

(b) Number of concurrent users

(c) Training/test instance offset (hours)

(d) Number of training instances

Fig. 3. Simulation results: influence of various parameters on proportion of correctly classified sessions (y-axis);

According to Fig. 3d the accuracy will increase if the attacker manages to obtain not only 1 but multiple consecutive training sessions of a given user or is able to correctly link multiple consecutive sessions of a user (cf. "learning" in Section 5.1). While the gain in accuracy caused by an additional training instance diminishes quite fast for immediately adjacent sessions, multiple training instances can be very useful when it comes to test instances whose offset to the training instance is larger. This becomes evident in Fig. 3d by comparing the slopes of the two curves supplied for 1-hour sessions with training/test offsets of 1 hour and 48 hours. For the latter the accuracy increases more rapidly for up to 5 additional training instances.

5.3   Linkability Metric

We analyzed the dataset for peculiarities that can explain the effectiveness of the classifier. Therefore, we constructed a numerical *host linkability* metric $L \in [0; 1]$ that captures the degree of re-identifiability of a user u that is caused by accessing

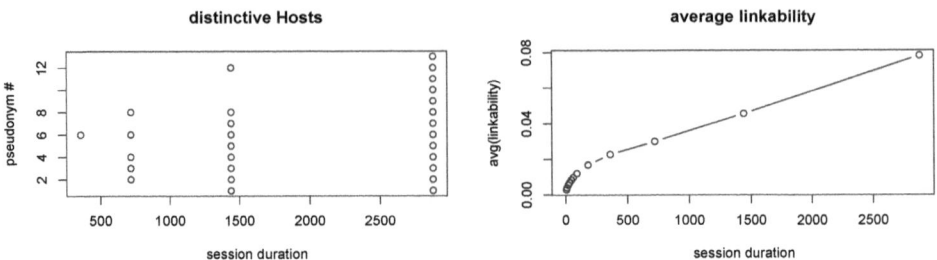

Fig. 4. Distinctive hosts and average linkability for various session durations

a specific host h. With this metric we can uncover hosts that almost immediately identify users once they request a website from them (cf. also [17, p. 62] for a different approach). Considering the multiset of website requests R^u of user u, the multiset of website requests R_h involving host h, the set of sessions S^u of user u and the set of sessions S_h involving host h, we obtain the host linkability as follows:

$$L(h, u) = \frac{|R^u \cap R_h|}{|R_h|} \cdot \frac{|S^u \cap S_h|}{|S^u|}$$

In words: A host h allows for immediate re-identification of a user u, if h is only accessed by u and if u visits h in each of his sessions; this is expressed by a host linkability value of $L(h, u) = 1$. If an attacker knew the hosts with $L = 1$ – we call them *distinctive hosts* – he wouldn't have to rely on our classification technique but could directly re-identify the respective users. We found 17 distinctive hosts in our dataset for nine users with a session time of 1440 minutes (cf. Fig 4). If a host is *distinctive* for a user for a session duration d_a, it will also be distinctive for this user for all session durations $d_b > d_a$. With decreasing session duration the linkability values for all hosts are decreasing as well, i. e. it is less likely to encounter a distinctive host in shorter sessions.

6   Countermeasures

A user can blur his behavioral profile by distributing his web requests over multiple (non-colluding) proxy servers (similar to the ideas proposed by Olivier [26]). A single server will then only see a subset of the requests of the user. There are many conceivable variants of such a distribution scheme: e. g. based on time (switching the server at regular intervals) or based on destination (all requests for hosts (h_1, h_2, h_3) are sent to server s_1, requests for hosts (h_4, h_5, h_6) are sent to a different server s_2. We leave the design and evaluation of various strategies open for future work. Instead we only analyse a basic strategy, which may serve as a baseline for benchmarking: randomly distributing all the requests of a user over multiple proxies. According to the results for 1, 10, 20 and 50 servers (cf. Fig. 5a), this strategy is effective, but not very efficient.

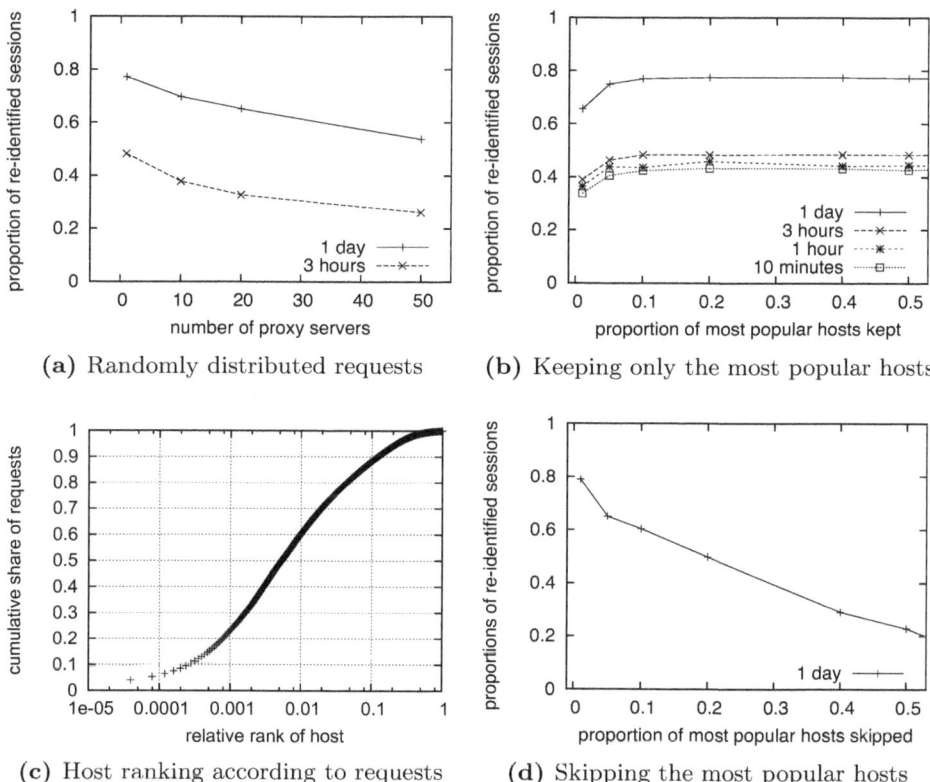

(a) Randomly distributed requests   (b) Keeping only the most popular hosts

(c) Host ranking according to requests   (d) Skipping the most popular hosts

Fig. 5. Effectiveness of countermeasures

Removing Requests from Log Files. In principle the web user re-identification attack is also applicable to log files of proxy servers that are shared or publicly available. There is a number of obfuscation tools that help to protect the privacy of the users whose requests are contained in the logs. Some tools (such as *tcpmkpub*, *tcpdpriv* or the Perl module *NetAddr::IP::Obfuscate*) rely on a consistent hashing or obfuscating scheme of IP addresses, which ensure that a given input address is always mapped to the same obfuscated output address. Thus, our web user re-identification attack can be applied to track users with dynamic IP addresses in such log files without modification. It could also be applied, if the proxy operator changed the mapping scheme from time to time.

In order to counter the attack a proxy operator may come to the conclusion to only share requests to the most popular hosts, which are not supposed to convey any personally identifying information. To evaluate the validity of this assumption we have repeated the simulation, restricting it to the most popular 1 %, 5 %, 10 %, 20 %, 40 % and 50 % of the hosts according to a descending ranking of hosts, which is based on the total number of requests they attracted (see Fig. 5c). The somewhat surprising results indicate that this approach cannot prevent the user re-identification attack: the classifier can still link more than

65 % of the 1-day sessions (cf. Fig. 5b) if instances are only based on the 1 % (= 251) most popular hosts. Due to the long-tailed distribution of access frequencies the log files contain only 60 % of the total requests in this case (cf. Fig. 5c). The utility of this countermeasure degrades fast: if 10 % or more of the most popular hosts are kept in the log file, accuracy values will not be affected significantly any more. Classification accuracy is also only moderately affected if the most popular hosts are *skipped* (cf. Fig. 5d): training the classifier on 1-day sessions after having removed the 50 % most popular hosts (which is equivalent to skipping 99.91 % of all requests!) still results in an accuracy of 22.9 %. Whether log files that have been stripped in such a way are of any practical use any more, certainly depends on the particular application at hand.

Anonymization Services. Instead of distributing their requests over multiple proxy servers, users can also rely on anonymisation services like Tor or JonDonym. These services prohibit eavesdropping by local adversaries and consequently also protect against any re-identification attacks carried out by them. The use of anonymisation services may also introduce new risks, though: in mix networks the exit node learns the true destination hosts as requested by its users. The Tor network uses circuits, which relay a user's traffic over a single exit router. After 10 minutes a circuit is abandoned and a new circuit with another exit node is set up. If a Tor user relayed all web requests over a single exit node (which is the default as of now), the exit node could apply our methodology to construct user session and create a MNB classifier to re-identify users. Collaborating exit nodes could share such profiles to track users across multiple exit nodes, which would seriously degrade their privacy. The attack could be prevented, if the Tor client routed web traffic over multiple exit nodes concurrently.

7   Discussion

Due to the limited scope of our study, we cannot precisely assess the real threat of user re-identification on the web. The small number of users may limit the generalisability of our results, but not of our methodology. We are already in the process of applying it to large DNS log files with several thousand users. Even for this different, more difficult problem our first results are promising: we are able to re-identify up to 50 % of the users about 80 % of the time.

For the purpose of evaluation we modelled a *user session* as a rigid time span (e. g. 10 minutes or 24 hours). As a matter of fact, our evaluation tools will erroneously distribute contiguous requests across two sessions, if the true user session crosses our session boundaries, which decreases the difficulty of the classification problem – at least for immediately adjacent sessions. This bias could be cured with a more realistic session splitting method, e. g. by taking into account the results of [6,30], which empirically derive actual session boundaries.

The presented basic form of the attack can not only be carried out by proxy servers or DNS servers, but by any eavesdropper in general. We are aware of the fact that we disregard promising pieces of information, which may be available to some attackers, such as the whole URL or request timing. Web proxies could also inspect the contents of the HTTP messages for identifying information, e. g. usernames and street addresses. While our methodology can be extended to support such attributes, we believe that in reality the biggest improvements will stem from the inclusion of context knowledge: a user who just received his driver's license might visit many hosts like *myfirstcar.com* and *firstcar.com* over a period of several days. Future work might take this into account by employing a semantic model to group hosts according to activities or actual interests.

Finally, we want to point out that our scenario in mind, a closed user group using a single proxy server, allows us to make a closed-world assumption, i. e. each instance belongs to a user of that group. Consequently, our classifier will output a prediction for each and every test instance no matter how likely it is. In some real-world situations, e. g. tracking one user among thousands of unknown users, this approach will cause a false alarm for the majority of instances. Adapting the methodology to cope with such scenarios (e. g. by using a probability threshold or reject class) is certainly an interesting area for future work.

8   Conclusion

Using a privacy-preservingly collected real-world dataset we have demonstrated that an adversary can re-identify web users based on their past browsing behaviour. Thus, malicious providers of (small-scale) web proxies may be able to track their users. Profile degradation over time is only moderate and it can be alleviated using multiple training instances. According to our results, counter-measures such as distributing web requests over multiple proxies can reduce the accuracy of our attack, but they come at a considerable cost.

Our technique is based on the observed access frequencies of hosts. It does not depend on any timing information or context knowledge, and it is totally agnostic of the type of host or the actual contents retrieved. Instead, we exploit the diversity on the World Wide Web: specific user interests (such as reading news or social networking) can be satisfied at a large number of different sites, which is reflected by the long-tailed distribution of access frequencies. Consequently, web user re-identification may even succeed for users with very similar interests – as long as they have a distinct preference regarding the websites where they pursue them.

Acknowledgments. This work has been partially sponsored and supported by the European Union EFRE project. The authors are grateful to the participants of the study who contributed their web requests. This paper has benefitted from fruitful discussions with Jacob Appelbaum, Karl-Peter Fuchs, Nico Görnitz, Konrad Rieck, Florian Scheuer, Rolf Wendolsky, Benedikt Westermann and from helpful comments by the anonymous reviewers.

References

1. Adamic, L., Huberman, B.: Zipf's Law and the Internet. Glottometrics 3(1), 143–150 (2002)
2. Baeza-Yates, R., Ribeiro-Neto, B.: Modern information retrieval. Addision Wesley, New York (1999)
3. Barbaro, M., Zeller, T.: A Face is Exposed for AOL Searcher No. 4417749. The New York Times, August 9 (2006)
4. Breslau, L., Cue, P., Cao, P., Fan, L., Phillips, G., Shenker, S.: Web Caching and Zipf-like Distributions: Evidence and Implications. In: INFOCOM, pp. 126–134 (1999)
5. Brickell, J., Shmatikov, V.: The cost of privacy: destruction of data-mining utility in anonymized data publishing. In: KDD 2008: Proceeding of the 14th ACM SIGKDD International Conference on Knowledge Discovery and Data Mining, pp. 70–78. ACM, New York (2008)
6. Catledge, L.D., Pitkow, J.E.: Characterizing Browsing Behaviors on the World-Wide Web. Georgia Institute of Technology (1995)
7. Coull, S.E., Collins, M.P., Wright, C.V., Monrose, F., Reiter, M.K.: On Web Browsing Privacy in Anonymized NetFlows. In: Proceedings of the 16th USENIX Security Symposium, Boston, MA (August 2007)
8. Coull, S.E., Wright, C.V., Keromytisz, A.D., Monrose, F., Reiter, M.K.: Taming the devil: Techniques for evaluating anonymized network data. In: Proceedings of the 15th Network and Distributed Systems Security Symposium (2008)
9. Coull, S.E., Wright, C.V., Monrose, F., Collins, M.P., Reiter, M.K.: Playing devil's advocate: Inferring sensitive information from anonymized network traces. In: Proceedings of the Network and Distributed System Security Symposium, pp. 35–47 (2007)
10. Crovella, M.E., Bestavros, A.: Self-similarity in World Wide Web traffic: evidence and possible causes. IEEE/ACM Trans. Netw. 5(6), 835–846 (1997)
11. Eckersley, P.: How Unique Is Your Web Browser? Technical report, Electronig Frontier Foundation (2009)
12. Erman, J., Mahanti, A., Arlitt, M.: Internet Traffic Identification using Machine Learning. In: Proceedings of IEEE Global Telecommunications Conference (GLOBECOM), San Francisco, CA, USA, pp. 1–6 (November 2006)
13. Herrmann, D., Wendolsky, R., Federrath, H.: Website fingerprinting: attacking popular privacy enhancing technologies with the multinomial naïve-bayes classifier. In: CCSW 2009: Proceedings of the 2009 ACM Workshop on Cloud Computing Security, pp. 31–42. ACM, New York (2009)
14. Kellar, M., Watters, C., Shepherd, M.: A field study characterizing Web-based information-seeking tasks. Journal of the American Society for Information Science and Technology 58(7), 999–1018 (2007)
15. Koukis, D., Antonatos, S., Anagnostakis, K.G.: On the Privacy Risks of Publishing Anonymized IP Network Traces. In: Leitold, H., Markatos, E.P. (eds.) CMS 2006. LNCS, vol. 4237, pp. 22–32. Springer, Heidelberg (2006)
16. Kumpošt, M.: Data Preparation for User Profiling from Traffic Log. In: The International Conference on Emerging Security Information, Systems, and Technologies, pp. 89–94 (2007)

17. Kumpošt, M.: Context Information and user profiling. PhD thesis, Faculty of Informatics, Masaryk University, Czech Republic (2009)
18. Kumpošt, M., Matyáš, V.: User Profiling and Re-identification: Case of University-Wide Network Analysis. In: Fischer-Hübner, S., Lambrinoudakis, C., Pernul, G. (eds.) TrustBus 2009. LNCS, vol. 5695, pp. 1–10. Springer, Heidelberg (2009)
19. Liberatore, M., Levine, B.N.: Inferring the Source of Encrypted HTTP Connections. In: CCS 2006: Proceedings of the 13th ACM Conference on Computer and Communications Security, pp. 255–263. ACM Press, New York (2006)
20. Malin, B., Airoldi, E.: The Effects of Location Access Behavior on Re-identification Risk in a Distributed Environment. In: Privacy Enhancing Technologies, pp. 413–429 (2006)
21. Manning, C.D., Raghavan, P., Schütze, H.: Introduction to Information Retrieval. Cambridge University Press, Cambridge (2008)
22. Moore, A.W., Zuev, D.: Internet traffic classification using bayesian analysis techniques. In: SIGMETRICS 2005: Proceedings of the 2005 ACM SIGMETRICS International Conference on Measurement and Modeling of Computer Systems, pp. 50–60. ACM Press, New York (2005)
23. Narayanan, A., Shmatikov, V.: Robust de-anonymization of large sparse datasets. In: IEEE Symposium on Security and Privacy, pp. 111–125 (2008)
24. Obendorf, H., Weinreich, H., Herder, E., Mayer, M.: Web Page Revisitation Revisited: Implications of a Long-term Click-stream Study of Browser Usage. In: CHI 2007, pp. 597–606. ACM Press (May 2007)
25. Ohm, P.: Broken Promises of Privacy: Responding to the Surprising Failure of Anonymization. In: Social Science Research Network Working Paper Series (August 2009)
26. Olivier, M.S.: Distributed Proxies for Browsing Privacy: a Simulation of Flocks. In: SAICSIT '05: Proceedings of the 2005 Annual Research Conference of the South African Institute of Computer Scientists and Information Technologists on IT Research in Developing Countries, pp. 104–112. South African Institute for Computer Scientists and Information Technologists, Republic of South Africa (2005)
27. Padmanabhan, B., Yang, Y.: Clickprints on the Web: Are there signatures in Web Browsing Data? Working Paper Series (October 2006)
28. Pang, J., Greenstein, B., Gummadi, R., Seshan, S., Wetherall, D.: 802.11 user fingerprinting. In: MobiCom 2007: Proceedings of the 13th Annual ACM International Conference on Mobile Computing and Networking, pp. 99–110. ACM, New York (2007)
29. Pang, R., Allman, M., Paxson, V., Lee, J.: The devil and packet trace anonymization. SIGCOMM Comput. Commun. Rev. 36(1), 29–38 (2006)
30. Srivastava, J., Cooley, R., Deshpande, M., Tan, P.-N.: Web usage mining: discovery and applications of usage patterns from Web data. SIGKDD Explor. Newsl. 1(2), 12–23 (2000)
31. Sweeney, L.: k-anonymity: A model for protecting privacy. International Journal of Uncertainty Fuzziness and Knowledge Based Systems 10(5), 557–570 (2002)
32. Williams, N., Zander, S., Armitage, G.: A preliminary performance comparison of five machine learning algorithms for practical IP traffic flow classification. SIG-COMM Comput. Commun. Rev. 36(5), 5–16 (2006)
33. Witten, I.H., Frank, E.: Data Mining. Practical Machine Learning Tools and Techniques. Elsevier, San Francisco (2005)

34. Wondracek, G., Holz, T., Kirda, E., Kruegel, C.: A Practical Attack to De-Anonymize Social Network Users, `iseclab.org`
35. Yang, Y.: Web user behavioral profiling for user identification. Decision Support Systems 49, 261–271 (2010)
36. Yang, Y.C., Padmanabhan, B.: Toward user patterns for online security: Observation time and online user identification. Decision Support Systems 48, 548–558 (2008)
37. Zipf, G.K.: The psycho-biology of language. An introduction to dynamic philology, 2nd edn. M.I.T. Press, Cambridge (1968)
38. Zuev, D., Moore, A.W.: Traffic Classification using a Statistical Approach. In: Dovrolis, C. (ed.) PAM 2005. LNCS, vol. 3431, pp. 321–324. Springer, Heidelberg (2005)

A Framework for the Modular Specification and Orchestration of Authorization Policies

Jason Crampton[1] and Michael Huth[2]

[1] Information Security Group, Royal Holloway, University of London
jason.crampton@rhul.ac.uk
[2] Department of Computing, Imperial College London, United Kingdom
M.Huth@imperial.ac.uk

Abstract. Many frameworks for defining authorization policies fail to make a clear distinction between policy and state. We believe this distinction to be a fundamental requirement for the construction of scalable, distributed authorization services. In this paper, we introduce a formal framework for the definition of authorization policies, which we use to construct the policy authoring language APOL. This framework makes the required distinction between policy and state, and APOL permits the specification of complex policy orchestration patterns even in the presence of policy gaps and conflicts. A novel aspect of the language is the use of a switch operator for policy orchestration, which can encode the commonly used rule- and policy-combining algorithms of existing authorization languages. We define denotational and operational semantics for APOL and then extend our framework with statically typed methods for policy orchestration, develop tools for policy analysis, and show how that analysis can improve the precision of static typing rules.

1 Introduction

One of the fundamental security services in computer systems is *access control*, a mechanism for constraining the interaction between (authenticated) users and protected resources. Generally, access control is implemented by an authorization service, which includes an *authorization decision function* (ADF) for deciding whether a user request to access a resource (an *access request*, which we abbreviate by *request* henceforth) should be permitted or not. The output of an authorization decision function is usually determined by evaluating the request with respect to *authorization state*.

The protection matrix [14] is one of the earliest techniques for encoding authorization state. It assumes the existence of a set of subjects S (those entities that generate requests), a set of objects O (those entities to which access is requested), and a set of actions A (the types of interactions with objects that subjects may request). Mathematically, the protection matrix M is a total function $S \times O \to \mathbb{P}(A)$ where $M[s, o]$ is the set of interactions that subject s is authorized to engage in with object o. A request is modeled as a triple (s, o, a) and is authorized if and only if $a \in M[s, o]$. This explicit enumeration of all authorized requests in the authorization state is appealing in its simplicity. The authorization *policy*, which is implemented by the ADF, is to authorize a request if it is listed in the authorization state.

T. Aura, K. Järvinen, and K. Nyberg (Eds.): NordSec 2010, LNCS 7127, pp. 155–170, 2012.

In recent years, this enumeration of authorized requests in authorization state has been refined, with authorized requests being grouped together into "targets". Authorization state can then be seen as a set of targets $\{T_1, \ldots, T_n\}$ where $T_i \subseteq S \times O \times A$. Typically, a request (s, o, a) is authorized if and only if $(s, o, a) \in T_i$ for some i. Access control lists (ACL) are one obvious example of this approach, where each target T_i is associated with a particular object o_i.

We may also extend what we call "*target-based*" authorization state by associating explicit deny and allow responses with targets, so that exceptions to requests authorized elsewhere in the authorization state can be articulated. Given an extended set of targets $\{(T_1, \text{allow}), (T_2, \text{deny})\}$, e.g., a request (s, o, a) is authorized if and only if $(s, o, a) \in T_1$ and $(s, o, a) \notin T_2$. Here we see that the authorization state may not be consistent: T_1 may allow a request, while T_2 may deny it. Most authorization frameworks provide a number of different ways of resolving such *conflicts* (such as "allow-overrides" or "deny-overrides"). Conversely, the authorization state could contain *gaps* and neither allows nor denies certain requests.

The literature includes many target-based specification languages for defining authorization state (e.g. [5,10,15]) – notably XACML [18] – and target-based policy algebras (e.g. [2,6,21]). In the case of XACML, we would define the authorization policy to be the specification of the policy decision point (PDP) – the algorithm that processes what the XACML standard refers to as "policies". Different implementations of the PDP may yield different authorized requests for the same "policies".

Motivation. Much recent work on access control has blurred the distinction between what we call *authorization state* and *authorization policy*. Consider the simple security property p_{SS}, defined in the Bell-LaPadula access control model [4], which says that subject s is authorized to read object o only if $\lambda(s) \geq \lambda(o)$, where $\lambda : S \cup O \to L$ is a labeling function and L is a lattice of security labels. The *policy* is that a subject is authorized to read an object only if its security classification is at least as high as that of the requested object. The *state* is defined by L and λ. To reinforce this distinction, suppose that $\lambda(o) = l_1$ at time t_1, and subsequently the contents of o are de-classified so that $\lambda(o) = l_2 < l_1$ at time $t_2 > t_1$. Now, for a subject s with $\lambda(s) = l_2$ at times t_1 and t_2, a request to read o is denied at t_1 and allowed at t_2. Thus, the decision depends on the request, the authorization state (λ is mutable), and the immutable policy ($\lambda(s) \geq \lambda(o)$).

Target-based "policies", however, do not make this distinction. The confusion arises because the protection matrix policy is to test for membership of a request in a set encoded by the protection matrix, and so the policy itself has become implicit. Although it is clearly possible to express most authorization policies using a protection matrix – by simply encoding all authorized triples in the matrix – such representations are very inefficient and "brittle": since state and policy are encoded in the matrix it will be necessary to change the matrix to re-encode the policy every time there is a state change. To encode the simple security property above, e.g., any change to $\lambda(o)$ requires adding action *read* into entry $M[s', o]$ for all subject s' with $l_2 \leq \lambda(s')$ and $l_1 \not\leq \lambda(s')$.

The evaluation of authorization policies may also be strongly dependent on system state. The Chinese wall policy [7], e.g., is a separation of duty policy designed to prevent conflict of interest. The evaluation of this policy requires historical information about which requests have previously been made and authorized. It is not clear how to represent or evaluate such policies using target-based policies. Similarly, stack-walking algorithms for evaluating requests in a virtual machine environment require information about the run-time state in order to determine whether a request is authorized [13].

Target-based "policies" encode authorization state and policy, so every instance of a target-based "policy" has to re-encode the semantics of the policy it seeks to enforce. In this sense, target-based policies are analogous to monolithic programs that neither benefit from the reuse of already existing authorization decision functions, nor cleanly separate authorization state from those policies. We thus believe that there is great value in a framework that supports the *modular* specification and realization of authorization policies, and that also provides for separation of state and policy.

The framework we propose has two types of policies: *decision policies* and *orchestration policies*. Decision policies are similar to Boolean functions, whereas orchestration policies are similar to policy combining algorithms in XACML [18] and operators in policy algebras (e.g. [6,19]).

Decision policies take parts of the request or authorization state (or both) as input and make either a Boolean decision or return a third value $\perp$, indicating that the policy is unable to provide a *conclusive* decision. A policy may return $\perp$ because

- the request either does not have the expected form for successful processing (e.g. the action is *delete* but needs to be *read* for p_{SS}), or
- the request cannot be evaluated in the authorization state (e.g. there may not be an ACL for the requested object).

Orchestration policies take other policies as input. We show that all possible orchestration requirements, even in the presence of inconsistency or lack of information, can be programmed with a single 4-case *switch operator*. Use of this operator should appeal to people familiar with such statements in mainstream programming languages. Indeed, we develop a simple typed, modular programming language in which decision and orchestration policies are distinguished by types and are declared and enforceable as parameterized methods.

Contributions. We develop a formal framework for authorization policies in which base policies encapsulate domain-specific aspects and offer an abstract interface for orchestration; all possible orchestration patterns for base policies are supported in the presence of conflict or lack of information; and authorization state and policy specifications are cleanly separated, facilitating maintenance and reuse. Policy orchestration is achieved with a switch operator that is formally analyzable and functionally complete for policy coordination (including conflict resolution). We add typed, parameterized methods to that core policy language. This not only facilitates reuse and modular analysis of policies, but these types and their analysis can also certify important run-time behavior of policy evaluation.

2   Authorization Using Trees

We first fix terminology and provide an overview of our approach. We then describe policy orchestration before introducing *policy trees* as formal foundations for APOL.

Overview. We assume the existence of three types of entities: policy enforcement points, policy orchestration points and policy decision points.[1] As in the XACML architecture, a policy enforcement point (PEP) is responsible for ensuring that (i) every request is evaluated to determine whether it is authorized and (ii) that the request is only allowed to proceed (i.e. granted) if it is authorized.

Unlike in XACML, a policy decision point (PDP) in our architecture exists to determine whether a request is authorized by a base policy (defined below). We introduce policy orchestration points (POP) to forward requests to PDPs or other POPs for evaluation. The POP combines the decisions returned in response to those requests, according to the orchestration pattern defined for that POP. The POP then returns a decision to the PEP (or a higher level POP).

Each base policy has its own PDP. Complex authorization policies are constructed by orchestrating base policies. Hence, the authorization architecture required to evaluate an orchestrated policy will be dependent on the policy. In this respect, our architecture is quite different from existing approaches, such as XACML, which assume a *single* PEP and a *single* PDP – reflecting that the policy in target-based approaches is implicit (and is based on membership of the request in one or more targets). Figure 1(a) illustrates schematically an example of this policy evaluation architecture. Henceforth, we will blur the distinction between a PDP and the base policy it enforces and use the two terms interchangeably.

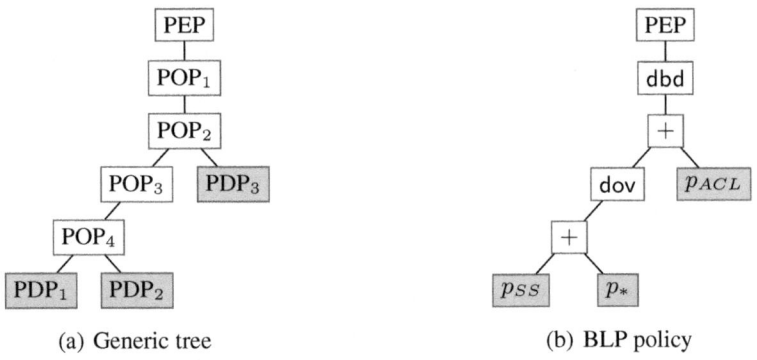

(a) Generic tree   (b) BLP policy

Fig. 1. Examples of policy evaluation trees

We assume that base policies are invoked by a policy orchestration point. A base policy returns an authorization decision based on the request *and* the current authorization state of the system. Returning to the example of the simple security property p_{SS} introduced in Section 1, informally speaking and writing σ_i to denote the state at time t_i, we have $p_{SS}((s, o, \textit{read}), \sigma_1) =$ deny and $p_{SS}((s, o, \textit{read}), \sigma_2) =$ allow. We model base policies as (partial) Boolean functions and authorization state is an input to a policy. This separation of concern allows us to decouple policy semantics from the specification of authorization state, in contrast to existing approaches such as XACML.

---

[1] We prefer this terminology to authorization enforcement function etc., as it is widely used and reflects the fact that access control in our setting is policy-based.

A POP or a PDP does not necessarily take a request of the form (s, o, a), or similar, as input. Consider, for example, an authorization service that implements a policy p_{ACL} that decides requests on the basis of membership in an ACL. Then the PEP may well receive a request of the form (s, o, a), but it actually passes s, a and the ACL for o to the PDP.[2] Hence, all requests of form (s, o, a) can be processed without error (assuming that o is a valid object identifier) and are processed in the same way. In contrast, p_{SS} does not process requests in this uniform manner: it is "silent" on the evaluation of *write* requests.

The ACL, however, is part of the authorization state, so policy p_{ACL} cannot be used to evaluate request (s, o, a) if it is not possible to locate and retrieve the ACL for object o. Indeed, the evaluation of all but the simplest policies (such as those that authorize all requests) will require authorization state as input, and is therefore acutely sensitive to the availability and consistency of such state. One cannot evaluate the simple security property p_{SS} if, e.g., $\lambda(s)$ is not available or does not belong to the security lattice L.

In summary: there will be requests for which a policy does not return a conclusive decision, simply because the policy is not designed to decide certain requests for particular authorization states; in addition, many policies cannot return a conclusive decision if there is incomplete knowledge of authorization state.

Base Policies. Base policies have total functions of type $\mathsf{Req} \times \Sigma \rightarrow \{0, 1, \bot\}$ as semantics, where Req is the set of requests and Σ the set of authorization states. Mathematically, a base policy is (semantically) equivalent to a partial function $b : \mathsf{Req} \times \Sigma \rightarrow \{0, 1\}$ that has been extended to a total function $\widehat{b} : \mathsf{Req} \times \Sigma \rightarrow \{\bot, 0, 1\}$ in the obvious way.

The intuition and assumption is that a base policy b returns a *conclusive* decision (0 for prohibitions or 1 for authorizations) for all well-formed requests as input that can be properly evaluated in the current state. Base policy p_{ACL}, e.g., makes a conclusive decision for requests (s, o, a) if object o has an ACL, and returns $\bot$ if o has no ACL. We can express the simple security property and the *-property [4] as the following base policies, where σ is understood to include an encoding of the security function λ.

$$p_{SS}((s, o, a), \sigma) = \begin{cases} 1 & \text{if } \lambda(s) \geq \lambda(o) \text{ and } a \text{ is read} \\ 0 & \text{if } \lambda(s) \not\geq \lambda(o) \text{ and } a \text{ is read} \\ \bot & \text{otherwise} \end{cases}$$

$$p_{*}((s, o, a), \sigma) = \begin{cases} 1 & \text{if } \lambda(s) \leq \lambda(o) \text{ and } a \text{ is write} \\ 0 & \text{if } \lambda(s) \not\leq \lambda(o) \text{ and } a \text{ is write} \\ \bot & \text{otherwise} \end{cases}$$

We work with a set of *base policies* $\mathcal{B}$ that have the above type and from which more complex policies are orchestrated. Actual members of $\mathcal{B}$ will depend on context and requirements. We might have $\mathcal{B} = \{p_{ACL}, p_{SS}, p_{*}\}$, for example. Base policies also fit

---

[2] The request received by the PEP may also be called an *application* request or *native* request, and the one passed to the PDP by the PEP may be called a *decision* or *authorization* request.

nicely with a view of authorization as a service, where the focus is on the orchestration of base policies informed by the known and trusted behavior of these base policies.

Joining Policies. Policy orchestration may be useful where policies are developed independently and their respective results need to be combined before reaching an authorization decision. Alternatively, we may simply need to construct authorization policies out of simpler sub-policies. The BLP model, for example, "orchestrates" three policies: the simple security property, the *-property and the discretionary security property (which requires that the request be authorized by a protection matrix M) [4].

Many existing languages, therefore, include the possibility of combining the decisions returned by two policies, and our language is no exception. We write $p_1 + p_2$ to denote the *join* of p_1 and p_2, and define

$$(p_1 + p_2)(r, \sigma) = p_1(r, \sigma) \oplus p_2(r, \sigma),$$

where $\oplus$ is a binary relation on $\{\bot, 0, 1, \top\}$ defined by the following table.

$\oplus$	$\bot$	0	1	$\top$
$\bot$	$\bot$	0	1	$\top$
0	0	0	$\top$	$\top$
1	1	$\top$	1	$\top$
$\top$	$\top$	$\top$	$\top$	$\top$

A similar join operator was proposed and used in the work of [8,9], but for policies of different types. We write $\mathcal{P}$ for the set of policies orchestrated from base policies in $\mathcal{B}$.

The orchestration of base policies means that policies in general have a richer type, as total functions p: Req $\times \Sigma \rightarrow \{\bot, 0, 1, \top\}$. By abuse of notation, we may write 0 and 1, respectively, for the constant policies $(r, \sigma) \mapsto 0$, and $(r, \sigma) \mapsto 1$. We also write 1_T, where $T \subseteq$ Req, to denote the base policy that returns 1 if $r \in T$ and 0 otherwise.

The Switch Operator. Many policy algebras and policy languages define ways of resolving gaps ($\bot$) and conflicts ($\top$) in policies as they occur [6,21], thereby reducing the range of all policies to some subset of $\{\bot, 0, 1, \top\}$. Reducing the range to $\{\bot, 0, 1\}$, e.g., removes conflicts, and reducing the range to $\{0, 1, \top\}$ removes gaps. XACML, e.g., uses *rule-combining* and *policy-combining algorithms* to remove conflicts [18].

We introduce the *switch* policy operator, which can be used *inter alia* to remove gaps and conflicts. Informally, this operator is a total function of type $\mathcal{P}^5 \rightarrow \mathcal{P}$, where the decision computed by evaluating the first policy determines which of the other four policies should be evaluated to obtain the overall decision. More formally, we have:

Definition 1. *Let* p, $q_\bot$, q_0, q_1 *and* $q_\top$ *be policies. Then the formal expression* $(p : q_\bot, q_0, q_1, q_\top)$ *is a policy with* switch policy p *such that for all* $(r, \sigma) \in$ Req $\times \Sigma$,

$$(p : q_\bot, q_0, q_1, q_\top)(r, \sigma) \stackrel{\text{def}}{=} \begin{cases} q_\bot(r, \sigma) & \text{if } p(r, \sigma) = \bot, \\ q_0(r, \sigma) & \text{if } p(r, \sigma) = 0, \\ q_1(r, \sigma) & \text{if } p(r, \sigma) = 1, \\ q_\top(r, \sigma) & \text{if } p(r, \sigma) = \top. \end{cases} \tag{1}$$

The switch operator is surprisingly versatile. We now describe some of its more immediate applications. We can define a policy $!p$ that reverses those decisions for which p is conclusive, and a policy (p/F) where F filters policy p as follows:

$$!p \stackrel{\text{def}}{=} (p : \bot, 1, 0, \top) \tag{2}$$

$$(p/F) \stackrel{\text{def}}{=} (1_F : \%, \bot, p, \%) \tag{3}$$

Since 1_F cannot output $\bot$ or $\top$, we use the reserved symbol $\%$ to denote "dead code", policies that cannot be reached by the switch operator. In particular, we write $\%$ for $q_\top$ whenever the switch policy p is a base policy (and so cannot produce $\top$ as a decision).

Policy p/F models the *if* operator of [8,9] where base policy F models what is called an "access predicate" in those papers. We may think of F as a filter and of p as the filtered policy. Indeed, if p is the constant 0 or 1 policy, p/F models an XACML rule with target F and effect p: policy expression $(1_F : \%, \bot, 0, \%)$, for example, encodes an XACML rule with target F and effect deny.

We may also express the join operator $p_1 + p_2$ (introduced above) using the switch operator:

$$(p_1 + p_2) \stackrel{\text{def}}{=} (p_1 : p_2, q_0, q_1, \top) \tag{4}$$

where $q_0 = (p_2 : 0, 0, \top, \top)$ and $q_1 = (p_2 : 1, \top, 1, \top)$. Moreover, all the usual policy modifiers can be expressed using the switch operator. We have, for example,

$$\mathsf{dov}(p) = (p : \bot, 0, 1, 0) \qquad \mathsf{aov}(p) = (p : \bot, 0, 1, 1) \qquad \mathsf{agr}(p) = (p : \bot, 0, 1, \bot)$$
$$\mathsf{dbd}(p) = (p : 0, 0, 1, \top) \qquad \mathsf{abd}(p) = (p : 1, 0, 1, \top)$$

where: dov denotes "deny-overrides; dbd denotes "deny-by-default"; aov denotes "allow-overrides"; abd denotes "allow-by-default"; and policy $\mathsf{agr}(p)$ returns the same decision as p if p returns a conclusive decision and returns $\bot$ otherwise. Most of these constructions are supported in XACML; agr, however, is not.

Clearly the switch operator provides a very economical and uniform way of specifying a wide variety of orchestration patterns. For example, we can easily specify an orchestration aed ("allow-overrides-else-deny") that returns 1 whenever p does and returns 0 otherwise: namely $\mathsf{aed}(p) = (p : 0, 0, 1, 1)$.

The switch statement $(p : p', 0, 1, p')$ is the policy that returns whatever policy p returns when p returns a conclusive decision, and returns whatever policy p' returns otherwise. In other words, $(p : p', 0, 1, p')$ is a "first-applicable" binary policy operator, commonly used to evaluate firewall rule-sets. Finally, one can also program "majority-out-of-n" for any odd natural number $n > 2$ with nested switch operators.

The policy $q_\top$ in (1) can be seen as a *conflict handler* for the switch policy p. The choice of this handler depends on the context within which $q_\top$ itself is orchestrated. For example, if the switch statement for $q_\top$ is the outermost policy, a conservative approach would make it always prohibit all requests. But $q_\top$ may have negative polarity (with respect to applications of $!$ above) as a sub-policy within an orchestration and so prohibiting all requests may be unwise. Polarity issues aside, $q_\top$ may be non-constant since it could make its decision depend on further switch statements that try to differentiate the source of conflict – a common idiom in programming with exceptions. In this context we note that the join operator distributes through all policies q_v in (1), but not through the switch policy p.

Example 1. We can orchestrate the full policy defined in the BLP model as

$$p_{\mathsf{BLP}} = \mathsf{dbd}(\mathsf{dov}(p_{\mathsf{SS}} + p_*) + p_{\mathsf{ACL}}).^3$$

Figure 1(b) shows the policy's evaluation architecture. An alternative, and perhaps more natural, orchestration can be defined using the switch operator:

$$p_{\mathsf{BLP}} = (p_{\mathsf{SS}} + p_* : \bot, 0, p_{\mathsf{ACL}}, 0)$$

Writing $p_{\mathsf{IF}} = \mathsf{dov}(p_{\mathsf{SS}} + p_*)$ to denote the *information flow* policy of the BLP model, we have $p_{\mathsf{BLP}} = \mathsf{dbd}(p_{\mathsf{IF}} + p_{\mathsf{ACL}})$. We may then view p_{IF} as a base policy since any conflicts arising from the evaluation of p_{SS} and p_* are resolved by the dov operator.

Note that an organization may choose to construct a new base policy (e.g. p_{IF} above) from existing ones and "hide" the original base policies (e.g. p_{SS} and p_*) from policy orchestrators. A modular policy language should therefore support such encapsulation.

Note also that the type of policy composition described in Example 1 is not possible in target-based policy languages, because the "policies" written in such languages encode state as well as policy and are therefore inextricably bound to the context in which they were authored.

The following result establishes that our language is powerful enough to realize any orchestration function.

Theorem 1. *For each $n > 0$, all total functions of type $\{\bot, 0, 1, \top\}^n \rightarrow \{\bot, 0, 1, \top\}$ can be generated from the constants $\bot$, 0, 1, $\top$ and the switch operator.*

Arieli and Avron [1] consider the expressive power of the language incorporating the connectives $\{\bot, 0, 1, \top, \neg, \vee, \wedge, \oplus, \otimes, \supset, \rightarrow, \leftrightarrow\}$. They prove that the language using connectives from $\{\neg, \wedge, \supset, \bot, \top\}$ is *functionally complete* and no proper subset of these connectives has this property [1, Theorem 3.8]. We use this result as the basis for the proof of Theorem 1.

Proof (Sketch). We show that the operators $\neg$, $\supset$ and $\wedge$ can be encoded using $\bot$, $\top$, 0, 1 and the switch operator. The definitions of $\supset$ and $\neg$ given below in (5) are equivalent to those given by Arieli and Avron (using connectives from $\{\neg, \wedge, \supset, \bot, \top\}$).

$$x \supset y \stackrel{\text{def}}{=} (x : 1, 1, y, y) \quad \text{and} \quad \neg x \stackrel{\text{def}}{=} (x : \bot, 1, 0, \top) \tag{5}$$

We now consider the $\wedge$ operator (which is analogous to conjunction in classical logic), the "truth" table for which is shown below.

x	y	$x \wedge y$	x	y	$x \wedge y$	x	y	$x \wedge y$	x	y	$x \wedge y$
$\bot$	$\bot$	$\bot$	0	$\bot$	0	1	$\bot$	$\bot$	$\top$	$\bot$	0
$\bot$	0	0	0	0	0	1	0	0	$\top$	0	0
$\bot$	1	$\bot$	0	1	0	1	1	1	$\top$	1	$\top$
$\bot$	$\top$	0	0	$\top$	0	1	$\top$	$\top$	$\top$	$\top$	$\top$

---

[3] We have chosen to implement the discretionary security property using the standard interpretation of a protection matrix as a set of ACLs.

$$p, q \; ::= \qquad\qquad\qquad\qquad \textit{(Policy Trees)}$$

allow | deny | na | conflict   Constant Policy

b Base Policy

$(p: q_\perp, q_0, q_1, q_\top)$ Policy Switch

(a) Grammar

$$[\![\text{allow}]\!](r, \sigma) \stackrel{\text{def}}{=} 1 \qquad [\![\text{deny}]\!](r, \sigma) \stackrel{\text{def}}{=} 0$$

$$[\![\text{na}]\!](r, \sigma) \stackrel{\text{def}}{=} \perp \qquad [\![\text{conflict}]\!](r, \sigma) \stackrel{\text{def}}{=} \top$$

$$[\![b]\!](r, \sigma) = \rho(b)(r, \sigma)$$

$$[\![(p: q_\perp, q_0, q_1, q_\top)]\!](r, \sigma) \stackrel{\text{def}}{=} [\![q_v]\!](r, \sigma) \quad \text{where } [\![p]\!](r, \sigma) = v$$

(b) Denotational semantics

$$\frac{}{(\text{allow}, r, \sigma) \rightsquigarrow 1} \, C1 \qquad \frac{}{(\text{deny}, r, \sigma) \rightsquigarrow 0} \, C0 \qquad \frac{}{(\text{conflict}, r, \sigma) \rightsquigarrow \top} \, C\top$$

$$\frac{}{(\text{na}, r, \sigma) \rightsquigarrow \perp} \, C\perp \qquad \frac{\rho(b)(r, \sigma) = v}{(b, r, \sigma) \rightsquigarrow v} \, Base \qquad \frac{(p, r, \sigma) \rightsquigarrow v \;\; (q_v, r, \sigma) \rightsquigarrow v'}{((p: q_\perp, q_0, q_1, q_\top), r, \sigma) \rightsquigarrow v'} \, Switch$$

(c) Inference rules for operational semantics

Fig. 2. Grammar and semantics for policy trees

Noting that $0 \wedge y = 0$ and $1 \wedge y = y$ for all $y \in \{\perp, 0, 1, \top\}$, it is easily seen that we can encode $x \wedge y$ as $(x : z, 0, y, z')$, where

$$z = (y : \perp, 0, \perp, 0) \quad \text{and} \quad z' = (y : 0, 0, \top, \top).$$

Note that: (i) we cannot encode $\supset$ without 1; (ii) we cannot encode $\wedge$ without 0; and (iii) we cannot encode $\neg$ without 0 and 1.

Grammar and Semantics for Policy Orchestration. We now summarize and formalize the preceding discussion by giving a grammar and formal semantics for policy trees. Figure 2(a) depicts the grammar for policies, which are built out of some set of base policies, constant policies (of which all except conflict are base policies), and the switch operator.

The denotational semantics for policy trees are shown in Figure 2(b), relative to an environment ρ that gives semantics $\rho(b)$: Req $\times \Sigma \rightarrow \{\perp, 0, 1\}$ to all base policies b. Figure 2(c) shows a "big-step" structural operational semantics of policy trees, again relative to an environment ρ. An induction on the height of derivation trees for judgments $(p, r, \sigma) \rightsquigarrow v$ can be used to establish that the operational and denotational semantics compute the same meaning:

pol ::=   (Policy)
    allow | deny | na | conflict   Constant Policy
    %   Dead Code
    base   Base Policy
    switch {pol: pol; pol; pol; pol}   Policy Switch

Fig. 3. Core policy-orchestration language APOL for some set of base policies

Theorem 2. *For all policy trees $p \in \mathcal{P}$ and environments ρ, equation $[\![p]\!](r, \sigma) = v$ holds if and only if $(p, r, \sigma) \rightsquigarrow v$ can be derived using the inference rules in Figure 2(c).*

3 APOL: A Typed, Modular Policy Language

We now develop a treatment of policies as *typed, modular programs*. Modularity facilitates compositionality, maintainability, and reuse of policies. Types are conservative mechanisms for preventing certain kinds of "run-time" errors during request evaluation. For example, types can certify that the use of % to represent dead code is safe for the evaluation of a policy for any request and authorization state.

The grammar of a core programming language APOL ("authorization policy orchestration language") is shown in Figure 3: it is essentially the grammar for policy trees shown in Figure 2(a), extended with a symbol % for dead code, and presented in a form more amenable to programming. Below, we present a static type system where types are inferred from the syntax of policies without evaluating them. We then also demonstrate that deeper semantic analysis is useful for such static type inference.

Let p be an expression of APOL and let $\rho(b)$ be defined for all base policies b occurring in p. Then we point out that the operational semantics of p in Figure 2(c) is well defined by matching clauses of the grammars in Figures 2(a) and 3. However, as there is no rule for $(\%, r, \sigma) \rightsquigarrow \ldots$, dead code does not evaluate to any value, meaning that its evaluation is stuck and constitutes an error.

Typed Methods for APOL. We extend our core policy language with typed, parameterized methods. The types τ in the extended language are base (for base policies, that cannot output $\top$), pol (for orchestrated policies), and prd (for base policies that cannot output $\bot$ and so represent Boolean predicates). Each method has $\tau \in \{\text{base}, \text{pol}, \text{prd}\}$ as return type, specifying that method invocations in-lined with correctly typed input policies render a policy of type τ. The following method, for example, explicitly implements the deny-overrides orchestration pattern. Note the return type base and the parameter type pol for its argument policy:

```
base deny-overrides(P:pol) { switch{P : na; deny; allow; deny} }
```

The type system for such methods is presented in Figure 4: judgments "expression e has type τ in context Γ" have the form $\Gamma \vdash e : \tau$, where $\tau \in \{\text{pol}, \text{base}, \text{prd}\}$ and Γ is a context binding variables x_i to types τ_i. Each rule specifies a possible inference: if all

$$\frac{}{\Gamma \vdash \mathtt{na : base}} \qquad \frac{}{\Gamma \vdash \mathtt{deny : prd}} \qquad \frac{}{\Gamma \vdash \mathtt{allow : prd}} \qquad \frac{}{\Gamma \vdash \mathtt{conflict : pol}}$$

$$\frac{X_i : \alpha_i \in \Gamma}{\Gamma \vdash X_i : \alpha_i} \qquad \frac{\Gamma \vdash e : \mathtt{rt} \;\; \Gamma \subseteq \Gamma'}{\Gamma' \vdash e : \mathtt{rt}} \qquad \frac{\Gamma \vdash e : \mathtt{prd}}{\Gamma \vdash e : \mathtt{base}} \qquad \frac{\Gamma \vdash e : \mathtt{base}}{\Gamma \vdash e : \mathtt{pol}}$$

$$\frac{\Gamma \vdash e : \mathtt{pol} \qquad \Gamma \vdash e_v : \mathtt{rt} \;\; (\forall v \in \{\bot, 0, 1, \top\})}{\Gamma \vdash \mathtt{switch}\{e : e_\bot;\; e_0;\; e_1;\; e_\top\} : \mathtt{rt}}$$

$$\frac{\Gamma \vdash e : \mathtt{prd} \qquad \Gamma \vdash e_v : \mathtt{rt} \;\; (\forall v \in \{0, 1\})}{\Gamma \vdash \mathtt{switch}\{e : \%;\; e_0;\; e_1;\; \%\} : \mathtt{rt}}$$

$$\frac{\Gamma \vdash e : \mathtt{base} \qquad \Gamma \vdash e_v : \mathtt{rt} \;\; (\forall v \in \{\bot, 0, 1\})}{\Gamma \vdash \mathtt{switch}\{e : e_\bot;\; e_0;\; e_1;\; \%\} : \mathtt{rt}}$$

$$\frac{\Gamma \cup \{\boldsymbol{X} : \boldsymbol{\alpha}\} \vdash e : \mathtt{rt}}{\Gamma \setminus \{\boldsymbol{X} \mid \boldsymbol{\alpha}\} \vdash \mathtt{rt}\, \mathtt{mname}(\boldsymbol{X} : \boldsymbol{\alpha})\{e\} : \boldsymbol{\alpha} \to \mathtt{rt}}$$

$$\frac{(\forall i)\, \Gamma \cup \{\boldsymbol{X} : \boldsymbol{\alpha}\} \vdash e_i : \alpha_i \;\; \Gamma \vdash \mathtt{rt}\, \mathtt{mname}(\boldsymbol{X} : \boldsymbol{\alpha})\{e\} : \boldsymbol{\alpha} \to \mathtt{rt}}{\Gamma \vdash \mathtt{mname}(e) : \mathtt{rt}}$$

Fig. 4. Rules for type checking judgments $\Gamma \vdash e : \mathtt{t}$ for **APOL** expressions, where Γ is a type context binding variables to types, $\mathtt{rt} \in \{\mathtt{base}, \mathtt{pol}, \mathtt{prd}\}$, and $\boldsymbol{X} : \boldsymbol{\alpha}$ is a list of typed parameters

judgments on top of the line of a rule have been inferred or are given, then the judgment below the line of that rule can be inferred.

The first row in Figure 4 states the types of constant policies, reflecting that $\mathtt{na}$ is a base policy, $\mathtt{conflict}$ a non-base policy, and that conclusive decisions are predicates. These are axioms as their inferences do not depend on any judgments. The second row uses standard structural and type casting rules for type inference in the presence of subtyping and states that prd is a subtype of base and that the latter is a subtype of pol. The third row handles type inference for the switch operator: the switch policy must have type pol (through casting of subtypes, if needed), and all argument policies must agree on the output type (again, through casting, if needed).

The next two rows depict two important patterns for reasoning about the safe use of the dead code symbol $\%$. The first one shows that $r = \mathtt{switch}\{e : \%;\; e_0;\; e_1;\; \%\}$ has return type $\mathtt{rt}$ by first showing that the switch policy e has type $\mathtt{prd}$, and then showing that both e_0 and e_1 have type $\mathtt{rt}$. These type inference rules are safe: for no request and for no authorization state does the operational semantics of r ever evaluate one of the two occurrences of $\%$. This rule can be used to certify that our definition of (p/F), when written in **APOL**, is type safe. The second rule is very similar but – since it only has a dead code symbol for the case when the switch policy outputs a conflict – it only has to show that the switch policy has type base. Again, such type inference guarantees that the symbol $\%$ will never be encountered in the operational semantics.

The final two rows show standard type inference rules for parameterized methods. The first rule assumes the type bindings of the method head, uses those bindings to infer a type for the method body, and that type is then the method return type (but in a type context that no longer relies on these assumptions). The second rule captures that well typed method invocations return the specified type.

Example 2. We illustrate the type system on method `deny-overrides` specified above. To show that this method has output type base, we assume that P has type pol as declared in the method header (and so Γ records that binding) and show that the switch statement has output type base under that assumption. But this follows easily from the type inference rule for the switch statement, since all argument policies have subtypes of base or have that type, and so all argument types can be cast into type base, if needed.

Note that variables occurring in a context Γ cannot be constants of APOL. In particular, it is not possible to assign a type to %, and so one can also not give a type to a policy switch with switch policy %.

Our type system can be fine-tuned to enable a richer semantic typing. For example, consider the typed APOL method `foo`, declared by

```
prd foo(P:pol) { switch{P : deny; P; P; deny} }
```

Its argument has type pol and so we cannot assume that this policy is a base policy or free of conflict. Our type system therefore forces that all four argument types of the switch statement be cast into their least common supertype, which is pol. Therefore, the type system can only infer pol as output type. But when P is executed as q_0 we know that its output is a `deny`. Similarly, when P is executed as q_1 its output is an `allow`. Therefore, it is intuitively safe to assume that all four arguments have type prd and so prd is a safe output type for method `foo`. We now sketch a semantic analysis that formalizes such intuitions. This analysis can then be used to extend our static type inference.

Analysis of APOL Policies. For any policy r, let $r \Uparrow 1$ be a propositional formula whose atoms are expressions of the form $b \Uparrow 1$ and $b \Uparrow 0$ for base or constant policies b occurring in policy r. Intuitively, $r \Uparrow 1$ is true if policy r authorizes the (implicit) request, and $r \Uparrow 0$ is true if policy r denies it. The constraint $r \Uparrow 1$ (respectively, $r \Uparrow 0$) therefore expresses the conditions on the base policy decisions for the orchestrated policy r to either authorize (respectively, deny) the request or to report a conflict.

The definition of $r \Uparrow 1$ and $r \Uparrow 0$ is by induction over terms of APOL. For constant policies, these conditions merely express the obvious meaning of these constants. For example, `conflict` $\Uparrow 1$ and `conflict` $\Uparrow 0$ both are the truth constant *true*, whereas na $\Uparrow 1$ and na $\Uparrow 0$ both are the truth constant *false*. For the other two logical constants, we set deny $\Uparrow 1 = false$, deny $\Uparrow 0 = true$ and allow $\Uparrow 1 = true$, allow $\Uparrow 0 = false$. Assuming that dead code is type safe, we set % $\Uparrow 1$ and % $\Uparrow 0$ both to be *false*.

The meaning of $b \Uparrow 1$ and $b \Uparrow 0$ for base policies b will depend on the application domain and concrete nature of those base policies. For example, base policies may be written over equations of attributes and so these constraints may be propositional formulas over such attribute conditions.

It remains to specify the conditions $r \Uparrow 1$ and $r \Uparrow 0$ when r is the switch statement $(p : q_\perp, q_0, q_1, q_\top)$. Then we can define $r \Uparrow 1$ in the following way:

$$r \Uparrow 1 = (\neg(p \Uparrow 0) \wedge \neg(p \Uparrow 1) \wedge (q_\perp \Uparrow 1)) \vee \qquad (6)$$
$$((p \Uparrow 0) \wedge \neg(p \Uparrow 1) \wedge (q_0 \Uparrow 1)) \vee$$
$$(\neg(p \Uparrow 0) \wedge (p \Uparrow 1) \wedge (q_1 \Uparrow 1)) \vee$$
$$((p \Uparrow 0) \wedge (p \Uparrow 1) \wedge (q_\top \Uparrow 1))$$

The definition of $r \Uparrow 0$ merely changes all $q_v \Uparrow 1$ in (6) to $q_v \Uparrow 0$. The intuition of these constraints should be clear. Each disjunct specifies, in its first two conjuncts, the intended continuation location of the switch statement, and captures the intended condition for that continuation in its third conjunct. These constraints are therefore disjunctions of conjunctions of similar constraints for subpolicies.

Given such formulas, one can then build other constraints, e.g., $\neg(r \Uparrow 0) \wedge (r \Uparrow 1)$, which states the conditions for policy r to authorize a request (and so, in particular, not to report a conflict). In order to determine whether a policy r has a conflict, for example, is equivalent to determining whether $(r \Uparrow 1) \wedge (r \Uparrow 0) \wedge \bigwedge_b \neg((b \Uparrow 1) \wedge (b \Uparrow 0))$ is satisfiable, where b ranges over all base policies occuring in r. Note that the third conjunct rules out spurious witnesses since base policies cannot return $\top$.

We can apply this analysis to infer the more informative type prd of method foo, which our static type system could not do. For that, it suffices to show that the body r of the method always returns 0 or 1, for any switch policy p of type pol; that is to say, that $r \Uparrow 1$ is equivalent to $\neg(r \Uparrow 0)$ if we interpret $p \Uparrow 0$ and $p \Uparrow 1$ as atomic propositions.

Applying (6) to that r, and noting that Deny $\Uparrow 1 = \mathit{false}$, we compute

$$
\begin{aligned}
r \Uparrow 1 &= (\neg(p \Uparrow 0) \wedge \neg(p \Uparrow 1) \wedge \mathit{false}) \vee \\
&\quad ((p \Uparrow 0) \wedge \neg(p \Uparrow 1) \wedge (p \Uparrow 1)) \vee \\
&\quad (\neg(p \Uparrow 0) \wedge (p \Uparrow 1) \wedge (q_1 \Uparrow 1)) \vee \\
&\quad ((p \Uparrow 0) \wedge (p \Uparrow 1) \wedge \mathit{false})) \\
&= \neg(p \Uparrow 0) \wedge (p \Uparrow 1)
\end{aligned}
\tag{7}
$$

Noting that Deny $\Uparrow 0 = \mathit{true}$, we similarly compute $r \Uparrow 0 = (p \Uparrow 0) \vee (\neg(p \Uparrow 0) \wedge \neg(p \Uparrow 1))$. But it is easily seen that $\neg(r \Uparrow 0)$ and $r \Uparrow 1$ are equivalent formulas.

4 Discussion

We now discuss our contributions and put them into perspective.

Separating State and Policies. We have argued that policy and state should be separated, and have developed a framework that meets this criterion. In a practical setting, enterprise security requirements must be encoded in authorization policies, which may require complex orchestration patterns. However, the authorization state is independent of these orchestrations, and different parts of the state would typically be maintained by different local administrators who are responsible for correctly associating users and resources with security-related attributes.

Informing Future Authorization Languages. We now consider how our work is related to target-based approaches to authorization and suggest how these connections might usefully inform the development of authorization languages.

Recall that the protection matrix authorizes a request if that request is encoded in the matrix. The policy is to allow if that request is encoded in the matrix and deny otherwise – the simplest possible way of deciding whether a request is authorized. In our view, the authorization state is the matrix M (or some other suitable data structure, such as a collection of ACLs). Accordingly, we define the base policy p_{allow}, where $p_{\mathsf{allow}}(r, M) = 1$ if $r \in M$, and $\bot$ otherwise.

We can, of course, prohibit certain requests using the orchestration $!p_{\text{allow}}$ for an appropriate choice of M. Complex policies can be built from authorization state components $M_1, \ldots, M_k$ and appropriate orchestrations using $+$ and $!$ (or the switch operator). Hence, policy authors can define orchestrations, while local administrators can update M_i to reflect changes to personnel and resources.

Informing XACML. We now reflect on how the features of our framework might usefully be applied in XACML. We focus our attention on XACML, because it is a well known standard that provides a framework for the specification and evaluation of target-based authorization policies. In conflating state and policy, target-based approaches such as XACML mean either that policy authors must be aware of authorization state or that local administrators must be able to author XACML policies. This makes it more difficult to author and maintain policies. In our framework, a component of authorization state can be regarded as (just) another resource and can be protected by an authorization policy like any other resource. In XACML, there is no structured support for policy updates, which therefore continue to be a problematic issue.

We believe the switch operator could usefully be deployed in XACML (and other authorization languages). Currently, the XACML standard requires that a number of rule- and policy-combining algorithms be supported by the PDP. Moreover, XACML rules and policies are indistinguishable in terms of semantics, so it is unnecessary to have both rule- and policy-combining algorithms. It has also been observed that there are certain pathological cases in which the combination of rule- and policy-combination algorithms (compliant with the XACML standard) leads to unexpected results [17]. Hence, we make three suggestions: (i) XACML should remove the (artificial) distinction between rules and policies; (ii) a single algorithm based on the switch operator should be supported (since we showed that it can encode the standard policy-combination algorithms); and (iii) types and modularity (as sketched in this paper) should be supported to provide safer policy orchestration for policy authors.

A feature of XACML and target-based policy languages and algebras is the immediate resolution of conflicts. As can be seen from our framework, there is no theoretical necessity for doing this and there may be good practical reasons for postponing the computation of a conclusive decision. A convincing case for decoupling policy composition from conflict resolution has been made in [8] already. In XACML terminology, the rule- and policy-combining algorithms should not be required attributes of policy and policy set elements, respectively, thereby enabling XACML policies and policy sets to return conflicts.

Related Work. The work of Bruns *et al.* [8,9] is closest to that reported in this paper. This work suggested the Belnap space $\{\perp, 0, 1, \top\}$ as carrier of meaning for authorization policies, built atomic policies of the form e/T (in our notation) where T is a subset of Req, employed policy combinators that act on policies in a pointwise manner, and showed that the resulting policy language is as expressive as it can be (thinking of targets T as predicates) [8]. Subsequently, various policy analyses are reduced to checking the satisfiability of formulae in an NP fragment of first-order logic, and such satisfiability checks are extended to a limited form of assume-guarantee reasoning [9]. Our work creates policy languages that have equal expressiveness of orchestration. But our framework separates requests from authorization state, supports types and modularity for policy orchestration and enforcement, and has a very simple policy analysis in the form of Boolean satisfiability checks (based on a sole policy operator `switch`).

There are a number of authorization frameworks in which policies are based on logic-programming languages such as Datalog (see [3,11,12], for example). Although these frameworks are not target-based and can easily express policies such as p_{SS}, the orchestration patterns that are available are limited by the semantics of rule evaluation in the underlying programming language.

5 Conclusions

Summary. The motivation of this paper was to overcome most of the shortcomings of existing target-based authorization-policy languages such as XACML. We began with a semantic view of a policy as a 4-valued function whose input comprises a request and relevant authorization state. This resulted in a language of policy trees with $\{0, 1, \bot\}$-valued base policies where $\bot$ models that a request is not applicable for the policy interface, or that it cannot be evaluated in the authorization state. We then transferred these ideas into the programming language APOL, first within a core language of policy trees and then for an extension of that core language to parameterized, typed methods. We also gave equivalent denotational and operational semantics to the core language. Finally, we discussed how our ideas and results could leverage policy analysis – for example to reason about the type safe identification of dead code – and inform new versions of the XACML standard and future authorization languages.

Future Work. Our most recent work shows that programs of type `pol` are representable, and hence implementable, as ternary decision diagrams [20]; that the remote evaluation of sub-programs can be accommodated by the use of decision diagrams that have four kinds of edges and terminals; and that our policy analysis methods can be used to enrich our type system with a notion of semantic (i.e. behavioral) types. We intend to continue our preliminary work in this area.

In our current approach, the output value $\bot$ is overloaded, as we use it to denote both the inapplicability of a base policy to a request and the inability to evaluate a request given current knowledge of the state. If we want to make a distinction between these cases, we would require a 5-valued meaning space $\{0, 1, \sharp, \flat, \top\}$, where 0, 1, and $\top$ retain their meaning and $\sharp$ and $\flat$ denote problems with policy evaluation and policy applicability (respectively). We also hope to develop an implementation of our framework, perhaps making use of XACML-like syntax to define platform-independent authorization state. Thirdly, we mean to devise a modular policy analysis for APOL based on the familiar idea of programming by contracts [16].

Acknowledgements. The authors would like to thank the anonymous referees for their helpful comments.

References

1. Arieli, O., Avron, A.: The value of the four values. Artificial Intelligence 102(1), 97–141 (1998)
2. Backes, M., Dürmuth, M., Steinwandt, R.: An Algebra for Composing Enterprise Privacy Policies. In: Samarati, P., Ryan, P.Y.A., Gollmann, D., Molva, R. (eds.) ESORICS 2004. LNCS, vol. 3193, pp. 33–52. Springer, Heidelberg (2004)
3. Becker, M.Y., Sewell, P.: Cassandra: Distributed access control policies with tunable expressiveness. In: Proc. of 5th IEEE International Workshop on Policies for Distributed Systems and Networks, pp. 159–168 (2004)
4. Bell, D.E., La Padula, L.: Secure computer systems: Unified exposition and Multics interpretation. Technical Report MTR-2997, Mitre Corporation, Bedford, Massachusetts (1976)
5. Bertino, E., Castano, S., Ferrari, E.: Author-$\mathcal{X}$: A comprehensive system for securing XML documents. IEEE Internet Computing 5(3), 21–31 (2001)
6. Bonatti, P., de Capitani di Vimercati, S., Samarati, P.: An algebra for composing access control policies. ACM Transactions on Information and System Security 5(1), 1–35 (2002)
7. Brewer, D., Nash, M.: The Chinese Wall security policy. In: Proc. of the 1989 IEEE Symp. on Security and Privacy, pp. 206–214 (1989)
8. Bruns, G., Dantas, D.S., Huth, M.: A simple and expressive semantic framework for policy composition in access control. In: Gligor, V.D., Mantel, H. (eds.) Proc. of the Fifth Workshop on Formal Methods in Security Engineering: From Specifications to Code, pp. 12–21 (2007)
9. Bruns, G., Huth, M.: Access control via Belnap logic: Effective and efficient composition and analysis. In: Sabelfeld, A. (ed.) Proc. of the 21st IEEE Computer Security Foundations Symp., pp. 163–176 (2008)
10. Damiani, E., di Vimercati, S.D.C., Paraboschi, S., Samarati, P.: A fine-grained access control system for XML documents. ACM Transactions on Information and System Security 5(2), 169–202 (2002)
11. DeTreville, J.: Binder, a logic-based security language. In: Proc. of the 2002 IEEE Symp. on Security and Privacy, pp. 105–113 (2002)
12. Dougherty, D.J., Fisler, K., Adsul, B.: Specifying and Reasoning about Dynamic Access-Control Policies. In: Furbach, U., Shankar, N. (eds.) IJCAR 2006. LNCS (LNAI), vol. 4130, pp. 632–646. Springer, Heidelberg (2006)
13. Gong, L.: Inside Java 2 Platform Security. Addison-Wesley (1999)
14. Harrison, M.A., Ruzzo, W.L., Ullman, J.D.: Protection in operating systems. Communications of the ACM 19(8), 461–471 (1976)
15. Jagadeesan, R., Marrero, W., Pitcher, C., Saraswat, V.: Timed constraint programming: A declarative approach to usage control. In: Proc. of the 7th International ACM SIGPLAN Conference on Principles and Practice of Declarative Programming, pp. 164–175 (2005)
16. Meyer, B.: Applying "Design by Contract". IEEE Computer 25(10), 40–51 (1992)
17. Ni, Q., Bertino, E., Lobo, J.: D-Algebra for composing access control policy decisions. In: Proc. of 4th ACM Symp. on Information, Computer and Communications Security, pp. 298–309 (2009)
18. OASIS. Xtensible Access Control Markup Language (XACML) Version 2.0, OASIS Committee Specification (T. Moses, editor) (2005)
19. Ribeiro, C., Zuquete, A., Ferreira, P., Guedes, P.: SPL: An access control language for security policies and complex constraints. In: Proc. of the Network and Distributed System Security Symp. (NDSS), pp. 89–107 (February 2001)
20. Sasao, T.: Ternary decision diagrams: Survey. In: Proc. of the 27th International Symp. on Multiple-Valued Logic (ISMVL 1997), pp. 241–250 (1997)
21. Wijesekera, D., Jajodia, S.: A propositional policy algebra for access control. ACM Transactions on Information and System Security 6(2), 286–325 (2003)

Credential Disabling
from Trusted Execution Environments

Kari Kostiainen, N. Asokan, and Jan-Erik Ekberg

Nokia Research Center, Helsinki
{kari.ti.kostiainen,n.asokan,jan-erik.ekberg}@nokia.com

Abstract. A generic credential platform realized using a hardware-based trusted execution environment (TrEE) provides a usable and inexpensive way to secure various applications and services. An important requirement for any credential platform is the ability to *disable* and *restore* credentials. In this paper, we raise the problem of temporary credential disabling from embedded TrEEs and explain why straightforward solutions fall short. We present two novel credential disabling approaches: one based on the presence check of a personal element, such as SIM card, and another utilizing a semi-trusted server. We have implemented the server-based credential disabling solution for mobile phones with M-Shield TrEE.

1 Introduction

Credentials are needed to secure various applications and online services. Traditional credentials, like passwords, are vulnerable to many attacks including phishing. Dedicated hardware tokens provide a higher level of security, but are too expensive for most use cases, and having to carry a separate token for each service is inconvenient for users. Credentials implemented using general-purpose hardware-based trusted execution environments (TrEEs), such as Trusted Platform Modules (TPM) [17], JavaCard [9], M-Shield [14] or ARM TrustZone [1], can provide good security and usability at the same time. By utilizing already deployed TrEEs, such credentials can also be cost-efficient; TPMs are already available on many high-end personal computers while several existing mobile phones are based on TrEEs like M-Shield and TrustZone. Examples of credential platforms implemented on top of these TrEEs include On-board Credentials [10] and Trusted Execution Module [4].

One important requirement for any credential platform is the ability to *disable* and *restore* credentials from TrEEs. To get a concrete example of the problem consider the following scenario: Alice has her on-line banking credential stored in the TrEE of her mobile phone. Alice damages her phone and has to leave it to a service point for repair. How can Alice (1) easily disable the banking credential from her phone for the duration of the repair, so that the service point personnel cannot use the credential, and (2) conveniently restore the credential once she gets the phone back? Another use case is device lending: Alice might want to disable important credentials from her phone before handing it over to a friend.

T. Aura, K. Järvinen, and K. Nyberg (Eds.): NordSec 2010, LNCS 7127, pp. 171–186, 2012.

Trusted execution environments are either removable or embedded. When a user's credentials are stored in a *removable* TrEE, in the form of physically distinct secure element like a smartcard, temporary credential disabling is intuitive and well-understood from the user's point of view: the user can simply remove the TrEE from the device, and the credentials can no longer be used in that device until the TrEE is re-inserted.

Storing credentials in embedded TrEEs is attractive for multiple reasons. First, embedded TrEEs, such as TPM, M-Shield and TrustZone, are available in a wide range of already deployed devices from mobile phones to laptops. Second, removable TrEEs are often controlled by the element issuer, e.g. in the case of SIM card the mobile phone operator; and using them for third-party credentials is not always possible. Third, embedded TrEEs are more cost-efficient, especially for low-end, mass market devices. Fourth, embedded TrEEs can be tightly integrated with the device OS so that a trusted path to the user can be realized.

When credentials are stored in an *embedded* TrEE credential disabling becomes more challenging. When the user e.g. leaves her device to a service point, the credentials must be disabled or removed from the embedded TrEE so that the new person in possession of the device, i.e. the attacker, cannot use the credentials even though he has physical access to the device itself.

In this paper we address the problem of temporary credential disabling from embedded TrEEs—a problem that has not been addressed before to the best of our knowledge. The contributions of this paper are two-fold: First, we raise the problem and explain why straightforward solutions are not adequate to solve this seemingly simple problem. Second, we present two novel credential disabling approaches: we outline credential disabling based on a *presence check* of a personal element, such as SIM card, and describe in more detail credential disabling that utilizes a *semi-trusted server*. Both of these solutions can be realized using commodity devices widely available today. We have implemented the server-based credential disabling solution for mobile phones with M-Shield TrEE.

2   Assumptions and Requirements

2.1   Assumptions

We make the following assumptions about the underlying hardware and software platform that is available on the user's device.

A1: Trusted execution environment. We assume that the device is equipped with a hardware-based trusted execution environment (TrEE) that provides: (1) isolated and integrity protected execution of trusted code (here "trusted" can mean e.g. code signed by a trusted authority, such as the device manufacturer), and (2) secure storage for a device-specific encryption key K. Integrity of the TrEE itself may be protected with secure boot. M-Shield [14] is an example of such TrEE.

A2: Operating system security framework. We also assume availability of an operating system (OS) security framework that provides: (1) isolated code execution, and (2) secure storage for each OS-level process/application. Additionally, (3) the OS security framework allows only trusted (e.g. signed) applications/processes to communicate with TrEE. Integrity of the OS security framework may be protected with secure boot that utilizes TrEE. Symbian OS is an example of such OS-level security framework [7].

2.2   Attacker Model

We make the following assumptions about the capabilities of the attacker.

C1: Network communication control. We assume that the attacker is able to read, modify and replay any network traffic between the user's device and any external storage media.

C2: External media control. We assume that the attacker has access to any data stored to *insecure* external storage media, such as removable memory elements like MMC cards and users' home PCs. This claim can be well justified with the users' careless handling of removable memory elements and prevalence of malware on users' PCs.

C3: TrEE control. We assume that the attacker *cannot* read or modify any processing that takes place within the TrEE, or read or modify any secrets, such as the device-specific encryption key K, stored within the TrEE. This assumption implies that the attacker is *not* able to tamper with the TrEE hardware or mount successful side-channel attacks.

C4: Operating system control. While in physical possession of the device, the attacker can install and remove any OS-level applications to and from the device. The attacker may also re-install the entire OS or reset the device back into factory state. We assume that the attacker *cannot* read or modify processing of existing applications (installed before the attacker acquired the possession of the device), or read or modify data stored to secure storage of existing applications, *as long as* the attacker cannot compromise the OS-level security framework. Due to the large size of modern operating systems we do not generally assume that the OS-level security framework remains uncompromised, and later in this paper we discuss the implications OS compromise to our credential disabling approaches.

2.3   Requirements

A credential platform that allows the user to disable and restore her credentials that are protected with an embedded TrEE should fulfill the following requirements.

R1: Automatic normal backup. Users are expected to (or at least allowed to) make frequent "normal backups" of their credentials into external insecure storage media, such as their home PC, MMC card or an on-line backup server. Normal backups should be encrypted to protected them from eavesdropping (attacker has access to backups due to assumption C2) and restoring them should be possible only to the *same device*. As long as the user is in

possession of her device, the normal backup operation should not require any
user interaction, so that the backup process can be automated for optimal
user experience.

R2: Easy disabling backup. Before lending her device, the user should be
able to trigger a so called "disabling backup" operation. This operation
should perform two tasks. First, it should create a new backup of the credentials that only the *same user* can restore into the *same device*. Second, it
should disable all the previously created normal backups, so that the attacker
in physical possession of the device cannot restore any of the normal backups
it may have access to (C2). Creating and restoring a disabling backup may
require some user interaction, since such an operation is performed considerably less often compared to normal backups, but nonetheless disabling and
restoring credentials should be as easy as possible for the user.

In this paper we explicitly do *not* address device theft (many mobile devices
already today support "remote kill" functionality to prevent usage of stolen
device), but instead focus on use cases in which the device is voluntarily handed
to an untrusted person for a limited period of time.

3   Straightforward Solutions

In this section we explain why the seemingly simple problem of credential disabling from embedded TrEEs cannot be solved with straightforward solutions.

3.1   Credential Disabling with Passwords

An obvious and simple approach would be to use a password for protecting the
recovery of disabling backups. In such a solution the *normal credential backups*
would be encrypted using the device-specific encryption key K (that is only
accessible within the TrEE) and the *disabling backups* would be additionally
bound to a password that the user defines either when the credential platform
is first taken into use or when the first backup is created. The user would have
to enter the same password into the device when a disabling backup is restored.
The credential platform would only allow recovery of disabling backup if the
password is correct.

This simple approach would have the typical usability and security issues of
password based approaches (user forget and re-use passwords, and pick passwords with low entropy). In addition, this approach would have the following
two problems. First, it would not meet our requirement R2: binding disabling
backups to a password would not prevent the attacker from restoring normal
backups that are not password protected (we assume that backups made to insecure storage media may leak to the attacker). Binding also normal backups to
a password would not meet our requirement R1. Second, implementing such a
scheme on existing devices would requite us to trust the entire operating system,
since passwords input to hardware-based TrEE without OS involvement is not
supported by majority of existing devices.

3.2   Credential Disabling with Removable Element

A natural following approach would be to bind the recovery of (both normal and disabling) backups to a key that is stored into a *removable general-purpose element* (RGE), such as MMC card or USB stick, that most PCs and mobile devices are equipped with or have interfaces for. During backup recovery the credential platform would check that a RGE with correct password is present on the device. As long as the RGE would remain present, normal backups could be created and restored automatically.

The user would be instructed to remove the RGE from the device when lending the device and re-insert the RGE back to the device when she regains the possession of the device. Such a straightforward approach would not meet our requirements because we assume that the attacker has access to any data stored to insecure external media, including RGEs. To be able to fulfill our requirements with the use of RGEs, we have to relax our initial attacker capability C2.

RC2: Relaxed external media control. In the relaxed attacker model we assume that the attacker has access to any data stored to insecure external media, except the *latest* data stored to removable general-purpose elements (RGE), such as MMC cards and USB sticks. In other words, we assume that the user can—when instructed correctly—take care of the RGE during device load period, but any data stored to RGE will *eventually* leak to the attacker.

Even with this relaxed attacker model, credential disabling from embedded TrEEs is not straightforward. By simply binding the recovery of backups to a recovery key that is stored to a RGE does not prevent the attacker from restoring *old* backups, since we assume that old recovery keys stored to RGE will *eventually* leak to the attacker (RC2). Thus, a mechanism for preventing recovery of old backups is needed.

3.3   Credential Disabling with Embedded Secure Counter

Preventing recovery of old backups is simple if the embedded TrEE supports secure non-volatile memory using which *secure monotonic counters* can be implemented. In such a solution, the current value of a secure counter would be bound to each normal backup (that is encrypted using the device specific key K). When the user in is possession of her device normal backups can be created and restored automatically. When the user triggers a disabling backup operation, the counter within the embedded TrEE is incremented and the new counter value and a recovery key (stored to RGE) are bound to the encrypted disabling backup. Again, the user is instructed to remove the RGE from the device for the duration of the device loan period. During backup recovery the credential platform will verify that the counter value in the backup matches the counter within the TrEE and that the user has inserted RGE with valid recovery key.

Assuming our relaxed attacker model (RC2) this mechanism would meet our requirements. The scheme would prevent the attacker from restoring normal backups when the device is disabled and prevent restoring of old disabling back-ups with old keys that may have leaked from the RGE. However, many existing and widely deployed TrEEs do not support secure non-volatile memory and secure counters (see e.g. [13] for discussion). Thus, to implement secure tempo-rary credential disabling using commodity devices available today, alternative approaches are needed.

4   Credential Disabling with Personal Element Presence

As explained in the previous section, disabling credentials from existing em-bedded TrEEs is not straightforward. Simple solutions based on passwords and removable elements do not meet our requirements and many existing devices do not support secure counter based credential disabling.

Conveniently, certain mobile devices are equipped with a removable element that the user is accustomed to remove from the device before lending it and taking good care of during the device loan period. We call such a storage ele-ment "personal element" (PE). PE is typically dedicated for single use and has monetary or other value so that the user has an incentive to remove it and not to insert it into untrusted devices. In mobile phones such an element is typically available in the form of a *SIM card*. We extend our attacker model to cover personal elements.

C5: Personal element control. We assume that the attacker *does not* have physical access to personal elements. This claim can be justified with (1) the users' existing habit and (2) monetary incentive to remove personal element from the device before lending it and taking good care during the device loan period.

An obvious approach would be to store all credentials to the personal element for the duration of the device loan. However, this is typically not possible. First, the storage space on many SIM cards is constrained (e.g. 128 kB on many existing SIM cards) while the credentials database may be arbitrary large.[1] Second, many existing SIM cards do not provide application programming interfaces (API) for using SIM cards as a generic, secure storage medium.[2]

Instead of using the personal element as *storage* for credentials during device loan, the recovery of backups can be bound to the *presence* of the personal element. The solution details are rather simple: A backup of the credentials can be made by encrypting the credentials using the device specific key K and

---

[1] Some credential platforms allow metadata, such as logo of credential issuer, to be attached to credentials

[2] Typically, SIM cards only provide an API for using the address book feature of the SIM card. The address book cannot be used as generic *secure* storage, since the data that can be stored into it is very limited and because the users are expected to (or at least allowed to) make backups of address book contents to external, *insecure* storage media.

including the PE *identifier* (e.g. IMSI number of SIM card) to the encrypted backup. When a backup is restored, the TrEE would simply check that PE with the same identity is present in the device.

For optimal user experience a backup of the credentials could be made (to an external storage medium) every time there is a change in one of the credentials, e.g. when a new credential is added to the credential platform. At any time the user may remove the personal element from the device. The credential platform notices the disappearance of the element and deletes the local copy of credentials from the device itself. The device may now be safely given to the attacker which cannot restore a backup without the same SIM card. When the user regains the possession of the device and re-inserts PE back to the device, the credentials platform can fetch the latest backup from the external storage and recover it.

Unfortunately, the above outlined simple PE presence check mechanism could be easily bypassed by the attacker. The attacker could e.g. insert a fake SIM card into the SIM card slot of the mobile device. The fake SIM would claim the required PE identity (IMSI) and restoring backups would be possible.

To prevent such attacks, the PE presence check should be based on a cryptographic protocol (e.g. challenge-response protocol) between the TrEE and the SIM card. The prerequisite of such a protocol is either the ability to setup a security association between the TrEE and the SIM card, or possibility to use an external and trusted server that has an established trust relationship with the SIM card issuer. The first alternative requires the possibility of installing new logic on the SIM card to support the setup and use of a security association. There is no standardized means to do this. The second alternative requires support from the operator who issued the SIM card. In Section 7.1 we discuss the latter alternative further, but for now we focus on alternatives that can be implemented without network operator involvement.

5   Credential Disabling with Semi-trusted Server

As discussed in the previous sections, credential disabling from embedded TrEEs can be implemented securely if the embedded TrEE provides support for secure counters, or a personal element is available and its presence can be checked in cryptographic manner. In many cases neither of these conditions hold. In this section we present a novel credential disabling solution that can be implemented using existing, widely deployed TrEEs without dependencies to external parties, such as network operators.

The basic idea of this approach is to bind disabling backups to a recovery key that is stored into a removable general-purpose element (RGE) and to use a *semi-trusted server* as a secure counter in order to prevent recovery of old backups (we call the server "semi-trusted" since it is only trusted to maintain integrity protected state information for each device and communicate this state information in an authenticated manner to each device). The user is expected to remove the RGE from the device before lending it and to take care of the RGE during the device loan period.

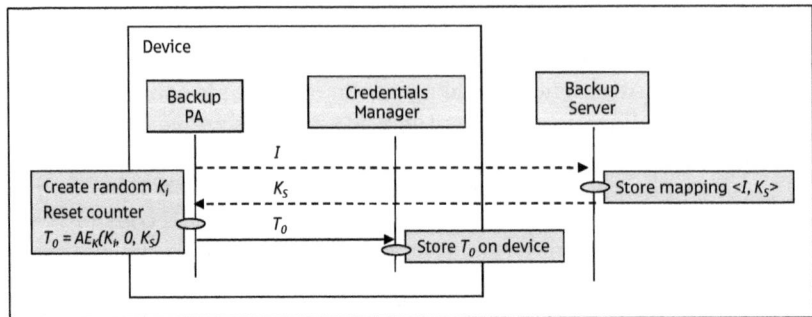

Fig. 1. Server-assisted credential system initialization

5.1   Definitions

We assume that the TrEE is equipped with a device specific *platform key* K that is only accessible inside the TrEE (assumption A1). The device and the server share a symmetric key K_S and the server is able to map a *platform key identifier* I to K_S shared between a particular device. K_S and I are setup during a system initialization phase.

On the device side we have two software components. Backup PA is a software component (protected application) that is executed inside the TrEE. Credentials Manager (CM) is a privileged operating system level component. The protocol that is run between the device and the server is called *credential disabling protocol*.

5.2   Initialization

The system initialization phase is shown in Figure 1. In this process shared I and K_S are established between the TrEE and the server. This negotiation should happen preferably at device manufacturing time. Another possibility is do the credential platform initialization when the credential platform is first taken into use. In such a case the exchange of I and K_S must be a part of an authenticated and encrypted protocol run between the server and the Backup PA to prevent an attacker from reseting the device (attacker capability C3) and initializing the system with an attacker chosen K_S.

The Backup PA creates a random key called *platform key instance* K_i that is used to seal individual credentials stored on device file system. The Backup PA also sets a secure monotonic counter to zero, and creates a *platform key token* T_0. This token is an authenticated encryption over K_i, counter value and K_S using device specific platform key K as the key; $T_0 = AE_K(K_i, 0, K_S)$ where $AE_k()$ denotes to authenticated encryption with k as the key.

CM saves T_0 to its OS-level secure storage. This token must be loaded to TrEE each time a new credential is created and sealed, or an existing sealed credential

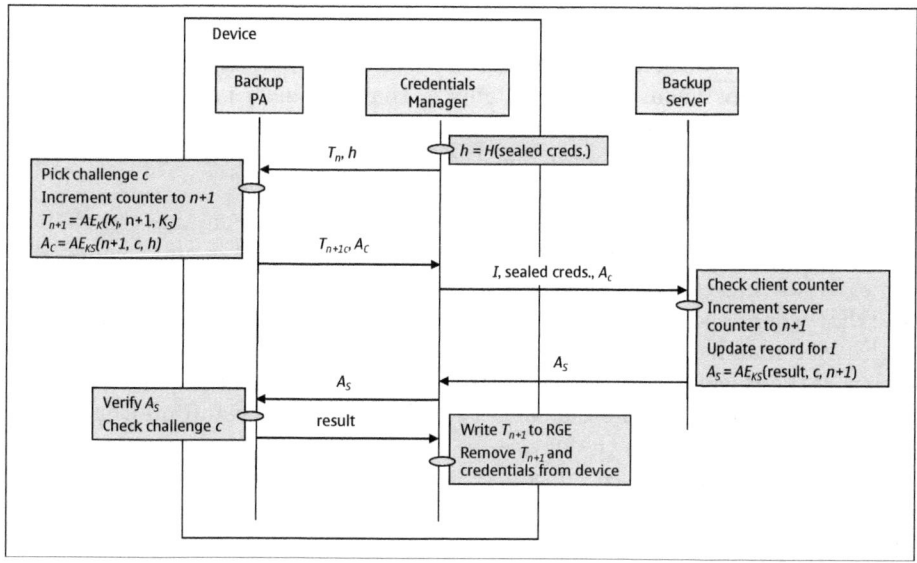

Fig. 2. Server-assisted credential disabling

is accessed. When a token is saved on the secure storage of CM, the device is considered "enabled". Normal backups can be created and restored simply by copying sealed credentials from the device to external, insecure storage media and from the storage media back to the device.

5.3   Credential Disabling

The server-assisted credential disabling operation is illustrated in Figure 2. The purpose of this operation is to create a new backup of the credentials to the backup server and disable all previous backups.

The disabling operation is triggered by the user. CM calculates a hash of all the sealed credentials that are stored on the device. The hash and current platform key token T_n are loaded to TrEE. The Backup PA picks a random challenge c for freshness of the credential disabling protocol, and saves it temporarily into *volatile* secure memory inside TrEE. The Backup PA also recovers the current counter value from T_n, increments the counter to $n + 1$, and creates a new platform key token $T_{n+1} = AE_K(K_i, n + 1, K_S)$. Additionally, the Backup PA creates a *client authenticator* A_C which is an authenticated encryption over counter value, challenge c and credentials hash h using K_S as the key: $A_C = AE_{K_S}(n + 1, c, h)$.

CM sends the sealed credentials and the authenticator A_C to the backup server together with a platform key identifier I. The server maintains a table with entries of the form $\langle$ I, counter, sealed credentials, K_S $\rangle$.[3] Upon receiving the client request the server determines which K_S to use based on identifier I, verifies the client authenticator A_C and recovers the client counter value and the sealed credentials hash. The server checks that the hash matches the received sealed credentials. If the client counter is larger than the one locally stored, the server updates its local counter and the local copy of sealed credentials in the database for this particular I.[4]

The server constructs a server authenticator A_S that contains the challenge c, the result of the backup operation and the incremented counter value: $A_S = AE_{K_S}(\text{result}, c, n + 1)$. Server sends authenticator A_S to CM which feeds it to TrEE where the Backup PA verifies the authenticator and checks that the challenge c matches the one it created and saved to the secure volatile memory earlier. If the Backup PA returns positive result, CM copies T_{n+1} to RGE, deletes the local copy of the credentials and T_{n+1} from the device and informs the user to remove the RGE from the device.

CM considers the device "disabled" as long as there is no token on its local storage. Restoring backups is possible only by running restore protocol with the server.

5.4   Credential Recovery

The server-assisted credential recovery is shown in Figure 3. The purpose of this operation is to restore previous disabling backup from the server provided that the user has re-inserted RGE with valid (latest) token to the device.

The restore operation is triggered when the user inserts RGE into the device. CM loads T_n from RGE to TrEE. The Backup PA constructs a client authenticator A_C that contains the counter value n and random challenge c: $A_C = AE_{K_S}(n, c)$. CM sends this authenticator A_C together with I to the server.

The server verifies authenticator A_C using K_S, and extracts the counter value. If the counter is less than in the local database of the server (old token read from RGE), the server returns an error. Otherwise, it increases its local counter and returns the sealed credentials together with an authenticator A_S that contains the operation result, hash of the sealed credentials h, the challenge c and the updated counter value: $A_S = AE_{K_S}(\text{result}, c, h, n + 1)$. CM hashes the received credentials and the Backup PA verifies that the credentials hash matches the one in the authenticator and that the challenge in the authenticator is valid. The Backup PA also creates T_{n+1} which CM stores on the device.

Now, CM considers the device "enabled" again and credentials can be used by loading an encrypted credential together with the token to TrEE.

---

[3] The server must protect the integrity of counter and confidentiality of K_S.

[4] Platform key identifier I can identify both the device and the currently used platform key instance, and thus allow multiple parallel backup branches to be be maintained for the same device, and thus multiple users using the same.

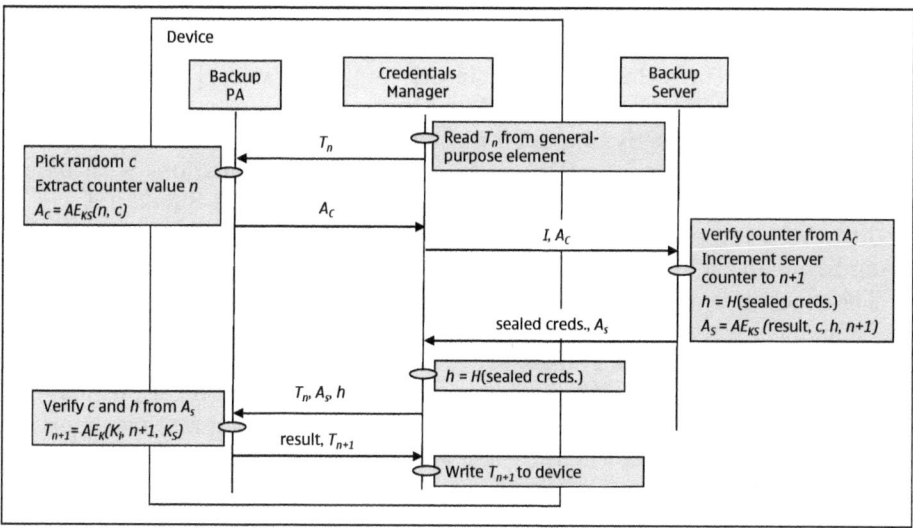

Fig. 3. Server-assisted credential recovery

6   Implementation

We have implemented the server-assisted credential disabling scheme described in the previous section for mobile phones with M-Shield secure environment. Our target implementation device was Nokia N96 with Symbian OS v9.3 and S60 platform.

M-Shield is a security architecture available for the OMAP platform used in mobile devices. It has a secure environment consisting of a small amount of on-chip ROM and RAM, as well as one-time programmable memory where unique device key(s) can be maintained. All of these are only accessible in a secure execution environment implemented as a special "secure processor mode". The secure mode is isolated from ordinary software, including the device operating system. In M-Shield architecture trusted (signed) code can be implemented as so called protected applications (PAs). For more detailed information on M-Shield see [15,14].

The Backup PA was implemented as an M-Shield protected application. The Backup PA was written in C and it is 6 kB in size in compiled format. We reuse the same the authenticated encryption operation (our own implementation of AES-EAX mode [2]) for local data sealing and disabling protocol authentication to minimize the Backup PA implementation footprint. The M-Shield environment provides existing primitives for encryption (AES), random number generation and hashing (SHA-1). The M-Shield TrEE provides small amount of volatile secure memory that persists its state between subsequent protected application executions (but not over device boots). We use this memory to store the challenge that is used to guarantee the freshness of the disabling backup protocol run.

The operating system level component Credentials Manager (CM) was implemented using C++ for Symbian OS. The Symbian OS platform security model provides two features that we utilize in our implementation [7]. First, each process has its own private directory. CM uses this feature for storing the platform key token. Second, the Symbian OS platform security provides capability model in which access to certain APIs can be restricted to applications with required capabilities (privileges). In our implementation, access to M-Shield TrEE is limited to CM using this model. The CM component itself is trusted due to signing using Symbian Signed infrastructure [16].

The Backup server was implemented with standard Apache server running on Linux. The credential disabling protocol was implemented with simple type-length-value encoded binary messages that are Base64 encoded for TLS based HTTP POST transport. We implemented the system initialization phase as a server-authenticated on-line protocol using similar encoding and transport. The trust root of the server authentication was fixed to our Backup PA implementation.

7   Analysis

7.1   Credential Disabling with Personal Element Presence

As already briefly discussed in Section 4 the PE presence check should be a cryptographic protocol between the TrEE and the PE. In case of SIM cards, one alternative to realize this would be to use Generic Bootstrapping Architecture (GBA) [8]. In GBA an application specific network entity called Network Authentication Function (NAF) and a software entity on the SIM-equipped device can bootstrap a shared secret from the SIM-resident secret that is shared with the network operator. The prerequisite is an established relationship between the NAF and the network operator.

One possible way to implement SIM-based credential disabling would be to fix the trust root of disabling specific NAF to the Backup PA. Then the check for the presence of a SIM card would be a protocol between the Backup PA and disabling NAF. If the valid SIM is present on the device, the device can prove this fact to the disabling NAF by using the bootstrapped GBA session key it shares with the NAF. The disabling NAF can sign a statement confirming this verification that the Backup PA can verify using the trust root. We leave working out the exact details of this protocol and implementation of this scheme as future work.

Personal element presence based credential disabling can be automatically triggered when the user removes the PE from the device. This significantly reduces the chance that the user would forget to disable her credentials before lending the device compared to solutions based on counters in which the user must explicitly trigger the disabling operation.

7.2   Credential Disabling with Semi-Trusted Server

In the server-assisted solution the freshness of the token is checked against the server to prevent recovery of backups using old tokens that the attacker may get access to (RC2). After a successful credential recovery, the token is stored on local storage of CM and loaded to TrEE every time a credential is used without connecting to the server. The security of this solution relies on the assumption that the attacker cannot replace a valid token on the local storage of CM with an old token (C4). In our implementation, the Symbian OS platform security model prevents an attacker from replacing data in CM private directory. The attacker may reset the whole device (e.g. many mobile phones provide an easy way to restore factory settings), but replacing a valid token with an old one is not possible without compromising the OS.

If similar OS-level secure storage is not available, or if we assume that the attacker is able to compromise the OS level security framework and thus replace the valid token with an old token, the attacker can restore old backups. This can be prevented by running an on-line protocol with the server either every time the device is booted or before every credential usage. The usage of this security mechanism could be based on credential specific policies. Freshness of the token could be checked before every credential invocation for credentials with high security level (e.g. online banking credentials), whereas for most credentials checking the freshness only during device boot might be enough.

The security of the solution is also based on the assumption that the semi-trusted server communicates correct counter values to the device. This means that the server must maintain integrity protected storage of counter values and secretly store keys that are used to authenticate the communication. In practice this could be done using hardware-based security module on the server. The sealed credential backups themselves are not confidential (i.e. they may leak to the attacker) which makes implementation and deployment of the server easier (the credential backups could be e.g. stored to external disks if needed).

If the server is malicious or gets compromised and send incorrect counter values, the device may accept an old token during recovery protocol. In such a case, the attacker can restore credentials from an old backup and use the old credentials. However, neither the attacker or the server can recover the content of the sealed credentials themselves.

The credential disabling protocol is not error-tolerant to network errors where the connection breaks after the server has received client request, but before the client has fully received server response. In such a case, the server has incremented its counter which invalidates the current token, but the client has not recovered credentials without a valid response from server. Two alternatives exist: (1) Allow multiple recovery attempts with the same token with the cost of increased attacker opportunities. (2) Introduce an additional round-trip to the protocol that would invalidate the current token, i.e. increment the server counter, only after successful recovery in client end. The client should check whether the server is reachable before performing a disabling backup. The credential disabling protocol provides freshness guarantee to the client device based

Table 1. Overview of different credential disabling solutions

Solution	Credential use	User failure	NV memory	Operator
1. PE presence	on-line	low	no	yes
2. Embedded counter	local	high	yes	no
3. Server-assisted	on-line	high	no	no

on the client nonce. The freshness guarantee to the server is based only on the counter.

The security of the server-assisted credential disabling is dependent on correct user behavior. First, the user may forget to trigger the *explicit* disabling operation. If this is the case, the credentials remain on the device and the attacker can use them. The likelihood of this failure is considerable. The user may also fail to remove the RGE that contains the platform key token from the device. If this is case, the attacker can recover the latest credential backup. This problem is less likely, since the credential platform can remind the user to remove the RGE once the disabling operation is completed. Second, the user may lose the RGE during the disabling period. In this case, she cannot recover the credential backup. To fully understand how likely these error cases are, users tests are needed. We leave these as future work.

The dependency on an explicit disabling operation also limits the applicability of the server-assisted solution. For example, the user cannot disable the device before leaving it at a service point, if the device is broken or malfunctioning in such a way that the disabling operation cannot be triggered from the device. To address such scenarios automatic credential backups are needed which can be supported in personal element presence check based credential disabling approach.

7.3   Comparison of Different Solutions

Table 1 presents an overview of the three primary credential disabling solutions discussed in this paper.

1. PE presence check based credential disabling has low probability of user failure (the user is likely to remove SIM before lending her device). If the OS-level security framework cannot be trusted, network based PE presence check should be performed before every credential invocation which requires on-line connectivity. The drawback of this solution is the dependency on network operators.
2. Credential disabling based on TrEEs with embedded secure counter has higher probability of user failures (user may forget to trigger disabling), but credential use without any server interaction is possible without having to assume trustworthiness of OS-level security. The drawback is that many existing and widely deployed TrEEs do not support non-volatile secure memory.

3. The server-assisted credential disabling can be implemented with many existing TrEEs (also the ones without counters). The drawbacks of this solution are higher probability of user failures (explicit user triggering) and the requirement to interact with the server before each credential invocation if we cannot rely on the trustworthiness of the OS-level security.

8   Related Work

To the best of our knowledge there is very little existing work addressing the problem of temporary credential disabling from embedded trusted execution environments. Most related work addresses either (1) credential transfer or migration from one TrEE to another, or (2) credential backup or storage to an on-line server.

The Trusted Platform Module (TPM) specification define migration and maintenance commands [17]. The migration commands enable transfer of a single credential from one TPM to another. The (optional) maintenance commands enable transfer of all TPM protected credentials, or more precisely the transfer of the storage root key that is used to protect TPM based credentials stored on the device. Several researchers have proposed extensions to the TPM migration and maintenance commands or built credential migration schemes and protocols using these commands (see e.g. [11,3]). The TrEE based credential transfer has also been studied in the context of digital right management (see e.g. [12]), and there has been some attempts to standardize credential storage servers and protocols [6,5]. However, none of the existing papers or specifications address the problem present in our scenario, i.e. how to prevent an attacker that has physical access to the device from restoring a valid credential backup.

Using a server to provide secure counters for client devices is not a new idea. van Dijk et al. show how an untrusted server that is equipped with a trusted time stamping device (in practice, a TPM) can be used to provide secure virtual monotonic counters for many client devices [18].

9   Conclusions

In this paper we have raised attention to a problem that has not been addressed before—temporary disabling and recovery of credentials from embedded trusted execution environments. We have explained why straightforwards solutions do not solve this seemingly simple problem, and presented two novel solutions: one using presence check of a personal element, such as SIM card, and another utilizing semi-trusted server as a secure counter. We have implemented the server-based solution for mobile phones with M-Shield secure environment.

Neither of the presented schemes is perfect: implementing SIM-based credential disabling securely requires network operator involvement and our server-based approach is dependent on correct user behavior. Thus, more work on temporary credential disabling is needed.

References

1. ARM. Trustzone,
   http://www.arm.com/products/processors/technologies/trustzone.php
2. Bellare, M., Rogaway, P., Wagner, D.: EAX: A conventional authenticated-encryption mode. Cryptology ePrint Archive: Re-port 2003/069 (September 2009),
   http://eprint.iacr.org/2003/069
3. Berger, S., Caceres, R., Goldman, K., Perez, R., Sailer, R., van Doorn, L.: vTPM - virtualizing the trusted platform module. In: Proceedings of 15th Usenix Security Symposium, pp. 305–320 (2006)
4. Costan, V., Sarmenta, L.F.G., van Dijk, M., Devadas, S.: The Trusted Execution Module: Commodity General-purpose Trusted Computing. In: Grimaud, G., Standaert, F.-X. (eds.) CARDIS 2008. LNCS, vol. 5189, pp. 133–148. Springer, Heidelberg (2008)
5. Fischl, J. (ed.): Certificate Management Service for The Session Initiation Protocol (SIP) draft-ietf-sip-certs-09. Internet Engineering Task Force (September 2009)
6. Farrell, S. (ed.): Securely Available Credentials Protocol. Internet Engineering Task Force, RFC 3767 (June 2004)
7. Heath, C.: Symbian OS Platform Security. Wiley (2006)
8. Holtmanns, S., Niemi, V., Ginzboorg, P., Laitinen, P., Asokan, N.: Cellular Authentication for Mobile and Internet Services. Wiley (2008)
9. JavaCard Technology,
   http://www.oracle.com/technetwork/java/javacard/overview/index.html
10. Kostiainen, K., Ekberg, J.-E., Asokan, N., Rantala, A.: On-board cre-dentials with open provisioning. In: Proc. of ACM Symposium on Information,Computer & Communications Security, ASIACCS 2009 (2009)
11. Kühn, U., Kursawe, K., Lucks, S., Sadeghi, A.-R., Stüble, C.: Secure Data Management in Trusted Computing. In: Rao, J.R., Sunar, B. (eds.) CHES 2005. LNCS, vol. 3659, pp. 324–338. Springer, Heidelberg (2005)
12. Nokia. Mobile Internet Technical Architecture - MITA. IT Press, Finland (2002)
13. Schellekens, D., Tuyls, P., Preneel, B.: Embedded Trusted Computing with Authenticated Non-volatile Memory. In: Lipp, P., Sadeghi, A.-R., Koch, K.-M. (eds.) TRUST 2008. LNCS, vol. 4968, pp. 60–74. Springer, Heidelberg (2008)
14. Srage, J., Azema, J.: M-Shield mobile security technology, TI White paper (2005),
    http://focus.ti.com/pdfs/wtbu/ti_mshield_whitepaper.pdf
15. Sundaresan, H.: OMAP platform security features, TI White paper (July 2003),
    http://focus.ti.com/pdfs/vf/wireless/platformsecuritywp.pdf
16. Symbian signed, https://www.symbiansigned.com
17. Trusted Platform Module (TPM) Specifications,
    https://www.trustedcomputinggroup.org/specs/TPM/
18. van Dijk, M., Rhodes, J., Sarmenta, L., Devadas, S.: Offline untrusted storage with immediate detection of forking and replay attacks. In: STC 2007: Proceedings of the 2007 ACM Workshop on Scalable Trusted Computing, pp. 41–48. ACM, New York (2007)

Java Card Architecture for Autonomous Yet Secure Evolution of Smart Cards Applications*

Olga Gadyatskaya, Fabio Massacci, Federica Paci, and Sergey Stankevich

DISI, University of Trento, Italy
surname@disi.unitn.it

Abstract. Open multi-application smart cards that allow post-issuance evolution (i.e. loading of new applets) are very attractive for both smart card developers and card users. Since these applications contain sensitive data and can exchange information, a major concern is the assurance that these applications will not exchange data unless permitted by their respective policies. We suggest an approach for load time application certification on the card, that will enable the card to make autonomous decisions on application and policy updates while ensuring the compliance of every change of the platform with the security policy of each application's owner.

1 Introduction

Open multi-application environments such as PCs and mobile phones are widespread. The main characteristics of such environments are co-existence of several applications on one single platform and the possibility of these platforms to evolve by adding new applications or updating of existing ones in a fully distributed and autonomous way. Such applications can exchange data locally or remotely or access local APIs and in order to protect our security we regulate their accesses by more or less stringent mechanisms of access control locally enforced by the platform. The problem of this approach is that we may end up downloading something that turns out to be unusable. An alternative solution could be to shift the security checks at loading time. This approach requires applications to come with a manifest of their security-relevant actions and check whether their behavior is acceptable before installing the code. The idea was explored by Sekar et al. when the notion of *model-carrying code* was introduced [13], has been demonstrated in the *Security-by-Contract* (S×C) approach [3], and was adopted by W. Enck et al. for Android security [4].

Modern smart cards could be another example of an open multi-application environment. But even examples of potentially multi-stakeholders applications are de facto single one: a loyalty Miles& More Lufthansa credit card [9], could include a Lufthansa application for collecting miles and a Bank application; in fact it is just a credit card and mileage is calculated by the back-end system.

---

* Work partially supported by the EU under grant EU-FP7-FET-IP-SecureChange. We thank B. Chetali, Q. Nguyen, and I. Symplot-Ryl for useful discussions.

T. Aura, K. Järvinen, and K. Nyberg (Eds.): NordSec 2010, LNCS 7127, pp. 187–192, 2012.
© Springer-Verlag Berlin Heidelberg 2012

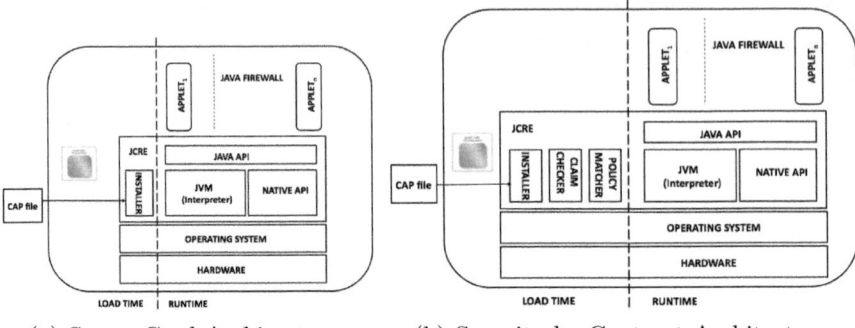

(a) Smart Card Architecture   (b) Security by Contract Architecture

Fig. 1. Architecture Evolution for Self-Certification

In order to support autonomous evolution on multi-application smart cards, we need a way for the platform to verify that applications arriving on the platform comply with the policy which is dynamically created by combining the policies of already installed applications. The task can be more complicated when applications can also be removed and we want to avoid loss of functionalities.

In this paper we propose an addition to the Java Card security architecture based on the Security-by-Contract approach that preserves security of the smart card when the content of the card changes, so that the smart card itself can ensure security after an update, when new applications arrive, old ones are updated or removed, or their security policies are changed.

2   Security-by-Contract Smart Card Architecture

Java Card architecture [10] consists of several layers as illustrated in Fig. 1(a):

- a device hardware,
- an embedded operating system (OS),
- a Java Card Runtime Environment (JCRE) on top of the embedded OS,
- the applications that are installed on the smart card, that are called *applets*.

Applets before being loaded on a smart card are converted into a CAP file, that is a binary executable representation of the Java classes that compose the applet. The JCRE is responsible for managing and executing applets. It is composed by a Java Virtual Machine (JVM), native API, framework APIs, and an application installer. The installer downloads and installs the applications on the card. To load an application, the installer interacts with an off-card installation program which transmits the CAP file. Once received the CAP file, the installer, first, checks the signature of the file to ensure integrity and to prove the identity of the application provider. Then, the installer saves the content of the file into the card's persistent memory, resolves the links with other applets already present on the card, creates an instance of the applet and registers it to the JCRE. Then JVM, which consists of a bytecode interpreter, executes the code contained in the CAP file.

The applets installed on the smart card are isolated by the Java firewall. The firewall allows only applets that belong to the same context to access the respective methods. If an applet (*server*) wants to share data with another applet (*client*) from a different context, it has to implement a *shareable interface* which defines a set of methods that are available to other applets. These methods (they are also called *services*) are the only methods of the server applet that are accessible through the firewall. The JCRE will pass the call to the shareable interface method from the client applet to the server applet. In the current Java Card security model the server has an access control list of the applets that are allowed to use this method, embedded into the server code. If the client is in the list, the access is granted, otherwise the client gets null. If the client has been updated, the server will still grant it an access, though now the server cannot really be sure of the trustworthiness of the client.

We have identified the requirements for an extension of the security mechanisms on Java Card in the presence of evolution from the requirements of the GlobalPlatform (GP) specification [8]. GP is a middleware, that can run on top of Java Card and provide more security mechanisms for applets management (for inter-application communications GP relies on the JCRE). GP specification provides explicit requirements for maintaining security (in terms of services access control enforcement) and functionality of the applications on the card during evolution.

The basic idea of our proposal is to add a contractual component to each applet detailing its security policy and its claims on the usage of other resources (services) on the platform (the latter can be also extracted from the CAP file). The architecture we propose is provided on Fig. 1(b). It is based on the addition of two components to the JCRE, the ClaimChecker and the PolicyChecker.

When a new applet has to be loaded on the card, the terminal sends the CAP file of the applet to the installer. The CAP file contains the binary code of the applet and its Contract. When the installer receives the CAP file of the new applet the ClaimChecker verifies that the claims are compliant with the applet's code. If this is the case, the PolicyChecker checks the applet's contract against the platform policy $\mathcal{P}$. If the PolicyChecker has returned True then the installer finalizes the loading and creates an instance of the applet. Otherwise, the applet is rejected. On the S×C-enhanced platform, when a method of the applet is called by another applet, the Java Card firewall simply checks that the method belongs to the shareable interface of the applet (this check is also a firewall's responsibility on the standard Java Card) and does not perform the run-time checks of the applet's privileges for an access to the services, since it was done at the loading time.

The security model behind the concepts in the architecture assumes that the card can be represented as a tuple $\langle \Delta_{\mathcal{A}}, \Delta_{\mathcal{S}}, \mathcal{A}, \mathsf{shareable}(), \mathsf{invoke}(), \mathsf{sec.rules}(), \mathsf{func.rules}() \rangle$, where $\Delta_{\mathcal{A}}$ is a domain of applications; $\Delta_{\mathcal{S}}$ is a domain of services; $\mathcal{A} \subseteq \Delta_{\mathcal{A}}$ is a set of applications installed (deployed) on the platform. The function $\mathsf{shareable}_{\mathsf{A}}$ defines the actual shareable interfaces of applet A available on the platform and the function $\mathsf{invoke}_{\mathsf{A}}$ the set of services called by A.

The functions sec.rules() and func.rules, define respectively the security policy and the functionality policy of each application. For every applet $A \in \mathcal{A}$ sec.rules$_A$(s) defines for each service of applet A which other applets on the platform are authorized to call it. The functional rules func.rules$_A$ specify the set of services on the platform that A needs in order to be functional (e.g. a transport applet normally needs a payment applet in order to be useful).

The contract Contract$_A$ of an application A includes the following sets: Provides$_A$ (a set of services that applet A has), Calls$_A$ (a set of services of other applets that A calls), sec.rules$_A$ (authorizations for A's services access) and func.rules$_A$ (set of functionally necessary services for A).

The ClaimChecker for an application B with a contract Contract$_B$ will return true if shareable$_B$=Provides$_B$ and invoke$_B$=Calls$_B$. A PolicyChecker algorithm for platform Θ and changed application B will allow the update if for all applications $A \in \mathcal{A}$ and services $s \in \mathcal{S}$

- **Security on contract level**: if service s of applet B is in Calls$_A$ then A is authorized by B to call s $((s, A) \in$ sec.rules$_B)$.
- **Functionality on contract level**: if service s of applet B is in func.rules$_A$ then $s \in$ Provides$_B$.

The main idea behind the security model is that if the ClaimChecker and the PolicyChecker are sound and they returned true for $\forall A \in \mathcal{A}$ then the platform Θ is secure.

3   Policy Checker Implementation

We have implemented the PolicyChecker for installation of a new application, as the most interesting and representative case, using Sun's Java Card simulator for Java Card 2.2.2 specification [10]. Contracts are implemented as instances of `Contract` Java class that are included in the CAP file of the applet. The PolicyChecker has been implemented as `Card` Java Card applet. The `Card` class has a field `Card.Pool` that stores the platform policy. `Card.Pool` is an instance of `Map` Java class that associates with each applet on the platform its contract. The applet is identified by a String that contains the AID while the contract is an instance of the `Contract` class. The method `validateContract(Contract)` of the class `Card` has as input parameter the `Contract` of a new applet and returns the result of the evaluation of `Contract` against the platform policy stored in field `Card.Pool`. If `Contract` is compliant with the platform policy, the new applet is installed, otherwise it is rejected.

We have tested the feasibility of installing the PolicyChecker on the card as an additional applet. In particular, we have evaluated the communication overhead associated with the installation of the PolicyChecker in terms of number of APDU commands exchanged between the terminal and the card to load the CAP file. In fact, when the Java classes are converted into the CAP file, the terminal converts them into data sequences (APDUs), which then are used to upload the code and make it selectable. This is a good indication of the cross-platform memory footprint of the applet as default APDUs are up to 255 bytes.

The CAP file generated for the PolicyChecker applet contains 18 Java classes and generates 118 APDUs commands to load the applet on the card. Thus, installing the PolicyChecker on the card does not require more APDUs than the installation of a normal applet. We have also evaluated the overhead of installing an applet along with its contract. We generated a Contract class for a sample *Transport* applet (*T* for short). The Contract$_T$ contains 3 services in Provides$_T$, 3 in Calls$_T$, 4 authorized applets in sec.rules$_T$ and 2 services in func.rules$_T$. The Contract$_T$ is rather complicated comparing with a contract an average smart card application can produce (usually applets have up to 2 services). The Java Card representation of the Contract$_T$ is only 7 APDUs.

We do not show here how to construct a ClaimChecker. An example can be found in Ghindici et al. [5]. The ClaimChecker they have built is working on more complex information flow models and it can be restricted to our Contract model.

4   Related Works and Conclusions

Ghindici et al. [5] propose a domain specific language for security policies capturing the information flow within small embedded systems. In the framework they propose each application is certified at loading time, having a information flow signature assigned to each method, describing the flow relations between method variables. Huisman et al. [7] present a formal framework and a tool set for compositional verification of application interactions on a multi-application smart card. Their method is based on construction of maximal applets, w.r.t structural safety properties, simulating all the applets respecting these properties. Model checking techniques can be then used to check whether a composition of two applets *A* and *B* respects some behavioral safety property.

Girard in [6] suggests to associate security levels (clearances) to application attributes and methods, using traditional Bell/La Padula model. Bieber et al. adopt this approach in [2] and propose a technique based on model checking for verification of actual information flows. The same approach is used by Schellhorn et al. in [12] for their formal security model for operating systems of multi-application smart cards. Avvenuti et al. in [1] propose a tool for off-card verification of Java bytecode files, that could be later installed on the card, their method explores the multi-level policy model and the theory of abstract interpretation.

Outside of the smart cards domain, the techniques for policy enforcement in multi-application environment are investigated also for mobile platforms and operation systems. Ongtang et al. in [11] have proposed the Saint framework for Android mobile platform applications to impose requirements on the usage of their services on other applications during installation time and run-time. Applications on a Saint-enabled Android platform can define permissions and demand fulfillment of certain requirements by both their callers and callees. The Kirin framework mentioned above was developed for Android by Enck et al. [4], it can check permissions application requests at installation time in order to capture possibly dangerous combinations of permissions and warn the user.

In this paper we have proposed an extension of the Java Card security mechanisms for open multi-application smart cards that makes it possible to do verify updates on the card. This extension adds two components to the JCRE, the ClaimChecker and the PolicyChecker. In a nutshell, all applications are arriving with specifications of their behavior and their requirements on other applications on the platform. These requirements merged together create platform security policy. The card can check autonomously whether they are acceptable and then either reject or accept the change.

References

1. Avvenuti, M., Bernardeschi, C., De Francesco, N., Masci, P.: A tool for checking secure interaction in Java Cards. In: Proc. of EWDC 2009 (2009)
2. Bieber, P., Cazin, J., Wiels, V., Zanon, G., Girard, P., Lanet, J.-L.: Checking secure interactions of smart card applets: Extended version. J. of Comp. Sec. 10(4), 369–398 (2002)
3. Dragoni, N., Massacci, F., Naliuka, K., Siahaan, I.: Security-by-Contract: Toward a Semantics for Digital Signatures on Mobile Code. In: López, J., Samarati, P., Ferrer, J.L. (eds.) EuroPKI 2007. LNCS, vol. 4582, pp. 297–312. Springer, Heidelberg (2007)
4. Enck, W., Ongtang, M., McDaniel, P.: On lightweight mobile phone application certification. In: Proceedings of CCS 2009, pp. 235–245. ACM (2009)
5. Ghindici, D., Simplot-Ryl, I.: On Practical Information Flow Policies for Java-Enabled Multiapplication Smart Cards. In: Grimaud, G., Standaert, F.-X. (eds.) CARDIS 2008. LNCS, vol. 5189, pp. 32–47. Springer, Heidelberg (2008)
6. Girard, P.: Which security policy for multiplication smart cards? In: USENIX Workshop on Smartcard Technology. USENIX Association (1999)
7. Huisman, M., Gurov, D., Sprenger, C., Chugunov, G.: Checking Absence of Illicit Applet Interactions: A Case Study. In: Wermelinger, M., Margaria-Steffen, T. (eds.) FASE 2004. LNCS, vol. 2984, pp. 84–98. Springer, Heidelberg (2004)
8. GlobalPlatform Inc. GlobalPlatform Card Specification. Specification 2.2 (2006)
9. Lufthansa. Miles&More credit cards, http://www.miles-and-more.com
10. Sun Microsystems. Runtime environment specification. Java Card^{TM} platform, version 2.2.2. Specification 2.2.2., Sun Microsystems (2006)
11. Ongtang, M., McLaughlin, S., Enck, W., McDaniel, P.: Semantically rich application-centric security in Android. In: Proceedings of ACSAC 2009, pp. 340–349 (2009)
12. Schellhorn, G., Reif, W., Schairer, A., Karger, P., Austel, V., Toll, D.: Verification of a Formal Security Model for Multiapplicative Smart Cards. In: Cuppens, F., Deswarte, Y., Gollmann, D., Waidner, M. (eds.) ESORICS 2000. LNCS, vol. 1895, pp. 17–36. Springer, Heidelberg (2000)
13. Sekar, R., Venkatakrishnan, V.N., Basu, S., Bhatkar, S., DuVarney, D.C.: Model-carrying code: a practical approach for safe execution of untrusted applications. In: Proc. of the 19th ACM Symp. on Operating Syst. Princ., pp. 15–28 (2003)

Implementing Erasure Policies
Using Taint Analysis

Filippo Del Tedesco, Alejandro Russo, and David Sands

Chalmers University of Technology, Göteborg, Sweden
{tedesco,russo,dave}@chalmers.se

Abstract. Security or privacy-critical applications often require access to sensitive information in order to function. But in accordance with the principle of least privilege – or perhaps simply for legal compliance – such applications should not retain said information once it has served its purpose. In such scenarios, the timely disposal of data is known as an *information erasure policy*. This paper studies software-level information erasure policies for the data manipulated by programs. The paper presents a new approach to the enforcement of such policies. We adapt ideas from dynamic taint analysis to track how sensitive data sources propagate through a program and erase them on demand. The method is implemented for Python as a library, with no modifications to the runtime system. The library is easy to use, and allows programmers to indicate information-erasure policies with only minor modifications to their code.

1 Introduction

Sensitive or personal information is routinely required by computer systems for various legitimate tasks: online credit card transaction may handle a card number and related verification data, or a biometric-based authentication system may process a fingerprint. Such systems often operate under informal constraints concerning the handling of sensitive data: once the data has served its purpose, it must not be retained by the system.

The notion of erasure studied here is higher-level than the system-level and physical notions of data erasure which might involve, e.g. ensuring that caches are flushed and that hard-drives are overwritten sufficiently often to eradicate magnetic traces of data. The approach to program-based high-level erasure stems from the work of Chong and Myers [3]. That work and its subsequent developments deal with a notion of erasure which is relative to a multilevel security lattice [7]. For the purpose of this paper, we will not consider this extra dimension – so we view data as either *available* or *erased*.

In this paper, we present a new approach to the enforcement of information-erasure policies on programs which adapts concepts from dynamic taint analysis.

Language-Based Erasure. Our approach for information-erasure has several key features: it is a purely dynamic mechanism, it is based on taint analysis, and it is realised completely as a Python library. To see the benefits of these features, it is useful to consider previous work on erasure in the context of a simple erasure scenario (one which we will further elaborate upon in Section 3): a fingerprint-activated left-luggage locker of the kind that is increasingly common at US airports and amusement parks. When depositing a bag, a fingerprint scan is recorded. The locker can only be opened with the

T. Aura, K. Järvinen, and K. Nyberg (Eds.): NordSec 2010, LNCS 7127, pp. 193–209, 2012.

same fingerprint that locked it. From a privacy perspective, there is a clear motivation for an erasure policy: the fingerprint (and any information derived from it) should be erased once a locker has been reopened.

Hunt and Sands [12] described the first approach to the enforcement of Chong-Myers-style erasure properties, reemphasizing two key features missing from [3]: the ability to associate erasure policies with IO (clearly needed in our erasure scenario), and a way to verify that a program correctly erases data by a purely static analysis (a type system). There are two key limitations in Hunt and Sands's approach. Firstly, in order to obtain a clean semantic model, the authors consider a restricted form of erasure policy which is specified in the code in the form: "the value received at this input statement must be erased by the end of the code block which follows it". This is suitable for the simple locker scenario (which is problematic for other reasons) but unsuitable for more complex conditional policies of the kind discussed by Chong and Myers. Secondly, the idea is only elaborated for a toy language. Scaling up to a real language is a nontrivial task for such a static analysis, and would require, among other things, a full alias analysis.

Chong and Myers [5] independently considered the problem of enforcing erasure policies and developed a hybrid static-dynamic approach. In their approach, data is associated with conditional erasure properties which state that data must be erased at the point when some (in principle arbitrary) condition becomes true. An implementation extending the Jif system uses a simple form of condition variables for this purpose [4]. To support such rich policies, they assume a combination of a static analysis and a runtime monitor. The static analysis ensures that all program variables are labeled with consistent policies. For example, if variable x is copied to y and x's policy says that it should be erased at some condition c, then the policy for y should be at least as demanding. It is then the job of the run-time system to detect when conditions become true, and implement the erasure on the behalf of the programmer (by overwriting all variables with a dummy value).

Neither of these approaches can satisfactorily handle the simple locker scenario (and certainly not the more complex variants we will consider later in this paper). The approach described in [5,4] does not consider input at all, but only one-time erasure of variables – although this is arguably not a fundamental limitation. More fundamentally, both approaches use a semantic notion of erasure which is based on a strict information-flow property. In the locker scenario described previously, there is a small amount of information which is inevitably "retained" by the system, namely the fact that the fingerprint used to unlock the container matches the one used to lock it. This requirement cannot be easily captured by [5,12] since no retention of information is allowed. Observe that the retained information is not enough to recover the fingerprint which produced it, and therefore we can consider the system as an erasing one. It is not difficult to imagine more complex scenarios (e.g. billing services) that need to retain portions of sensitive information to complete their task, but the amount of retained data is not enough to consider their behavior as a violation of some required erasure policies. Chong-Myers approach includes declassification, but what we need here is instead an erasure dual, the ability to selectively ignore that some information is remembered by the system.

This feature might be called *delimited retention*, as it resembles the *delimited release* [21] property that some non-interferent system may exhibit.

Overview. In the remainder of this paper we outline our alternative approach. We adopt the idea of *dynamic taint tracking* which is familiar from languages like Perl [1] and a number of recent pragmatic information-flow analysis tools [10,13,14,8,22]: a specific piece of data which is scheduled for erasure is labeled ("tainted"). As computation proceeds, the labels are tracked through the system ("taint propagation"). When it is time to erase the data, we can locate all the places to which the data has propagated and thereby erase all of them.

By performing a dynamic analysis, we obtain a system that is able to deal with complex conditional-erasure conditions. Taint analysis does not track all information flows; in particular the information flows which result purely from control-flow are not captured. This makes the approach unsuitable for malicious code (the approach presented in [16] could be integrated with our library in order to tackle such flows). However, when implicit information flows [7] are ignored, then the need for yet-more-complex *delimited retention* policies used at branching instructions seems to be unnecessary. In principle, it could be possible to encode any delimited retention policy using implicit flows at the price of writing complex and unnatural code, which supports the idea to explicitly include mechanisms for delimited retention.

We are able to implement erasure enforcement for Python, an existing widely-used programming language, simply by providing a library, with no modification of the language runtime system and no special purpose compiler needed. Python's dynamic dispatch mechanism is mainly responsible to facilitate the implementation of our approach as a library. It could be then possible to implement our enforcement for other programming languages with similar dynamic features as Python.

The programmer interface to the library does not require the program to be written in a particular style or using particular data structures, so in principle, it can be applied to existing code with minimal modifications.

The API for the library is particularly simple (Section 2) and its implementation builds on two well-known techniques from object-oriented programming and security, namely *delegation* [15] (Section 2.1) and *taint analysis* (Section 2.3). To use the library the programmer must identify *erasure sources* – in the case of the simple locker example, it is the input function which returns the fingerprint. Then, the programmer must mark in the code the point at which a given value must be erased. This allows the library to trace the origins of a given value and erase all its destination values (Section 2.4).

Section 3 illustrates the use of the library with an extended example based on the locker scenario, but with more involved policies.

In addition, we explore a new *lazy* form of erasure (Section 4). This form of erasure is triggered "just in time" at the points where data would otherwise escape the system and observably break the intended erasure policy. The advantage of lazy erasure is that it is able to easily express rich conditional-erasure policies, including those involving time constraints (e.g. "erase credit card numbers more than one week old"). Additional related work is described in Section 5.

2 The Erasure Library

This section presents the library to introduce information erasure policies into programs. Both its source code and the examples we are using in this paper are publicly available at http://www.cse.chalmers.se/~russo/erasure.

The library API essentially consists of three functions:

`erasure_source(f)` is used to mark that values produced by function f might be erased. Henceforth, we will say that such values are *erasure-aware*. In the locker scenario, suppose that the function responsible to perform the scan of a fingerprint and return its value is getFingerprint. Then, the programmer might declare (prior to any computation): getFingerprint=erasure_source(getFingerprint). The instruction above can be interpreted as t=erasure_source(getFingerprint); getFingerprint=t, where t is a temporary variable. As an alternative, if the code for the definition of getFingerprint() is available, Python's decorator syntax can be used to obtain the same effect:

```
@erasure_source
def getFingerprint() :
    # body of definition ...
```

`erasure(v)` erases all erasure-aware data which was directly used in the computation of value v. The effect is to overwrite the data with a default value. For example, if a locker is locked with a fingerprint stored in a variable of the same name, then the code for the locked state might be:

```
while locked
    tryprint=getFingerprint()                   # get attempt
    locked=not(match(tryprint,fingerprint))     # unlock?
    erasure(tryprint)                           # erase attempt
erasure(fingerprint)                            # now unlock
```

A simple variant erasure() erases all erasure-aware data (strings and numbers), and any data computed from them.

`retain(f)` provides an escape-hatch for erasure. It declares that the result of function f does not need to be erased. We say that f is a *retainer*. It corresponds to declaring an escape hatch in delimited release, or a sanitisation function in a taint analysis. In the example above, we might declare match as a retainer: match=retain(match).

Figure 1 contains two interactive sessions[1]. >>> is the interpreter prompt, while raw_input is the built-in function that reads a line from the standard input. In the left, line 1 gets the string 'A' as an input and stores it in variable x. Then, variable x is used in two elements of list y. Naturally, when printing the list, we can observe that the second element is x and the third one is some data derived from x, i.e. x concatenated with itself. Now, let us consider a replay of this session in which the programmer wants to delete the information related to the input x after list y is printed once, which constitutes an information erasure policy. To achieve that, the programmer needs to import our library, indicate that function raw_input returns erase-aware values, and call function erasure before printing the list for the second time. This revised session is illustrated on the right of Figure 1. Observe that erasure removes data related to x. It

---

[1] We refer to Python 2.7 here, but our techniques can also be applied to previous releases.

```
1   >>> x=raw_input()          1   >>> from erasure import *
2   A                          2   >>> raw_input=erasure_source(raw_input)
3   >>> y=['E',x, x+x]         3   >>> x=raw_input()
4   >>> y                      4   A
5   ['E','A','AA']            5   >>> y=['E',x,x+x]
                               6   >>> y
                               7   ['E','A','AA']
                               8   >>> erasure(x)
                               9   >>> y
                               10  ['E','','']
```

Fig. 1. Examples of interactive sessions, without and with erasure

is worth noting that the core part of the program has not drastically changed in order to introduce an information erasure policy. The next subsections provide some insights into the implementation of the library.

2.1 Delegation

```
1   >>> x=Erasure('A')
2   >>> type(x)
3   <type 'instance'>
4   >>> x
5   'A'
6   >>> y=x+x
7   >>> type(y)
8   <type 'instance'>
9   >>> y
10  'AA'
11  >>> x.erase()
12  >>> y.erase()
13  >>> (x,y)
14  ('', '')
```

Fig. 2. Mutable strings

Basic types are immutable in Python, which means they cannot be changed in-place after their creation. For instance, every string operation is defined to produce a new string as a result. Having immutable strings goes against the nature of erasure, since removing information stored in a string implies in-place overwriting of its contents by, for instance, the empty string. By using a coding pattern usually known as *delegation*, the library carefully implements a mechanisms that allows the value of a string to be changed as shown by lines 7 and 10 in Figure 1.

Delegation is a composite-based structure that manages a wrapped object and propagates method calls to it. In our library, it is implemented by the class Erasure, which wraps an immutable object. Most of the method calls on that class are forwarded to the wrapped object. The forwarding mechanism assures that the results of method calls are also wrapped by the class Erasure. By doing so, the only reference to the wrapped immutable object is by a field on the class Erasure. As a result, it is possible to encode mutable strings by simply using delegation. Let us consider the example in Figure 2. Line 1 creates an object of the class Erasure that contains the immutable string 'A', while line 3 states its type is instance and not str[2]. Line 6 calls the concatenation method on the object x, which is forwarded to the concatenation method of the string 'A'. The result of that, the immutable string 'AA', is wrapped by a new object of the class

---

[2] For semplicity Erasure was defined as an old-style class. For a new-style definition the return value of the type operator would be <**class** 'erasure.Erasure'>

Erasure and stored in y. Class Erasure provides the method erase to perform the concrete action of overwriting, with a default value, the class field where the immutable object is stored (see Lines 11–12). Consequently, the wrapped objects have now become the empty strings. The previous immutable objects, 'A' and 'AA', are no longer referenced and thus will be garbage collected on due course. Programmers are not supposed to deal with the class Erasure directly (observe that it is not in the interface of the library). Determining what data must be wrapped by the class Erasure is tightly connected to what information must be erasure-aware. The next two subsections describe the internal use of Erasure by the different mechanisms of the library.

2.2   The Primitive erasure_source

Erasure policies are expected to be only applied on a data source (i.e. an input) [12]. In fact, it does not make too much sense to erase information known at compile-time (e.g. global constants, function declarations, etc). In this light, the library provides the primitive erasure_source to indicate those sources of erase-aware values. More technically, the argument of erasure_source is a function, and the effect is to wrap, by using the class Erasure, the immutable values returned by it. As an example, we have the sequence of commands in Figure 3.

```
1    >>> from erasure import *
2    >>> raw_input=erasure_source(raw_input)
3    >>> x=raw_input()
4    A
5    >>> type(x)
6    <type 'instance'>
```

Fig. 3. Example of using erasure_source

Note that lines 1–3 are the same as the ones in Figure 1. In this case, the string 'A', returned by calling raw_input, is wrapped into an object of the class Erasure. As shown in Figure 1, users might want to delete a given input value as well as information computed from it. Therefore, the library must be able to automatically call the method erase on a given input as well as any piece of data computed from it. In order to do that, the library keeps track of how erasure-aware values flow inside programs by using taint analysis.

2.3   Taint Analysis

Taint analysis is an automatic approach to find vulnerabilities in applications. Intuitively, taint analysis keeps track how tainted (untrustworthy) data flow inside programs in order to constrain data to be untainted (trustworthy), or sanitised, when reaching sensitive sinks (i.e. security critical operations). Perl was the first scripting language to provide taint analysis as a special mode of the interpreter called *taint mode* [2]. Similar to Perl, some interpreters for Ruby [24], PHP [17], and Python [14] have been carefully modified to provide taint modes. Rather than modifying the interpreter, Conti and Russo in [6] show how to provide a taint mode via a library in Python.

There is a clear connection between the use of taint analysis for finding vulnerabilities and the problem of implementing an erasure policy. In taint analysis, data computed from untrustworthy values is tainted. In our library, data that is computed from erasure-aware values is erasure-aware. With this in mind, and inspired by Conti and Russo's work, we implement a mechanism to perform taint propagation, i.e. how to mark as erasure-aware data that is computed from other erasure-aware values. From now on, we use taint and erasure-aware as interchangeable terms.

Let us consider tainting and taint propagation in the following example, which is an extended version of the listing in Figure 1:

```
1   >>> raw_input=erasure_source(raw_input)
2   >>> x=raw_input()
3   A
4   >>> x.tstamps
5   set([datetime.datetime(2010, 7, 3, 14, 13, 49, 21585)])
6   >>> y=raw_input()
7   B
8   >>> y.tstamps
9   set([datetime.datetime(2010, 7, 3, 14, 13, 56, 324137)])
10  >>> z=x+y
11  >>> z.tstamps
12  set([datetime.datetime(2010, 7, 3, 14, 13, 49, 21585), datetime.
        datetime(2010, 7, 3, 14, 13, 56, 324137)])
```

As mentioned previously, erasure policies intrinsically refer to some input in the program. Consequently, to enforce erasure policies, it is necessary to identify specific inputs. Our library associates a timestamp to each input, representing the date and time at which the data was provided. Timestamps are stored in the attribute tstamps of the class Erasure. Thus, the assignment f=erasure_source(f) makes the result of f erasure aware, and in addition it ensures that each value produced by f is (uniquely) timestamped. Line 5 shows the timestamps corresponding to the input that variable x depends on. The content of x.tstamps is the date and time when the input in line 3 was provided (2010–7–3 at 14:13:49 and some microseconds).

When erasure-aware values are involved in computations, taint information (i.e. timestamps) gets propagated. More specifically, newly created erasure-aware objects are associated to the set of timestamps obtained by merging the timestamps found in the different objects involved in the computation. Taint propagation is implemented inside the delegation mechanism of the class Erasure and it is performed after forwarding method calls for a given object.

Line 10 combines two inputs (x and y) in order to create a new value, which is stored in z. Lines 11–12 show effect of taint propagation, as timestamps associated to z are those corresponding to the inputs x and y. At this point, the reader might wonder why timestamps are used rather than a simple input-event counter. By using timestamps, we will be able to program temporal erasure policies (Section 4).

Explicit and Implicit Flows. On most situations, taint analysis propagates taint information on assignments. Intuitively, when the right-hand side of an assignment uses tainted values, the variable appearing on the left-hand side becomes tainted. In fact, taint analysis is just a mechanism to track explicit flows, i.e. direct flows of information from one variable to another. Taint analysis tends to ignore implicit flows [7], i.e. flows through the control-flow constructs of the language.

```
1  if x == 'A': isA=True
2  else: isA=False
3  erasure(x)
```

Fig. 4. An implicit flow

Figure 4 presents an implicit flow where variable x is erasure-aware. Observe that variable isA is not erasure-aware. In fact, it is built from untainted Boolean constants. Although the value of x is erased (Line 3), information about x is still present in the program, i.e. the program knows if x referred to 'A'. It is not difficult to imagine programs that circumvent the taint analysis by copying the content of erasure-aware strings into regular strings by using implicit flows [19]. In scenarios where attackers have full control over the code (e.g. when the code is potentially malicious), implicit flows present an effective way to circumvent the taint analysis. There is a large body of literature on the area of language-based security regarding how to track implicit flows [20]. In this work, we only track explicit flows, and thus our method is only useful for code which is written without malice. Despite the good intentions and experience of programmers, some pieces of code might not perform erasure of information as expected. For example, a programmer might forget to overwrite a variable that is used to temporarily store some sensitive information. In this case, taint analysis certainly helps to repair such errors or omissions. How much information are implicit flows able to retain in non-malicious code? As it has been argued for taint analysis [19], we argue that implicit flows are unlikely to account for a large volume of unintended data retention. The reason is that data retention relies on the non-malicious programmer writing more involved and rather unnatural code in order to, for instance, copy tainted (erasure-aware) strings into untainted ones [19]. In contrast, to produce explicit flows, programmers simply need to forget to remove the content of a variable.

2.4 Erasing Data

The taint analysis described above allows the library to determine, given a value, which erasure-aware inputs were used to create it. These inputs are identified by a set of timestamps. To perform erasure, however, the library must take these timestamps and track down all primitive values which are built from those inputs (c.f. line 8 in Figure 1). To track which erasure-aware values depend on which inputs, the library internally maintains a dependency table. It is the interaction of taint analysis and this table what determines one of the differences between our approach and [6]. The table maps each timestamp to the set of (references to) erasure-aware values – i.e. objects of the class Erasure. If timestamp t is mapped to objects a and b, it means that the only values in the program created by the input value provided at time t are a and b. The dependency table is extended each time an erasure-aware input value is generated. It is updated when erasure-aware values are formed from already existing ones. Primitive erasure_source and the taint propagation mechanism are responsible for properly updating the dependency table. Primitive erasure(v), which performs the actual erasure of data, can be then easily implemented. More precisely, calling erasure(v) triggers the method erase (recall Figure 2) on all the objects which depend on the timestamps associated to v. As a result, erasure-aware values derived from the same inputs as v are erased from the program. Similarly, calling erasure() triggers the method erase on *every* object in the dependency table.

```
1  def lockerSystem():
2    while(True):
3      print 'Welcome to the locker system'
4      fingerprint=getFingerprint()
5      ts=datetime.today()
6      if fingerprint in ADM:
7        log.add('MEMORY DUMP -->'+fingerprint+': '+str(ts))
8        dump(log.getLog())
9      else:
10       suspect=local_police.check(fingerprint)
11       h = hash(fingerprint)
12       if locker.isFree():
13         key = h
14         locker.occupied()
15         print 'Please, do not forget to retrieve your goods'
16         log.add('LOCKED -->'+fingerprint+': '+str(ts))
17       else:
18         if key == h:
19           locker.free()
20           print 'Thanks for using the service'
21           log.add('UNLOCKED -->'+fingerprint+': '+str(ts))
22         else:
23           print 'You are not the right owner'
24           log.add('INVALID ACCESS -->'+fingerprint+': '+str(ts))
```

Fig. 5. Locker system

3   Extended Example

To give a fuller illustration of the capabilities of our approach, we add some extra functionalities to the locker system described previously that are likely to be found in a
real implementation. Firstly, the system is able to keep track of events in a log that a
group of special users, called *administrators*, can fetch using their fingerprints. Secondly, since such lockers are typically found in security-critical public infrastructures,
we anticipate that there will be communication with some external authority in order
to cross-check the input fingerprints with the ones contained in special records (terror-
ist suspects, wanted criminals etc.). For simplicity, and without losing generality, we
consider a system connected to just a single locker rather than several ones.

The code in Figure 5 shows an implementation of the locker system. As before,
function getFingerprint reads a fingerprint. Function datetime.today returns a
timestamp representing the current date and time. Object log implements logging facilities. Method log.add inserts a line into the log and method log.getLog provides
the log back inside a container.

When the fingerprint matches one of the administrator's fingerprints stored in the
container ADM, the dump function is executed using log.getLog as argument, and
the log is output (lines 7-8). Object local_police represents a connection to the external authority. Method local_police.check cross-checks the fingerprint given as
an argument against a database of suspects.

In all other cases (i.e. for locking and opening purposes), the locker only needs a hash of the fingerprint, which is assigned to h. locker represents the state of the locker, which is initially "free" and could become "occupied" during the execution. If the fingerprint does not belong to an administrator, the locker is tested with the isFree method. If the answer is positive, the user can store luggage; the hash is then saved in key and the locker state is set to occupied (lines 13-16). Otherwise, the locker is full and it is released only if the current hash matches with the one used to lock it. In this case the method free makes the locker available for the next user (lines 19-21).

When it comes to logging, it is crucial to define what we want and is allowed to log. The program logs four different responses corresponding to the system usage: 'LOCKED', 'UNLOCKED', 'INVALID ACCESS', and 'MEMORY DUMP'. Naturally, it is important to register the actions performed by the system as well as the time when they occur. Clearly, information erasure emerges as a desirable property when it comes to handle fingerprints. On one hand, *fingerprints corresponding to regular users must be removed from the system (including from its log) after they are used for the intended purpose*, which constitutes the information erasure policy of the locker system (observe the hash of the fingerprint is stored in the system for the authentication purpose, and for the purposes of this example is considered to be OK to store). Fingerprints corresponding to suspects, on the other hand, can be logged as evidence in case of a police investigation. In order to give credit for his or her work, fingerprints from administrators can also be logged. In other words, fingerprints from regular users must be erased after using them, while fingerprints from suspects and administrators can remain in the system. The code shown in Figure 5 does not fulfill the information erasure policy described before. It actually logs the fingerprints of any user, which violates citizens privacy. Although it is relatively simple to detect the violation of the information erasure policy in this example, the same task could be very challenging in a more complex system where there could be multiple sources of sensitive information in several thousands lines of codes.

Figure 6 shows how programmers can use the library to make the code fulfill the erasure policy regarding fingerprints. Line 1 imports our library. Line 4 identifies that

```
1    from erasure import erasure_source, retain, erasure
2
3    # Erasure-aware sources
4    getFingerprint=erasure_source(getFingerprint)
5
6    # Retention statement
7    hash=retain(hash)
8
9    def lockerSystem():
10       ...
11       suspect=local_police.check(fingerprint)
12       h = hash(fingerprint)
13       if not(suspect):
14          erasure(fingerprint)
15       ...
```

Fig. 6. Locker system patched to fulfill the erasure policy regarding fingerprints

fingerprints are subjected to erasure policies, i.e. they are erasure-aware values. Line 7 states that `hash` is properly written, namely its outputs cannot be related to its input, and therefore they are not considered to violate any erasure policy. Then, the implementation of function `lockerSystem` is only changed to call `erasure` when the user of the locker is not a suspect (lines 13-14). The rest of the code remains unchanged.

4 Lazy Erasure

The notion of erasure presented in the previous section is very intuitive. To remove all erasure-aware inputs used to compute a given value `v`, it is enough to call `erasure(v)`. When calling `erasure`, the library immediately triggers the mechanism to perform erasure over the current state of the program. Due to that fact, we call the mechanism implemented by the API in Section 2 *eager erasure*[3].

Eager erasure does not easily capture some classes of erasure policies without major encoding overhead, which might drastically modify the code of the program. In particular, let us consider conditional policies that cannot be immediately decided, e.g. a certain value can only remain in the system for a period of time, after which it has to be erased. Clearly, it is not possible to trigger the erasure mechanism straight away, but the need for erasure has to be remembered in the system and triggered at the right time. To deal with such policies without any additional major runtime infrastructure, the library provides *lazy erasure* as a mechanism to perform erasure at the latest possible moment, i.e. when needed.

Lazy erasure deletes information "just in time" at the points where data would otherwise escape the system and observably break the intended erasure policy. Programmers only need to state what is supposed to be erased and the library triggers the erasure mechanisms at certain output points, i.e. when information is leaving the system.

4.1 The Lazy Erasure API

Lazy erasure adds some additional functions to the API of the library. The other primitives such as `erasure_source` have the same semantics as before.

`erasure_escape(f)` This function is used syntactically in the same manner as `erasure_source` – i.e. as a function wrapper. It is used to identify the functions which are to be considered as "outputs" for the system. These are the functions where an erasure policy could be observable violated – for example writing to a file or communicating with the outside world in some other manner. The lazy erasure policies are enforced by inspecting the arguments to the functions which have been wrapped by the primitive `erasure_escape`.

`lazy_erasure(v,p)` Primitive `lazy_erasure` introduces an erasure policy into the program, but does not perform any actual erasure of information. It receives as arguments a value `v` and a policy function `p`. The policy function (henceforth an *erasure policy*) is a function from timestamps (i.e. timestamps of inputs) to Boolean values. Internally, a policy can use any of the program state, together with the timestamp ar-

---

[3] In functional languages, eager and lazy evaluation are commonly used terms to indicate when evaluation is performed. We use the same terminology for erasure of data rather than evaluation of terms.

gument (representing the timestamp of the value to be erased) to make judgment on whether the value should be erased or not. Thus, declaring `lazy_erasure(v,p)` indicates that any input values (and values computed from them) which were used in the creation of `v` should be erased if policy `p` holds for their timestamps. Erasure is then enforced at the output functions indicated by `erasure_escape`.

Two abbreviations are supported: `lazy_erasure(v)`, which is equivalent to `lazy_erasure(v,(lambda t:True))` and thus unconditionally enforces erasure at the erasure-escape points, and `lazy_erasure(p)`, which is an abbreviation for calling `lazy_erasure` with the policy `p` applied to every erasure-aware value in the system.

4.2 Lazy Erasure Examples

To illustrate how lazy erasure works, we start by encoding a temporal erasure policy that allows to only keep fingerprints (administrators and suspects' ones) for a limited time of five days. The following piece of code implements the condition for such a policy:

```
1  def fivedays_policy(time):
2      return (datetime.today()-time)>timedelta(days=5)
```

Policy `fivedays_policy` takes a timestamp as input and returns whether the timestamp is more than five days old. In Figure 7, we show how to apply the policy in our locker system. Line 8 indicates that before extracting the log from the system, erasure must be performed. Line 10 introduces the erasure policy `fivedays_policy` into the system. As a result, dumping the log triggers erasure on each of its entries which are older than 5 days.

```
1   from datetime import datetime, timedelta
2   from erasure import *
3
4   getFingerprint=erasure_source(getFingerprint)
5
6   hash=retain(hash)
7
8   dump=erasure_escape(dump)
9
10  lazy_erasure(fivedays_policy)
11
12  def lockerSystem():
13      ...
```

Fig. 7. Locker system with a lazy erasure policy

Lazy erasure is particularly useful to express policies that cannot be immediately decided when input data enters the system. To illustrate this, we extend the locker scenario a bit further.

A common experience with network connections is the loss of connectivity. To handle this situation properly, we introduce the constant `'no_connection'` to be returned by method `local_police.check` when the connection with the police department cannot be established. Enforcing an erasure policy that depends on the connection to the police department is not as simple as the policies considered previously. On one hand, we would like to have in the log the fingerprints which got the `'no_connection'` answer since they could belong to suspects. On the other hand, fingerprints that got the `'no_connection'` answer and do not belong to suspects must be erased in order to avoid violating users privacy when administrators dump the log.

As a trade-off between preserving fingerprints of suspects and privacy of regular citizens is represented by the enforcement of an erasure policy which depends on the person doing the dumping of the log. If a police agent is included in the set of administrators, then he or she can dump the log if necessary. Since a police agent represents the public authority, the agent has full access to the fingerprints stored in the log. Therefore, all the entries are included in the log, including those ones with the `'no_connection'` answer. In contrast, if the dumper is a regular administrator, the entries with `'no_connection'` are removed from the log. In this way, suspect-related data may get lost but privacy is not compromised. Clearly, the erasure policy is more involved than the ones that we have been considered so far. However, we show that it can be easily encoded by our library.

We start by introducing the Boolean global variable `police_mode` to represent when a police agent is dumping the log. Then, the function `lockerSystem` has to signal whether the person dumping the log is the police agent. Figure 8 shows an extension to `lockerSystem`. In line 3, `police_mode` is initially set to `False`. Immediately before dumping the log (line 9), the administrator identity is checked. If it is a police agent, `police_mode` is set to `True` (line 8). The state is then reset at line 10. If the person

```
1   def lockerSystem():
2       global police_mode
3       police_mode=False
4       ...
5       if fingerprint in ADM:
6           log.add('MEMORY DUMP -->'+fingerprint+': '+str(ts))
7           if fingerprint=='police':
8               police_mode=True
9           dump(log.getLog())
10          police_mode=False
11      else:
12          suspect=local_police.check(fingerprint)
13          h = hash(fingerprint)
14          if suspect==False:
15              lazy_erasure(fingerprint)
16          elif r=='no_connection':
17              lazy_erasure(fingerprint,role_policy)
18          else:
19              pass
20      ...
```

Fig. 8. `lockerSystem` reimplemented for lazy erasure

```
1  def role_policy(time):
2     global police_mode
3     return not(police_mode)
```

Fig. 9. Example of a lazy policy based on roles

dumping the log is a regular administrator, the value of `police_mode` does not change. Observe that line 17 associates the erasure policy `role_policy` to those fingerprints received when the connection to the policy department cannot be established. Consequently, the erasure of the fingerprint depends on the value returned by the policy *at the time of dumping the log*. Figure 9 defines `role_policy`. This policy only returns true when the dumping is done by a regular administrator (line 3). As a consequence, those fingerprints associated with `'no_connection'` are erased immediately before dumping the log provided that `police_mode` is false.

5   Related Work

As we have already explained in the introduction, application level erasure has been studied in [3] and [12]. A simpler form of erasure for Java bytecode is discussed in [11]. In [23], the counterpart of erasing systems (according to the definition given in [12]) has been explored, providing some insights into the obligations of a user who interacts with a system which promises erasure. These works all deal with an attacker model where an attacker can in the worst case inject arbitrary code into the system at a point in time at which erasure is supposed to have occurred. At lower levels of abstraction, for example [9], conditions and techniques to guarantee physical erasure on storage devices are considered. The need for physical erasure comes from a much stronger attacker model where the attacker is not hindered by any abstraction layers. An end-to-end view linking the high-level application level and the low level physical views should be possible, but it has not been previously considered.

To the best of our knowledge, Jif_E [4] is the only system currently implementing application-level erasure. This is based on the Jif compiler which deals with a subset of Java extended with security labels. Unlike the very general model on which it is based [5], the only conditions allowed in Jif_E's conditional erasure policies are a special class of Boolean condition variables. The implementation ensures that whenever such a condition variable changes, any necessary erasures are triggered. It would be simple to mimic this style of implementation (modulo implicit flows) using our primitives.

Erasure can be also related to *usage control*, since it is based on the idea of changing the way data is handled in the system after a certain moment. In [18], the authors present a model to reason on usage control, based on *obligations* the data receiver has to enforce through some *mechanisms*. The model is very general, and erasure can be described as an obligation (actually it is explicitly mentioned as a data owner requirement), but its purpose does not correspond to our approach, which deals with techniques to implement that obligation. The work in [26] extends access control with temporal and times-consuming features, leading to what they call TUCON (Times-based Usage Control) model. This approach allows to reason with policies that deal with the period of time in which a given object is available. Although it would not be very natural (policies here seem to be more user-oriented), it should be also possible to reason about erasure in this framework as well; similar considerations about implementation holds in this case as well. However, concepts from the usage control literature could provide inspiration for a study of the enforcement of a wider class of usage policies at code level.

6   Conclusions and Future Work

We have presented a library-approach to enforce erasure policies. The library transparently adds taint tracking to data sources, making it easy to use and permitting programmers to indicate information-erasure policies with only minor modifications to their code. To the best of our knowledge, this is the first implementation of a library that connects taint analysis and information-erasure policies. From our limited experience, the imperfections of taint analysis (the inability to track implicit flows) serve to keep the policy specifications simple, and enable us to handle examples for which existing approaches would not be sufficiently expressive. We have also introduced the concept of lazy erasure – an observational form of erasure which supports richer erasure policies, including temporal policies, with a simple implementation.

There are a number of directions for further work. One challenge ahead is how to deal with permanent storage like databases or file systems when specifying erasure policies. Policies like "user information must be erased when his or her account is closed" are out of scope in the existing approaches [3,12], where erasure is performed on internal data structures. User information, on the other hand, is usually placed in databases (e.g. web application) or file systems (e.g. Unix-like operating systems). We believe that it is possible to extend the interfaces for accessing files and databases in order to store data as well as erasure information (timestamps). Those interfaces usually involve handling objects and thus the library needs to be extended to consider them. To achieve that, we could threat objects as just mere containers and apply similar tainting techniques as the ones used for dictionaries. Another important aspect is the evaluation of the overheads caused by the library – in particular, how taint propagation and updates in the dependency table impact on performance. It would also be interesting to evaluate how *precise tainting* [17,8] could be exploited to obtain more precision when erasing data. Precise tainting associates taint information to characters rather than to whole strings. In our library, if an small part of an string contains some information that should be erased, then the whole string is deleted. By using *precise tainting*, it would be possible, in principle, to only delete those pieces of the string containing the information to erase. Precise tainting usually requires to fully understand the semantics of each function that manipulates erasure-aware values. As for most approaches to dynamic taint analysis, our approach ignores implicit flows. As a consequence programs might retain information indirectly via their control constructs. Rather than fixing this problem, a reasonable alternative might be to bound it. Inspired by preserving confidentiality, the work in [16] develops a mechanism to obtain bounds on the information leaked by implicit-flows. We believe that it is feasible to adapt such mechanism to obtain bounds on the information retained by control constructs. On the theoretical side, it could be important to describe precisely the security condition that taint analysis is enforcing in the presence of delimited retention policies. In fact, to the best of our knowledge, the work by [25] is the only one that presents a security condition for taint analysis using formal semantics.

Acknowledgements. Thanks are due to Juan José Conti for his contributions during the library development, to Aslan Askarov for suggesting the luggage-locker example and to our colleagues of the Prosec group, who shared with us their impressions on the topic. This work was partially supported by VR (`vr.se`), SSF (`stratresearch.com`) and the EU FP7 WebSand project.

References

1. The Perl programming language, `http://www.perl.org/`
2. Bekman, S., Cholet, E.: Practical mod_perl. O'Reilly and Associates (2003)
3. Chong, S., Myers, A.C.: Language-based information erasure. In: Proc. IEEE Computer Security Foundations Workshop, pp. 241–254 (June 2005)
4. Chong, S.: Expressive and Enforceable Information Security Policies. Ph.D. thesis, Cornell University (August 2008)
5. Chong, S., Myers, A.C.: End-to-end enforcement of erasure and declassification. In: CSF 2008: Proceedings of the 2008 21st IEEE Computer Security Foundations Symposium, pp. 98–111. IEEE Computer Society, Washington, DC (2008)
6. Conti, J.J., Russo, A.: A taint mode for python via a library. OWASP AppSec Research (2010)
7. Denning, D.E., Denning, P.J.: Certification of programs for secure information flow. Comm. of the ACM 20(7), 504–513 (1977)
8. Futoransky, A., Gutesman, E., Waissbein, A.: A dynamic technique for enhancing the security and privacy of web applications. In: Black Hat USA Briefings (August 2007)
9. Gutmann, P.: Data remanence in semiconductor devices. In: SSYM 2001: Proceedings of the 10th Conference on USENIX Security Symposium, pp. 4–4. USENIX Association, Berkeley (2001)
10. Haldar, V., Chandra, D., Franz, M.: Dynamic Taint Propagation for Java. In: Proceedings of the 21st Annual Computer Security Applications Conference, pp. 303–311 (2005)
11. Hansen, R.R., Probst, C.W.: Non-interference and erasure policies for java card bytecode. In: 6th International Workshop on Issues in the Theory of Security, WITS 2006 (2006)
12. Hunt, S., Sands, D.: Just Forget it – The Semantics and Enforcement of Information Erasure. In: Gairing, M. (ed.) ESOP 2008. LNCS, vol. 4960, pp. 239–253. Springer, Heidelberg (2008)
13. Jovanovic, N., Kruegel, C., Kirda, E.: Pixy: A Static Analysis Tool for Detecting Web Application Vulnerabilities (Short Paper). In: 2006 IEEE Symposium on Security and Privacy, pp. 258–263. IEEE Computer Society (2006)
14. Kozlov, D., Petukhov, A.: Implementation of Tainted Mode approach to finding security vulnerabilities for Python technology. In: Proc. of Young Researchers' Colloquium on Software Engineering (SYRCoSE) (June 2007)
15. Lutz, M.: Learning Python. O'Reilly & Associates, Inc., Sebastopol (2003)
16. Newsome, J., McCamant, S., Song, D.: Measuring channel capacity to distinguish undue influence. In: PLAS 2009: Proceedings of the ACM SIGPLAN Fourth Workshop on Programming Languages and Analysis for Security, pp. 73–85. ACM (2009)
17. Nguyen-Tuong, A., Guarnieri, S., Greene, D., Shirley, J., Evans, D.: Automatically Hardening Web Applications Using Precise Tainting. In: 20th IFIP International Information Security Conference, pp. 372–382 (2005)
18. Pretschner, A., Hilty, M., Basin, D., Schaefer, C., Walter, T.: Mechanisms for usage control. In: ASIACCS 2008: Proceedings of the 2008 ACM Symposium on Information, Computer and Communications Security, pp. 240–244. ACM, New York (2008)
19. Russo, A., Sabelfeld, A., Li, K.: Implicit flows in malicious and nonmalicious code. Marktoberdorf Summer School. IOS Press (2009)

20. Sabelfeld, A., Myers, A.C.: Language-based information-flow security. IEEE J. Selected Areas in Communications 21(1), 5–19 (2003)
21. Sabelfeld, A., Myers, A.C.: A Model for Delimited Information Release. In: Futatsugi, K., Mizoguchi, F., Yonezaki, N. (eds.) ISSS 2003. LNCS, vol. 3233, pp. 174–191. Springer, Heidelberg (2004)
22. Seo, J., Lam, M.S.: InvisiType: Object-Oriented Security Policies. In: 17th Annual Network and Distributed System Security Symposium, Internet Society, ISOC (February 2010)
23. Del Tedesco, F., Sands, D.: A user model for information erasure. In: 7th International Workshop on Security Issues in Concurrency, SecCo 2009. Electronic Proceedings in Theoretical Computer Science (2009)
24. Thomas, D., Fowler, C., Hunt, A.: Programming Ruby. The Pragmatic Programmer's Guide. Pragmatic Programmers (2004)
25. Volpano, D.: Safety Versus Secrecy. In: Cortesi, A., Filé, G. (eds.) SAS 1999. LNCS, vol. 1694, pp. 303–311. Springer, Heidelberg (1999)
26. Zhao, B., Sandhu, R., Zhang, X., Qin, X.: Towards a Times-Based Usage Control Model. In: Barker, S., Ahn, G.-J. (eds.) Data and Applications Security 2007. LNCS, vol. 4602, pp. 227–242. Springer, Heidelberg (2007)

A Taint Mode for Python via a Library

Juan José Conti[1] and Alejandro Russo[2]

[1] Universidad Tecnológica Nacional, Facultad Regional Santa Fe, Argentina
[2] Chalmers University of Technology, Sweden

Abstract. Vulnerabilities in web applications present threats to on-line systems. SQL injection and cross-site scripting attacks are among the most common threats found nowadays. These attacks are often result of improper or none input valida-tion. To help discover such vulnerabilities, popular web scripting languages like Perl, Ruby, PHP, and Python perform taint analysis. Such analysis is often im-plemented as an execution monitor, where the interpreter needs to be adapted to provide a taint mode. However, modifying interpreters might be a major task in its own right. In fact, it is very probably that new releases of interpreters require to be adapted to provide a taint mode. Differently from previous approaches, we show how to provide taint analysis for Python via a library written entirely in Python, and thus avoiding modifications in the interpreter. The concepts of classes, dec-orators and dynamic dispatch makes our solution lightweight, easy to use, and particularly neat. With minimal or none effort, the library can be adapted to work with different Python interpreters.

1 Introduction

Over the past years, there has been a significant increase on the number of activities performed on-line. Users can do almost everything using a web browser (e.g. watching videos, listening to music, banking, booking flights, planing trips, etc). Considering the size of Internet and its number of users, web applications are probably among the most used pieces of software nowadays. Despite its wide use, web applications suffer from vulnerabilities that permit attackers to steal confidential data, break integrity of systems, and affect availability of services. When development of web applications is done with little or no security in mind, the presence of security holes increases dramatically. Web-based vulnerabilities have already outplaced those of all other platforms [4] and there are no reasons to think that this tendency has changed [12].

According to OWASP [32], cross-site scripting (XSS) and SQL injection (SQLI) at-tacks are among the most common vulnerabilities on web applications. Although these attacks are classified differently, they are produced by the same reason: *user supplied data is sent to sensitive sinks without a proper sanitation*. For example, when a SQL query is constructed using an unsanitize string provided by a user, SQL injection at-tacks are likely to occur. To harden applications against these attacks, the implemen-tations of some popular web scripting languages perform taint analysis in a form of execution monitors [23, 2]. In that manner, not only run interpreters code, but they also perform security checks. Taint analysis can also be provided through static analysis [15, 16]. Nevertheless, execution monitors usually produce less false alarms than tradi-tional static techniques [28]. In particular, static techniques cannot deal with dynamic

T. Aura, K. Järvinen, and K. Nyberg (Eds.): NordSec 2010, LNCS 7127, pp. 210–222, 2012.

code evaluation without being too conservative. Most of the modern web scripting languages are capable to dynamically execute code. In this paper, we focus on dynamic techniques.

Taint analysis is an automatic approach to find vulnerabilities. Intuitively, taint analysis restricts how tainted or untrustworthy data flow inside programs. Specifically, it constrains data to be untainted (trustworthy) or previously sanitized when reaching sensitive sinks. Perl was the first scripting language to provide taint analysis as an special mode of the interpreter called *taint mode* [6]. Similar to Perl, some interpreters for Ruby [30], PHP [22], and recently Python [17] have been carefully modified to provide taint modes. Adapting interpreters to incorporate taint analysis present two major drawbacks that directly impact on the adoption of this technology. Firstly, incorporating taint analysis into an interpreter might be a major task in its own right. Secondly, it is very probably that it is necessary to repeatedly adapt an interpreter at every new version or release of it.

Rather than modifying interpreters, we present how to provide a taint mode for Python via a library written entirely in Python. Python is spreading fast inside web development [1]. Besides its successful use, Python presents some programming languages abstractions that makes possible to provide a taint mode via a library. For example, Python decorators [20] are a non-invasive and simple manner to declare sources of tainted data, sensitive sinks, and sanitation functions. Python's object-oriented and dynamic typing mechanisms allows the execution of the taint analysis with almost no modifications in the source code.

```
import sys                                        1
import os                                         2
                                                  3
usermail = sys.argv[1]                            4
file = sys.argv[2]                                5
                                                  6
cmd = 'mail -s "Requested file" '                 7
      + usermail + ' < ' + file                   8
os.system(cmd)                                    9
```

Fig. 1. Code for `email.py`

The library provides a general method to enhance Python's built-in classes with tainted values. In general, taint analysis tends to only consider strings or characters [23, 22, 14, 17, 13, 29]. In contrast, our library can be easily adapted to consider different built-in classes and thus providing a taint analysis for a wider set of data types. By only considering tainted strings, the library provides a similar analysis than in [17], but without modifying the Python interpreter. To the best of our knowledge, a library for taint analysis has not been considered before.

1.1   A Motivating Example

We present an example to motivate the use of taint analysis in order to discover and repair vulnerabilities. The example considers an scenario of a web application where users can send their remotely stored files by email. Figure 1 shows the simple module `email.py` that is responsible to perform such task. For simplicity, the code takes the user input from the command line (lines 4 and 5) rather than from the web server. Figure 2 shows some invocations to the module from the shell prompt. Line 1 shows a

```
1   python email.py alice@domain.se ./reportJanuary.xls
2   python email.py devil@evil.com '/etc/passwd'
3   python email.py devil@evil.com '/etc/passwd ; rm -rf / '
```

Fig. 2. Different invocations for email.py

request from Alice to send her own file reportJanuary.xls to her email address alice@domain.se. In this case, Alice's input produces a behavior which matches the intention of the module. In contrast, lines 2 and 3 show how attackers can provide particular inputs to exploit unintended or unforeseen behaviors of email.py. Line 2 exploits the fact that email.py was written assuming that users only request their own files. Observe how devil@evil.com gets information regarding users accounts by receiving the file /etc/passwd. Line 3 goes an step further and injects the command rm -rf / after sending the email. These attacks demonstrate how, what was intended to be a simple email client, can become a web-based file browser or a terminal. To avoid these vulnerabilities, applications need to rigorously check for malicious data provided by users or any other untrustworthy source. Taint analysis helps to detect when data is not sanitize before it is used on security critical operations. In Section 2.2, we show how to harden email.py in order to reject the vulnerabilities shown in Figure 1.

The paper is organized as follows. Section 2 outlines the library API. Section 3 describes the most important implementation details of our approach. Section 4 covers related work. Section 5 provides some concluding remarks.

2   A Library for Taint Analysis

On most situations, taint analysis propagates taint information on assignments. Intuitively, when the right-hand side of an assignment uses a tainted value, the variable appearing on the left-hand side becomes tainted. Taint analysis can be seen as an information-flow tracking mechanism for integrity [27]. In fact, taint analysis is just a mechanism to track explicit flows, i.e. direct flows of information from one variable to another. Taint analysis tends to ignore implicit flows [11], i.e. flows through the control-flow constructs of the language. Figure 3 presents an im-

```
<<<<<<< implicit.py
if t == 'a':
        u = 'a'
else:
        u = ''
=======
if t == 'a': u = 'a'
else: u = ''
>>>>>>> 1.2
```

Fig. 3. An implicit flow

plicit flow. Variables t and u are tainted and untainted, respectively. Observe that variable u is untainted after the execution of the branch since an untainted value ('a' or '') is assigned to it. Yet, the value of the tainted variable t is copied into the untainted variable u when t == 'a'. It is not difficult to imagine programs that circumvent the taint analysis by copying the content of tainted strings into untainted ones by using implicit flows[26].

In scenarios where attackers has full control over the code (e.g. when the code is potentially malicious), implicit flows present an effective way to circumvent the taint

```
1   v = taint(d)                              13   eval = ssink(T)(eval)
2                                             14
3   web.input = untrusted(web.input)          15   @ssink(T)
4                                             16   def f(...) :
5   @untrusted                                17      ...
6   def f(...) :                              18
7      ...                                    19   w = cleaner(T)(wash)
8                                             20
9   class MyProtocol(LineOnlyReceiver):       21   @cleaner(T)
10          @untrusted_args([1])              22   def f(...) :
11          def lineReceived(self,line):      23      ...
12              ...
```

Fig. 4. API for taint analysis

analysis. In this case, the attackers' goal is to craft the code and input data in order to circumvent security mechanisms. There is a large body of literature on the area of language-based security regarding how to track implicit flows [27].

There exists scenarios where the code is non-malicious, i.e. written without malice. Despite the good intentions and experience of programmers, the code might still contain vulnerabilities as the ones described in Section 1.1. The attackers' goal consists on craft input data in order to exploit vulnerabilities and/or corrupt data. In this scenario, taint analysis certainly helps to discover vulnerabilities. How dangerous are implicit flows in non-malicious code? We argue that they are frequently harmless [26]. The reason for that relies on that non-malicious programmers need to write a more involved, and rather unnatural, code in order to, for instance, copy tainted strings into untainted ones. In contrast, to produce explicit flows, programmers simply need to forget a call to some sanitization function. For the rest of the paper, we consider scenarios where the analyzed code is non-malicious.

2.1   Using the Library

The library is essentially a series of functions to mark what are the sources of untrust-worthy data, sensitive sinks, and sanitation functions. Figure 4 illustrates how the API works. Symbol . . . is a place holder for code that is not relevant to explain the pur-pose of the API. We assume that v is a variable, d is an string or integer, and f is a user-defined function. Symbol T represents a tag. By default, tags can take values XSS, SQLI, OSI (Operating System Injection), and II (Interpreter Injection). These val-ues are used to indicate specific vulnerabilities that could be exploited by tainted data. For instance, tainted data associated with tag SQLI is likely to exploit SQL injection vulnerabilities. Function taint is used to taint values. For example, line 1 taints vari-able d. The call to untrusted(web.input) establishes that the results produced by web.input are tainted. Line 5 shows how untrusted can be used to mark the values returned by function f as untrustworthy. Observe the use of the decorator syntax (@untrusted). Function untrusted_args is used to indicate which functions' arguments must be tainted. This primitive is particularly useful when programming frameworks require to redefine some methods in order to get information from external sources. As an example, Twisted[3], a framework to develop network applications, calls method `lineReceived` from the class `LineOnlyReceiver` every time that an string is received from the network. Lines 9–12 extend the class `LineOnlyReceiver` and implement the method `lineReceived`. Line 10 taints the data that Twisted takes from the network. Functions `taint`, `untrusted`, and `untrusted_args` associate all the tags to the tainted values. After all, untrustworthy data might exploit any kind of vulnerability. Line 13 marks `eval` as a sensitive sink. If eval receives a tainted data with the tag `T`, a possible vulnerability T is reported. Line 15 shows how to use `ssink` with the decorator syntax. Line 19 shows how `cleaner` establishes that function `wash` sanitizes data with tag `T`. As a result of that, function w removes tag `T` from tainted values. Line 21 shows the use of `cleaner` with the decorator syntax. Sensitive sinks and sanitization functions can be associated with more than one kind of vulnerabilities by just nesting decorators, i.e. `ssink(OSI)(ssink(II)(critical_operation))`.

2.2 Hardening `email.py`

We revise the example in Section 1.1. Figure 5 shows the secure version of the code given in Figure 1. Line 3 imports the library API. Line 4 imports some sanitization functions. Line 6 marks command `os.system` (capable to run arbitrary shell instructions) as a sensitive sink to OSI attacks. Tainted values reaching that sink must not contain the tag `OSI`. Lines 7 and 8 establish that functions `s_usermail` and `s_file` sanitize data in order to avoid OSI attacks. Lines 10 and 11

```
import sys                                   1
import os                                    2
from taintmode import *                      3
from sanitize import *                       4
                                             5
os.system = ssink(OSI)(os.system)            6
s_usermail = cleaner(OSI)(s_usermail)        7
s_file = cleaner(OSI)(s_file)                8
                                             9
usermail = taint(sys.argv[1])               10
file = taint(sys.argv[2])                   11
#usermail = s_usermail(usermail)            12
#file = s_file(file)                        13
cmd = 'mail -s "Requested file" '           14
      + usermail + ' < ' + file             15
os.system(cmd)                              16
```

Fig. 5. Secure version of module `email.py`

mark user input as untrustworthy. When executing the program, the taint analysis raises an alarm on line 16. The reason for that is that variable `cmd` is tainted with the tag `OSI`. Indeed, `cmd` is constructed from the untrustworthy values `usermail` and `file`. If we uncomment the lines where sanitization takes place (lines 12 and 13), the program runs normally, i.e. no alarms are reported. Observe that the main part of the code (lines 14–16) are the same than in Figure 1.

3 Implementation

In this section we present the details of our implementation. Due to lack of space, we show the most interesting parts. The full implementation of the library is publicly available at [10].

```
1   def taint_class(klass, methods):
2       class tklass(klass):
3           def __new__(cls, *args, **kwargs):
4               self = super(tklass, cls).__new__(cls, *args, **kwargs)
5               self.taints = set()
6               return self
7       d = klass.__dict__
8       for name, attr in [(m, d[m]) for m in methods]:
9           if inspect.ismethod(attr) or
10          inspect.ismethoddescriptor(attr):
11              setattr(tklass, name, propagate_method(attr))
12      if '__add__' in methods and '__radd__' not in methods:
13          setattr(tklass, '__radd__',
14              lambda self, other: tklass.__add__(tklass(other),
15              self))
16      return tklass
```

Fig. 6. Function to generate taint-aware classes

One of the core part of the library deals with how to keep track of taint information for built-in classes. The library defines subclasses of built-in classes in order to indicate if values are tainted or not. An object of these subclasses posses an attribute to indicate a set of tags associated to it. Objects are considered untainted when the set of tags is empty. We refer to these subclasses as *taint-aware classes*. In addition, the methods inherited from the built-in classes are redefined in order to propagate taint information. More specifically, methods that belong to taint-aware classes return objects with the union of tags found in their arguments and the object calling the method. In Python, the dynamic dispatch mechanism guarantees that, for instance, the concatenations of untainted and tainted strings is performed with calls to methods of taint-aware classes, which properly propagates taint information.

3.1 Generating Taint-aware Classes

Figure 6 presents a function to generate taint-aware classes. The function takes a built-in class (klass) and a list of its methods (methods) where taint propagation must be performed. Line 2 defines the name of the taint-aware class tklass. Objects of tklass are associated to the empty set of tags when created (lines 3–6). At-

```
def propagate_method(method):               1
    def inner(self, *args, **kwargs):       2
        r = method(self, *args, **kwargs)   3
        t = set()                           4
        for a in args:                      5
            collect_tags(a, t)              6
        for v in kwargs.values():           7
            collect_tags(v, t)              8
        t.update(self.taints)               9
        return taint_aware(r,t)             10
    return inner                            11
```

Fig. 7. Propagation of taint information

tribute taints is introduced to indicate the tags related to tainted values. Using Python's introspection features, variable d contains, among other things, the list of methods for the built-in class (line 7). For each method in the built-in class and in methods (lines 8–10), the code adds to tklass a method that has the same name and computes the same results but also propagates taint information (line 11). Function propagate_method is explained below. Lines 12–15 set method __radd__ to taint-aware classes when built-in classes do not include that method but __add__. Method __radd__ is called to implement the binary operations with reflected (swapped) operands[1]. For instance, to evaluate the expression x+y, where x is a built-in string and y is a taint-aware string, Python calls __radd__ from y and thus executing y.__radd__(x). In that manner, the taint information of y is propagated to the expression. Otherwise, the method x.__add__(y) is called instead, which results in an untainted string. Finally, the taint-aware class is returned (line 16).

The implementation of propagate_method is shown in Figure 7. The function takes a method and returns another method that computes the same results but propagates taint information. Line 3 calls the method received as argument and stores the results in r. Lines 4–9 collect the tags from the current object and the method's arguments into t. Variable r might refer to an object of a built-in class and therefore not include the attribute taints. For that reason, function taint_aware is designed to transform objects from built-in classes into taint-aware ones. For example, if r refers to a list of objects of the class str, function taint_aware returns a list of objects of the taint-aware class derived from str. Function taint_aware is essentially implemented as a structural mapping on list, tuples, sets, and dictionaries. The library does not taint built-in containers, but rather their elements. This is a design decision based on the assumption that non-malicious code does not exploit containers to circumvent the taint analysis (e.g. by encoding the value of tainted integers into the length of lists). Otherwise, the implementation of the library can be easily adapted. Line 11 returns the taint-aware version of r with the tags collected in t.

```
STR = taint_class ( str , str_methods )
INT = taint_class ( int , int_methods )
```

Fig. 8. Taint-aware classes for strings and integers

To illustrate how to use function taint_class, Figure 8 produces taint-aware classes for strings and integers, where str_methods and int_methods are lists of methods for the classes str and int, respectively. Observe how the code presented in Figures 6 and 7 is general enough to be applied to several built-in classes.

3.2 Decorators

Except for taint, the rest of the API is implemented as decorators. In our library, decorators are high order functions [7], i.e. functions that take functions as arguments and return functions. Figure 9 shows

```
def untrusted (f):                          1
    def inner (*args , **kwargs ):          2
        r = f (*args , **kwargs )           3
        return taint_aware (r , TAGS)       4
    return inner                            5
```

Fig. 9. Code for untrusted

the code for untrusted. Function f, given as an argument, is the function that returns untrustworthy results (line 1). Intuitively, function untrusted returns a

---

[1] The built-in class for strings implements all the reflected versions of its operators but __add__.

function (`inner`) that calls function `f` (line 3) and taints the values returned by it (line 4). Symbol `TAGS` is the set of all the tags used by the library. Readers should refer to [10] for the implementation details about the rest of the API.

3.3 Taint-aware Functions

Several dynamic taint analysis [23, 22, 16, 17, 13, 29] do not propagate taint information when results different from strings are computed from tainted values. (e.g. the length of a tainted string is usually an untainted integer). This design decision might affect the abilities of taint analysis to detect vulnerabilities. For instance, taint analysis might miss dangerous patterns when programs encode strings as lists of numbers. A common workaround

```
def propagate_func(original):                         1
    def inner(*args, **kwargs):                       2
        t = set()                                     3
        for a in args:                                4
            collect_tags(a,t)                         5
        for v in kwargs.values():                     6
            collect_tags(v,t)                         7
        r = original(*args,**kwargs)                  8
        if t == set([]):                              9
            return r                                  10
        return taint_aware(r,t)                       11
    return inner                                      12
```

Fig. 10. Propagation of taint information among possibly different taint-aware objects

to this problem is to mark functions that perform encodings of strings as sensitive sinks. In that manner, sanitization must occur before strings are represented in another format. Nevertheless, this approach is unsatisfactory: the intrinsic meaning of sensitive sinks may be lost. Sensitive sinks are security critical operations rather than functions that perform encodings of strings. Our library provides means to start breaching this gap.

Figure 10 presents a general function that allows to define operations that return tainted values when their arguments involve taint-aware objects. As a result, it is possible to define

```
len = propagate_func(len)
ord = propagate_func(ord)
chr = propagate_func(chr)
```

Fig. 11. Taint-aware functions for strings and integers

functions that, for instance, take tainted strings and return tainted integers. We classify this kind of functions as *taint-aware*.

Similar to the code shown in Figure 7, `propagate_func` is a high order function. It takes function `f` and returns another function (`inner`) able to propagate taint information from the arguments to the results. Lines 3–7 collect tags from the arguments. If the set of collected tags is empty, there are no tainted values involved and therefore no taint propagation is performed (lines 9–10). Otherwise, a taint-aware version of the results is returned with the tags collected in the arguments (line 11).

To illustrate the use of `propagate_func`, Figure 11 shows some taint-aware functions for strings and integers. We redefine the standard functions to compute lengths of lists (`len`), the ASCII code of a character (`chr`), and its inverse (`ord`). As a result, `len(taint('string'))` returns the tainted integer 6. It is up to the users of the library to decide which functions must be taint-aware depending on the scenario. The library only provides redefinition of standard functions like the ones shown in Figure 11.

3.4   Scope of the Library

In Figure 6, the method to automatically produce taint-aware classes does not work with booleans. The reason for that is that class `bool` cannot be subclassed in Python[2]. Consequently, our library cannot handle tainted boolean values. We argue that this shortcoming does not restrict the usability of the library for two reasons. Firstly, different from previous approaches [23, 22, 16, 17, 13, 29], the library can provide taint analysis for several built-in types rather than just strings. Secondly, we consider that booleans are typically used on guards. Since the library already ignores implicit flows, the possibilities to find vulnerabilities are not drastically reduced by disregarding taint information on booleans.

When generating the taint-aware class STR (Figure 8), we found some problems when dealing with some methods from the class `str`. Python interpreter raises exceptions when methods `__nonzero__`, `__reduce__`, and `__reduce_ex__` are redefined. Moreover, when methods `__new__`, `__init__`, `__getattribute__`, and `__repr__` are redefined by function `taint_class`, an infinite recursion is produced when calling any of them. As for STR, the generation of the taint-aware class INT exposes the same behavior, i.e. the methods mentioned before produce the same problems. We argue that this restriction does not drastically impact on the capabilities to detect vulnerabilities. Methods `__new__` is called when creating objects. In Figure 6, taint-aware classes define this method on line 3. Method `__init__` is called when initializing objects. Python invokes this method after an object is created and programs do not usually called it explicitly. Method `__getattribute__` is used to access any attribute on a class. This method is automatically inherited from `klass` and it works as expected for taint-aware classes. Method `__nonzero__` is called when objects need to be converted into a boolean value. As mentioned before, the analysis ignores taint information of data that is typically used on guards. Method `__repr__` pretty prints objects on the screen. In principle, developers should be careful to not use calls to `__repr__` in order to convert tainted objects into untainted ones. However, this method is typically used for debugging [3]. Methods `__reduce__` and `__reduce_ex__` are used by Pickle [4] to serialize strings. Given these facts, the argument `method` in function `taint_class` establishes the methods to be redefined on taint-aware classes (Figure 6). This argument is also useful when the built-in classes might vary among different Python interpreters. It is future work to automatically determine the lists of methods to be redefined for different built-in classes and different versions of Python.

It is up to the users of the library to decide which built-in classes and functions must be taint-aware. This attitude comes from the need of being flexible and not affecting performance unless it is necessary. Why users interested on taint analysis for strings should accept run-time overheads due to tainted integers?

---

[2] http://docs.python.org/library/functions.html#bool
[3] http://docs.python.org/reference/datamodel.html
[4] An special Python module.

It is important to remark that the library only tracks taint information in the source code being developed. As a consequence, taint information could be lost if, for example, taint values are given to external libraries (or libraries written in other languages) that are not taint-aware. One way to tackle this problem is to augment the library functions to be taint-aware by applying `propagate_func` to them.

As a future work, we will explore if it is possible to automatically define taint-aware functions based on the built-in functions (found in the interpreter) and taint-aware classes in order to increase the number of taint-aware functions provided by the library. At the moment, the library provides taint-aware classes for strings, integers, floats, and unicode as well as some taint-aware functions (e.g. `len`, `chr`, and `ord`).

4   Related Work

A considerable amount of literature has been published on taint analysis. Readers can refer to [8] for a description of how this technique has been applied on different research areas. In this section, we focus on analyses developed for popular web scripting languages.

Perl [23] was the first scripting language to include taint analysis as a native feature of the interpreter. Perl taint mode marks strings originated from outside a program as tainted (i.e. inputs from users, environment variables, and files). Sanitization is done by using regular expressions. Writing to files, executing shell commands, and sending information over the network are considered sensitive sinks. Differently, our library gives freedom to developers to classify the sources of tainted data, sanitization functions, and sensitive sinks. Similar to Perl, Ruby [30] provides support for taint analysis. Ruby's taint mode, however, performs analysis at the level of objects rather than only strings. Both, Perl and Ruby, utilize dynamic techniques for their analyses.

Several taint analysis have been developed for the popular scripting language PHP. Aiming to avoid any user intervention, authors in [15] combine static and dynamic techniques to automatically repair vulnerabilities in PHP code. They propose to use static analysis (type-system) in order to insert some predetermined sanitization functions when tainted values reach sensitive sinks. Observe that the semantic of programs might be changed when inserting calls to sanitization functions, which constitutes the dynamic part of the analysis in [15]. Our approach, on the other hand, does not implement a type-system and only reports vulnerabilities, i.e. it is up to developers to decide where, and how, sanitization procedures must be called. In [22], Nguyen-Toung et al. adapt the PHP interpreter to provide a dynamic taint analysis at the level of characters, which the authors call *precise tainting*. They argue that precise tainting gains precision over traditional taint analyses for strings. Authors need to manually exploit, when feasible, semantics definitions of functions in order to accurately keep track of tainted characters. Our approach, on the other hand, uses the same mechanism to handle tainted values independently of the nature of a given function. Consequently, we are able to automatically extend our analysis to different set of data types but without being as precise as Nguyen-Toung et al.' work. It is worth seeing studies indicating how much precision (i.e. less false alarms) it is obtained with *precise tainting* in practice. Similarly to Nguyen-Toung et al.'s work, Futoransky [13] et al. provide a precise dynamic taint analysis for PHP. Pietraszek and Berghe [24] modify the PHP runtime environment to assign *metadata* to user-provided input as well as to provide metadata-preserving string operations. Security critical operations are also instrumented to evaluate, when taken strings as input, the risk of executing such operations based on the assigned metadata. Jovanovic et al. [16] propose to combine a traditional data flow and alias analysis to increase the precision of their static taint analysis for PHP. They observe a 50% rate of false alarms (i.e. one false alarm for each vulnerability). The works in [5, 21] combine static and dynamic techniques. The static techniques are used to reduce the number of program variables where taint information must be tracked at run-time.

A taint analysis for Java [14] instruments the class `java.lang.String` as well as classes that present untrustworthy sources and sensitive sinks. The instrumentation of `java.lang.String` is done offline, while other classes are instrumented online. The authors mention that a custom class loader in the JVM is needed in order to perform online instrumentation. Another taint analysis for Java [31], called TAJ, focus on scalability and performance requirements for industry-level applications. To achieve industrial demands, TAJ uses static tecniques for pointer analysis, call-graph construction, and slicing. Similarly, the authors in [19] propose an static analysis for Java that focus on achieving precision and scalability.

A series of work [18, 9, 25] propose to provide information-flow security via a library in Haskell. These libraries handle explicit and implicit flows and programmers need to write programs with an special-purpose API. Similar to other taint analysis, our library does not contemplate implicit flows and programs do not need to be written with an special-purpose API.

Among the closest related work, we can mention [17] and [29]. In [17], authors modify the Python interpreter to provide a dynamic taint analysis. More specifically, the representation of the class `str` is extended to include a boolean flag to indicate if a string is tainted. We provide a similar analysis but without modifying the interpreter. The work by Seo and Lam [29], called InvisiType, aims to enforce safety checks without modifying the analyzed code. Similar to our assumptions, their approach is designed to work with non-malicious code. InvisiType is more general than our approach. In fact, authors show how InvisiType can provide taint analysis and access control checks for Python programs. However, InvisiType relies on several modifications in the Python interpreter in order to perform the security checks at the right places. For example, when native methods are called, the run-time environment firstly calls the special purpose method `__nativecall__`. As a manner to specifying policies, the approach provides the class `InvisiType` that defines special purposes methods to get support from the run-time system (e.g. `__nativecall__` is one of those methods). Subclasses of this class represent security policies. The approach relies on multiple inheritance to extend existing classes with security checks. To include or remove security checks from objects, programs need to explicitly call functions *promote* and *demote*. Being less invasive, our library uses decorators instead of explicit function calls to taint and untaint data. Our approach does not require multiple inheritance.

5 Conclusions

We propose a taint mode for Python via a library entirely written in Python. We show that no modifications in the interpreter are needed. Different from traditional taint analysis, our library is able to keep track of tainted values for several built-in classes. Additionally, the library provide means to define functions that propagate taint information (e.g. the length of a tainted string produces a tainted integer). The library consists on around 300 LOC. To apply taint analysis in programs, it is only needed to indicate the sources of untrustworthy data, sensitive sinks, and sanitization functions. The library uses decorators as a noninvasive approach to mark source code. Python's object classes and dynamic dispatch mechanism allow the analysis to be executed with almost no modifications in the code. As a future work, we plan to use the library to harden frameworks for web development and evaluate the capabilities of our library to detect vulnerabilities in popular web applications.

Acknowledgments. Thanks are due to Arnar Birgisson for interesting discussions. This work was funded by the Swedish research agencies VR and SSF, and the scholarship program for graduated students from the Universidad Tecnológica Nacional, Facultad Regional Santa Fe.

References

[1] List of Python software,
     http://en.wikipedia.org/wiki/List_of_Python_software
[2] The Ruby programming language, http://www.ruby-lang.org
[3] The Twisted programming framework, http://twistedmatrix.com
[4] Andrews, M.: Guest Editor's Introduction: The State of Web Security. IEEE Security and Privacy 4(4), 14–15 (2006)
[5] Balzarotti, D., Cova, M., Felmetsger, V., Jovanovic, N., Kirda, E., Kruegel, C., Vigna, G.: Saner: Composing static and dynamic analysis to validate sanitization in web applications. In: Proceedings of the 2008 IEEE Symposium on Security and Privacy. IEEE Computer Society, Washington, DC (2008)
[6] Bekman, S., Cholet, E.: Practical mod_perl. O'Reilly and Associates (2003)
[7] Bird, R., Wadler, P.: An introduction to functional programming. Prentice Hall International (UK) Ltd. (1988)
[8] Chang, W., Streiff, B., Lin, C.: Efficient and extensible security enforcement using dynamic data flow analysis. In: Proceedings of the 15th ACM Conference on Computer and Communications Security. ACM, New York (2008)
[9] Tsai, T.C., Russo, A., Hughes, J.: A library for secure multi-threaded information flow in Haskell. In: IEEE Computer Security Foundations Symposium, pp. 187–202 (2007)
[10] Conti, J.J., Russo, A.: A Taint Mode for Python via a Library. Software release (April 2010), http://www.cse.chalmers.se/~russo/juanjo.htm
[11] Denning, D.E., Denning, P.J.: Certification of programs for secure information flow. Comm. of the ACM 20(7), 504–513 (1977)
[12] Federal Aviation Administration (US). Review of Web Applications Security and Intrusion Detection in Air Traffic Control Systems (June 2009), http://www.oig.dot.gov/sites/dot/files/pdfdocs/ATC_Web_Report.pdf Note: thousands of vulnerabilities were discovered.

[13] Futoransky, A., Gutesman, E., Waissbein, A.: A dynamic technique for enhancing the security and privacy of web applications. In: Black Hat USA Briefings (August 2007)

[14] Haldar, V., Chandra, D., Franz, M.: Dynamic Taint Propagation for Java. In: Proceedings of the 21st Annual Computer Security Applications Conference, pp. 303–311 (2005)

[15] Huang, Y., Yu, F., Hang, C., Tsai, C., Lee, D., Kuo, S.: Securing web application code by static analysis and runtime protection. In: Proceedings of the 13th International Conference on World Wide Web, pp. 40–52. ACM (2004)

[16] Jovanovic, N., Kruegel, C., Kirda, E.: Pixy: A Static Analysis Tool for Detecting Web Application Vulnerabilities (Short Paper). In: 2006 IEEE Symposium on Security and Privacy, pp. 258–263. IEEE Computer Society (2006)

[17] Kozlov, D., Petukhov, A.: Implementation of Tainted Mode approach to finding security vulnerabilities for Python technology. In: Proc. of Young Researchers' Colloquium on Software Engineering (SYRCoSE) (June 2007)

[18] Li, P., Zdancewic, S.: Encoding information flow in Haskell. In: Computer Security Foundations Workshop, IEEE, p. 16 (2006)

[19] Livshits, V.B., Lam, M.S.: Finding security vulnerabilities in Java applications with static analysis. In: Proceedings of the 14th Conference on USENIX Security Symposium. USENIX Association, Berkeley (2005)

[20] Lutz, M., Ascher, D.: Learning Python. O'Reilly & Associates, Inc. (1999)

[21] Monga, M., Paleari, R., Passerini, E.: A hybrid analysis framework for detecting web application vulnerabilities. In: IWSESS 2009: Proceedings of the 2009 ICSE Workshop on Software Engineering for Secure Systems, pp. 25–32. IEEE Computer Society, Washington, DC (2009)

[22] Nguyen-Tuong, A., Guarnieri, S., Greene, D., Shirley, J., Evans, D.: Automatically Hardening Web Applications Using Precise Tainting. In: 20th IFIP International Information Security Conference, pp. 372–382 (2005)

[23] Perl. The Perl programming language, http://www.perl.org/

[24] Pietraszek, T., Berghe, C.V.: Defending Against Injection Attacks Through Context-Sensitive String Evaluation. In: Valdes, A., Zamboni, D. (eds.) RAID 2005. LNCS, vol. 3858, pp. 124–145. Springer, Heidelberg (2006)

[25] Russo, A., Claessen, K., Hughes, J.: A library for light-weight information-flow security in Haskell. In: Proceedings of the First ACM SIGPLAN Symposium on Haskell, pp. 13–24. ACM (2008)

[26] Russo, A., Sabelfeld, A., Li, K.: Implicit flows in malicious and nonmalicious code. Marktoberdorf Summer School. IOS Press (2009)

[27] Sabelfeld, A., Myers, A.C.: Language-based information-flow security. IEEE J. Selected Areas in Communications 21(1), 5–19 (2003)

[28] Sabelfeld, A., Russo, A.: From Dynamic to Static and Back: Riding the Roller Coaster of Information-Flow Control Research. In: Pnueli, A., Virbitskaite, I., Voronkov, A. (eds.) PSI 2009. LNCS, vol. 5947, pp. 352–365. Springer, Heidelberg (2010)

[29] Seo, J., Lam, M.S.: InvisiType: Object-Oriented Security Policies. In: 17th Annual Network and Distributed System Security Symposium, Internet Society, ISOC (February 2010)

[30] Thomas, D., Fowler, C., Hunt, A.: Programming Ruby. The Pragmatic Programmer's Guide. Pragmatic Programmers (2004)

[31] Tripp, O., Pistoia, M., Fink, S.J., Sridharan, M., Weisman, O.: TAJ: effective taint analysis of web applications. In: Hind, M., Diwan, A. (eds.) Proc. ACM SIGPLAN Conference on Programming language Design and Implementation, pp. 87–97. ACM Press (2009)

[32] van der Stock, A., Williams, J., Wichers, D.: OWASP Top 10 2007 (2007), http://www.owasp.org/index.php/Top_10_2007

Security of Web Mashups: A Survey

Philippe De Ryck, Maarten Decat, Lieven Desmet,
Frank Piessens, and Wouter Joosen

IBBT-DistriNet
Katholieke Universiteit Leuven
3001 Leuven, Belgium
`firstname.lastname@cs.kuleuven.be`

Abstract. Web mashups, a new web application development paradigm, combine content and services from multiple origins into a new service. Web mashups heavily depend on interaction between content from
multiple origins and communication with different origins. Contradictory, mashup security relies on separation for protecting code and data.
Traditional HTML techniques fail to address both the interaction/com-
munication needs and the separation needs. This paper proposes concrete
requirements for building secure mashups, divided in four categories: separation, interaction, communication and advanced behavior control. For
the first three categories, all currently available techniques are discussed
in light of the proposed requirements. For the last category, we present
three relevant academic research results with high potential. We conclude
the paper by highlighting the most applicable techniques for building
secure mashups, because of functionality and standardization. We also
discuss opportunities for future improvements and developments.

1 Introduction

The evolution within web 2.0 has led to a new application type, called a web
mashup – simply *mashup* from now on. A mashup is a composed application,
using elements from different sources. The most simple form of mashups are web
pages incorporating advertisements, which come from an external origin. More
complex examples combine content from multiple sources into a new service.
The classical example case is *HousingMaps*, which collects listings of real estate
from *Craigslist* and visualizes their location on *Google Maps*. There are numerous
mainstream mashup examples, of which *iGoogle* and *Facebook* are widely known.
Mashups have also found their way into enterprise scenarios, where they can
be used to create quick views on data coming from multiple sources within
and outside the enterprise. Development tools for mashup scenarios have been
included in the portfolio of IT application and service providers [12,16,17,18].

A mashup can be defined as "a web application that combines content or services from more than one origin to create a new service". By combining multiple
separate services into a new application, a mashup generates added value, which
is one of the most important incentives behind building mashups. Mashups also
succeed in maximizing content reuse, even from services that never intended to

T. Aura, K. Järvinen, and K. Nyberg (Eds.): NordSec 2010, LNCS 7127, pp. 223–238, 2012.

produce reusable data. Additionally, mashups are flexible and lightweight applications, since they merely gather and combine information, thus do not need complex application logic. These three advantages have driven the growth of mashups, which has led to the need of support for strong security requirements.

The discussion of the security requirements will become more concrete if applied to an example application: a financial mashup, which provides integrated access to your financial and stock information. The mashup contains a component from your bank, an advising component from a brokerage firm and an advertising component. The bank and brokerage component need to interact, to provide relevant advice regarding your stock portfolio and interests; the brokerage and banking component provide the advertising component with keywords about your financial habits, so that you receive targeted advertisements. The bank component and brokerage component need to communicate with the servers of their firm, to retrieve the most recent information. The advertising component needs to communicate with servers from multiple advertising firms, to retrieve relevant advertisements.

A first contribution of this paper is the concrete definition of the security requirements for mashup applications, which can be used to examine existing security mechanisms. Second, we contribute a detailed overview of the current state-of-practice and adopted state-of-the-art concerning mashup security techniques. Third, we highlight a few important academic results, as well as discuss potential future improvements and developments to enhance support for the mashup security requirements.

In the remainder of this paper, we will specify the security requirements for mashups (Section 2), followed by a detailed overview of the currently available techniques (Section 3, 4 and 5). We also discuss a few promising state-of-the-art techniques, which can contribute to the future of mashup security (Section 6). We conclude the paper in Section 7 with an overview of the presented techniques and their capabilities, as well as a detailed discussion of potential future improvements or evolutions of mashup security mechanisms.

2   Problems with Mashup Security

Examining the security requirements for mashups has led to the specification of four specific categories, of which the security-specific requirements have been determined. The following overview discusses these categories and requirements, which will be used to discuss existing security mechanisms.

C1. Separation Components need to be separated from each other, to ensure the following security properties:
   a. **DOM**: ensures that the component's part of the DOM tree is separated from other components.
   b. **Script**: ensures that the component's scripts can not be influenced by other components.
   c. **Applicable in same domain**: ensures that the separation techniques can also be applied to different components belonging to the same domain.

C2. Interaction Regardless of their separation, a component requires interaction with other components and the host page. This interaction is subject to the following requirements:

  a. Confidentiality: ensures that sensitive information can not be stolen from interactions between components.

  b. Integrity: ensures that the contents of an interaction can not be modified without the knowledge of the interacting components.

  c. Mutual authentication: ensures that the interacting components can establish who they are interacting with.

C3. Communication Components need to be able to communicate with the mashup provider, as well as with other parties. This requires the following properties:

  a. Cross-domain: components should be able to communicate with other origins than the origin to which they belong.

  b. Authentication: a service receiving messages should be able to identify the origin of the message.

C4. Behavior Control Control over specific behavior of components is needed to selectively allow or disallow specific functionality. This category is currently state-of-the-art and too broad to grasp in a few categories.

Currently, mashup security is based on the de facto security policy of the web: the Same Origin Policy (SOP) [34]. The SOP states that scripts from one origin should not be able to access content from other origins. This prevents scripts from stealing data, cookies or login credentials from other sites. Additionally to the SOP, browsers also apply a frame navigation policy, which restricts the navigation of frames to its descendants [3].

The security provided by the traditional mechanisms for building mashups relies on the application of these browser security policies. Loading components from different origins in Iframes causes them to be separated by the SOP. Using script inclusion causes the script to be loaded in the protection domain of the including page, which is a straightforward way to achieve interaction between components. Communication with the origin of the page containing the script can be achieved using the XHR object of the JavaScript language.

These traditional mechanisms have led to two different approaches for building mashups: server-side composition and client-side composition (Figure 1). The former combines the entire mashup at the server side and serves it as a whole to the client, while the latter provides a template to the client, which retrieves all pieces separately and composes the mashup at the client side, conform to the provided template. The difference between both approaches is fading as hybrid models are being used, where separate components and pre-composed content are combined. In either model, there are no significant technical challenges. The responsibility for security always lies with the mashup integrator, taking into account the security requirements of the different components and their stakeholders.

Examining the traditional techniques in the light of the previously proposed security requirements yields some interesting results. Iframes offer full separation between different origins, but not within the same origin, and provide no

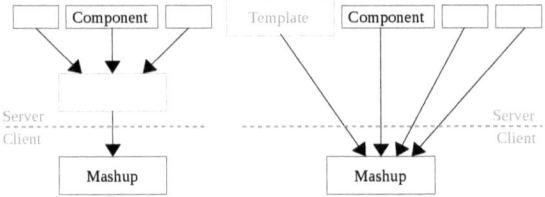

Fig. 1. Server-side mashup (left) and client-side mashup (right)

interaction between components. Script inclusion offers no separation at all, but provides full interaction. This interaction is not authenticated, nor can confidentiality or integrity be ensured. As far as communication is concerned, XHR does not offer any cross-domain communication. These results show the pressing need for secure techniques to enable separation while still allowing secure interaction, as well as secure communication. Additionally, providing behavior control for components will only strengthen the security of mashups.

In the following sections, we provide a detailed discussion of both state-of-practice and state-of-the-art in mashup security. Section 3 focuses on specific techniques enabling separation and providing interaction. Section 4 presents techniques that enable the isolation of JavaScript modules within the same execution environment. Section 5 discusses techniques which help to achieve communication with remote parties. In Section 6, we discuss state-of-the-art academic research that supports fine-grained control over specific security-related aspects.

3   Separation and Interaction

The security requirements demand stronger separation guarantees, but also require the possibility of interaction between separated components. In this section we discuss several techniques which approach this problem on a document basis. Script-based solutions are discussed in the next section.

The solutions proposed here use three different points of view to address the needed security requirements: (i) leverage existing separation mechanisms and provide controlled interaction (Subspace, Fragment Identifier Messaging and postMessage), (ii) strengthen the existing separation mechanisms, while preserving interaction (module tag and sandbox attribute), and (iii) start from scratch, while honoring the already existing legacy by ensuring some form of backwards compatibility (MashupOS and OMash).

3.1   Subspace

Subspace [19] enables interaction across the boundaries of an iframe, using a shared JavaScript object and relying on domain relaxation. In a nutshell (Figure 2), a JavaScript object is created by frame A and shared with a nested intermediate iframe of the same domain (B). This intermediate iframe has a nested frame belonging to the component (C), which needs to obtain the JavaScript object to enable interaction. This is achieved by having both frames B and C relax their domain, so the JavaScript object can be shared. Interaction is now possible using the shared JavaScript object. More complex scenarios, involving multiple components and origins, are also supported.

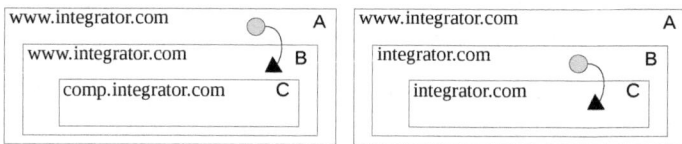

Fig. 2. Subspace: initial setup (left) and after domain relaxation (right) (Source: [19])

Subspace effectively enables interaction between frames, even with the restrictions imposed by the SOP. albeit with a few disadvantages. Apart from the fairly expensive setup phase, the burden of subdomain management for each component is another disadvantage of Subspace.

The security requirements for separation are addressed by the use of iframes. As for the security requirements regarding interaction, Subspace achieves confidentiality and integrity, as long as the shared objects are protected. Mutual authentication is inherent to the owners of the shared object, which are determined during the setup phase.

3.2   Fragment Identifier Messaging

Fragment Identifier Messaging (FIM) [3], also known as Iframe Cross-Domain Communication [10,31], builds a communication channel based on frame navigation. If the URL of a frame is set, but only the fragment[1] changes, the page is not reloaded. This allows JavaScript within the page to read this fragment, thus providing a one-way channel. Two-way interaction can be achieved using nested frames.

Even though FIM enables interaction without violating the browser's security policies, it is not a designed interaction channel. This brings a few disadvantages, such as a restricted message length, the lack of a notification system for new messages or the fact that messages can easily be overwritten.

Compared to the proposed security requirements, FIM is dependent on the use of iframes for separation. In terms of the security requirements for interaction, FIM does achieve confidentiality, since the browser's security policies prevent the frame location to be read by other origins. Integrity is also preserved, since the frame's location can only be overwritten as a whole, so no fragment can be partially modified. Mutual authentication is not available, since the sender of a message is not known, but an authentication mechanism can be implemented.

---

[1] The part of a URL after the # symbol, used to navigate to an anchor within the page.

The issues with FIM can be addressed, as is shown by component framework SMash [7], the OpenAjax Hub [28], OMOS [35] and the Microsoft API for using FIM [31].

3.3 PostMessage

PostMessage is an extension of the browser API, providing a designed interaction channel between frames [14]. The specification introduces a new DOM event, `message`, which is fired if messages are received, as well as an API function that can be used to send messages to a frame, `postMessage()`. When sending a message, the destination origin has to be specified, which is validated by the browser upon message delivery [3]. For received messages, the browser provides the origin of the sender as part of the message object.

PostMessage is an improved version of FIM and addresses specific issues. Similar to FIM, the separation requirements are met by the underlying use of iframes. When compared to the security requirements for enabling interaction, postMessage does achieve confidentiality and integrity. Mutual authentication is also supported on the level of domains: the browser checks the destination when sending a message and the receiver can check the origin of a message.

PostMessage is part of the HTML5 standard, which is currently still a draft [13]. Nonetheless, postMessage is already supported by major browsers. It can also be used to replace FIM, as will be done in SMash [7] and the OpenAjax Hub [28].

3.4 Module Tag

The module tag allows content separation in modules, which are only accessible through a message-passing interface for sending and receiving messages [5]. This message-passing interface is restricted to the JSON format, to prevent security issues through the leaking of JavaScript objects. Additionally, the module tag assigns a unique origin to each module, thus effectively enabling separation between multiple components from the same origin.

Compared to the security requirements for separation and interaction, the module tag effectively separates components from each other. Separation is enforced within the same domain, both for scripts as DOM elements. As for interaction between modules, confidentiality and integrity are achieved by the separation of internal state. Mutual authentication is not achieved, since there is no authentication of the sender, but can be implemented.

The module tag is not implemented by major browser vendors and is, as far as we know, not used in practice. It does however provide valuable insights and inspiration for the design of other standardized solutions, such as the sandbox attribute, discussed next.

3.5 Sandbox Attribute

The sandbox attribute [15] is an extension of the iframe tag and augments the origin-based separation of iframes. The sandbox attribute imposes a set of restrictions, such as assigning a unique origin to the content, preventing scripts or browser plugins to run or preventing forms from being submitted. These restrictions, except for running plugins, can be relaxed by specifically allowing them when specifying the attribute.

Within the separation category, the sandbox attribute achieves all three security requirements. The interaction requirements are achieved by the chosen interaction technique. This can be any interaction technique available for iframes, but the standardized postMessage is a favorite, with one caveat: if a component is assigned a unique origin, the postMessage-origin is set to a globally unique identifier for outgoing messages. This may be problematic to achieve mutual authentication with sandboxed components.

The sandbox attribute is part of HTML5, which is currently a draft [13]. Major browsers are starting to support the sandbox attribute though, with Chromium/Chrome taking the lead.

3.6 MashupOS

MashupOS [33] arguments the need for additional trust levels within a mashup. Next to the "no trust" provided by iframes, known as isolated content, and "full trust" provided by script inclusion, known as open content, they propose access-controlled content, which provides separation with the possibility of message-passing across domains, and unauthorized content, which can not assume any privileges associated with a domain, such as authentication credentials or origins.

Technically, these levels of trust are achieved by introducing new HTML tags. These tags do not only provide separation and interaction, but also enable the separation of physical resources, which is out of scope here. MashupOS also provides a way for modules to expose a specific API.

Mapping MashupOS to the proposed security requirements is not easy, because there are multiple levels of trust. Using the different levels of trust, MashupOS is able to provide strong separation for both DOM elements and scripts. Separation within the same origin is dependent on the technique used (e.g. unauthorized content is not associated with a domain). As for interaction, confidentiality and integrity can be ensured using the provided API specification mechanism, but no support for mutual authentication is provided. This can however be implemented on top of the provided interaction mechanism.

MashupOS is not implemented in a major browser, but the four trust levels can be simulated using iframes and postMessage. MashupOS also serves a valuable role in the research on mashups.

3.7 OMash

A totally different approach is taken by OMash [4], where web pages are represented as objects, which have public interfaces for interaction. Such an object encapsulates the internal state of a web page, including associated resources such as cookies or authentication credentials. By separating pages, using an object representation, OMash eliminates the need for the SOP. Resource sharing is done by passing the needed resources between objects, but only if they can be safely shared (e.g. session cookies are shared when a link within a site is followed).

OMash satisfies the separation requirements, since DOM objects and scripts belong to an object's private data. Since all objects are separated, OMash also supports separation within the same origin. Interaction is possible using the exposed interfaces, which provide confidentiality and integrity. Mutual authentication is not inherently present, but can be implemented using shared secrets.

OMash is not adopted by any major browser vendor, but is available as a prototype implementation.

4   Script Isolation

Script isolation techniques leverage the interaction possibilities present in a script environment, and try to introduce separation between different components. The general approach is restricting JavaScript to a subset, which adheres to the object-capability security model. This security model is based on the fact that separated objects have no capabilities and can only achieve capabilities on an object if they are handed a reference to that object. For example, if an object in the language has no reference to the Image object, it can not construct new images. By giving it a reference to the Image object, it obtains the capability to create images.

The three techniques presented here, i.e. ADsafe, Facebook JavaScript and Caja, follow this object-capability security model, thus achieving component separation, regardless of domain. Separation for DOM elements and built-in script objects is achieved using subset restrictions and run-time control over specific operations, such as DOM access. The isolated modules can interact using explicitly shared objects, which offer confidentiality and integrity. Mutual authentication can be implemented if desired.

4.1   ADsafe

The ADsafe subset [6] is aimed at putting guest code, such as advertisements, in a web page, without suffering security consequences. This is achieved by restricting scripts to a safe subset of JavaScript. Safe interaction with their environment, such as the DOM tree, is possible using a provided **ADSAFE** object.

ADsafe is not an active protection mechanism, but is enforced using a static code verification tool. This tool can determine whether a script adheres to the ADsafe subset or not, but will not actively rewrite code. Next to preventing access to the global object or well-known insecure language features, such as `eval` or `with`, ADsafe also prohibits the use of `this`, since it has subtle properties that can be used to obtain a reference to the global object.

In recent research on the security of JavaScript subsets, specific issues with ADsafe have been discovered [23]. These issues are minor design oversights, which do not break the fundamental model of the language. Continued formal verification is needed to prove that the ADsafe language fully adheres to the object-capability security model.

4.2   Facebook JavaScript

Facebook, the social networking site, supports an extension model based on applications, which are developed by external parties. To ensure the safe incorporation, Facebook provides Facebook JavaScript (FBJS) [11], which is a secure JavaSript subset. FBJS is an active protection mechanism, which applies a rewriting process to normal JavaScript. This rewriting process includes rewriting variable and function names to a unique namespace, as well as defining Facebook-specific DOM objects, which do not implement insecure features. Remote communication is available through an `Ajax` object, which uses a server-side proxy to retrieve cross-domain content. More importantly, this retrieved content is rewritten to FBJS, to ensure continuous protection.

The major advantage of the approach taken by Facebook is the active protection mechanism, which allows the dynamic addition of content. This is particularly useful in mashup applications. The disadvantage however is that every request needs to go through the Facebook servers, which might not be feasible for each integrator.

Recent research on the security of JavaScript subsets has also identified issues with FBJS [23]. These issues do not have an impact on the fundamental model of the language, and can be further eliminated using strong formal models.

4.3   Caja

Caja [27], a safe JavaScript subset designed by Google, takes a similar approach to FBJS. It analyzes JavaScript to detect subset violations and it rewrites the code to create isolated modules, as well as to mediate DOM access. Caja is a fairly flexible subset, since it allows the use of `this`, albeit in a limited way. Caja does more than subsetting JavaScript, it also introduces a new feature: frozen objects. Frozen objects can not be changed, which makes them ideal for information sharing between components. Objects in the default global environment are automatically frozen.

An advantage of the way Caja is introduced is that it is aimed at supporting existing scripts, with some exceptions such as `eval` or `with`. This allows a gradual transition towards the Caja subset. Underneath, a second subset is defined, named Cajita. Cajita can be considered "Caja without `this`", since `this` is considered a dangerous and unnecessary language feature. Cajita is meant to be the subset for writing new applications, while Caja is meant to be backwards compatible with current applications. Similar to FBJS, a server-side rewrite process ensures continuous protection of dynamic code.

Recent research on the security of JavaScript subsets has been able to prove that a subset based on Caja is capability safe [22]. This important result shows that a JavaScript subset can adhere to an object-capability security model, and can thus be used to achieve the proposed security requirements.

Caja is currently used by several OpenSocial gadget integrators, such as Yahoo! Application Platform, Shindig, iGoogle, Code Wiki and Orkut.

5 Communication

In this section, we discuss several techniques to achieve cross-domain communication. These techniques are mostly workarounds, to enable communication under the restrictions of the SOP. The last technique, i.e. cross-origin resource sharing, is designed to extend the SOP to allow safe, controlled cross-domain communication.

5.1 XMLHttpRequest Proxies

XHR does not allow cross-domain requests, a restriction that can be circumvented by providing a server-side proxy within the origin of the page initiating the request. The proxy receives a request for some content, retrieves it and sends it back to the requesting page. This solution is elegant in the sense that it allows the client-side implementation to use XHR, the standardized communication mechanism. The solution lacks elegance however in the fine details, such as the difficulty in handling authentication credentials of the remote site, where the information needs to be retrieved from. Another disadvantage is the fact that every component provider needs to provide a proxy. Furthermore, this proxy has to be fully trusted by the client, since it can manipulate both request and response.

When compared against the proposed security requirements, this solution does offer cross-domain communication, but offers no authentication. Even when an authentication mechanism is implemented on top of this communication channel, the proxy effectively acts as a man in the middle, which makes the authentication process untrustworthy.

This technique is currently used by Facebook JavaScript and iGoogle.

5.2 Script Communication

Scripts can be included from any origin, but their content is included in the protection domain of the page that includes it. Furthermore, the page does not get access to the contents of the received script file, which is executed immediately. This does not prevent the use of script inclusion as a communication channel: outgoing information is embedded using GET parameters and incoming information is encoded as JavaScript code. This code can be anything, but will most likely be JSON data.

This technique achieves cross-domain communication, but can not guarantee any authentication. Depending on the degree of separation between the components, an authentication mechanism may be implemented on top of this channel.

A major issue with this technique however is the fact that the response has full privileges within the requesting page. This means that if an attacker can manipulate the response, the whole requesting page is vulnerable to attack.

This technique is used in practice, for instance in Google's mail service, Gmail.

5.3 Using Browser Plugins

By interacting with browser plugins, such as Flash or Java, cross-domain communication can be achieved. These plugins are not bound to the SOP of the browser and are free to implement their own policy. The implemented policies resemble the SOP of the browser, with some exceptions [34]. The origin to which the plugin is bound is typically the origin where it was downloaded from, not the origin of the including document. One noteworthy extension to the SOP of the browser is that Flash and Java, among others, use a cross-domain policy file (called `crossdomain.xml`) [1], which is used to selectively allow cross-domain requests. This policy file is created and served by the destination of a cross-domain request and identifies the origins where the request can come from. The plugin checks this policy file before executing a cross-domain request.

The use of browser plugins enables cross-domain communication and offers more fine-grained controls that other techniques do. Authentication can be achieved using cookies or HTTP authentication headers, but the browser plugin, which acts as a client-side proxy component, is still responsible for identifying the component behind the request. Disadvantageous to this technique is the need for browser plugin support, which can have an impact on the security of the browser platform, as shown by numerous vulnerabilities in both the Flash and Java plugin environment. Additional disadvantages are the potential lack of plugin support on mobile devices and the elevated resource consumption caused by the loaded browser plugin objects.

This technique is currently in use by Facebook JavaScript.

5.4 Cross-Origin Resource Sharing

Cross-Origin Resource Sharing (CORS) is an extension of the HTTP protocol to support cross-domain requests [32]. CORS allows a remote server to indicate whether the given origin has access to its resources or not, a decision which is enforced by the browser. The server can formulate fine-grained decisions for particular resources, such as the HTTP methods that can be used or whether credentials (cookies, HTTP authentication) are allowed.

Technically, CORS adds request headers to provide the server additional information, such as the origin or the need for credentials, to which the server responds with response headers specifying the fine-grained decision that the browser needs to enforce. The specification preserves the protection of legacy operations, which have no knowledge about CORS, using a deny-by-default approach.

This solution is a durable, long-term approach to enabling cross-domain communication. It even offers support for authentication, using cookies or HTTP authentication. A disadvantage with the specification is the domain-based identification of origins, which makes it hard for a remote server to distinguish requests coming from two different components from within the same origin. As experiments have shown, using CORS in conjunction with the unique origin of the `sandbox` attribute leads to a `null`-origin being associated with the request. This behavior can be attributed to the sandbox being a "privacy-sensitive" context [2].

The CORS specification is still a W3C working draft, but is already supported in major browsers. Since CORS only specifies an algorithm, browser vendors are free to implement it how they see fit. Firefox and Chrome have extended the traditional XHR communication mechanism with this additional functionality. Internet Explorer has implemented it as the new XDomainRequest API, due to previous security issues with the implementation of XHR [9].

6   Advanced Fine-Grained Control

In this section, we present three approaches which are aimed at providing fine-grained control over component behavior in a mashup. The first approach focuses on enforcing a policy on JavaScript code, either with or without specific browser-side support. A second approach mediates access to specific objects, thus enabling the enforcement of a security policy. A third approach is aimed at enabling information flow control for JavaScript.

6.1   Policy Enforcement Techniques for JavaScript

ConScript enables the specification and enforcement of fine-grained security policies for JavaScript in the browser [21]. Such policies can be used to control the script behavior, such as disallowing calls to certain functions (e.g. `eval`), or preventing the script from accessing cookies. To ease the task of writing policies, ConScript supports automatic policy generation trough static analysis of server-side code or run-time analysis of client-side code. Technically, ConScript supports the enforcement of security advice within the JavaScript engine. The advantage of this approach is its effectivity, since all indirections and ambiguities, such as different paths to the same function, are eliminated inside the JavaScript engine.

Self-protecting JavaScript [29] provides similar security features, but does not require specific support within the browser. Policy enforcement is achieved by wrapping security-sensitive JavaScript operations before normal script execution. As a consequence of not depending on browser-support, this technique faces several challenges, such as covering all access paths to a specific function or preventing wrapped operations to be restored by the malicious script. Several of these issues have been addressed in a follow-up paper [25], while others will be resolved in future research.

6.2   Mediating Access to Objects

Object views offer a fine grained control over shared objects in a JavaScript environment [26]. By creating and sharing a view of an object, instead of the full object, all calls to the object pass through the view, where a security policy can be enforced. An example application scenario is a document sharing policy, where the HTML document is a shared object. A view of this document can enforce the security policy, where a component can have read-only access to the entire DOM tree, and only gets write access to within its boundaries.

AdJail [30] offers a technique to mediate access to advertisements, which are embedded as a DOM object. Advertisements are executed separately in a sandboxed environment, where they can cause no harm. In order to preserve the user experience and to enable ad-specific services, such as compatibility with ad network targeting algorithms or billing operations, a mediation technique selectively forwards specific operations, such as visualizing content and forwarding of user interface events, between the sandbox and hosting page.

6.3   Information Flow Control for JavaScript

Applying information flow control (IFC) to mashup components on the client-side can prevent the leaking of sensitive data. A lattice-based approach to mashup composition [24] prevents unauthorized leaking between origins. Authorized sharing can be enabled by so-called *escape hatches*, which allow the declassification of specific content items. Related work is Mash-IF [20], which presents a client-side solution for enabling information flow control by means of a browser extension. The extension supports the identification of sensitive data and uses a reference monitor to prevent unauthorized disclosure within the mashup.

Additionally, secure multi-execution achieves non-interference between different levels in the security lattice, by executing a script for each security level, which results in only a limited run-time overhead on multi-core client machines [8].

7   Discussion

The overview in Figure 3 shows the compliance of the discussed solutions with the security requirements for separation and interaction. The table also indicates whether a technique is currently supported by mainstream browsers or not. From this table – and the earlier discussion – it can be concluded that the use of iframes combined with postMessage offers separation and interaction in a standardized way, without much overhead. Stronger separation can be achieved by using sandboxed iframes. For script separation within the same execution environment, Caja is most widely used and has the strongest formal background. The techniques to enable communication have not been summarized in a table, because there are too many differences between different techniques. The conclusion for this category is that the use of CORS is the recommended solution, since it is a soon-to-be-standardized approach, with very limited overhead.

If we revisit the running example from the beginning of the paper, we can use the following techniques to meet the security requirements: a client-side mashup composes the application by separating the components using iframes

	Separation			Interaction			
	DOM	Script	Applicable in same domain	Confidentiality	Integrity	Mutual Authentication	Standardized/ Supported
iframe	yes	yes	no	N/A	N/A	N/A	yes
script	no	no	no	no	no	no	yes
iframe + postmessage	yes	yes	no	yes	yes	yes	yes
sandbox + postmessage	yes	yes	yes	yes	yes	yes	yes
subspace	yes	yes	no	yes	yes	yes	yes
smash	yes	yes	no	yes	yes	yes	yes
module	yes	yes	yes	yes	yes	possible	no
mashupOS	yes	yes	yes	yes	yes	possible	no
Omash	yes	yes	yes	yes	yes	possible	no
Adsafe	yes	yes	yes	yes	yes	possible	yes
Facebook JavaScript	yes	yes	yes	yes	yes	possible	yes
Caja	yes	yes	yes	yes	yes	possible	yes

Fig. 3. Overview: Separation/Isolation and Interaction. Note: mutual authentication is most of the time not available, but can be implemented (indicated by "possible").

(all different domains, so no need to use sandboxes). Interaction between banking an brokerage component is enabled using postMessage, with access-control to ensure that the advertising component does not try to request private information. Both banking an brokerage component also expose an API to retrieve relevant keywords, which is publicly available, and can be used by the advertising component. The banking and brokerage component can communicate with their servers using traditional XHR. The advertising component can retrieve specific advertisements using CORS, where the remote server allows requests coming from the domain of the advertising component.

Opportunities for future work and developments for building secure mashups are available both within the currently existing techniques as in the evolution of mashups. One way currently existing techniques can be improved is by solving the remaining issues, such as the authentication problems with the use of unique-origin sandboxes [2]. Another important improvement is the support for web developers. The proposed security mechanisms, such as the postMessage API and CORS specification serve their purpose, but expose too many low level details to the developers. An abstraction on top of the postMessage API could allow developers to define a public interface in some form of interface definition language, which is then translated to the corresponding, low level message handler. Similarly, the CORS specification enables cross-domain communication, but the header injection at the server-side needs to be encapsulated by frameworks and management tools, to relieve the implementation and management burden.

A growing mashup popularity will lead to changing requirements, especially the need for fine-grained control techniques. The selective restrictions introduced by the sandbox attribute are a step in the right direction, but more fine-grained control will be needed in the future, an evolution started by the techniques presented in Section 6. Providing secure, fine-grained policy enforcement techniques will enable developers and integrators to compose mashups, which respect specified policies. This is especially important for complex enterprise mashups, where regulations, service level agreements or contracts may need to be respected.

Acknowledgements. This research is partially funded by the Interuniversity Attraction Poles Programme Belgian State, Belgian Science Policy, IBBT, the Research Fund K.U. Leuven and the EU-funded FP7-projects WebSand and NESSoS.

References

1. Adobe Systems Inc. Cross-domain policy file specification (January 2010), `http://www.adobe.com/devnet/articles/crossdomain_policy_file_spec.html`
2. Barth, A., Jackson, C., Hickson, I.: The web origin concept (June 2010), `http://tools.ietf.org/html/draft-abarth-origin-07`
3. Barth, A., Jackson, C., Mitchell, J.C.: Securing frame communication in browsers. In: In Proceedings of the 17th USENIX Security Symposium (USENIX Security 2008) (2008)
4. Crites, S., Hsu, F., Chen, H.: Omash: Enabling secure web mashups via object abstractions. In: Proceedings of the 15th ACM Conference on Computer and Communications Security, pp. 99–108. ACM (2008)
5. Crockford, D.: The module tag (October 2006), `http://www.json.org/module.html`
6. Crockford, D.: Adsafe (December 2009), `http://www.adsafe.org/`
7. De Keukelaere, F., Bhola, S., Steiner, M., Chari, S., Yoshihama, S.: Smash: Secure component model for cross-domain mashups on unmodified browsers. In: Proceedings of the 17th International Conference on World Wide Web, pp. 535–544. ACM (2008)
8. Devriese, D., Piessens, F.: Non-interference through secure multi-execution. In: 2010 IEEE Symposium on Security and Privacy Proceedings, pp. 109–124 (2010)
9. Dutta, S.: Client-side cross-domain security (June 2008), `http://msdn.microsoft.com/library/cc709423.aspx`
10. Facebook Developer Wiki. Cross domain communication (January 2009), `http://wiki.developers.facebook.com/index.php/Cross_Domain_Communication`
11. Facebook Developer Wiki. FBJS (August 2010), `http://wiki.developers.facebook.com/index.php/FBJS`
12. Harmonia, Inc. Liquidapps (2010), `http://www.liquidappsworld.com/`
13. Hickson, I., Hyatt, D.: Html 5 working draft (June 2010), `http://www.w3.org/TR/html5/`
14. Hickson, I., Hyatt, D.: Html 5 working draft - cross-document messaging (June 2010), `http://www.w3.org/TR/html5/comms.html#crossDocumentMessages`
15. Hickson, I., Hyatt, D.: Html 5 working draft - the sandbox attribute (June 2010), `http://www.w3.org/TR/html5/the-iframe-element.html#attr-iframe-sandbox`
16. IBM. IBM Mashup Center (2010), `http://www-01.ibm.com/software/info/mashup-center/`
17. Intel Corporation. Mash Maker (2010), `http://mashmaker.intel.com/web/`
18. JackBe Corporation. Presto: Powering the enterprise app store (2010), `http://www.jackbe.com/products/`
19. Jackson, C., Wang, H.J.: Subspace: secure cross-domain communication for web mashups. In: Proceedings of the 16th International Conference on World Wide Web, p. 620 (2007)

20. Li, Z., Zhang, K., Wang, X.F.: Mash-if: Practical information-flow control within client-side mashups. In: 2010 IEEE/IFIP International Conference on Dependable Systems and Networks (DSN), pp. 251–260 (2010)

21. Livshits, B., Meyerovich, L.: Conscript: Specifying and enforcing fine-grained security policies for javascript in the browser. Technical report, Microsoft Research (2009)

22. Maffeis, S., Mitchell, J.C., Taly, A.: Object capabilities and isolation of untrusted web applications. In: Proceedings of IEEE Security and Privacy 2010. IEEE (2010)

23. Maffeis, S., Taly, A.: Language-based isolation of untrusted javascript. In: 22nd IEEE Computer Security Foundations Symposium, pp. 77–91 (2009)

24. Magazinius, J., Askarov, A., Sabelfeld, A.: A lattice-based approach to mashup security. In: Proceedings of the 5th ACM Symposium on Information, Computer and Communications Security, pp. 15–23 (2010)

25. Magazinius, J., Phung, P., Sands, D.: Safe wrappers and sane policies for self protecting javascript. In: 15th Nordic Conference on Secure IT Systems (2010)

26. Meyerovich, L.A., Felt, A.P., Miller, M.S.: Object views: Fine-grained sharing in browsers. In: Proceedings of the 19th International Conference on World Wide Web, pp. 721–730 (2010)

27. Miller, M.S., Samuel, M., Laurie, B., Awad, I., Stay, M.: Caja: Safe active content in sanitized javascript (January 2008),
http://google-caja.googlecode.com/files/caja-spec-2008-01-15.pdf

28. OpenAjax Alliance. Openajax hub 2.0 specification (July 2009),
http://www.openajax.org/member/wiki/index.php?
title=OpenAjax_Hub_2.0_Specification&oldid=12174

29. Phung, P.H., Sands, D., Chudnov, A.: Lightweight self-protecting javascript. In: Proceedings of the 4th International Symposium on Information, Computer, and Communications Security, pp. 47–60 (2009)

30. Ter Louw, M., Ganesh, K.T., Venkatakrishnan, V.N.: Adjail: Practical enforcement of confidentiality and integrity policies on web advertisements. In: 19th USENIX Security Symposium (2010)

31. Thorpe, D.: Secure cross-domain communication in the browser (July 2007),
http://msdn.microsoft.com/en-us/library/bb735305.aspx

32. van Kesteren, A.: Cross-origin resource sharing (2009)

33. Wang, H.J., Fan, X., Howell, J., Jackson, C.: Protection and communication abstractions for web browsers in mashupos. ACM SIGOPS Operating Systems Review 41(6), 16 (2007)

34. Zalewski, M.: Browser security handbook (2010),
http://code.google.com/p/browsersec/wiki/Main

35. Zarandioon, S., Yao, D.D., Ganapathy, V.: Omos: A framework for secure communication in mashup applications. In: Annual Computer Security Applications Conference, ACSAC 2008, pp. 355–364 (2008)

Safe Wrappers and Sane Policies
for Self Protecting JavaScript

Jonas Magazinius, Phu H. Phung, and David Sands

Chalmers University of Technology, Sweden

Abstract. Phung *et al* (ASIACCS'09) describe a method for wrapping built-in functions of JavaScript programs in order to enforce security policies. The method is appealing because it requires neither deep transformation of the code nor browser modification. Unfortunately the implementation outlined suffers from a range of vulnerabilities, and policy construction is restrictive and error prone. In this paper we address these issues to provide a systematic way to avoid the identified vulnerabilities, and make it easier for the policy writer to construct declarative policies – i.e. policies upon which attacker code has no side effects.

1   Introduction

Even with the best of intentions, a web site might serve a page which contains malicious JavaScript code. Preventing e.g. cross-site scripting (XSS) attacks in modern web applications has proved to be a difficult task. One alternative to relying on careful use of input validation is to focus on code *behavior* instead of code integrity. Even if we cannot be sure of the origins (and hence functionality) of all the code in a given page, it may be enough to guarantee that the page does not behave in an unintended manner, such as abusing resources or redirecting sensitive data to untrusted origins.

One way to do this is to specify a policy which says under what conditions a page may perform a certain action, and implement this by a *reference monitor* [2] which grants, denies or modifies such action requests. In this paper we study this approach in a JavaScript/browser context, where the policy is enforced by using software wrappers. In the remainder of this introduction we review the background of policy enforcement mechanism in protecting web pages from malicious JavaScript code. A number of recent proposals implement policy enforcement by using wrappers to intercept security-relevant events. Here we sample the various approaches to implementing wrappers – each with their own advantages and disadvantages, before focusing in more detail on the approach, *self-protecting JavaScript*, that forms the main focus of this article.

1.1   The Wrapper Landscape

One key dimension for comparing security wrapper and sandboxing approaches is whether they require browser modification or not. Full browser integration offers some clear advantages. For example, the wrapping mechanism has direct access to the scripts as seen by the browser so there can be no inconsistency between the wrapper's and the browser's view of the code. Such inconsistencies are the basis for attacks, as is well

T. Aura, K. Järvinen, and K. Nyberg (Eds.): NordSec 2010, LNCS 7127, pp. 239–255, 2012.
© Springer-Verlag Berlin Heidelberg 2012

known from the evasion attacks on script filters. The wrapping mechanism also has access to lower-level implementation details that would not be accessible at the Java-Script level, and permits modifications and extensions, for the greater good, to Java-Script's semantics. The state-of-the-art in this approach is CONSCRIPT [21], which modifies Internet Explorer 8 to provide aspect-oriented programming constructs for JavaScript.

Avoiding browser modification, on the other hand, is an advantage in itself. For example it could allow a server to protect its own code from XSS attacks using an application-specific policy. The user would receive this protection without being proactive. Within this area one can roughly divide the approaches into those which transform the whole program (thus requiring the program to be parsed) and those which perform wrapping without having to modify the code. Phung *et al* [25] refer to these styles as *invasive* vs *lightweight*, respectively. The former approach is taken by the BrowserShield tool [28] which performs a deep wrapping of code, requiring run-time parsing and transformation of the code. In more recent work, Ofuonye and Miller [23] show that the high runtime overheads witnessed in BrowserShield can be improved in practice by optimising the instrumentation technique. The *lightweight* approach refers to techniques which do not require any aggressive code manipulation. There are many JavaScript programming libraries which provide this kind of functionality; the lightweight self-protecting JavaScript work of Phung *et al* [25] is the only one of these which is security specific. More details of this approach are given below.

A number of approaches involve using well-behaved subsets of JavaScript. These can be though of as a hybrid of an invasive pass (to check that the code is in the intended sub-language), followed by wrapping. By syntactically filtering the language, the wrapping problem becomes much simpler, since problematic language features can be disallowed (these invariably must include, among other things, all dynamic code creation features such as `eval` and `document.write`). This approach is exemplified in FBJS [12], a JavaScript subset provided by Facebook to sandbox third-party applications. A principled perspective on this approach is provided in the work of Maffeis *et al*, e.g. [19].

Each approach has potential advantages and disadvantages, and each must both overcome numerous technical problems to be practically applicable.

1.2   Self Protecting JavaScript

In this paper we focus on problems and improvements in the *self protecting JavaScript* approach [25]. Here we outline the key ingredients of that approach.

Policies are defined in terms of security relevant events, which are the API calls – the so-called *built-in* methods of JavaScript. These are the methods which have an intrinsic meaning independent of the code itself. The attacker is assumed to have injected arbitrary JavaScript into the body of a web page. A policy is a piece of JavaScript which, in an aspect-oriented programming (AOP) style, specifies which method calls are to be intercepted (the *pointcut* in AOP-speak), and what action (*advice*) is to be taken.

The key to being "lightweight" is that the method does not need to parse or transform the body of the page at all. This is achieved by assuming that the server, or some trusted proxy, injects the policy code into the header of the web page. Integrity of this policy code is assumed (so attacks to the page in transit are not considered). Injecting the policy code into the header ensures that the policy code is executed first, so the policy code gets to wrap the security critical methods before the attacker code can get a handle on them. This is a strikingly simple idea that does not have any particular difficulty with dynamic language features such as on-the-fly code generation. The price paid for this is that it can only provide security policies for the built-in methods, and cannot patch arbitrary "code patterns" as e.g. the BrowserShield approach.

Phung *et al* implemented this idea via an adaptation of a non security-oriented aspect-oriented programming library. But in a security context the ability to ensure that the code and policy are tamper-proof, and that the attacker cannot obtain pointers to the unwrapped methods is crucial. In this paper we study and fix vulnerabilities of both kinds in the implementation outlined by Phung *et al*, and propose a way to make it easier to write sane policies which behave in a way which is not unduly influenced by attacker code.

We divide the study into issues relating to the generic wrapper code (Section 2), and issues relating to the construction of safe policies (Section 3). Before discussing this work in more detail below, we summarize the attacks which motivate the present work, most of which are either well-known or based on well-known mechanisms:

Prototype poisoning. Prototype poisoning is a well-known attack vector: trusted code can be compromised because it inherits from a global prototype which is accessible to the attacker. We address several flavours of poisoning attack:

- *Built-in subversion* Built-in methods used in the implementation of the generic *wrapper code* can be subverted by modifying the prototype object.
- *Global setter subversion* Setters defined on prototype objects are executed upon instantiation of new objects. This opens up for external code to access information in a supposedly private scope. In the case of the wrapper implementation, inconsiderate use of temporary objects leads to compromise. This issue has been discussed previously in the context of JSON Hijacking [24,8].
- *Policy object subversion* Any object implicitly or explicitly manipulated by the *policy code* is vulnerable to subversion via its global prototype. Meyerovich *et al* [20] provide a good example of this attack in the subversion of a URL whitelist stored in a policy.

Aliasing issues. A specific built-in may have several aliases pointing to the same function in the browser. Knowing what to wrap given one of these aliases is imperative for the monitor in order to control access to the built-in. Meyerovich *et al* [20] call this *incomplete mediation*. Also, each window instance has its own set of built-ins but can under some circumstances access and execute a built-in of another instance. This sort of dynamic aliasing needs to be controlled so that one instance with wrapped built-ins cannot not access the unprotected built-ins of another.

Abusing the caller-chain. When a function is called, the `caller` property of that function is set to refer to the function calling it. The called function can thereby get a handle on its caller and access to and modify part of the information which is supposed to be local to it e.g. the `arguments` property. This implies that if user code in one way or another is called from either a built-in, the wrapper, or from the policy, it could potentially bypass the monitor. This general attack vector is described in the Caja end-user's guide [13] ("Reflective call stack traversal leaks references").

Non declarative arguments. If a policy inspects a user-supplied parameter the parameter can masquerade as a "good" value at inspection time, and change to a "bad" value a the time of use. This is because JavaScript performs an implicit type conversion. This attack was already addressed in [25] where it is credited to Maffeis (see also [19]). It is also the basis of a recently described attack on ADsafe [18]. (This paper significantly extends the defence mechanism of [25] for this class of attack).

2   Breaking and Fixing the Wrapping Code

Upon analyzing the wrapper implementation by Phung *et al.* [25] (see Listing 1.1), we found that it was vulnerable to a number of attacks. In this section we discuss the attacks, potential solutions and how the attacks apply to other wrapping libraries.

```
1   var wrap = function(pointcut, Policy) {
2       ...
3       var aspect = function() {
4           var invocation = { object: this, args: arguments };
5           return Policy.apply(invocation.object,
6               [{ arguments: invocation.args,
7                   method: pointcut.method,
8                   proceed: function() {
9                       return original.apply(...);
10                  }}]);
11      } ...
12  }
```

Listing 1.1. The main wrapper function in Phung *et al* [25]

2.1   Function and Object Subversion

Since the header is executed before the page is processed, any malicious code in the page will only have access to wrapped methods. But since wrapped methods are executed in the attacker's environment, the attacker can subvert functions that are used in the wrapping function to bypass the policies or extract the original unwrapped methods. As an example, the wrapper in Listing 1.1 uses the `apply`-function to execute the policy and the original method. The `apply`-function is inherited from the `Function`-prototype, which is part of the environment accessible to the attacker. By modifying the `apply`-function of `Function`-prototype an attacker can bypass the execution of the policy or even extract the original built-in. Suppose that the wrapped built-in is the function `window.alert`. The following code (Listing 1.2) illustrates this attack by extracting the original `window.alert` and restoring it. If the monitor were to rely on inherited properties of objects it could be influenced in a similar way.

```
1  var recover_builtin;
2  Function.prototype.apply = function(thisObj, args){
3          if (args[0].proceed) args[0].proceed();
4          else recover_builtin = this; };
5  //call the wrapped built-in, so that the wrapper will execute
6  window.alert('XSS');
7  //then recover the built-in
8  if (recover_builtin) window.alert = recover_builtin;
```

Listing 1.2. Illustration of subverting built-in to recover the wrapped method

To prevent attacker code from subverting objects we can try to ensure that each object reference used in the policy is a local property of the object and not something inherited from its low-integrity prototype. The built-in function `hasOwnProperty` can be used for this purpose (of course the integrity of the function `hasOwnProperty` must be maintained as well). But this approach requires all object accesses to be identified and checked. This is potentially tricky for implicit accesses, e.g., the `toString`-function is called implicitly when an object is converted to a string.

Since the monitor code is the first code to be executed it can store local references to the original built-in methods used in the advice function. Our solution is to ensure that the wrapper code only uses the locally stored copies of the original methods. As an example, `o.toString()` would be rewritten as `original_toString.apply(o, [])`. To prevent an attacker from subverting the apply function of the stored methods, it is made local to each stored function by assignment, i.e. `original_toString.apply= original_apply`. Now even if the prototype of the function is subverted, the `apply` function local to the object remains untouched. Again, this is not entirely foolproof since it could be hard to determine which functions are being called *implicitly*.

A simpler alternative approach (supported in e.g. Firefox, Chrome and Safari, but not in e.g. IE8 or Opera) is to set an object's __proto__ to **null**. This has the effect of disconnecting the object from its prototype chain, thus preventing it from inheriting properties defined outside of the policy code. Since they are no longer inherited, any required properties of the prototype must be reattached to the object from the stored originals. This technique is used in the implementation of the function `safe` in Section 3.1.

2.2 Global Setter Subversion

A special case of function subversion involves setters. A setter is a function for a property of an object, that is executed whenever the property is assigned a new value.

Defining a setter on a prototype object will affect all objects inheriting from that prototype, which is our definition of a global setter. If a setter is defined for `Object.`
`prototype`, it will be inherited by *all* objects.

An issue that has been discussed recently [32,29] is that global setters will be executed upon object instantiation. This creates an unexpected behavior where external
code is able to extract values from a private scope. When considering the code in Listing 1.1, an attacker could define a global setter for the property *proceed* of all objects.
The below snippet illustrates this attack in the wrapper in Listing 1.1.

```
1  var recover_builtin;
2  Object.prototype.__defineSetter__('proceed',
3                      function(o) { recover_builtin = o });
```

When the advice is executed, a temporary argument object for the policy is created.
Since this object contains a *proceed*-property, the setter will be executed and the function containing the original method will be passed as an argument. The attacker can now
bypass the policy by executing the function in the setter. Note also that the argument
object as a whole will be accessible to the setter through the **this**-keyword. The same
holds for any object created in the execution of the advice or in the policy itself. This
vulnerability also applies to arrays and functions.

While the correctness of this behaviour is debatable [32], it is implemented in most
browsers (at the time of writing). The exceptions are Internet Explorer (which only implement setters for DOM-objects) and Firefox which have recently [29] changed this
behavior so that setters are not executed upon instantiation of objects and arrays (although for functions the problem still remains). This issue has been discussed previously in the context of JSON Hijacking [24,8].

One possibility to protect against this problem would be to prevent the wrapping
code from creating any new objects, arrays or functions. This severely restricts how
the advice function could be implemented, in such a way that it might not be possible
to implement at all. Checking for the existence of setters for every property before
creating an object is another alternative, but it would be infeasible in general. The advice
code could define its own getters and setters on the object instead of just assigning the
property a value. The custom getters and setters would overshadow the inherited ones,
making the object safe to use. Again this might be a bit too cumbersome.

As mentioned in the previous section, the chain of inheritance can be broken by
setting the __proto__ property to **null**. This is our current solution. Developing a solution which works for platforms not supporting this feature would require very careful
implementation and is left for future work.

2.3   Issues Concerning Aliases of Built-ins

Although policies are specified in terms of built-in function *names*, semantically speaking they refer to the native code to which the function points. This gives rise to an
aliasing problem as there may be several aliases to the same built-in. This is a problem
since a crucial assumption of the approach is that wrappers hold the *only* references to

the security relevant original functions. This problem is highlighted in [21] (where it is solved by pointer comparison – something that is not possible at the JavaScript level).

Static Aliases. Most functions have more than one alias within the window, and if one is wrapped, then the others need to be wrapped as well. Otherwise, the original function can be restored by using an alias. As an example, in Firefox the function alert can be reached through at least the following aliases: `window.alert`, `window.__proto__.alert`, `window.constructor.prototype.alert`, `Window.prototype.alert`. Enumerating these different aliases for each method is browser specific and somewhat tedious, but we conjecture that in most cases there is a "root" object at the top of the prototype inheritance chain for which wrapping of the given method takes care of all the aliases. For a given `object` and `method` this root object can be computed by:

```
1  while(!object.hasOwnProperty(method) && object.__proto__)
2    object = object.__proto__;
```

Any aliases not captured by this scheme must be handled on an *ad hoc* basis. But the main point here is that this should be the job of the wrapping library and not the policy writer. Thus we propose to extend the wrapping library with a means to compute aliases, and ensure that a policy applied to one function is applied to all its static aliases.

Dynamic Aliases. Another class of aliases are those which can be obtained from other window object (window, frame, iframe). In [25], several attempted solutions were introduced to deal with the problem, including disabling the creation of new window, frame/iframe or disable the access to `contentWindow` property of frame/iframe objects from where references to unwrapped methods can be retrieved. Unfortunately the proposed approach seems both incomplete (does not provide full mediation) and overly restrictive. In this work, we allow window objects to be created, but user code should not be able to obtain a reference to one. If user code gets a reference to a foreign window object, even if it is enforced with the same policies, that window object could be navigated to a new location which would reset all the built-ins. To implement this we provide pre-defined policies which enforce methods that potentially return a window object. This boils down to two cases: static frames that are defined as part of the HTML code, and dynamic frames that are generated on the fly.

For static frames the problem is that they do not exist at the time the policy code in the header is executed, and there is no way to intervene just after they have been created. This means we have to proactively prevent access to an unspecified number of frames that *might* be created. If we disable `contentWindow` for all frames, the only other way for user code to obtain a reference to the window is through the `window.frames` or `window` array. By defining getters for "enough" indices in this array we can fully prevent inappropriate access. The remaining problem is determining how many indices will be enough – here we must rely on some external approximation.

For dynamic iframes a similar approach is used. By wrapping all actions that may result in the creation of an iframe, we can intervene and replace the `contentWindow` property and the right number of indices in the `window` array.

2.4   Abusing the Caller-Chain

Built-in Subversion. The following core assumption is formalised in [25]: *we are effectively assuming that the built-in methods do not call any other methods, built-in or otherwise.* This assumption does not hold for all built-ins, and its failure has consequences. Specifically, (i) some built-ins run arbitrary user functions by design, such as `filter`, `forEach`, `every`, `map`, `some`, `reduce`, and `reduceRight`, and (ii) some built-ins implicitly access object properties e.g. `pop` which sets the `length` property or `alert` that implicitly calls `toString` on its argument. These property accesses can, in turn, trigger arbitrary code execution via user-defined getters and setters.

Both of these cases are problematic because of a nonstandard but widely implemented[1] `caller` property of function objects. For a function `f`, `f.caller` returns a pointer to the function which called `f` (assuming `f` is currently on the call stack). Thus any user code which is called from within a built-in can obtain a pointer to that built-in using `caller`.

As an example, suppose that the `alert` function has been wrapped. In Listing 1.3 the user defines an object with a `toString` which sets `alert` to the function calling it. Now the user code calls `alert(x)`, thus invoking the wrapped `alert` function. Now suppose that the wrapper eventually calls the original `alert` built-in. The built-in will internally make a call to `x.toString`. The modified `toString` can now obtain a reference to the built-in from the caller chain and restore the original built-in.

```
1  var x ={toString:function(){ alert=arguments.callee.caller;}};
2  alert(x);
```

Listing 1.3. An example of the caller attack

Wrapper Subversion. The caller attack does not only apply to built-ins. In several places the wrapper code must traverse user-supplied objects in order to inspect or assign to properties. This might trigger the execution of getters or setters or other user supplied code which can abuse the caller chain to influence the wrapper, extract information, or dynamically change its behavior upon inspection.

Mitigating the Caller Attack. For type-(i) functions this is not a real problem – we simply ban them from wrapping. From a policy perspective the built-ins are really just a way to get a handle on *behaviours*. Functions like those listed are simply programming utilities and have nothing to do with the extensional behaviour of the system at all, and policies have no business trying to control them.

Type-(ii) functions, on the other hand, do indeed involve built-ins that may need to be wrapped, e.g. `document.appendChild`. For each built-in, the wrapper needs to know (an upper bound on) the properties that it might access directly. Before calling the original built-in the wrapper must unset any user-defined getters or setters for the accessed properties before calling the built-in; to preserve functionality these are restored after the built-in returns.

---

[1] Not part of any ECMA standard but implemented in all major browsers.

As for subversion of the wrapper, there is no upper bound on which properties might be accessed. Therefore the wrapper must ensure that user code is not implicitly executed when traversing the object. This could be achieved as for type-(ii) functions above, but a simpler approach works in this case. If there is a recursive function on the stack then the caller operation can never get past it. So by wrapping operations on untrusted data in a dummy recursive function, the caller operation can be prevented from reaching the sensitive context.

2.5   Browser Specific Issues

It seems unlikely that one can come up with a solution which works for all browsers. One thorny problem that is specific to Firefox is the behavior of the delete operator which when applied to the name of a built-in simply deletes any wrappers and restores the original method. This problem is discussed in [25], and also plagues the Torbutton anonymous browsing plug-in, which is unable to properly disable access to the Date object for precisely this reason [30]. We are not optimistic that there is a workaround for this in the current versions of Firefox, although future versions supporting object attributes from the recent ECMAScript 262 standard [11] will certainly see an end to this problem.

2.6   Other Lightweight AOP Libraries

As an experiment we tried to adjust the attacks to other AOP-wrapping libraries to see if any of them were more suitable candidates for implementing a reference monitor. The libraries used were jQuery AOP [15], dojo AOP [10], Ajaxpect [1], AspectJS [3], Cerny.js [7], AspectES [4], PrototypeJS [27]. One thing to note is that none of these libraries were designed for security purposes, but rather as general implementations of AOP-functionality. The results were discouraging: all of the libraries were vulnerable to all the attacks described above. In addition the way they are designed opens up for new attacks which had been considered in the design of [25]. For example, since the the wrapping code (the AOP library) is not in the same local scope as the policy code, the library must export its wrapping functions, thus making them vulnerable to simple redefinition from attacker code.

3   Declarative Policies

Let us suppose that the mechanism for enforcing policies provides full mediation of security relevant events. Then all one needs to do is to write policies which enforce the desired security properties. Unfortunately, due to the complexities of JavaScript, this is not a simple task. It is all too easy to write policies which look reasonable, but whose behavior can be controlled by the attacker (who controls the code outside of the policy).

In this section we describe this problem and propose a method to structure policy code which makes them *declarative*, in the sense that code outside the policy and wrapper library cannot have side-effects on the policy.

As a running example consider a policy implementing a URL white-list which is used to filter calls to e.g. window.open(url,..): calls to whitelisted URL's are allowed, other calls are dropped.

3.1 Object and Function Subversion in Policies

In [20] an additional problem with policy subversion is noted. Let us consider the example given there: suppose that the policy writer models a URL whitelist by an object: **var** whitelist ={"*good.com*":**true**, "*good2.org*":**true**}. Then for a policy, which also allows subdomains of the domains in the whitelist, the code would involve a check similar to the one in Listing 1.4.

```
1  var l = url.lastIndexOf('.',url.length-5) + 1;
2  if (whitelist[url.substring(l)] === true) { ... }
```

Listing 1.4. Policy sample code

This looks like the desired policy, but unfortunately the attacker can easily bypass it by assigning to Object.prototype["*evil.com*"]=**true**; this will add an "*evil. com*" field to all objects *including the whitelist*. Alternatively the attacker could redefine substring to always return a string that is in the whitelist. The *url* would then pass the check regardless of its actual value.

The solution we adopt here is the same as for the wrapper code. For functions the policy writer must use local copies of the originals, and for objects we can ensure that they cannot access a poisoned prototype by simply removing it from its prototype chain.

Let us refer to such an object as a *safe* object. How can we make it easy for the policy author to work only with safe objects? Our current approach is to provide a function safe, which recursively traverses an object, detaching it and all sub-objects from the prototype chain that can be modified by the user. As explained in Section 2.1 detaching the object is done by setting its __proto__ property to **null**. Since detaching implies that the object will no longer inherit any of the methods expected to be associated with the type of the object, this functionality needs to be restored. Since determining the type of an object is difficult the safe function takes an optional argument to specify the type. Safe versions of the functions associated with this type are added to the object. The safe versions of the functions are stored locally and are detached from the prototype chain to prevent attacker influence. The format of the object type is similar to the types described in Section 3.2. Programming with a whitelist would then be written as:

```
1  var whitelist = safe({"good.com":true, "good2.org":true});
```

The policy writer must, in general, ensure that any object which is accessed is made safe. But objects are also constructed implicitly – for example a string might get implicitly converted to a string object. When this happens the string object in question will be unsafe. Because of this the policy author should apply the safe function to all types, preemptively (and recursively) converting all values to (safe) objects.

The question of how to obtain complete and optimal insertion of the "safe" operation in order to avoid all unsafe objects is left for further work. Note that it is not enough to wrap safe around object literals (as we initially believed). Suppose *e* is some expression which returns a value of primitive type. Now consider the expression e.toString (). This is unsafe because in order to apply the toString method the primitive type constructed by e is implicitly converted to an object (e.g. a Boolean object). This object is unsafe and thus an attacker-defined `toString` method could return any value. To fix this we could apply `safe` to e, but this would be redundant if e is already safe (by virtue of having being built from safe objects).

3.2 Non Declarative Arguments

Phung *et al* [25] (following Maffeis *et al* [17]) note a problem with inspecting call parameters. In the case of the whitelist example, note that the argument to such a call might not actually be a string, but any object with a `toString` method. Since this object comes from outside, it can be malicious. In the case of the whitelist example it could be a stateful object which returns `"goodurl.org"` when inspected by the policy, but in doing so it redefines its `toString` method to return `"evil.com"` when subsequently passed to the original e.g. `window.open(url,..)` method. Phung *et al* [25] suggested a solution to solve this problem by implementing *call-by-primitive-value* for all policy parameters using appropriate helper functions to force each argument into an expected primitive type. The idea is that the policy writer decides which arguments of the wrapped call will be inspected, and at what type. These arguments are then forcibly coerced to that type before being passed to the policy code, thus ensuring that what you see (in the policy logic) is what you get (in any subsequent call to the wrapped built-in).

Types for Declarative Arguments. The approach of Phung *et al* has some shortcomings: (i) it does not provide a clear declarative way for the policy writer to specify the parameters and their intended types; (ii) it only only applies to primitive types and not objects; (iii) it does not deal with the return value of the wrapped function (iv) it relies on the policy writer not accessing unsanitized parameters; (v) it uses functions such as `toString` for implementing coercion, but leaves this function open to subversion.

We provide a policy calling mechanism which addresses these shortcomings. Here we provide a brief outline of the design. The idea is that the policy writer writes a policy and an *inspection type* for the argument and the result. The policy code can assume that the parameters are declarative and the wrapper library will ensure this using an inspection type. An inspection type is a specification of the types of the call parameters that will be inspected by the policy code.

As an example (listing 1.5) suppose we have a policy for the `appendChild` method of the `document.body` object. The argument of the `appendChild` method should be an HTML node object which has several properties and methods. The policy (function `ipolicy`) intends to check whether the argument is an iframe by looking at the property `tagName` of the argument; if so then it should only proceed if the `src` property of the argument is an allowed URL. If the argument is not an iframe it should just proceed. (It should be noted that `tagName` is not reliable enough for this policy, but it suffices as an example.) Code to install this policy using our wrapper constructor is given in listing 1.5 below.

The first two arguments of `wrap` specify the object and method to be wrapped (the "pointcut"). The third parameter is the policy function (the "advice") and the fourth parameter is the argument inspection type – a specification of how the parameters will

```
1   var ipolicy = function(args, proceed) {
2       var o = args[0];
3       if (o.tagName == 'iframe') {
4           if (allowedUrls(o.src))
5               return proceed();
6       } else
7           return proceed();
8   }
9   wrap(document.body, 'appendChild',        // object and method
10      ipolicy,                              // policy function
11      [{src:'string', tagName:'string'}]); // arg inspection type
```

Listing 1.5. Example of using the wrapper

be inspected by the policy. In the example call above we are specifying that only the first argument to `appendChild` will be inspected by the policy code, and it will do so assuming type {src: `'string'`, tagName: `'string'`}. Not shown in the example is an optional return inspection type. This is needed if the policy will also inspect and modify the return type of the wrapped builtin.

The parameter inspection type is an array of types. The following simple grammar of JavaScript literals represents the types used in our current implementation:

$$\text{type} ::= \text{'string'} \mid \text{'number'} \mid \text{'boolean'} \mid \text{'*'} \mid \text{undefined}$$
$$\mid \{\text{field}_1 : \text{type}_1, \dots, \text{field}_n : \text{type}_n\}$$

The `'*'` type provides a reference to a value without providing access to the value itself. We expect that experience will reveal the need for a more expressive type language, such as sum-types and more flexible matching for parameter arrays – but these should not be problematic to add.

Policies are enforced as follows: the inspection type is used as a pattern to create a clone of the argument array. We will call this the *inspection argument array*. This is the generalization of the idea of *call-by-primitive-value*, except that the cloned parameters also *remove* any parts of the arguments which are not part of the type. The policy logic can only access the inspection argument array. However, when passing the parameters on to any built-in function, we permit the function access to the whole of the argument array. To do this we *combine* the original argument array with the inspection argument array. Figure 1 illustrates this process and Listing 1.6 outlines the code.

When cloning, the reference type `'*'` is replaced by a fresh dummy object. When combining, each such object is replaced with original value that it represented. Note that the type language does not include functions. This means that policy code cannot inspect any function parameters. However, this does not mean that we cannot have policies on built-in functions which e.g. have callbacks as arguments – it just means that we cannot make policy *decisions* based on the behavior of the callbacks. This restriction to "shallow" types does not seem to be a serious limitation, but more experience is needed to determine if this is indeed the case.

Example policy computation for some built-in called with (a,b,c). In this example the policy inspects **b** at type string and removes the last character, and sets the third parameter to 42 before calling `proceed()` in order to access the original built-in function. The **foo** field of the return value is incremented before it is returned to the caller. In the diagram ⊥ is an abbreviation for **undefined**, and array objects are depicted as boxes.

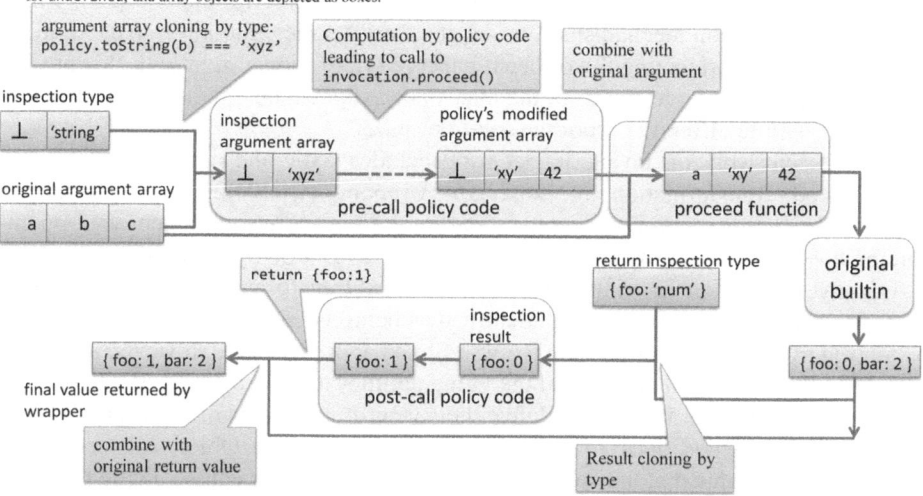

Fig. 1. Illustration of policy parameter manipulation

```
1    var wrap = function(object, method, policy, inType, retType) {
2        // Find function corresponding to alias
3        while(!object.hasOwnProperty(method) && object.__proto__)
4            object = object.__proto__;
5        var original = object[method];
6
7        object[method] = function wrapper() {
8            var object = this;
9            var orgArgs = arguments, orgRet;
10           var polArgs = cloneByType(inType, arguments);
11           var proceed = function() {
12               orgRet = original.apply(object,
13                           combine(polArgs, orgArgs));
14               return cloneByType(retType, orgRet);
15           }
16           var polRet = policy(polArgs, proceed);
17           return combine(polRet, orgRet);
18       };
19   }
```

Listing 1.6. Outline of the revised wrapper function supporting inspection types

The treatment of the return value of the method is analogous to the treatment of the arguments: a return type specifies what the policy may inspect from the return value. If this is not specified then a return type of * is assumed. The return value of the policy function is combined with the return value produced by the actual built-in.

4   Related Work

This work is based on the lightweight self-protecting JavaScript method [25], which embeds the protection mechanism in terms of security policy into a web page to make the web page self-protecting. Two recent papers [21,20] (concurrent with this present work) also discuss a large subset of the attacks investigated here, but with the purpose motivating a quite different part of the solution space.

Other recent work on JavaScript security includes static and runtime analysis e.g. [5,6,22], code transformation e.g. [28,23,16], wrapping e.g. [21,20], and safe subsets e.g. [19,14]. In this section, we compare our work to more recent related work on enforcing fine-grained security policies for JavaScript execution by wrapping.

Ofuonye and Miller [23] introduced an optimized transformation method to implement wrappers by rewriting objects identified as being vulnerable. Their approach can be viewed as an optimization of the BrowserShield approach [28]. However, it appears that the authors have not considered the vulnerabilities that we discussed in Section 2, and it seems that these attacks can defeat their security mechanism. For example, their transformation method does not protect against Function and Object subversion (cf. Section 2.1). It seems that the solutions described in this paper can be applied directly to their implementation – including not only solutions to function and object subversion, but also e.g. the use of alias-sets to apply a policy consistently across all aliases of a given built-in method.

A similar approach concurrent to our work is *object views* proposed by Meyerovich *et al* [20] that provides wrappers as a library in JavaScript. Object views, however, focus on the safe sharing of objects between two principals in the browser, e.g. between two frames of different origins or privileged code and untrusted code, whereas we focus on controlling the use of built-in methods to mitigate the extensional effects of cross-site scripts. Because policies do not control built-in functions, they need to deal with the flexibility of user defined objects and functions. In order to do so, they provide recursive "deep" wrapping and use reference equality checking of user defined objects to ensure the full mediation of each operation. Meyerovich *et al* also provide a policy system where policy writers can specify policies in declarative rules which is later compiled into wrapper functions.

CONSCRIPT [21] is more closely related to our work in the sense that it provides a JavaScript aspect-oriented programming system for enforcing security policies including those studied here. However, as mentioned in the introduction, the realisation of CONSCRIPT is different from our work in the sense that it extends JavaScript language with new primitive functions to support aspect-oriented programming and provides safe methods replacing vulnerable native JavaScript prototype functions. In order to deploy such extensions, the authors have to modify the JavaScript engine (i.e. the browser itself). CONSCRIPT also provides a type system that can be used to validate the defined policies to ensure that the policies do not contain vulnerabilities. This feature is more advanced than our declarative policies since we provide tools for the policy writer to construct sensible policies, but our method does not guarantee the correctness of the policies. A possible extension of our work to include a similar type system is left to further work.

Typed interfaces in JavaScript The use of a typed interface to enable the safe inspection and manipulation of user values is a direct generalisation of the earlier *call-by-primitive value* idea. The use of JavaScript-encoded typed interfaces is not uncommon in Java libraries. For example the Cerny.js library [7] provides a similar type language to the one used here in order to improve code quality and documentation. As mentioned above, the policy language of the ConScript system has a type system that plays an essential role in eliminating a number of security issues such as malicious user objects masquerading as primitive types. But types are only used for type checking. Thus type coercions to primitive types must be added manually to the code where needed in order for type checking to succeed. Our approach is different in that the types themselves are interpreted as coercion operations.

Aspect-oriented programming In the context of aspect-oriented programming for JavaScript, besides the AOP libraries we analysed in Section 2.6 (i.e. jQuery AOP [15], dojo AOP [10], Ajaxpect [1], AspectJS [3], Cerny.js [7], AspectES [4] and PrototypeJS [27]), there have been several AOP frameworks for JavaScript in literature. AOJS [33] is a framework supporting the separation between aspects and JavaScript code where aspects are defined in a XML-based language and then woven to JavaScript by a tool (similar to the proxy-based approach like [28,23,16] reviewed in the introduction). Current implementation of AOJS only support *before* and *after* advice, as the aspect system cannot control the behavior of operations.

Similar to our work (and the self protecting JavaScript approach), AspectScript [31] is another AOP library for JavaScript that supports richer set and pointcuts in JavaScript. AspectScript also supports stateful pointcuts that is similar to security states in Phung et al [25]. More interestingly, AspectScript provides a library as a weaver tool to transform JavaScript code into aspect-based code and the weaving process is performed at runtime. However, the mentioned libraries or frameworks have not paid attention to securing their aspect systems (see e.g. [9]), thus they are subject to the vulnerabilities that we have presented here.

5 Future Work

Most of the solutions and policy mechanisms presented here have been implemented in JavaScript and a prototype library suitable for the Safari and/or Chrome browsers is available on [26]. A number of more substantial extensions remain to be investigated.

Idiot-Proof Policies. The current policy language is intended to make it easy for the policy writer to construct sensible policies, but it does not enforce this. A natural extension of this work would be to find ways to guarantee that the policy code does not, e.g. create unsafe objects or use subverted built-in functions. We see two possible directions to achieve this. One approach would be to provide a proper separation between policy code and attacker code rather than trying to handle this on a per-method and per-object basis as we do here. Another approach is to constrain the way that policies are written, for example using JavaScript sub-languages which can be more easily constrained (see e.g. the ConScript approach and [19]) or by designing a policy language which can be compiled to JavaScript, but for which we can construct a suitable static type system. Recent work by Guha *et al* seems well suited for this purpose [14].

Session Policies. Policies should not be associated with pages but with a session and an origin. One issue that we have not addressed in this paper is writing policies which span multiple frames/iframes. This, in general, requires sharing and synchronization of policy state information between frames in a tamper-proof manner.

Acknowledgments. This work was partly funded by the European Commission under the WebSand project and the Swedish research agencies SSF and VR. This work was originally presented at OWASP AppSec Research 2010; thanks to the anonymous referees and Lieven Desmet for numerous helpful suggestions.

References

1. Ajaxpect: Aspect-Oriented Programming for Ajax (2008),
   `http://code.google.com/p/ajaxpect/`
2. Anderson, J.P.: Computer security technology planning study. Technical Report ESD-TR-73-51, US Air Force, Electronic Systems Division, Deputy for Command and Management Systems, HQ Electronic Systems Division (AFSC), USA (1972)
3. AspectJS: A JavaScript MCI/AOP Component-Library. Version 1.1, commercial (2008),
   `http://www.aspectjs.com/`
4. Balz, C.M.: The AspectES Framework: AOP for EcmaScript,
   `http://aspectes.tigris.org/` (accessed in January 2010)
5. Barth, A., Jackson, C., Mitchell, J.C.: Securing frame communication in browsers. Commun. ACM 52(6), 83–91 (2009)
6. Barth, A., Weinberger, J., Song, D.: Cross-origin JavaScript capability leaks: Detection, exploitation, and defense. In: Proc. of the 18th USENIX Security Symposium (USENIX Security 2009) (2009)
7. Cerny, R.: Cerny.js: a JavaScript library. Version 2.0,
   `http://www.cerny-online.com/cerny.js/`
8. Chess, B., O'Neil, Y.T., West, J.: JavaScript Hijacking, `http://cli.gs/jshijack` (accessed in January 2010)
9. Dantas, D.S., Walker, D.: Harmless advice. In: POPL 2006: Conference Record of the 33rd ACM SIGPLAN-SIGACT Symposium on Principles of Programming Languages, pp. 383–396. ACM, New York (2006)
10. dojo AOP library (2008), `http://cli.gs/dojoaop`
11. Ecma International. Standard ECMA-262: ECMAScript Language Specification. 5th edn., (December 2009), `http://cli.gs/ecma2625e`
12. Facebook. FBJS, `http://cli.gs/facebookjs`
13. Google. Attackvectors,
    `http://code.google.com/p/google-caja/wiki/AttackVectors` (accessed January 2010)
14. Guha, A., Saftoiu, C., Krishnamurthi, S.: The Essence of JavaScript,
    `http://www.cs.brown.edu/research/plt/dl/CS-09-10/` (accessed in January 2010)

15. jQuery AOP. Version 1.3 (October 17, 2009),
    `http://plugins.jquery.com/project/AOP`
16. Kikuchi, H., Yu, D., Chander, A., Inamura, H., Serikov, I.: Javascript Instrumentation in Practice. In: Ramalingam, G. (ed.) APLAS 2008. LNCS, vol. 5356, pp. 326–341. Springer, Heidelberg (2008)
17. Maffeis, S., Mitchell, J., Taly, A.: Run-Time Enforcement of Secure JavaScript Subsets. In: Proc of W2SP 2009. IEEE (2009)
18. Maffeis, S., Mitchell, J., Taly, A.: Object capabilities and isolation of untrusted web applications. In: Proc of IEEE Security and Privacy 2010. IEEE (2010)
19. Maffeis, S., Mitchell, J.C., Taly, A.: Isolating JavaScript with Filters, Rewriting, and Wrappers. In: Backes, M., Ning, P. (eds.) ESORICS 2009. LNCS, vol. 5789, pp. 505–522. Springer, Heidelberg (2009)
20. Meyerovich, L., Felt, A.P., Miller, M.: Object Views: FineGrained Sharing in Browsers. In: WWW2010: Proceedings of the 16th International Conference on World Wide Web. ACM (2010)
21. Meyerovich, L., Livshits, B.: ConScript: Specifying and Enforcing Fine-Grained Security Policies for JavaScript in the Browser. In: SP 2010: Proceedings of the 2010 IEEE Symposium on Security and Privacy. IEEE Computer Society (2010)
22. Nadji, Y., Saxena, P., Song, D.: Document Structure Integrity: A Robust Basis for Cross-site Scripting Defense. In: Proc. of Network and Distributed System Security Symposium, NDSS 2009 (2009)
23. Ofuonye, E., Miller, J.: Resolving JavaScript Vulnerabilities in the Browser Runtime. In: 19th International Symposium on Software Reliability Engineering, ISSRE 2008, pp. 57–66 (November 2008)
24. Open Ajax Alliance. Ajax and Mashup Security, `http://cli.gs/ajaxmashupsec` (accessed in January 2010)
25. Phung, P.H., Sands, D., Chudnov, A.: Lightweight Self-Protecting JavaScript. In: ASIACCS 2009: Proceedings of the 4th International Symposium on Information, Computer, and Communications Security, pp. 47–60. ACM, New York (2009)
26. ProSec Security group, Chalmers. Self-Protecting JavaScript project,
    `http://www.cse.chalmers.se/~phung/projects/jss`
27. Prototype Core Team. Prototype - A JavaScript Framework,
    `http://www.prototypejs.org/` (accessed in January 2010)
28. Reis, C., Dunagan, J., Wang, H.J., Dubrovsky, O., Esmeir, S.: BrowserShield: Vulnerability-driven filtering of dynamic HTML. ACM Trans. Web 1(3), 11 (2007)
29. The Mozilla Development Team. New in JavaScript 1.8.1, `http://cli.gs/newjs181` (accessed in January 2010)
30. The Tor Project. Torbutton FAQ; Security Issues, `http://cli.gs/torsec` (accessed in February 2010)
31. Toledo, R., Leger, P., Tanter, E.: AspectScript: Expressive Aspects for the Web. Technical report, University of Chile Santiago, Chile (2009)
32. Walden, J.: Web Tech Blog - Object and Array initializers should not invoke setters when evaluated, `http://cli.gs/mozillasetters` (accessed in January 2010)
33. Washizaki, H., Kubo, A., Mizumachi, T., Eguchi, K., Fukazawa, Y., Yoshioka, N., Kanuka, H., Kodaka, T., Sugimoto, N., Nagai, Y., Yamamoto, R.: AOJS: Aspect-Oriented JavaScript Programming Framework for Web Development. In: ACP4IS 2009: Proceedings of the 8th Workshop on Aspects, Components, and Patterns for Infrastructure Software, pp. 31–36. ACM, New York (2009)

Protocol Implementation Generator

Jose Quaresma and Christian W. Probst

Technical University of Denmark
{jncq,probst}@imm.dtu.dk

Abstract. Users expect communication systems to guarantee, amongst others, privacy and integrity of their data. These can be ensured by using well-established protocols; the best protocol, however, is useless if not all parties involved in a communication have a correct implementation of the protocol and all necessary tools. In this paper, we present the *Protocol Implementation Generator* (PIG), a framework that can be used to add protocol generation to protocol negotiation, or to easily share and implement new protocols throughout a network. PIG enables the sharing, verification, and translation of communication protocols. With it, partners can suggest a *new protocol* by sending its specification. After formally verifying the specification, each partner generates an implementation, which can then be used for establishing communication. We also present a practical realisation of the *Protocol Implementation Generator* framework based on the LySatool and a translator from the LySa language into C or Java.

1 Introduction

The Internet, and network technology in general, are increasingly used for providing central functionality for applications and systems, most notably through, *e.g.*, infrastructure services such as the cloud or web services, or any kind of client-server architecture. This seamless integration of network facilities into user applications has enabled development of new application domains, which in turn resulted in increased integration of networks. While in the past data was mostly stored locally, today, due to the wide availability of networks, data is often being communicated or accessed via local or wide-area networks. Most of the time, users do not need to be aware of where their data is located, and how it is communicated. In fact, being able to access data from wherever one wants to is one of the driving forces behind network integration.

Being able to access data via the network is only half the story, of course. What is (often implicitly) expected is that data is secured by the application and system, both when stored and in transit. Users expect communication systems to guarantee, amongst others, privacy and integrity of their data. When storing data, this can be achieved, *e.g.*, by (a combination of) access control and cryptography. In communication, this can be ensured by using well-established protocols.

Protocols are usually specified by means of protocol narrations, which describe in detail how the involved partners communicate with each other, and

T. Aura, K. Järvinen, and K. Nyberg (Eds.): NordSec 2010, LNCS 7127, pp. 256–268, 2012.

which messages they exchange. Protocol narrations serve two purposes: they can be used for formally verifying the protocol, and for guiding the implementation of the protocol. Recently, researchers have looked into generating protocol implementations from specifications [1–3] and extracting protocol specifications from implementations [4], thereby narrowing the gap between the formal, verified specification, and the usually unverified implementation.

The best protocol, however, is useless if not all parties involved in a communication "speak it", that is, have an implementation of the protocol and all necessary tools. This is why protocols such as "Secure Socket Layer" (SSL) [5, 6] start with a negotiation phase where the partners agree on a suite of algorithms necessary for establishing a connection using the protocol. Whenever no such common algorithms are found, the negotiation phase fails.

In this paper we present the *Protocol Implementation Generator* (PiG) [7], a framework for adding protocol *generation* to protocol *negotiation*. In PiG, when the negotiation phase fails, one of the partners can suggest a *new protocol* by sending its specification. After formally verifying the specification against a set of security properties, each partner generates an implementation, which then can be used for establishing communication. We also present a practical realisation of the *Protocol Implementation Generator* based on the LySatool and a LySa to C and Java translator.

The rest of this paper is structured as follows. We start with a general overview of the *Protocol Implementation Generator* in Section 2, followed by a presentation of a prototype realisation in Section 3. After discussing related work (Section 4), Section 5 concludes the paper and gives an outlook on future work.

2   The Protocol Implementation Generator

In this section we describe the overall layout of the PiG framework, as well as the individual components necessary to realise it. In the next section we will present a concrete implementation of PiG based on the LySatool [8].

The idea behind the PiG framework is to allow communication partners to establish a secure communication channel *without* previously sharing an implementation for the protocol. Instead, one of the partners can suggest a new protocol by sending its formal specification, *e.g.*, as a protocol narration. This formal specification can be verified by the other partner, and if the verification succeeds, the specification can be used to automatically generate a protocol implementation.

Deriving the protocol implementation directly from the specification is an important aspect of our approach, closing the often found gap between the two when protocols are implemented by hand.

Figure 1 shows the process implemented in the PiG framework. When protocol negotiation fails (steps 1,2), Alice sends a specification for a "new" protocol (step 3). Bob checks the specification against the desirable security requirements (step 4) and, if it is found to be safe, he generates the implementation for the protocol (step 6), and Alice and Bob start communication using the new protocol (step 7).

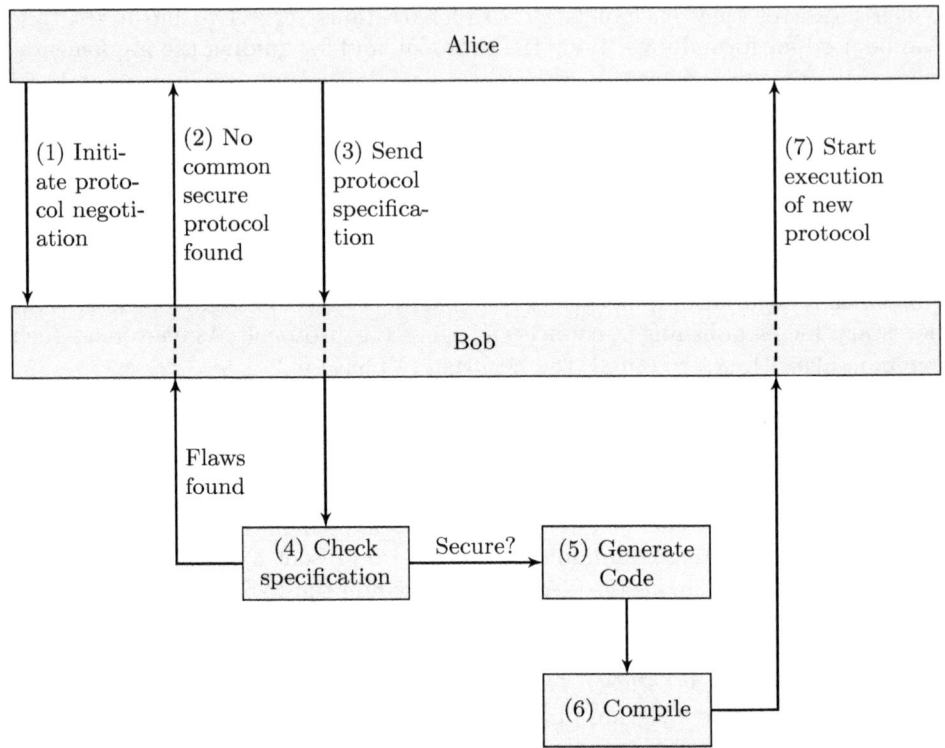

Fig. 1. The process implemented in the *Protocol Implementation Generator*

The *Protocol Implementation Generator* is based on three core components:

- the protocol specification language,
- the protocol verifier, and
- the code generator.

The only requirement for a realisation is that all involved partners have these components. While the components used in the framework can be freely chosen, they must fulfil the requirement that the verifier and the code generator work on the same formalism. Furthermore, the code generator must be complete with respect to the elements of the specification formalism. This is essential, since the *Protocol Implementation Generator* should be transparent to the user, and therefore code generation should be automated, with no need for human interaction.

A possible extension is the use of proof-carrying code [9] techniques to avoid a full re-analysis of the specification before code generation. Instead, the protocol specification would be annotated with the proof for a verification condition that guarantees the protocol to pass verification.

Another extension in the same direction targets a slightly different arrangement of the steps described above. The overall process would be similar, but in step 3 Alice would send to Bob an implementation of the "new" protocol and Bob, in step 4, would need to extract the protocol specification from the received implementation. Only then he would verify the correctness of the protocol. If found to be correct, Alice and Bob could start the execution of the protocol.

This idea of extracting the protocol specification from its implementation could also be useful in proving the correctness of the translation from the protocol specification to the protocol implementation—after the translation one could derive the specification from the generated implementation and verify it against the original specification.

3   A Practical Realisation of PiG

Having presented the *Protocol Implementation Generator* framework in the previous section, we now discuss a specific instance of the framework. The used configurable components are LySa [10] as protocol specification language, which is analysed using the LySatool [8], and a code generator based on ANTLR [11]. These components are at the core of a prototype realisation of PiG [7].

In order to give an example of the functioning of the prototype, we use as a running example the Otway-Rees protocol [12], which, while not in wide-spread use, is simple enough to be covered in an article. The Otway-Rees protocol is used in order to mutually authenticate two principals, Alice (A) and Bob (B) via a mutually trusted third party (S), and to generate a secret shared key that they can use to securely communicate.

```
1.  A->B  :  M,A,B,{M,A,B,NA}:KA
2.  B->S  :  M,A,B,{M,A,B,NA}:KA,{M,A,B,NB}:KB
3.  S->B  :  M,{NA,KAB}:KA,{NB,KAB}:KB
4.  B->A  :  M,{NA,KAB}:KA
5.  B->A  :  {MSG}:KAB
```

Fig. 2. Pseudo-code specification of the Otway-Rees protocol

As seen in the protocol definition, in Figure 2, this is achieved with the exchange of four messages in total. A starts by sending B a message (line 1) encrypted with a shared key between A and S, which contains a nonce NA generated by A, a running serial M, and both principals' identities.

B, after receiving this message — that he cannot decrypt — sends it to S, together with another message encrypted with a key shared between B and S, with similar content to the one A sent, but in this case with a nonce NB generated by B (line 2). After S has received those two encrypted elements from B, it will verify the identities of the principals and the running serial M, and generate a symmetric key KAB that A and B will use to securely communicate.

S then encrypts that key together with the nonce generated by A with the key shared between S and A and, similarly, also encrypts that same key together with the nonce generated by B with the key shared by S and B.

S then sends those two elements to B (line 3), which decrypts the one encrypted with the key it shares with S. If the nonce matches, it will be ready to use the new key in future communications with A.

In the last step of the protocol (line 4), B sends to A the other element that it received from S. A decrypts it with the key it shares with S and, if the nonce matches, uses the new key for future communications with B.

In this example, an extra message *MSG* is sent in line 5 to illustrate the use of the new key shared between Alice and Bob.

3.1   LySa and the LySatool

LySa [10] is a process algebra aimed at specifying communication protocols. A LySa protocol specification consists of a standard protocol narration extended with annotations in order to remove analysis ambiguity that could arise from vague protocol narrations. This is especially beneficial in a setting like PIG, where the analysis and code generation should be automatic and transparent.

LySa is based on the Spi Calculus [13], which extends the π Calculus with cryptographic primitives that are used in the description and analysis of cryptographic protocols. In Spi Calculus, protocols are represented as processes and their security properties are stated by protocol equivalence.

The main difference between LySa and these calculi is that LySa assumes a single, global communication medium, to which all processes have access. The LySa approach seems, therefore, more natural when considering communication scenarios on the Internet, where it is not difficult to eavesdrop a conversation.

In LySa, only the legitimate part of the protocol in question is described, while the illegitimate, malicious part is implicitly modelled as a Dolev-Yao attacker [14]. The attacker can be equipped with some initial knowledge, which can be expanded by eavesdropping the network or by decrypting messages using known keys, it may encrypt messages using those keys, and is also able of initiating new sessions.

Protocols specified in the LySa calculus can be analysed for security properties using the LySatool [8]. The checked properties include authenticity, secrecy, and confidentiality and are fixed by the tool. The LySatool is implemented in Standard ML and uses the Succinct Solver [15]. It receives a LySa specification of a communication protocol as input, and performs a static analysis assuming the presence of the strongest possible attacker previously mentioned. The analysis result either indicates that the protocol is found to be secure, or not. In the latter case, further analyses have to be performed to distinguish between a false negative and a real security problem. These false negatives can happen due to the over-approximation analysis performed by LySa. This has to be taken into account when designing or choosing a protocol specification for use in the *Protocol Implementation Generator*.

In the initial phase of PiG, as described in the previous section, one of the principals is waiting for another principal to connect. When that happens, the latter will send a LySa protocol specification to the former. After receiving the protocol specification, the principal checks the protocol's security by verifying the specification with the LySatool. As mentioned above, in the current version, those security properties are implicit in the tool. If the protocol specification is found to be insecure, the tool reports that, and the process is terminated. If the protocol analysis identifies the protocol specification to be secure (which means that the security properties were guaranteed for the new protocol), the principal will execute the next step, starting the translation process.

LySa Specification of the Otway-Rees Protocol. When converting from pseudo-code, or Alice and Bob notation, to LySa notation there are several steps that need to be performed. It is necessary to model the principals running in parallel —in this case there are 3 principals— and each message exchanged in the pseudo-code needs to be modelled as being sent by one principal and being received by another. For example, line 1 of Figure 2 specifies that Alice sends a message to Bob (A->B:M,A,B,{M,A,B,NA}:KA), and that same message in the LySa specification consists of the sending on Alice's specification (<A,B,M,A,B,{M,A,B,NA}:KA>), and the receiving on Bob's specification ((A,B,M,A,B;y1)).

Another detail that needs to be taken into account is the pattern matching and the assignment of variables. This might not be trivial because, sometimes what is supposed to be pattern matched and assigned is not explicitly shown in the pseudo-code description of the protocol, and so it is necessary to interpret the protocol in order to make those details explicit in the LySa specification. Using the same first message as an example, when Bob receives it ((A,B,M,A,B;y1)), it will check if A is Alice's address, if B is its own address and if M is equal to the session running serial. Furthermore, it will assign the last element of the message sent by Alice, which is the encrypted block {M,A,B,NA}:KA, to the variable y1. In fact, Bob cannot decrypt that block since he does not have the key that was used for its encryption.

Another point to consider is that, regardless of what the elements of the messages are, LySa requires that the address of the sender and the address of the receiver are the first two elements of the sent and received messages. This is easily solved by tagging the messages from the pseudo-code description with these two elements in the LySa specification.

The full LySa specification of the Otway-Rees protocol can be seen in Figure 3.

3.2   ANTLR

ANTLR, which stands for "ANother Tool for Language Recognition", is a framework for generating recognisers, interpreters, compilers and translators based on grammatical descriptions. Besides providing support for building lexers and parsers, it also supports tree construction and tree walking. Parsers can generate

```
(new M)( (new KA)( (new KB)(

/* Initiator - A */
((new NA)
<A,B,M,A,B,{M,A,B,NA}:KA>.        //line 1, send with encr.
(B,A,M;x1).                       //line 4, receive
decrypt x1 as {NA;xk}:KA in       //line 4, decryption
(B,A;x2).                         //line 5, receive
decrypt x2 as {;xmsg}:xk in       //line 5, decryption
0)                  //termination
|


/* Responder - B */
((new NB)
(A,B,M,A,B;y1).                   //line 1, receive
<B,S,M,A,B,y1,{M,A,B,NB}:KB>.     //line 2, send with encr.
(S,B,M;y2,y3).                    //line 3, receive
decrypt y3 as {NB;yk}:KB in       //line 3, decryption
<B,A,M,y2>.                       //line 4, send
(new MSG)                         //line 5, message creation
<B,A,{MSG}:yk>.                   //line 5, send with encr.
0)                  //termination
|

/* Server - S */
((B,S,M,A,B;z1,z2).               //line 2, receive
decrypt z1 as {M,A,B;zna}:KA in   //line 2, decryption
decrypt z2 as {M,A,B;znb}:KB in   //line 2, decryption
(new K)                           //line 3, new shared key
<S,B,M,{zna,K}:KA,{znb,K}:KB>.    //line 3, send with encr.
0)                  //termination
)))
```

Fig. 3. LySa specification of the Otway-Rees protocol. The comments refer to the lines on the specification.

Abstract Syntax Trees, which can be further analysed with Tree Parsers (also called Tree Walkers). The framework has a tight integration with StringTemplate [16], which makes it ideal for translating from one language to another. It is this feature that we use for generating C and Java code from LySa specifications.

After the protocol as been verified, the ANTLR-based code generator translates the specification to a programming language that can then be compiled and executed. The presented prototype implementation translates the specification to C code as well as to Java code. ANTLR to generates the Lexer, the Parser, and the Tree Walker that performs the actual translation.

The first phase of the translator transforms the LySa specification into an abstract syntax tree (AST), which is used as input for the code generation, performed by the Tree Walker. A node in the AST represents an action in the protocol, and one of its children represents the next action taken by the principal.

The Tree Walker traverses the AST and, using string templates, generates the code that corresponds to the AST structure, and consequently to the original LySa protocol specification. Using StringTemplate is not only of advantage when extending the translation to support more target languages, but it is also advantageous when generating code for the different actors in a protocol. Due to supporting inheritance, StringTemplate enables the specification of generic templates together with specific ones. The latter are used to define actor-specific code — which depends on the role of the actor in the protocol — and can be loaded individually when performing the translation.

Figure 4 shows a SEND block that belongs to the Otway-Rees AST generated after parsing the initiator code. This block corresponds to the sending of the first message of the protocol.

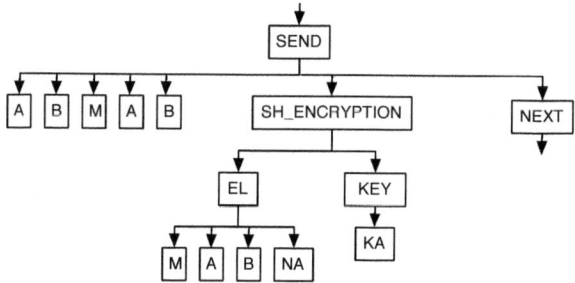

Fig. 4. Part of the AST subtree showing the send block of the initiator of the (first line of the) protocol specified in Figure 3

3.3   Retargeting the PiG

An important part regarding the implementation of the framework is the generation of the String Templates that will be used by the Tree Walker. For this prototype, the LySa specification has to be analysed and its main components identified, which need to have a direct correspondence to the main components of the String Templates.

The full version of the LySa specification language [10] contains artefacts that are not relevant for the actual protocol, but only help to increase the precision of the analysis tool. Taking this into consideration, the following main components can be identified:

- sending and receiving messages on the network,
- encryption and decryption (symmetric and asymmetric), and
- generation of fresh values (nonces, symmetric and asymmetric keys).

When implementing the translation from a specification language, identifying its main components is the first step because the templates are a direct implementation of the main components of the specification language. It is important to note that adding new languages as a target of the framework to an existing realisation of the PIG is very simple. As said before, it is only necessary to specify the StringTemplate for the main components.

An improvement on this part of the framework would be to make this translation provably correct, similar to the method presented by Pironti *et al.* [17]. They define a type-system and a translation function that allow to prove that the generated code simulated the process represented by the protocol specification, thus proving the correctness of the translation.

One of the main challenges when specifying template functions is that they need to fit together in the generated code, *e.g.*, how values are communicated between different functions. This can be tricky, since the same value may be used in different roles by different components, depending on the LySa specification.This resembles building the small parts of a puzzle before ensuring that the whole puzzle can be solved.

Another detail requiring special attention when specifying templates for a new language are variables reused between different blocks that are generated from the same template component. These cannot be be declared globally in each of the individual blocks, and consequently must be declared before any of the individual blocks and cleared before usage.

Last but not least, all the target languages must use the same format for message exchange, to allow interoperability. In our current prototype we apply the following straightforward format, which can be easily changed:

- firstly, the **number of elements** in the message;
- then, the **size of each element** in the message;
- finally, the **payload**: all the elements in the protocol message are concatenated without any separation between them.

As an illustrative example, if one wants to send a message with two elements, the first being "Hello" and the second being "Reader", the sent message would have the following format:

$$\text{``}2, 5, 6, HelloReader\text{''}$$

4   Related Work

Recently, a lot of work has been done in the automatic verification of security protocols as well as in the automatic translation from a protocol specification into a real programming language such as C, Java or F#. The goal of this paper is to present a framework that uses and implements both automatic processes—the verification and the translation—so there is an automatic and secure way from the writing of the specification protocol, over its verification, to its translation and execution. This is done in a way that enables the sharing of the specification (and consequently verification and translation) of protocols.

Possible Similar Tool Combinations. Several existing tools could be combined in order to realise a *Protocol Implementation Generator* implementation, providing the same functionality as described in the previous section.

The same high-level specification used in this paper could be used together with other tools. A protocol can be described in the LySa language, verified with LySatool and, with some extra annotations, can be translated using the YALT [18] tool, which automatically translates a LySa specification into Java code.

Another option would be to use Spi Calculus together with Spi2Java or S3A and Spi2F#.

After using the Spi Calculus to describe a security protocol, one could use Spi2Java [1] to verify and translate the description into a protocol implementation. Another option would be to use S3A [19] to verify the protocol specification and Spi2F# [20] that specification into a protocol implementation.

Using F# together with FS2PV [4] and ProVerif [21, 22] one could achieve a similar tool chain, although with a big difference. While our framework verifies the protocol specification and then translates it to some implementation language, this combination would translate the implementation of the protocol into a verifiable specification and only then would verify it. This setup, as already mentioned in Section 2, could also be seen as an extension/improvement to our framework. In this combination, the functional language F# would be used for protocol specification. Then, FS2PV would derive a formal model from that protocol code and symbolic libraries. FS2PV currently only supports a first-order subset of F#, with simple formal semantics facilitating model extraction, and primitives for communication and concurrency. The tool would translate the protocol implementation into π Calculus, which can be verified by ProVerif, an automatic cryptographic protocol verifier based on a simple representation of the protocol using Prolog rules.

Existing Frameworks. Some frameworks aim at combining protocol specification, verification, and implementation.

In the AGVI framework [23] the designer describes the security requirements and the system specification. The toolkit will attempt to find a protocol according to the demands. If found, it will translate it into Java. The SPEAR II Framework [24, 25] is a GUI-based framework that enables secure and efficient security protocol design and implementation, combining formal specification, security and performance analysis, meta-execution and automatic code generation. ACG-C# [2] automatically generates a C# implementation of a security protocol verified in Casper and FDR. Casper translates from high level to CSP, which can be verified using FDR, and translated by ACG-C#.

All these approaches differ significantly from the work presented in this paper. For example, AGVI does not support a protocol specification, but only receives the security requirements, and SPEAR II receives the protocol specification in a GUI environment, which hinders automating the implementation generation.

Furthermore, none of these frameworks offer support for sharing the protocol specification, making it impossible to rapidly enable two hosts to share the same protocol and to spread new protocols.

Last but not least, Kiyomoto *et al.* [3] present a tool that translates a high-level XML protocol specification into C, without any verification of the protocol specification.

5   Conclusions and Future Work

In this work we present a new approach to securing the communication in scenarios where partners do not initially share a protocol. This is especially important for the kind of networked applications we are relying on today, where the location of data is mostly hidden from users.

The *Protocol Implementation Generator* allows communication partners to exchange protocol specifications that can be verified and implemented on the fly; both the verification and the implementation, or code generation, are based on the same formal specification of the protocol, resulting in a direct link between the two.

We have implemented and presented a prototype realisation of PiG based on the process calculus LySa, its verifier the LySatool, and a standard code generation tool, ANTLR, which was set to generate C and Java code. The same functionality can be achieved with other combinations, as long as they share the protocol specification formalism.

We are currently investigating several extensions of the presented framework; we are investigating how to use proof-carrying code techniques [26] or lightweight verification [27] to avoid a full re-analysis of the specification before code generation. We are also interested in combining our approach with techniques that extract protocol specifications from implementations. This would allow to perform sanity checks by comparing the specification extracted from the generated implementation with the original specification.

Another thread of future work has to do with the security properties that are used by the verification tool of our framework. In the current version of our implementation, the security properties are implicit in the used tool (LySatool). A way of extending this version would be to enable the principals of the framework to negotiate security properties as part of the initial phase. Another possible way of approaching this would be to automate the download of general security properties from a set of trusted servers. With this, the PiG principals would have updated security properties that they would use for protocol verification.

The ideas behind PiG are being extended, and will be used to develop a framework for Service Oriented Systems, composed of different levels of abstraction, that includes verification (with different tools) and translation (into different languages) of abstractly specified Service Oriented Systems.

Finally, a word of warning seems in place. Approaches like PiG allow to add new protocols on the fly, and this might seem like a well-suited technique to updating large parts of a network by feeding newly designed protocols using a framework like ours. However, the underlying automatism also allows to exploit shortcomings in the used tools to distribute a protocol that is known to pass verification but to result in faulty implementations. How to mitigate this threat remains a topic for future work.

References

1. Pozza, D., Sisto, R., Durante, L.: Spi2java: automatic cryptographic protocol java code generation from spi calculus. In: 18th International Conference on Advanced Information Networking and Applications, AINA 2004, vol. 1, pp. 400–405 (2004)
2. Jeon, C., Kim, I., Choi, J.: Automatic generation of the C# code for security protocols verified with casper/FDR. In: Proc. IEEE Int. Conf. on Advanced Inf. Networking and Applications (AINA), Taipei, Taiwan (2005)
3. Kiyomoto, S., Ota, H., Tanaka, T.: A security protocol compiler generating c source codes. In: 2008 International Conference on Information Security and Assurance (ISA 2008), pp. 20–25 (2008)
4. Bhargavan, K., Fournet, C., Gordon, A.D., Tse, S.: Verified interoperable implementations of security protocols. ACM Transactions on Programming Languages and Systems (TOPLAS) 31(1), 5 (2008)
5. Hickman, K., Elgamal, T.: The SSL protocol. Netscape Communications Corp. (1995)
6. Frier, A., Karlton, P., Kocher, P.: The SSL 3.0 protocol. Netscape Communications Corp. 18 (1996)
7. Quaresma, J.: A protocol implementation generator. Master's thesis, Kgs. Lyngby, Denmark (2010)
8. Buchholtz, M.: User's Guide for the LySatool version 2.01. DTU (April 2005)
9. Necula, G.C.: Proof-carrying code. In: POPL 1997: Proceedings of the 24th ACM SIGPLAN-SIGACT Symposium on Principles of Programming Languages, pp. 106–119. ACM, New York (1997)
10. Bodei, C., Buchholtz, M., Degano, P., Nielson, F., Nielson, H.: Static validation of security protocols. Journal of Computer Security 13(3), 347–390 (2005)
11. Parr, T.: The Definitive ANTLR Reference: Building Domain-Specific Languages. Pragmatic Bookshelf (2007)
12. Otway, D., Rees, O.: Efficient and timely mutual authentication. Operating Systems Review 21(1), 8–10 (1987)
13. Abadi, M., Gordon, A.D.: A calculus for cryptographic protocols: The spi calculus. Information and Computation 148(1), 1–70 (1999)
14. Dolev, D., Yao, A.C.: On the security of public key protocols. In: Annual IEEE Symposium on Foundations of Computer Science, pp. 350–357 (1981)
15. Nielson, F., Riis Nielson, H., Sun, H., Buchholtz, M., Rydhof Hansen, R., Pilegaard, H., Seidl, H.: The Succinct Solver Suite. In: Jensen, K., Podelski, A. (eds.) TACAS 2004. LNCS, vol. 2988, pp. 251–265. Springer, Heidelberg (2004)
16. Parr, T.: Stringtemplate documentation (May 2009),
http://www.antlr.org/wiki/display/ST/StringTemplate+Documentation
17. Pironti, A., Sisto, R.: Provably correct java implementations of spi calculus security protocols specifications. Computers & Security 29(3), 302–314 (2010); Special issue on software engineering for secure systems
18. Vind, S., Vildhøj, H.W.: Secure protocol implementation with lysa. Bachelor's Thesis, DTU (2009)

19. Durante, L., Sisto, R., Valenzano, A.: Automatic testing equivalence verification of spi calculus specifications. ACM Trans. Softw. Eng. Methodol. 12(2), 222–284 (2003)
20. Tarrach, T.: Spi2f# – a prototype code generator for security protocols. Master's thesis, Saarland University (2008)
21. Blanchet, B.: An efficient cryptographic protocol verifier based on prolog rules. In: Proceedings of 14th IEEE Computer Security Foundations Workshop, pp. 82–96 (2001)
22. Abadi, M., Blanchet, B.: Analyzing security protocols with secrecy types and logic programs. Journal of the ACM (JACM) 52(1), 102–146 (2005)
23. Song, D., Perrig, A., Phan, D.: Agvi - Automatic Generation, Verification, and Implementation of Security Protocols. In: Berry, G., Comon, H., Finkel, A. (eds.) CAV 2001. LNCS, vol. 2102, pp. 241–245. Springer, Heidelberg (2001)
24. Saul, E., Hutchison, A.: SPEAR II-The Security Protocol Engineering and Analysis Resource (1999)
25. Lukell, S., Veldman, C., Hutchison, A.: Automated attack analysis and code generation in a unified, multi-dimensional security protocol engineering framework. Comp. Science Hon (2002)
26. Necula, G.C.: Proof-carrying code. In: Conference Record of the Annual ACM Symposium on Principles of Programming Languages, pp. 106–119 (1997)
27. Rose, E.: Lightweight bytecode verification. Journal of Automated Reasoning 31(3-4), 303–334 (2003)

Secure and Fast Implementations of Two Involution Ciphers

Billy Bob Brumley*

Aalto University School of Science, Finland
billy.brumley@aalto.fi

Abstract. Anubis and Khazad are closely related involution block ciphers. Building on two recent AES software results, this work presents a number of constant-time software implementations of Anubis and Khazad for processors with a byte-vector shuffle instruction, such as those that support SSSE3. For Anubis, the first is serial in the sense that it employs only one cipher instance and is compatible with all standard block cipher modes. Efficiency is largely due to the S-box construction that is simple to realize using a byte shuffler. The equivalent for Khazad runs two parallel instances in counter mode. The second for each cipher is a parallel bit-slice implementation in counter mode.

Keywords: Anubis, Khazad, involution ciphers, block ciphers, software implementation, timing attacks.

1   Introduction

Anubis and Khazad are two block ciphers by Barreto and Rijmen submitted during the NESSIE project (see [12] for a summary). Anubis [2] works on 128-bit blocks and is quite similar in many respects to AES. Khazad [3] is a "legacy-level" cipher working on 64-bit blocks and is closely related to Anubis. These are both involution ciphers: decryption differs from encryption only in the key schedule.

The motivation for this work comes largely from cache-timing attacks, where an attacker attempts to recover parts of the cryptosystem state by observing the variance in timing measurements due to processor data caching effects. These attacks can be time-driven and carried out remotely by measuring the latency of a high level operation, or trace-driven and locally by exploiting the cache structure to determine the sequence of lookups the cryptosystem performs. The vulnerability exists when part of the state is used as an index into a memory-resident table.

A high-speed table-based implementation of AES unrolls lower level operations such as SubBytes, ShiftRows, and MixColumns into four tables of size

---

* Supported in part by Helsinki Doctoral Programme in Computer Science - Advanced Computing and Intelligent Systems (Hecse) and the European Commission through the ICT program under contract ICT-2007-216499 CACE.

T. Aura, K. Järvinen, and K. Nyberg (Eds.): NordSec 2010, LNCS 7127, pp. 269–282, 2012.

256 containing 32-bit values. Lookups into these tables, indexed by state values, are combined with XOR to carry out AES rounds in a more software-friendly manner, relaxing the need to manipulate a large number of single byte values and bits within those bytes. Similar versions of both Anubis and Khazad exist, in fact provided as the C reference implementations and discussed in both specifications [2,3, Sect. 7.1].

Cache-timing attacks are a serious threat and can easily lead to leakage of key material. Although there are numerous published attacks on such implementations, a practical noteworthy one is Bernstein's AES time-driven attack [5]. Anubis and Khazad are presumably susceptible to this and other timing attacks. In light of these attacks, a reasonable security requirement for any cipher is that it can be implemented to use a constant amount of time. In this context, Bernstein defines constant as "independent of the AES key and input" [5, Sect. 8]. The concept of security within this paper is with respect to timing attacks.

To this end, this work shows that constant-time and efficient implementations of both Anubis and Khazad are possible. Four such implementations appear herein, summarized as follows.

- The first Anubis implementation runs only one instance of the cipher, compatible with all standard block cipher modes. This is efficient due to a byte-vector shuffle instruction, allowing elegant realization of the nonlinear layer in constant-time. The Khazad implementation is otherwise analogous but with a smaller state runs two parallel cipher instances, here in counter mode under the same key.
- The second Anubis implementation bit-slices the state and runs eight parallel instances, here in counter mode. Not surprisingly, this is faster but requires a parallel block cipher mode. Analogously, the Khazad implementation runs 16 parallel instances.

This work builds upon two recent results on AES software implementations that remarkably manage to achieve constant-time and exceptional performance at one stroke.

- A common hardware technique to compute the AES S-box uses an isomorphism $\mathbb{F}_{2^8} \to \mathbb{F}_{2^4}^2$ and subsequently reduces the problem of inversion in the latter field to that of one in in the ground field; [13,14,7] are good examples of this. Using a similar technique in software when equipped with a byte-vector shuffle instruction and using a novel field element representation, Hamburg presents techniques for fast and constant-time software implementation of AES [10]. Running only a single instance of the cipher, the implementation is compatible with all standard block cipher modes.
- Käsper and Schwabe present AES bit-slice techniques, aligning individual bits of state bytes in distinct registers [11]. The implementation runs eight parallel streams in counter mode under the same key. Not only does this provide a constant-time implementation, but also is currently the fastest published AES counter mode implementation in software (not considering newer Intel models equipped with AES instruction set extensions). Table-based AES implementations on common platforms that can perform only

one load instruction per cycle are inherently limited to ten cycles per byte; there are ten rounds requiring sixteen lookups each. The authors show that bit-slicing circumvents this limit.

2   Cipher Descriptions

This section gives a description of the Anubis and Khazad primitives, specifically each component of the ciphers. The ciphers share some components verbatim and others only differ slightly. The notation here follows style of the specifications; see them for a more formal treatment [2,3].

2.1   The Anubis Cipher

Although Anubis supports variable length keys, this work only explicitly considers 16-byte keys; generalizations are straightforward. Analogous to AES-128, Anubis consists of a 16-byte state. The state is either viewed as a vector in $\mathbb{F}_{2^8}^{16}$ or a 4×4 matrix with entries in $\mathbb{F}_{2^8}$ depending on the context. The specification denotes this by a map μ, but this work omits this formalization; flattening the matrix row-wise (concatenating the rows) yields the vector representation.

The Nonlinear Layer γ. This layer is otherwise analogous to the AES Sub-Bytes step, but with a different S-box. It applies an S-box $S : \mathbb{F}_{2^8} \to \mathbb{F}_{2^8}$ to each byte of the input. To facilitate efficient hardware implementation, the designers chose to build S using a three layer substitution-permutation network (SPN), where each layer includes two S-boxes $P, Q : \mathbb{F}_{2^4} \to \mathbb{F}_{2^4}$ termed "mini-boxes". Fig. 1 depicts this structure.

The Transposition τ. Viewing the input as a 4×4 matrix, this mapping outputs the transpose. To illustrate:

$$\begin{bmatrix} 0 & 1 & 2 & 3 \\ 4 & 5 & 6 & 7 \\ 8 & 9 & A & B \\ C & D & E & F \end{bmatrix} \mapsto \begin{bmatrix} 0 & 4 & 8 & C \\ 1 & 5 & 9 & D \\ 2 & 6 & A & E \\ 3 & 7 & B & F \end{bmatrix}.$$

The Linear Diffusion Layer θ. This layer shares some similarities with the AES MixColumns step. It multiplies the input in matrix form by the symmetric matrix

$$H = \begin{bmatrix} 01 & 02 & 04 & 06 \\ 02 & 01 & 06 & 04 \\ 04 & 06 & 01 & 02 \\ 06 & 04 & 02 & 01 \end{bmatrix} = \begin{bmatrix} 1 & x & x^2 & x^2+x \\ x & 1 & x^2+x & x^2 \\ x^2 & x^2+x & 1 & x \\ x^2+x & x^2 & x & 1 \end{bmatrix}$$

and $\theta : a \mapsto a \cdot H$ with all operations done in $\mathbb{F}_{2^8} = \mathbb{F}_2[x]/(x^8+x^4+x^3+x^2+1)$.

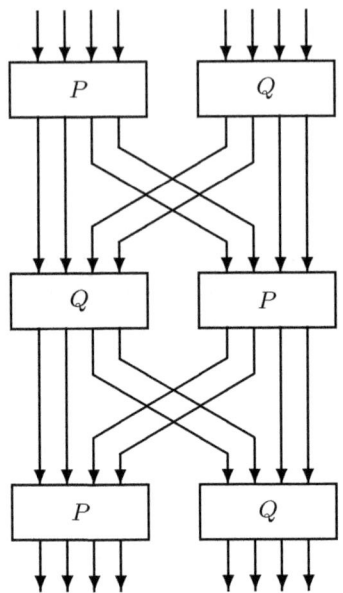

Fig. 1. S-box S as a three layer SPN with mini-boxes P and Q

The Cyclical Permutation π. This operation is otherwise analogous to the AES ShiftRows step, but cyclically shifts column i of the matrix downward i positions instead. This map only appears in the key schedule. To illustrate:

$$\begin{bmatrix} 0 & 1 & 2 & 3 \\ 4 & 5 & 6 & 7 \\ 8 & 9 & A & B \\ C & D & E & F \end{bmatrix} \mapsto \begin{bmatrix} 0 & D & A & 7 \\ 4 & 1 & E & B \\ 8 & 5 & 2 & F \\ C & 9 & 6 & 3 \end{bmatrix}.$$

The Key Extraction ω. This is a linear mapping involving the Vandermonde matrix

$$V = \begin{bmatrix} 01 & 01 & 01 & 01 \\ 01 & 02 & 02^2 & 02^3 \\ 01 & 06 & 06^2 & 06^3 \\ 01 & 08 & 08^2 & 08^3 \end{bmatrix} = \begin{bmatrix} 1 & 1 & 1 & 1 \\ 1 & x & x^2 & x^3 \\ 1 & x^2+x & x^4+x^2 & x^6+x^5+x^4+x^3 \\ 1 & x^3 & x^6 & x^5+x^4+x^3+x \end{bmatrix} = \begin{bmatrix} 01 & 01 & 01 & 01 \\ 01 & 02 & 04 & 08 \\ 01 & 06 & 14 & 78 \\ 01 & 08 & 40 & 3A \end{bmatrix}$$

and $\omega : a \mapsto V \cdot a$. This map also only appears in the key schedule.

The Key Schedule. Given the cipher key K, round keys K^i for $0 \leq i \leq 12$ satisfy $K^r = (\tau \circ \omega \circ \gamma)(\kappa^r)$ where $\kappa^0 = K$ and $\kappa^r = (\sigma[c^r] \circ \theta \circ \pi \circ \gamma)(\kappa^{r-1})$ for $r > 0$, σ is addition in $\mathbb{F}_{2^8}^{16}$, and c^r are vector constants dependent only on S. Note the shared application of γ.

The Complete Cipher. Anubis initializes the state as $\sigma[K^0]$ applied to the input. This gets iteratively transformed through 12 rounds by $\sigma[K^r] \circ \theta \circ \tau \circ \gamma$ where the last round omits θ.

2.2   The Khazad Cipher

The Khazad block cipher [3] works on 8-byte blocks and uses a 16-byte key. The state is viewed as an element of $\mathbb{F}_{2^8}^8$. The components are similar to those of Anubis in many respects; the nonlinear layer γ remains the same. A description of the other components follows.

The Linear Diffusion Layer θ. This linear layer multiplies the input vector by the symmetric matrix

$$H = \begin{bmatrix} 01 & 03 & 04 & 05 & 06 & 08 & 0B & 07 \\ 03 & 01 & 05 & 04 & 08 & 06 & 07 & 0B \\ 04 & 05 & 01 & 03 & 0B & 07 & 06 & 08 \\ 05 & 04 & 03 & 01 & 07 & 0B & 08 & 06 \\ 06 & 08 & 0B & 07 & 01 & 03 & 04 & 05 \\ 08 & 06 & 07 & 0B & 03 & 01 & 05 & 04 \\ 0B & 07 & 06 & 08 & 04 & 05 & 01 & 03 \\ 07 & 0B & 08 & 06 & 05 & 04 & 03 & 01 \end{bmatrix}$$

and $\theta : a \mapsto a \cdot H$.

The Key Schedule. Round keys satisfy $K^r = (\sigma[K^{r-2}] \circ \sigma[c^r] \circ \theta \circ \gamma)(K^{r-1})$ where $0 \le r \le 8$ and K^{-2} and K^{-1} are the first and second eight bytes of the key K, respectively. There is no component corresponding to the key extraction ω in Anubis.

The Complete Cipher. Khazad initializes the state as $\sigma[K^0]$ applied to the input. This gets iteratively transformed through eight rounds by $\sigma[K^r] \circ \theta \circ \gamma$ where the last round omits θ.

3   Implementations

This section presents constant-time yet efficient implementations of both Anubis and Khazad. It begins with some background on SIMD vector operations, focusing on Intel processors. Then, for each cipher, a discussion on two implementation strategies appears. The first is more of a SIMD approach, running one instance in the Anubis case and two for Khazad. The second is a bit-slice approach running eight and sixteen instances, respectfully.

3.1   Vector Operations

In 64-bit mode, processors with Streaming SIMD Extensions 3 (SSE3) can operate on 16 128-bit SIMD registers xmm0 through xmm15. SSE3 and predecessors contain a wealth of instructions for parallel computation amongst these registers. Cryptosystem implementations usually restrict to a smaller subset of these instructions dealing with integer values. Supplemental SSE3 (SSSE3) introduces a handful of new instructions, the most interesting for this work being a byte shuffler pshufb. Note that recent AMD processors implement SSE3 but not SSSE3, although a related instruction is slated for the eXtended Operations (XOP) extension.

Byte Shuffling. Since the implementations in this work make heavy use of pshufb, a brief description of the instruction is in order. The name already implies the ability to shuffle bytes around in a vector, but perhaps hides an important aspect of the instruction. Aranha, López, and Hankerson note its versatility [1, Sect. 2.1]:

> "A powerful use of this instruction is to perform 16 simultaneous lookups in a 16-byte lookup table."

Formally, given 16-signed-byte vector operands a and b, components of the 16-byte vector output r of pshufb satisfy

$$r_i = \begin{cases} a_{b_i \bmod 16} & \text{if } b_i \geq 0, \\ 0 & \text{otherwise,} \end{cases}$$

so b holds the indices into the table and a the values. Indeed, this allows to implement any $\mathbb{F}_2^4 \to \mathbb{F}_2^8$ function in parallel: this is a constant-time hardware lookup table, shuffling the values in a based on the indices in b. To summarize, typical use of pshufb is either that of shuffling bytes around in a fixed manner (b is fixed) or implementing lookups into a fixed table (a is fixed), and the distinction is in the operand order.

Linear Maps. Given the above, one can implement a linear map $\phi : \mathbb{F}_2^8 \to \mathbb{F}_2^8$ on 16 bytes in parallel. Denote $\alpha \in \mathbb{F}_{2^8}$ by $\alpha = \alpha_H x^4 + \alpha_L$ where α_i are the 4-bit nibbles. Linearity ensures $\phi(\alpha) = \phi(\alpha_H x^4) + \phi(\alpha_L)$ and each input on the right is effectively only four bits. Denote 16-byte vectors $t_{\phi H}$ and $t_{\phi L}$ that map the corresponding input to the output; these are the a from the previous section. The following steps realize ϕ in parallel:

1. Mask the lower nibble (α_L) of each byte in the input vector. (pand)
2. Bit-shift the input four positions towards LSB and mask again (α_H). (psrlq, pand)
3. Shuffle $t_{\phi L}$ and $t_{\phi H}$ with their respective indices from the above steps. (pshufb × 2)
4. Bitwise XOR the two outputs together. (pxor)

The second mask is a minor inconvenience due to the lack of an instruction to shift bits of individual bytes in a 16-byte vector (there are no `psllb` and `psrlb` instructions). The following implementations uses this strategy often. Note that when applying multiple maps to the same input, the first two steps are needed only once.

3.2   Implementing Anubis

This following presents SSSE3 implementation techniques for Anubis; it discusses two different approaches. The first is serial in the sense that it employs only one cipher instance, while the second runs eight instances in parallel.

A SIMD Approach. Beginning with the nonlinear layer γ, the authors state that the choice to build it as an SPN with mini-boxes was influenced by efficient hardware implementation [2, 6.2]. A key observation in this work is that as a consequence of the underlying smaller $\mathbb{F}_{2^4} \to \mathbb{F}_{2^4}$ mini-boxes, the composition can be implemented elegantly using `pshufb`. Since P and Q are four bits to four bits but the instruction allows a parallel four bit to eight bit lookup, the bit permutations following P and Q can be unrolled for each layer to provide shifted and spread versions of their output. For example, $Q(\texttt{0x1}) = \texttt{0xE} = 1110_2$ but following the first layer the upper two bits get shifted two positions towards the MSB: here the lookup provides $Q_0(\texttt{0x1}) = \texttt{0x32} = 110010_2$. This unrolling yields the following six lookup tables for the corresponding layers:

$$t_{Q0} = \texttt{0x200123133110003330030222212113221}$$
$$t_{P0} = \texttt{0x0408804C488488C4C08C404400C8CC0C}$$
$$t_{P1} = \texttt{0x01022013122122313023101100323303}$$
$$t_{Q1} = \texttt{0x80048C4CC44000CCC00C08884844C884}$$
$$t_{Q2} = \texttt{0x08010B070D04000F0C03020A06050E09}$$
$$t_{P2} = \texttt{0x102080706090A0D0C0B0405000E0F030}.$$

As the last layer does not permute the bits, note t_{P2} and t_{Q2} are simply the nibble-shifted and original contents as bytes, respectively, of P and Q.

With these tables in hand, the following steps implement layer i of S:

1. Mask the lower nibble of each byte in the input vector. (**pand**)
2. Bit-shift the input four positions towards LSB and mask again. (**psrlq, pand**)
3. Shuffle t_{Pi} and t_{Qi} with their respective indices from the above steps. (**pshufb** × 2)
4. Bitwise OR the two outputs together. (**por**)

Iterating this concept for all layers shows that S can be realized in parallel on all 16 input bytes using six **pand**, three **psrlq**, six **pshufb**, and three **por**. Another option is to pair-wise reverse the wires on one mini-box per layer and use an XOR swap on two bits instead to implement the permutations between layers. It seems this does not reduce the operation count for current Intel processors.

Moving on to other components, the naïve way to implement the transpose τ requires a single `pshufb` instruction with indices defined as

$$t_\tau = \text{0x0F0B07030E0A06020D0905010C080400}$$

but in fact, by modifying the cipher and key schedule appropriately τ can be omitted. Consider the operation of rounds 1 and 2:

$$\sigma[K^2] \circ \theta \circ \tau \circ \gamma \circ \sigma[K^1] \circ \theta \circ \tau \circ \gamma.$$

With H a symmetric matrix ($H^T = H$), observe that the composition $\theta \circ \tau$ yields $a^T \cdot H = (H \cdot a)^T$. Denote $\hat{K}^1$ as τ applied to K^1 and $\hat{\theta} : a \mapsto H \cdot a$. Note γ is invariant under τ; it is not affected by any byte ordering. Then the following expression, essentially relying on the fact that τ is an involution, yields the same output:

$$\sigma[K^2] \circ \theta \circ \gamma \circ \sigma[\hat{K}^1] \circ \hat{\theta} \circ \gamma.$$

Hence all even rounds use the unmodified round keys and θ while odd rounds use transposed round keys and $\hat{\theta}$. With an even number of rounds, τ never needs to be applied during cipher operation. This is similar in spirit to Hamburg eliminating ShiftRows when implementing AES [10, 4.2].

For the linear layers θ and $\hat{\theta}$, viewing the input vector components as $a_i \in \mathbb{F}_{2^8}$, examining the matrix products reveals we need $a_i b_j$ for all i and all $b_j \in \{1, x, x^2, x^2 + x\}$. That is, we need the result of three distinct linear maps applied to the input. Applying the machinery from Sect. 3.1 yields $t_2 = ax$ and $t_4 = ax^2$, then the final product is $t_6 = t_4 + t_2$. The outputs of θ and $\hat{\theta}$ differ only in how these t_i are subsequently shuffled. For θ, these vectors are shuffled using the following indices corresponding to their positions in the columns of H:

$$t_{\theta 2} = \text{0x0E0F0C0D0A0B08090607040502030001}$$
$$t_{\theta 4} = \text{0x0D0C0F0E09080B0A0504070601000302}$$
$$t_{\theta 6} = \text{0x0C0D0E0F08090A0B0405060700010203}$$

and the output is the XOR-sum of these three shuffled vectors with the input. This strategy realizes θ using seven `pshufb`, six `pxor`, two `pand`, and one `psrlq`. Note the `pand` can be eliminated by merging these layers with γ; the last layer of S does not permute the bits so the output from the final P and Q can be used directly as the indices for the linear maps. The byte shuffles for $\hat{\theta}$ are much more regular; for example

$$t_{\hat{\theta} 2} = \text{0x0B0A09080F0E0D0C0302010007060504}$$

which in fact is not a byte shuffle but a dword shuffle `pshufd` that is more efficient since it takes an immediate operand.

For the key schedule, it remains to implement both the permutation π and key extraction ω; the former requires only one `pshufb` instruction with indices defined as

$$t_\pi = \text{0x0306090C0F0205080B0E0104070A0D00}.$$

Unfortunately ω is quite a different situation compared to θ, where the product of every entry in the matrix with every component of the input vector a is required. For example, here $(x^2 + x)a_i$ is only needed for $4 \le i < 8$. When computing with 16-component vectors, this kind of selective computation is difficult to accomplish in an elegant fashion.

On the other hand, realizing multiple linear maps as in Sect. 3.1 with the same input amortizes the cost of the first two steps: the nibbles (indices into tables) need be produced only once. In light of this, one strategy is over-computation by producing $a_i b_j$ for all i and all b_j as distinct entries in V. Computing six of the maps (02, 04, 08, 14, 3A, and 40) is enough to reach the remaining two with XOR chains (06 and 78). This strategy uses twelve `pshufb`, nine `pxor`, two `pand`, and one `psrlq`.

Denote the resulting vectors by r_i; these need to be combined at different indices before XOR-summing them to arrive at the result (three `pxor`). For column j of V with entries $[v_{0j}, v_{1j}, v_{2j}, v_{3j}]$ the needed vector is

$$[v_{0j}[a_{4j}], \ldots, a_{4j+3}], v_{1j}[a_{4j}, \ldots, a_{4j+3}], v_{2j}[a_{4j}, \ldots, a_{4j+3}], v_{3j}[a_{4j}, \ldots, a_{4j+3}]].$$

One way to achieve this is through a series of interleaves: `punpckldq` interleaves the lower two 4-byte values in the first operand with those in the second, and `punpckhqdq` the high 8-byte value.

The following illustrates this concept with $j = 1$ where vectors $\{r_1 = a, r_2 = ax, r_6 = a(x^2 + x), r_8 = ax^3\}$ facilitate constructing the vector

$$[a_4, a_5, a_6, a_7, 02a_4, 02a_5, 02a_6, 02a_7, 06a_4, 06a_5, 06a_6, 06a_7, 08a_4, 08a_5, 08a_6, 08a_7].$$

Here the r_i are filled with dummy data to help observe the interleaving action:

$$r_1 = \text{0x33333333222222221111111100000000}$$
$$r_2 = \text{0x77777777666666665555555544444444}$$
$$r_6 = \text{0xBBBBBBBBAAAAAAAA9999999988888888}$$
$$r_8 = \text{0xFFFFFFFFEEEEEEEEDDDDDDDDCCCCCCCC}$$
$$t_0 = \text{0x55555555111111114444444400000000} \quad (\texttt{punpckldq})$$
$$t_1 = \text{0xDDDDDDDD99999999CCCCCCCC88888888} \quad (\texttt{punpckldq})$$
$$t_2 = \text{0xDDDDDDDD999999995555555511111111} \quad (\texttt{punpckhqdq}).$$

These operations accomplish the goal of extracting bytes $v_4, \ldots, v_7$ from each of the given $v = r_i$ to a vector in a specific order corresponding to column j of V. The vectors for other j are obtained similarly with three instructions, but different interleaves. The exception being $j = 0$, using only one `pshufd` to broadcast the lower 4-byte value of the input across the vector.

A Bit-slice Approach. Käsper and Schwabe use the SIMD registers to represent eight AES instances running in parallel [11]. While these can be unrelated instances with different keys, parallel block cipher modes such as counter mode are where this method is particularly interesting: encrypting the next eight counter values under one key in parallel. Eight SIMD registers hold the entire state for these eight instances, but each register represents one bit-slice of the state bytes for all instances.

Naturally, the same approach can be used to implement Anubis in counter mode. Denote 128-bit SIMD registers r_i for $0 \le i < 7$ each holding bit i of all state bytes. Byte j of r_i holds bit i of the jth state byte for all eight instances, each instance at a fixed offset within these bytes. Figure 2 depicts this structure.

With this representation, some of the components from the previous section remain unchanged and are simply iterated for each r_i. For example, τ, π, and the shuffles at the end of θ. As this counter mode implementation uses only a single key, the key schedule components stay the same, but the resulting round keys must be subsequently converted into bit-slice format using eight times the storage. See [11, Sect. 4.1] for a brief discussion on general data conversion to and from bit-slice format. This implementation uses the same code for said conversion.

The two components that differ significantly in implementation compared to the serial case are the nonlinear layer γ and linear layer θ ($\hat{\theta}$), the only layers where any time consuming operations are carried out during encryption. The previous serial implementation relies heavily on pshufb as a lookup table to realize γ. In contrast, bit-slicing relies on boolean expressions alone to evaluate the S-box, facilitated by access to individual bits of all state bytes collected in one register. Indeed, this is the allure of bit-slicing.

The specification gives boolean expressions for P and Q with 18 gates each, implementing S with 108 gates [2, Appx. B]. This is not significantly lighter than the current smallest published AES S-box with 115 gates [6], although the former appeared at inception while the later took roughly a decade of research to whittle down, and further they are not immediately comparable as the later employs XNOR gates. Regardless, in software register-to-register moves must also be considered since most SSE instructions, particularly those for bitwise operations, do not allow passing a separate destination operand. The simple construction of S as an SPN using smaller P and Q easily allows the implementation to remain entirely within the working register set: the stack is not required, and in this work the implementation of γ uses 148 instructions. Table 1 compares the instruction counts to that of AES [11, Tbl. 2] and the result suggests, when bit-slicing in software, the Anubis S-box is slightly more efficient compared to that of AES. In practice, instruction scheduling is equally important: alas a succinct, meaningful comparison is not straightforward.

	byte 15								⋯	byte 1								byte 0							
bit 0 (xmm0)	instance 7	instance 6	instance 5	instance 4	instance 3	instance 2	instance 1	instance 0	⋯	instance 7	instance 6	instance 5	instance 4	instance 3	instance 2	instance 1	instance 0	instance 7	instance 6	instance 5	instance 4	instance 3	instance 2	instance 1	instance 0
bit 1 (xmm1)																									
⋯																									
bit 7 (xmm7)	instance 7	instance 6	instance 5	instance 4	instance 3	instance 2	instance 1	instance 0	⋯	instance 7	instance 6	instance 5	instance 4	instance 3	instance 2	instance 1	instance 0	instance 7	instance 6	instance 5	instance 4	instance 3	instance 2	instance 1	instance 0

Fig. 2. Bit-slice state representation for Anubis

For the linear layer, similar to an AES MixColumns, viewing the input and output of θ as matrices one can derive a formula for each byte of the output:

$$b_{ij} = a_{ij} + x(a_{i1-j} + a_{i3-j} + x(a_{i2+j} + a_{i3-j}))$$

where all the subscripts are modulo 4. Each multiplication by x implies three XOR gates for reduction. This leads to a cost of 38 `pxor` and 24 `pshufb` (`pshufd` for $\hat{\theta}$), notably heavier than the 27 `pxor` and 16 `pshufd` of MixColumns [11, Sect. 4.4]. The difference in `pxor` counts is simply due to the fact that the entries of H have higher degree than those for MixColumns, and the above formula for each byte contains one extra term in the sum. The difference in shuffle counts is due to the fact that the shuffles for MixColumns are simple dword rotations, and one can reduce the required shuffles per bit from three to two. The shuffles for H are not as simple and do not seem to allow this.

3.3   Implementing Khazad

This section presents two Khazad implementations, analogous to the previous two Anubis implementations. Both require a parallel block cipher mode when only a single key is used. The strategies are in fact so similar to those of Anubis that only a brief summary is provided. The implementations of the nonlinear layer γ stay the same; the key extraction ω and permutations π and τ in Anubis have no equivalent in Khazad, so the only component to consider is the linear layer θ.

Two Parallel Instances. As the SIMD registers are 16-byte and Khazad maintains an 8-byte state, here the analogous SIMD implementation of Khazad runs two instances in parallel, for convenience restricted here to the same key using counter mode. The strategy to compute θ is the same as the corresponding layer in Anubis. First compute three linear maps (02, 04, and 08) and derive the remaining maps with XOR chains. The output is the XOR-sum of the input and the seven shuffled vectors resulting from the linear maps. This implementation uses 15 `pxor`, 13 `pshufb`, two `pand` and one `psrlq`.

Table 1. S-box instruction counts compared

	pxor	pand/por	movdqa	Total
AES	93	35	35	163
Anubis	66	42	39	147

Sixteen Parallel Instances. Lastly, the bit-slice implementation of Khazad in counter mode. Khazad works on 8-byte blocks and with 128-bit SIMD registers aligning the bits of bytes in the state, this implies 16 parallel streams. The approach to implement θ is exactly the same as with the bit-slice Anubis implementation: derive a formula for the output bytes and accumulate the result in output bits iteratively. For each of the eight input bits, this works out to 14 `pxor` and seven `pshufb` to produce a degree-10 polynomial. Similarly the reduction uses a total of 12 `pxor` to clear the three top bits.

4   Results

This section presents the timing results for all of the implementations described in this paper. The machine used for benchmarking is an Intel Core 2 Duo E8400 "Wolfdale" (45 nm) with 4GB of memory running Ubuntu 9.10, kernel 2.6.31-21, and gcc 4.4.1. Table 2 contains the timings for long streams. Timings are median over 1K runs obtained from the CPU time stamp counter `rdtsc`.

To place the results in some context, benchmark results of existing AES code running on the same machine are included as well. Hamburg's AES implementations includes a benchmarking script and the reported time is for encrypting 4kB [10]. Käsper and Schwabe implement the eSTREAM API that benchmarks a number of different metrics; the reported time is the best result from the test suite, that of "Encrypted 60 packets of 1500 bytes (under 1 keys, 60 packets/key)".

Note that one purpose of this work is to improve the security and, if possible, speed of Anubis and Khazad software implementations. Hence the AES timings are only included as a rough benchmark and are not for direct comparison. In particular, AES-128 has 10 rounds while Anubis-128 has 12. They have very different code footprints: AES encryption and decryption are implemented separately, while with Anubis and Khazad they only differ in the key schedule.

Table 2. Timing results in cycles per byte

Cipher	Method	Language	Mode	Instances	"Wolfdale"
Anubis	SSSE3	C	CTR	1	21.7
Anubis	SSSE3	C	CBC	1	20.7
Anubis	SSSE3	C	CBC^{-1}	1	20.3
Anubis	SSSE3	asm	CTR	8	9.2
Anubis	Table	C [2]	CTR	1	20.7
Anubis	Table	C [2]	CBC	1	21.3
Anubis	Table	C [2]	CBC^{-1}	1	21.2
Khazad	SSSE3	asm	CTR	2	18.6
Khazad	SSSE3	asm	CTR	16	10.3
Khazad	Table	C [3]	CTR	1	19.8
AES	SSSE3	asm [10]	CTR	1	11.6
AES	SSSE3	asm [10]	CBC	1	11.0
AES	SSSE3	asm [10]	CBC^{-1}	1	13.6
AES	SSSE3	asm [11]	CTR	8	8.0

The timings in Table 2 show that the serial Anubis implementations outline here are very competitive with the purely table-based implementation. In particular, there is no significant penalty to realize protection against cache-timing attacks on this platform. The compiler is able to optimize the C implementation using compiler intrinsics for SIMD operations quite well; it is unclear how to improve it by hand-crafted assembly. For parallel modes, the bit-slice approach is significantly more efficient than the serial approach for both Anubis and Khazad.

5   Conclusion

This paper presents a number of constant-time implementations of the Anubis and Khazad block ciphers. The results show that constant-time and efficient are not mutually exclusive with respect to their software implementation. The work here also further showcases the potential of a vector-byte shuffle instruction to provide both secure and fast software implementations of cryptosystems.

It is worth mentioning that at least two other primitives make use of the compact S-box used in Anubis and Khazad [4,15]. Its particularly efficient software implementation here, in serial using `pshufb` or parallel when bit-slicing, greatly encourages further use: perhaps as a building block for other primitives.

Realizing the threat that timing attacks pose to software implementations, more recent trends in cipher design are away from the rather traditional view of an S-box as a lookup table towards methods that better suit constant-time implementations using native instructions supported by common processors. For example, the Threefish block cipher explicitly states this as a design criteria [9, Sect. 8.1], using an extremely simple nonlinear function MIX consisting of a rotation, XOR, and addition modulo 2^{64} iterated during a large number of rounds. However, equipped with powerful instructions like `pshufb` it will be interesting to see how cryptologists harness this machinery and what the future holds for cipher design.

References

1. Aranha, D.F., López, J., Hankerson, D.: High-Speed Parallel Software Implementation of the η_T Pairing. In: Pieprzyk, J. (ed.) CT-RSA 2010. LNCS, vol. 5985, pp. 89–105. Springer, Heidelberg (2010)
2. Barreto, P.S.L.M., Rijmen, V.: The Anubis block cipher (2001),
   http://www.larc.usp.br/~pbarreto/anubis-tweak.zip
3. Barreto, P.S.L.M., Rijmen, V.: The Khazad legacy-level block cipher (2001),
   http://www.larc.usp.br/~pbarreto/khazad-tweak.zip
4. Barreto, P.S.L.M., Simplício Jr., M.A.: CURUPIRA, a block cipher for constrained platforms. In: 5th Brazilian Symposium on Computer Networks and Distributed Systems, pp. 61–74 (2007),
   http://www.sbrc2007.ufpa.br/anais/2007/ST02%20-%2001.pdf
5. Bernstein, D.J.: Cache-timing attacks on AES (2004),
   http://cr.yp.to/papers.html#cachetiming
6. Boyar, J., Peralta, R.: New logic minimization techniques with applications to cryptology. Cryptology ePrint Archive, Report 2009/191 (2009),
   http://eprint.iacr.org/
7. Canright, D., Osvik, D.A.: A More Compact AES. In: Jacobson Jr., M.J., Rijmen, V., Safavi-Naini, R. (eds.) SAC 2009. LNCS, vol. 5867, pp. 157–169. Springer, Heidelberg (2009)
8. Clavier, C., Gaj, K. (eds.): CHES 2009. LNCS, vol. 5747. Springer, Heidelberg (2009)
9. Ferguson, N., Lucks, S., Schneier, B., Whiting, D., Bellare, M., Kohno, T., Callas, J., Walker, J.: The Skein hash function family. Submission to NIST (Round 2) (2009), http://www.skein-hash.info/sites/default/files/skein1.2.pdf

10. Hamburg, M.: Accelerating AES with vector permute instructions. In: Clavier and Gaj [8], pp. 18–32
11. Käsper, E., Schwabe, P.: Faster and timing-attack resistant AES-GCM. In: Clavier and Gaj [8], pp. 1–17
12. Preneel, B.: The NESSIE project: towards new cryptographic algorithms. In: 3rd International Workshop on Information Security Applications, WISA 2002, pp. 16–33 (2002)
13. Rudra, A., Dubey, P.K., Jutla, C.S., Kumar, V., Rao, J.R., Rohatgi, P.: Efficient Rijndael Encryption Implementation with Composite Field Arithmetic. In: Koç, Ç.K., Naccache, D., Paar, C. (eds.) CHES 2001. LNCS, vol. 2162, pp. 171–184. Springer, Heidelberg (2001)
14. Satoh, A., Morioka, S., Takano, K., Munetoh, S.: A Compact Rijndael Hardware Architecture with S-Box Optimization. In: Boyd, C. (ed.) ASIACRYPT 2001. LNCS, vol. 2248, pp. 239–254. Springer, Heidelberg (2001)
15. Simplício Jr., M.A., Barreto, P.S.L.M., Carvalho, T.C.M.B., Margi, C.B., Näslund, M.: The CURUPIRA-2 block cipher for constrained platforms: Specification and benchmarking. In: Bettini, C., Jajodia, S., Samarati, P., Wang, X.S. (eds.) PiLBA. CEUR Workshop Proceedings, vol. 397, CEUR-WS.org (2008)

The PASSERINE Public Key Encryption and Authentication Mechanism

Markku-Juhani O. Saarinen

Aalto University
Department of Communications and Networking
P.O. Box 13000, 00076 Aalto, Finland
m.saarinen@tkk.fi

Abstract. PASSERINE[1] is a lightweight public key encryption mechanism which is based on a hybrid, randomized variant of the Rabin public key encryption scheme. Its design is targeted for extremely low-resource applications such as wireless sensor networks, RFID tags, embedded systems, and smart cards. As is the case with the Rabin scheme, the security of PASSERINE can be shown to be equivalent to factoring the public modulus. On many low-resource implementation platforms PASSERINE offers smaller transmission latency, hardware and software footprint and better encryption speed when compared to RSA or Elliptic Curve Cryptography. This is mainly due to the fact that PASSERINE implementations can avoid expensive big integer arithmetic in favor of a fully parallelizable CRT randomized-square operation. In order to reduce latency and memory requirements, PASSERINE uses Naccache-Shamir randomized multiplication, which is implemented with a system of simultaneous congruences modulo small coprime numbers. The PASSERINE private key operation is of comparable computational complexity to the RSA private key operation. The private key operation is typically performed by a computationally superior recipient such as a base station.

Keywords: Rabin Cryptosystem, Randomized Multiplication, RFID, Wireless Sensor Networks.

1 Introduction

Public key encryption is often viewed as unimplementable for extremely low-resource devices such as sensor network nodes and RFID tags. However, public key cryptography offers clear security advantages as fixed secret keys do not have to be shared between the two communicating parties. The PASSERINE public key encryption operation is very light, but the private key operation is approximately as computationally demanding as the private key operation of RSA.

For (RFID) authentication purposes a protocol can be devised that requires the tag to only perform public key encryption using the interrogator's public key.

In a military application a large number of sensors may be dispersed to an area of operations to lay passively dormant until an a particular combination of events triggers

---

[1] PASSERINE 0.7 of October 2010. This is a short "work in progress" report.

T. Aura, K. Järvinen, and K. Nyberg (Eds.): NordSec 2010, LNCS 7127, pp. 283–288, 2012.

their activation. In such a scenario, key management with symmetric-only encryption may become exceedingly difficult. A single captured and reverse-engineered sensor unit may reveal all shared keys that it contains, possibly compromising the entire sensor network. Use of public-key cryptography simplifies key management and also reduces the need to protect keying information contained in the node. Each node only needs to store its unique identifier and the public key of the secure receiving station. The adversary can only impersonate a single physically captured sensor unit.

In this scenario the devices are controlled by a base station that stores their private identifiers. The devices only need to be able to perform the public key operation - to broadcast messages to the base station. A sensor unit can securely authenticate an another node with the aid of the trusted base station.

1.1 Previous Work

The use of Rabin encryption in low-resource platforms has been investigated by Shamir [19], Gaubatz et al. [6,7] and more recently by Oren and Feldhofer [14]. The approaches considered in these papers differ significantly from PASSERINE; Gaubatz et al. do not consider randomized multiplication but only bit-serial multiplication. Shamir, Oren and Feldhofer use randomized multiplication but not CRT arithmetic nor payload encoding into the random mask. Systems described in [14,19] require substantial amounts of real randomness, which may be difficult to generate in a resource-strained device. PASSERINE requires only a single random 128-bit key for each message. Naccache et al. [12] use randomized multiplication and CRT arithmetic (which they call Brugia-di Porto-Filipponi number system after [4]) in a low-resource implementation of a related identification protocol which was subsequently broken in [5].

2 The PASSERINE Randomized Rabin Cryptosystem

Rabin's public key cryptosystem [18] is in many ways similar to the RSA cryptosystem. Let n be a product of two large primes p and q. In order to facilitate implementation, these primes are often chosen so that $p \equiv q \equiv 3 \pmod{4}$. To encrypt a message x, one simply squares it modulo the public modulus n:

$$z = x^2 \pmod{n}. \tag{1}$$

The Rabin private key operation requires computation of modular square roots and is of comparable complexity to the RSA private key algorithm. Since there are a total of four possible square roots ($\sqrt{z} \equiv \pm x \mod p$ and $\sqrt{z} \equiv \pm x \mod q$), a special mechanism is required in to mark and find the correct root. We refer to standard cryptography textbooks such as [9] for a discussion about implementation options.

The main distinguishing factor for the Rabin cryptosystem, in addition to being slightly faster than RSA in encryption, is that it is provably as secure as factoring. This equivalence may or may not hold for RSA [1,3].

2.1 Shamir's Randomized Variant

In Eurocrypt '94 [19] Shamir proposed a randomized variant of the Rabin cryptosystem that avoids arithmetic mod n by using a random masking variable $r > n$. The encryption operation is

$$z = x^2 + r \cdot n. \tag{2}$$

The private key operation is essentially the same as with the standard Rabin scheme.

Randomized multiplication was originally considered by Naccache [11], albeit for a different application. Shamir proved that this randomized variant has equivalent security properties to the standard version. The main drawback from avoiding modular arithmetic is that the ciphertext roughly doubles in size and that a large amount of high quality random bits must be generated for r. We avoid this problem using an encoding technique described in Section 2.3.

2.2 Arithmetic Modulo a Set of Coprime Numbers

A large majority of the implementation footprint of traditional public key encryption schemes such as RSA or ECC tends to be consumed by implementing large finite field multiplication and exponentiation. We avoid this by using arithmetic modulo a set of coprime numbers.

Let $b_1, b_2, \ldots, b_k$ denote a *base*, a set of coprime numbers, and $B = \prod_{i=1}^{k} b_i$ their product. The Chinese Remainder Theorem (CRT) states that any number $x, 0 \leq x < B$ can be uniquely expressed as a vector x_i that represents a set of k congruences $x_i = x \mod b_i$ when $i = 1, 2, \ldots, k$. Furthermore, ring arithmetic modulo B can be performed in this domain. To compute the sum, difference or a product of two numbers mod B, all one needs to do is to is to add or multiply the individual vector components i, each mod b_i. Multiplication modulo B therefore has essentially linear complexity. Looking at Equation 2, one notices that when $z < B$, the entire public key computation can be performed in the CRT domain. This observation was first made in [4,12].

Encryption Latency. One of the main advantages of a CRT implementation of PASSERINE is that serial transmission of encrypted data may be started immediately after the first word of $x^2 + r \cdot n$ has been computed. This is not the case with RSA or in ECC cryptography. This technique also helps to reduce the memory requirements of a PASSERINE implementation.

2.3 Carrying Payload Data in the Randomization Mask

An important and novel feature of PASSERINE is that r is used to carry payload data that has been encrypted using a random symmetric key, contained in x. This encoding technique allows us to essentially double the transmission bandwidth of the channel when compared to the original proposal by Shamir in [19].

3   Implementing PASSERINE Public Key Operation on a Low-Resource Platform

We targeted our implementation of PASSERINE encryption for low-power 8/16 - bit microprocessors and microcontrollers typically found in active RFID and wireless sensor network applications. We chose to use a 1025-bit public modulus, which offers a reasonable level of security [8]. For highly sensitive data, a larger modulus should be used. For symmetric encryption, we use AES-128 in counter mode.

The total code size is about 750 bytes on the ultra-low power MSP430 microcontroller architecture (we used TI CC430F6137 which has a 32-bit hardware multiplier and an AES accelerator and is therefore well suited for this application). For a 32-bit x86 platform the implementation size was 1136 bytes, including a tiny AES implementation. These implementations do not call any external functions. The implementations were in C and compiled with GCC-MSP430 4.4.3 and GCC 4.4.3.

The CRT base (Section 2.2) was chosen to consist of 64 primes 4294965793 ... 4294967291 and the word 2^{32}. The encoding capacity is $\prod_{i=1}^{65} b_i \approx 2^{2079.999982}$, which is very close to the maximum channel capacity of 2080 bits.

Encoding parameters:

$n =$	A 1025-bit public modulus.		

$m = $ | k | d_0 | d_1 | d_2 | d_3 | d_4 | d_5 | d_6 | d_7 | d_8 | d_9 | d_{10} | d_{11} | d_{12} | d_{13} | d_{14} | c

$x = $ | First 1024 bits of m.

$r = $ | Remaining 1055 bits of m.

Public Key Encryption Operation:

$x^2 = $ | A 2048-bit square.

$+$

$rn = $ | A 2080-bit randomization mask.

$=$

$z = $ | Ciphertext (2080 bits).

Transmission in CRT format:

$z' = $ | 65×32 - bit words (2080 bits, capacity 2079.99998)

Fig. 1. Encoding of key and payload in PASSERINE. Encryption is actually performed using CRT representation (modulo small primes in base b), not in standard two's complement representation

Figure 1 illustrates PASSERINE data encoding. We use AES-128 [13] in counter mode (CTR) for encryption of data blocks d_i. The first 1024 bits ($m[0..31]$) of the message are used as x and the latter 1056 bits ($m[32..64]$) as r in Equation 2.

Current v0.7 implementation sacrifices some message integrity protection for simplicity and only a 31-bit checksum c is used. Incorporating an authenticated encryption mode such as the EAX [2], CCM [15] or GCM [16] is straightforward. Our final hardware design will use GCM, which is also a part of NSA's "Suite B cryptography" [17].

4   PASSERINE Private Key Operation and Decryption

We implemented the private key operation in C using the OpenSSL library for both fast big number arithmetic and AES. The implementation required only about 230 code lines. In this section we will only give the relevant mathematics.

A straightforward method for converting the ciphertext to conventional two's complement binary representation is given in Equation 3. Here b_i is the base with $k = 65$ coprime numbers, $B = \prod_{i=1}^{k}$, and the CRT ciphertext vector z_i satisfies $0 \leq z_i < b_i$ for each i.

$$z = \left(\sum_{i=1}^{k} z_i \cdot \frac{B}{b_i} \cdot \left(\frac{B}{b_i} \right)_{b_i}^{-1} \right) \mod B. \tag{3}$$

The de-CRT coefficients $d_i = (B/b_i) \cdot (B/b_i)_{b_i}^{-1}$ in Equation 3 can be precomputed as they do not depend on the private parameters used.

Computing the square root. For decryption, one needs the private factorization pq of n. Rabin decryption is significantly easier to implement when $p \equiv q \equiv 3 \mod 4$ and we will assume that this is the case. There are four square roots for every quadratic residue mod pq:

$$x_p = (z^{\frac{p+1}{4}} \mod p) \cdot q \cdot q_p^{-1}. \tag{4}$$

$$x_q = (z^{\frac{q+1}{4}} \mod q) \cdot p \cdot p_q^{-1}. \tag{5}$$

The four square roots of z are given by $x = \{x_p + x_q, x_p - x_q, -x_p + x_q, -x_p - x_q\} \pmod{n}$. The correct root can be recognized using authenticator c.

Symmetric decryption. Once the correct square root x is found, the mask r can be derived from

$$r = \frac{z - x^2}{n}. \tag{6}$$

We can then concatenate the two values and obtain the full message $m = x \parallel r$, which contains the symmetric decryption key and proceed to decrypt the entire data payload.

5   Further Work

The PASSERINE system has been implemented on the Texas Instruments CC430F6137, which is a MSP430 architecture MCU with an integrated sub-1-GHz wireless transceiver.

We are currently implementing wireless sensor applications in the 433 MHz band using the CC430F6137. Further implementation details and applications will be discussed in a separate report.

Acknowledgements. The author gratefully acknowledges financial support from Matine (Project 776). Further work on the PASSERINE project has been undertaken with Revere Security Corp. after the publication of this initial report.

References

1. Aggarwal, D., Maurer, U.: Breaking RSA Generically is Equivalent to Factoring. In: Joux, A. (ed.) EUROCRYPT 2009. LNCS, vol. 5479, pp. 36–53. Springer, Heidelberg (2009)
2. Bellare, M., Rogaway, P., Wagner, D.: The EAX Mode of Operation. In: Roy, B., Meier, W. (eds.) FSE 2004. LNCS, vol. 3017, pp. 389–407. Springer, Heidelberg (2004)
3. Boneh, D., Venkatesan, R.: Breaking RSA May Not Be Equivalent to Factoring. In: Nyberg, K. (ed.) EUROCRYPT 1998. LNCS, vol. 1403, pp. 59–71. Springer, Heidelberg (1998)
4. Brugia, O., di Porto, A., Filiponi, P.: Un metodo per migliorare l'efficienza degli algoritmi di generazione delle chiavi crittografiche basati sull'impiego di grandi numeri primi. Note Recesioni e Notizie, Ministero Poste e Telecommunicazioni 33(1-2), 15–22 (1984)
5. Coron, J., Naccache, D.: Cryptanalysis of a Zero-Knowledge Identification Protocol of Eurocrypt '95. In: Okamoto, T. (ed.) CT-RSA 2004. LNCS, vol. 2964, pp. 157–162. Springer, Heidelberg (2004)
6. Gaubatz, G., Kaps, J., Özturk, E., Sunar, B.: State of the Art in Ultra-Low Power Public Key Cryptography for Wireless Sensor Networks. In: PerCom 2005 Workshops, pp. 146–150. IEEE (2005)
7. Gaubatz, G., Kaps, J.-P., Sunar, B.: Public Key Cryptography in Sensor Networks—Revisited. In: Castelluccia, C., Hartenstein, H., Paar, C., Westhoff, D. (eds.) ESAS 2004. LNCS, vol. 3313, pp. 2–18. Springer, Heidelberg (2005)
8. Kleinjung, T., Aoki, K., Franke, J., Lenstra, A., Thomé, E., Bos, J., Gaudry, P., Kruppa, A., Montgomery, P., Osvik, D.A., te Riele, H., Timofeev, A., Zimmermann, P.: Factorization of a 768-bit RSA modulus. IACR Cryptology ePrint Archive: Report 2010/006 (2010), http://eprint.iacr.org/2010/006
9. Menezes, A., van Oorschot, P., Vanstone, S.: Handbook of Applied Cryptography. CRC Press (1996)
10. Lowe, G.: An Attack on the Needham-Schroeder Public-Key Authenticaion protocol. Information Processing Letters 56, 131–131 (1995)
11. Naccache, D.: Method, Sender Apparatus And Receiver Apparatus For Modulo Operation. US patent: US5479511 (December 26, 1995), European patent application: EP0611506 (August 24, 1994), World publication: WO9309620 (1993)
12. Naccache, D., M'Raïhi, D., Wolfowicz, W., di Porto, A.: Are Crypto-Accelerators Really Inevitable? In: Guillou, L.C., Quisquater, J.-J. (eds.) EUROCRYPT 1995. LNCS, vol. 921, pp. 404–409. Springer, Heidelberg (1995)
13. NIST. Specification for the Advanced Encryption Standard (AES) Federal Information Processing Standards Publication. FIPS-197, NIST (2001)
14. Oren, Y., Feldhofer, M.: A Low-Resource Public-Key Identification Scheme for RFID Tags and Sensor Nodes. In: WiSec 2009, pp. 59–68. ACM (2009)
15. NIST. Recommendation for Block Cipher Modes of Operation: The CCM Mode for Authentication and Confidentiality. NIST Special Publication 800-38 C, NIST (2004)
16. NIST. Recommendation for Block Cipher Modes of Operation: Galois/Counter Mode (GCM) and GMAC. NIST Special Publication 800-38 D, NIST (2007)
17. National Security Agency. NSA Suite B Cryptography, http://www.nsa.gov/ia/programs/suiteb_cryptography/
18. Rabin, M.C.: Digitalized Signatures and Public-Key Functions as Intractable as Factorization. MIT / LCS / TR-212, Massachusetts Institute of Technology (1979)
19. Shamir, A.: Memory Efficient Variants of Public-Key Schemes for Smart Card Applications. In: De Santis, A. (ed.) EUROCRYPT 1994. LNCS, vol. 950, pp. 445–449. Springer, Heidelberg (1995)

Author Index